2 HOUR RESERVE

LIBRARY USE ONLY

Due at Langsam Circulation
Desk
2 hours after check out
$1.00 overdue fine per hour
(or part of an hour)

NO RENEWALS

After the Imperial Turn

Thinking with and through the Nation

Edited by ANTOINETTE BURTON

DUKE UNIVERSITY PRESS

Durham and London 2003

© 2003 Duke University Press

All rights reserved

Printed in the United States of America on acid-free paper ∞

Designed by Amy Ruth Buchanan

Typeset in Carter & Cone Galliard by Keystone Typesetting, Inc.

Library of Congress Cataloging-in-Publication Data and permissions
information appear on the last printed page of this book.

FRONTIS Turning toward the Antipodes: Prince Philip and
Queen Elizabeth II framed by two aboriginal men. Reprinted with
permission from the *Guardian Weekly,* March 7–13, 2002. Photo
by Fiona Hanson.

For Nicholas, Jonah, and Fiona,

whose turn is all too soon to come

Contents

Acknowledgments

My thanks go to all the contributors for their endless forbearance and good cheer as I put them through draft after draft and asked for changes both large and small. I would also like to acknowledge my colleagues who participated in the NEH seminar on globalization at the University of Illinois, 2001–2002; it was an experience that has greatly influenced my thinking about the nation, empires, and the politics of geopolitics itself. I am especially grateful to Jim Barrett, Herman Bennett, Ann Curthoys, Elena Delgado, Ian Fletcher, Lara Kriegel, Hannah Rosen, and Hsu-Ming Teo, all of whom read the introduction and offered very helpful feedback. Tony Ballantyne, for his part, has been the sine qua non of this project. I am equally indebted to Miriam Angress at Duke University Press, who shepherded this manuscript so helpfully and generously through the process. Many thanks to her for being an ideal editor.

Down to the last, Paul and Nicholas have indulged my need to work: thanks to them for their love, their patience, and their regular weeknight trips to the playland.

ANTOINETTE BURTON

Introduction: On the Inadequacy and the Indispensability of the Nation

By now it is practically axiomatic that obituaries of the nation are premature.[1] Less readily accepted is Etienne Balibar's contention that "in a sense, every modern nation is a product of colonization," let alone Frantz Fanon's simple but eloquent formula: "Europe is literally the creation of the Third World."[2] *After the Imperial Turn* grapples with precisely these crosscurrents. For even as claims about the durability of the nation multiply in response to postcolonial critique and regimes of globalization, evidence of the constitutive impact of modern European imperialism on metropolitan politics and society accumulates in scholarship, in academic jobs, and hence in North American classrooms, raising questions about the coherence, presumed originality, and boundedness of the modern, Western, Euro-American nation as a historical form. At first glance, such "cross-talk" may appear to be nothing more than a paradoxical by-product of the collision of the nation-state with global capitalism at the end of the twentieth century. But to dismiss the continued vigor of the nation in an era of postcoloniality merely as an ironic counterpoint to narratives of European postmodernity is to remain complicit with the staging of historical time through which the West has traditionally managed "the rest."[3] In the first instance, historians of the early modern period, and especially of China and other Eastern political economies before 1800, have cast doubt on the newness of the global idea, giving lie to the notion that globalization is either a uniquely modern or an originally Western phenomenon. Their work does more than write Asia back into the history of Western civilization or update hidebound histories of Western supremacy. It challenges "modernity," and the modern European nation with it, as the originary site of transnational streams and global influences.[4] Equally significant for our purposes are the ways in which Enlightenment claims not just about the universality but also the originality of "European" ideas and practices of justice, social order, and domesticity have been subject to interrogation in recent years.[5] The work of Dipesh Chakrabarty has been especially important in this regard because of its insistence on the role of modern imperialism in shaping not just European national culture(s), but the project of history writing in the West as well. Attempts like his to "provincialize Europe" have the potential to prize open still dominant evolutionary narratives about the boundaries of the Western nation and to create the possibility of a political space in which a more nuanced account of the work of imperial nation-states can be imagined.[6]

Contributors to this volume offer a variety of reflections on and pathways out of the post-Enlightenment box within which the academic disciplines remain constrained, history primary but by no means unique among them. They do so by engaging with the impact of "the imperial turn" on the scholarship and culture of the humanities in order to assess the fate of the nation as a subject of disciplinary inquiry and, more particularly, as the traditional investigative modality of history and literature. We take "the imperial turn" to mean the accelerated attention to the impact of histories of imperialism on metropolitan societies in the wake of decolonization, pre- and post-1968 racial struggle and feminism in the last quarter century. The democratization of the North American academy, however glacial and incomplete at the twentieth century's end, is partly the result of these social/political movements. They have in turn created new constituencies insistent on histories that explain the experiences of colonial and ex-colonial peoples — and account for the structural disadvantages of persistently racialized "Others" — in postcolonial metropolitan societies.[7] Those constituencies are the legacy of several generations of black Europeans — and here I refer not just to the colonized in distant lands, but also to those "at the other end of the imperial chain, inside Europe as citizens, bystanders and sojourners."[8] And although there is no natural or necessary connection between historically subordinate status (whether of color, class, or political affiliation) and ideological conviction, most often the practitioners of the imperial turn have been feminists, socialists, people of color, and/or former colonial subjects who have linked political agendas for social struggle and transformation to academic work — as the controversial careers of Edward Said, Paul Gilroy, Stuart Hall, Gayatri Spivak, and Hazel Carby all testify. What these critics (and countless others) have provoked is not a turn toward empire so much as *a critical return* to the connections between metropole and colony, race and nation, which imperial apologists and dissenters have appreciated at least since the nineteenth century, if not before.[9] In the context of Euro-American colonial histories, then, what we might properly call the return to empire is one symptom of the pressure of postcolonial social, political, and demographic realities on the production of modern knowledge.

The impact of this pressure on Britain and its histories is illustrative — if not wholly representative — of the fate of Western nations and empires in the wake of both decolonization and the shifting balance of geopower in the post-1945 era. Although it is still a contested claim in some quarters, it nonetheless requires a herculean effort at the dawn of the new millennium to gainsay Edward Said's argument that "we are at a point in our work when we can no longer ignore empires and the imperial context in our studies."[10] As Peter Hulme has pointed out, the enduring purchase of Said's work—its "irritative process of critique"—lies in its insistence that what is at risk from attention to orientalism is the integrity of the European "heartland" itself because "the principal motifs and tropes of . . . European cultural tradition, far from being self-generated, were the product of constant, intricate, but mostly unacknowledged traffic with the non-European world."[11] Recent scholarship in British history has documented the traces of empire that were everywhere to be found "at home" before World War I — in spaces as diverse as the Boy Scouts, Bovril advertisements, and biscuit tins; in productions as varied as novels, feminist pamphlets, and music halls; in cartographies as particular as Oxbridge, London, and the Franco-British Exhibition; and in halls as hallowed as Westminster itself.[12] And either because they were part of permanent communities with long histories and traditions in the British Isles or because they were travelers or temporary residents in various metropoles and regions throughout the United Kingdom, a variety of colonial "Others" circulated at the very heart of the British Empire before the twentieth century. They were, as Gretchen Gerzina has noted, a "continual and very English presence" from the Elizabethan settlement onward.[13] Empire was, in short, not just a phenomenon "out there," but a fundamental and constitutive part of English culture and national identity at home, where "the fact of empire was registered not only in political debate . . . but entered the social fabric, the intellectual discourse and the life of the imagination."[14]

If these claims would seem to make good historical sense, they have met with an opposition so vociferous that it would be easy to imagine that they pose some kind of threat to national security. Studies that seek to rematerialize the presence of nonwhite Britons in the United Kingdom before 1945 have attracted the most attention, in part because, as Paul Gilroy has argued with regard to the emergence of black history in Britain, they are perceived as "an illegitimate intrusion into a vision of authentic national life that, prior to their arrival, was as stable and peaceful as it was ethnically undifferentiated."[15] Accusations by a British government minister in 1995 that the elevation of historical figures like Olaudah Equiano and Mary Seacole to the status of British heroes constituted a "betrayal" of true British history and "national identity" certainly testify to the political contests that representation has the power to set in motion.[16] But recent attention to empire's influences at home has provoked a response even when the topics are commodities and aesthetics, ideologies and politics, rather than an "alien" presence. Whether by a calm, cool refutation of claims about empire's centrality or via the impassioned denunciations of Said, those in charge of safeguarding Britain's national heritage, from Whitehall to the Senior Common Room, have raised the standard in defense of the nation's impenetrability to outside forces. This "no fatal impact" argument has come to be known as the Marshall Thesis after an essay of the same name by P. J. Marshall of King's College, London, appeared in the *Times Literary Supplement* in 1993.[17] Although scholars like Catherine Hall and Bill Schwarz see empire's constitutive impact on metropolitan society as the starting point for new critical geographies of British imperial culture, empire cannot be viewed as having made Britian "what it was" for Marshall because it was so centripetal and uneven—and by implication, perhaps, untraceable—in its impact.[18]

Clearly some of the claims of the new imperial history in Britain have touched a nerve, even if they are scarcely represented in the footnotes of a new reactionary imperial history, which seeks to reestablish the idea that home and empire were separate spheres—or, alternatively, to blunt the impact of the colonial encounter on "domestic" society.[19] In doing so, critics implicitly acknowledge that history writing is one terrain upon which political battles are fought out and admit the persuasive power of recent scholarship that seeks to recast the nation as an imperialized space—a political territory that could not, and still cannot, escape the imprint of empire. Such work—often grouped under the rubric of "the new imperial studies"—strikes at the heart of Britain's long ideological attachment to the narratives of the splendid isolation and of European exceptionalism. It materializes the traffic of colonial goods, ideas, and people across metropolitan borders and indeed throws into question the very Victorian distinctions between "home" and "away" that defined the imagined geography of empire in the nineteenth century, helping to challenge the equally Victorian conviction that "England possesses an unbroken history of cultural homogeneity and territorial integrity."[20] The reactionary response that the new imperial history has often provoked should not prevent us from appreciating that what it potentially leaves intact is the sanctity of the nation itself as the right and proper subject of history. For even some of the most critically engaged work runs the risk of remaking Britain (itself a falsely homogeneous whole) as the centripetal origin of empire, rather than insisting on the interdependence, the "uneven development," as Mrinalini Sinha calls it, of national/ imperial formations in any given historical moment.[21] And—perhaps most significant—it leaves untouched the conviction that "national" history can be tracked through a linear chronological development (with empire added in) rather than as "a set of relations that are constantly being made and remade, contested and refigured, [and] that nonetheless produce among their contemporaneous witnesses the conviction of historical *difference.*"[22] Anne McClintock, in her influential book, *Imperial Leather,* for example, tends to see empire and nation precisely as *two,* and in a sequential relationship at that — for example, "as domestic space became racialized," to quote from *Imperial Leather,* "colonial space became domesticated."[23] Here not only is the binary reinstantiated, not only is the "nation" represented as a privileged and cohesive subject, but also empire follows nation in a fairly conventional linearity.[24] The fact that this relationship is a classically *imperial* concept of nation-empire relations should be our first clue to the limits of its critical usefulness (not to mention its historically specific constructedness). Rather than emerging as an unstable subject-in-the-making, the nation is in danger of functioning as a pretext for postmodern narrative in the same way it functioned as the foundation for post-Enlightenment historicism. Such a coincidence implicates them both, though differently, in the metanarrative(s) of Western imperial discourse, where the nation has historically served as the sovereign ontological subject.[25]

Despite the veritable explosion of work in the field, in other words, few have been willing to embrace or even engage the notion of deracinated, mobile identities posed by Paul Gilroy's *Black Atlantic* (a text that has been woefully underengaged by British historians at any rate). Britain — and England within it — tends to remain the fixed referent, the a priori body upon which empire is inscribed. Even when it is shown to be remade by colonialism and its subjects, "the nation" often stands as the mirror to which imperial identities are reflected *back.*[26] This is perhaps because not many historians are willing to fully countenance the notion that the nation is not only *not* antecedent to empire, but that as both a symbolic and a material site the nation — as Judith Butler has argued for identity and Joan Scott for gender and experience — has no originary moment, no fixity outside of the various discourses of which it is itself an effect. So, to paraphrase Anna Marie Smith, the fiction of a preexisting England is left largely unchallenged.[27] Some observers of the imperial turn in British history have suggested that it differs little from old imperial history because "metropolitan Britain still remains the main point of departure for embarking upon the study of its empire, rather than the reverse."[28] This is a misreading, but it testifies to the persistence of "home" and "empire" as segregated domains and of imperialism as a force with directional vectors rather than as a spatialized terrain of power — a persistence that speaks, in turn, to the resilience of older models of empire as much as it does to that of nation in contemporary (even postcolonial) scholarly discourses. Rarely is the starting point of the newly imperialized British history the "precarious vulnerability" of imperial systems, as Ann Stoler has strenuously argued for the Dutch East Indies context.[29]

Indeed, the very concept of Britain seems to have a "fantasy structure" that is more resilient and more resistant to its own displacement than almost any other "national" imaginary today.[30] Even the naming of Britain as an imperial space — a maneuver that challenges the colonial status quo by implying that "home" was not hermetically sealed from the colonies — potentially works to naturalize the distinctions between "home" and "empire" when it seems clear that the nineteenth century is one particular historical moment during which such discursive categories were being affirmed (if not invented) and circulated as evidence of "modernity" and civilization in the first place.

"Why the need for nation?" — a question posed, significantly, by the contemporary black British cultural critic Kobena Mercer — is not, therefore, simply rhetorical.[31] Those who need it tend to require that their historical subjects be national at heart — not only fixed by borders, but equally unfragmented and coherent, as stable as the rational post-Enlightenment subjects that postcolonial studies, feminist theory, and postmodernism together have revealed as a kind of self-interested, if historically intelligible, modernist Western fantasy. Nostalgia for and attachment to the nation are thus connected with regret for the passage of that historical moment when the subjects of history were as yet uncontaminated by the critical apparatus set in motion by the historical events of the past quarter century.[32] As historians of American women in the 1950s have argued, one historically engaged response to such nostalgia is to remind its advocates that the power of her image notwithstanding, there never was a June Cleaver (the famous postwar TV mom) — or, rather, that she was a fiction, the invention of a cultural moment that has continued to displace and obscure the material conditions under which such iconography (like that of the nation) emerged.[33] This is not to say that we should disregard the historical "fact" of nation. Rather, the return to empire reminds us that as we struggle to interpret its historical significance, we need to pay more attention to the question of who needs it, who manufactures the "need" for it, and whose interests it serves. In this sense, "Who needs the nation?" might profitably be imagined as a question of "Who can *afford* to need the nation?", thus writing social class, material dispossession, and political disenfranchisement back into historical narratives about imperial culture. This kind of refiguration also requires us to ask how — that is, through what kinds of practices — it is possible to write national histories like those of "Britain" so that they do not continue to act as colonial forms of knowledge in the context of postcoloniality.

At their most self-critical, scholars writing in the wake of the imperial turn commit themselves to unmasking the instabilities of conventional historical narrative and exposing the fictions of an apparently insular "British" culture by insisting that narratives of the nation (like all stories) are never "found" in nature but are always construed by historians for implicit and explicit political purposes and in discrete historical circumstances.[34] This remains the intriguing and unsettling paradox of the "new" imperial history and studies, for the work of unmasking, however valuable, can and often still does leave the nation in pride of place, rather than staging it as precarious, unmoored, and, in the end, finally unrealizable. Fully countenancing such a possibility is a challenge precisely because modern history writing (and not just in the West) has historically been a "narrative contract" with the territorially bounded nation-state.[35] Prying the nation from that contract is nothing less than a struggle to reorganize and reconstitute the spatial bases of power.[36] If narratives of geography are at stake in narratives of history, then loosening the narrative contract may mean displacing nation-states like Britain from center stage.[37] In the British context, more work surely needs to be done to follow the trajectory of Tom Nairn's *After Britain* and Peter Hitchens's *The Abolition of Britain* — to examine, in other words, the genealogy of the paradox of the British empire's apparent "disappearance" and the British nation's subsequent revival at the end of the twentieth century.[38]

The political urgency of such projects can scarcely be gainsaid. As Enoch Powell (1912–1998; Tory MP for three decades) worried in 1985, "What sort of country will England be when its capital, other cities and areas . . . consist of a population of which at least one-third is of African and Asian descent? My answer . . . is that it will be a Britain unimaginably wrecked by dissension and violent disorder, not recognizable as the same nation it had been, or perhaps as a nation at all."[39] In this view, Britain itself is in danger of being no longer recognizable as a nation because of the legacies of empire. In the context of the summer 2001 riots of "Asian youth" in the north of England, such sentiments, already an echo of Powell's famous 1968 "Rivers of Blood" speech, were replayed in public discourse, prompting one to wonder why many Britons appear nostalgic for Powell's Britain — had it ever existed — and what role the Raj nostalgia of the 1980s and 1990s has played in that phenomenon. The party political stakes are equally high. Like John Major and Margaret Thatcher before him, Tony Blair has been plagued by the problem of race and national identity, as the furor over the publication of the Runnymede Trust report, *The Future of Multi-Ethnic Britain* (2000) — which called for an end to "Englishness" in light of the growing presence of racial minorities in the U.K. — suggests.[40] The unease of Blair's cabinet ministers as they defended "the English nation" in the perpetually fragmenting "British Isles" signals not just the political necessity of the nation, but also the way it is occasioned by the specter of empire's diasporas and by anxieties about the ex-colonial bodies — black, brown, and various shades of white — that it continues to bring "home" as well.[41]

The work that is both mapped out and called for in *After the Imperial Turn* involves more than just challenging the parameters of "national" histories like Britain's. It means unmasking the complicity of history writing in patrolling the borders of national identity as well. Taking up the task of imagining unstable national histories may well end up letting the nation in through the back door. Such effects may in the last analysis be a testimony to how difficult it is to escape the grasp of national investigative frameworks even when one attempts a highly self-conscious and, hopefully, principled critique of the allure of nationness for Western historians — especially since the nation itself has historically served as "the ideological alibi of the territorial state."[42] Though the nation may be indispensable, it is also woefully inadequate to the task of representation for which it is apparently historically determined. The essays collected here engage the question of how — and even whether — historians can succeed in displacing the nation from center stage in part because the authors herein recognize that such a project depends on *our* willingness to take seriously the ramifications of the claim that a nation is never fully realized but always in the making and to interrogate the ways in which our own narrative strategies help to fetishize or denaturalize one of history's most common explanatory frameworks, if not its most seductive investigative modalities. This is surely a significant, if not hopeful, conviction, for it suggests that one does not have to give up on history in order to interrogate and ultimately to denaturalize the narrative strategies of its practitioners.

Indeed, British history has arguably been galvanized by renewed interest in things imperial, even if the institutional bodies that oversee it are of two minds about the desirability of British studies (in North America at least) being saved from irrelevance by empire.[43] As has been indicated above, in the British context the imperial turn has taken the form of monographs on the presence of colonial and ex-colonial peoples in metropolitan spaces; books on the impact of state-sponsored racial policies "at home"; critiques of the imbrication of imperial politics on the making of domestic legislation; articles and essays on the role of spectacle in producing imperial citizens in the metropole; work on the influence of empire on romanticism, the novel, and "English" literature more generally; and arguments that attempt to reorient the home/empire model by positing new concepts of political and social formation.[44] Elsewhere the approach has a more state-centered history, though cultural analysis has had a major impact on the development of continental and U.S. imperial histories as well.[45] Like the multisited and often inchoate intellectual currents that have been frozen somewhat unnaturally in rubrics like "the linguistic turn" and "the cultural turn," the imperial turn is hardly unified methodologically or politically, drawing (as the essays below amply demonstrate) on a variety of approaches and experiences. Like those "other" turns, the imperial one, which we aim to bring more clearly into view, is hardly monolithic. It is also recent enough that its histories have yet to be written and its several genealogies fully appreciated, offering us an opportunity to begin to think through some of its limits and possibilities.

Despite the role of postcolonial studies in shaping debates about empire and colonial hegemony since the 1980s (if not before), we do not necessarily see the imperial turn as coterminous with postcolonialism in all its academic varieties. Though these are not, admittedly, narratives that tend to structure accounts of the emergence of postcolonialism as an academic phenomenon, the work of critical race and feminist theorists, together with the pluralization — in race and ethnic as well as class terms — of North American undergraduate student bodies has helped to shape the return to empire as a site of analytical investigation in often contradictory ways. In the context of modern Britain, so have a variety of "riots" in the period since World War II. Such demonstrations have been motivated by resentment about racial inequality, postcolonial discontent at the limits of "national" citizenship, and resistance to the citizenship machinery of passports, visas, and racial profiling — from Notting Hill to Brixton down to Bradford in the summer of 2001, as contributors were thinking through their essays for this volume. Rarely are the connections among social action, theoretical innovation, and establishment history so clearly visible as they are in Tony Blair's Britain, where the revival of a reactionary imperial history can be read as one effect of the postimperial crises that have, in part, prompted the imperial turn. David Cannadine's *Ornamentalism: How the British Saw Their Empire*, which appeared in the summer of 2001, is just one in a long line of such reactions. An attempt to reclaim old, hallowed ground not just for the nation but for the classes and the masses, *Ornamentalism* aims to revalorize a hidebound narrative of social order in an attempt to sideline questions of race, violence, and domination from the Island Story, asserting even as it attempts to attenuate the constitutive impact of imperialism on British society at home.[46] Such intellectual projects are linked to a long-standing denial of, or at best amnesia about, the impact of empire on domestic political forms and social relations. They are also a response to the ways in which new imperial histories have begun to recast national narratives as inherently imperial and to destabilize Englishness at a moment when that identity is being very publicly and passionately debated.[47] That this occurred as Britain debated and then rejected the euro as its currency *and* in the wake of the

Runnymede Trust report on the future of "multi-ethnic Britain" reminds us of the very real stakes of the imperial turn for reconceptualizations of the nation.[48] It also dramatizes the ways in which traditional history is invoked as a justification for the reconsolidation of a resurgent white nationalism and the pleasures it brings to that genuinely paradoxical constituency of late postmodernity: dominant communities under siege — those suffering from what Ien Ang calls "identity panic."[49] To be sure, the events of September 11, 2001, have given such panic new kinds of political legitimacy in ways that have produced ostensibly new fantasies about globalization (both "Western" and Islamic) and helped to reconstitute a variety of nations in newly militarized ways. In the long run, the "new world" that 9/11 is believed to have inaugurated will be understood as having been emergent well before the events of that infamous day and will be reintegrated, one hopes, into the longer story of neocolonialism at century's end.[50] Meanwhile, the convergence of discussions about Europe and multicultural Britain is timely evidence of what Paul Gilroy calls the "tangle" of race and nation, as well as proof of the need to ask what the imperial turn in history writing can and should do to remain relevant and useful to contemporary political and social crises.[51]

The centrality of Britain to these questions is as much a limitation as it is a possibility when it comes to untangling — and hopefully retangling in productive ways — empire, nation, race, colony, and globe. Scholars working in the fields of modern Western history and literature cannot help but notice, and rightly lament and resent, the reproduction of British imperial dominance in the new imperial history and postcolonial studies.[52] The work of Latin Americanists is especially apposite here: not only have they been doing what has come to be called "postcolonial critique" for a long time, but also the empires with which they engage do not necessarily follow the models laid out as implicitly British and putatively universal in some postcolonial studies scholarship.[53] As Britain's "jewel in the crown," India has enjoyed a similarly privileged — and perhaps disproportionate — place in the imperial turn. The perniciousness of this state of affairs is perhaps most startlingly evident from one reviewer's comments on the back cover of Achille Mbembe's 2001 book, *On the Postcolony*, which is about power and subjectivity in Africa: "Finally," says George Marcus, "a powerful African alternative and complement to the now-canonical postcolonial literature on South Asia." Whether alternative or complement, work on postcolonial sites other than South Asia runs the risk of appearing derivative, just as Indian nationalism and other colonial political and cultural forms were seen as derivative at the height of the Raj and beyond.[54] De-exceptionalizing India ought to be entailed by deparochializing British history, though this is obviously an ongoing project.[55] The conflation of India with the postimperial, and indeed with the colonial *tout court*, has persisted in part because historical and ethnographic work has followed if not the flag, then the archive, which is arguably densest and richest for Britain's most valued colonial possession, whether that archive is literature or state-sponsored documentation. Given the role of both the British Empire and British history in shaping the historiographies of former settler states like the United States, Canada, Australia, and South Africa—not to mention India, China, and other ex-colonial sites—interrogating this legacy is crucial to a critically engaged postcolonial politics.[56] Whether scholarly attention to the global and the transnational ends up interrogating imperial histories or continues to do their ideological work through reconstituted forms of the nation is an important intellectual and political question that authors in this volume engage both directly and allusively as they critique old paradigms, chart new subjects, and struggle with new methods of research and writing.

After the Imperial Turn reflects the historical and historiographical legacy of the Raj insofar as it begins with Britain; makes clear the claims to splendid isolationism that have undergirded narratives of modern British history; and explores how, whether, and to what effect the nation can be decentered by new histories of what Sinha calls "imperial social formation."[57] I trust that foregrounding Britain will be viewed as a strategic maneuver designed not to reinstantiate it but, rather, to subject its presumptive centrality to interrogation and to submit the "new imperial history" that has grown out of the British experience to critique. Is it possible to challenge the dichotomies of "home" and "away" that underwrite national and imperial histories; to merge center and periphery and posit an imaginative and material space where metropole and colony emerge simultaneously, rather than in a teleological, imperialized sequence?[58] What kinds of disruptions does such a maneuver really make to the model of core and periphery—and to whose core and periphery, given the role of Ireland, Scotland, and Wales in empire, not to mention the ongoing processes of devolution they are currently experiencing? How does a turn toward empire break with the colonial logic that Chakrabarty and others have suggested is embedded in history writing per se; what kinds of logics and methods does it put into play?[59] In many respects, scholars working on polities other than Britain are in a better position to evaluate these possibilities, as well as to ask how particular these questions are and whether the answers they have so far produced are generalizable beyond Britain. Hence the volume features essays on the impact of the imperial turn in French, German, Spanish, Australian, and American "national" historiographies in order to interrogate the Anglocentric presumptions of new imperial histories and to open postcolonialism itself to critique as a carrier of unseen and subtle traces of British imperial hegemony.[60] These are, of course, just a few of the historiographies engaging these questions: work on Russia, East Asia, and elsewhere did not, for one reason or another, make it into the volume (which does not, in any event, attempt to be comprehensive). At the same time, encouraging students of Britain and its empire to come to terms with the ways in which historians of other national cultures are addressing the imperial turn, or not, is one of the chief purposes of this collection.

Given the very real geopolitical conditions and contests (both local and global) that have given energy to the turn to empire as a constitutive force in national histories and historiographies, the fact that nearly all the contributors save four work and live in the United States is surely significant. Indeed, there are many for whom the trends detailed below mark the Americanization of history — a way of making the past intelligible to a certain segment of the twenty-first century "global village," the most economically privileged and possibly the most politically naive segment at that. Racial tension and the spectral presence of racialized Others are perhaps the most legible idioms through which Americans are able to read social disorder elsewhere in the West. These are idioms of which the new imperial studies make repeated use for understanding both European empires of the past and the eruptions of ethnic and communal struggle in "fortress Europe" that cross American media screens, however briefly and episodically. The extent to which American scholars working on Europe have brought a generalized racial lens to bear on British and continental histories and literatures remains a matter for further exploration. The relationship between the generation of '68 in the academy and the institutionalization of (and resistance to) the imperial turn also remains to be fully explored. While these institutional and political phenomena cannot be reduced to either a simple cause or a simple set of effects, they would seem to point to the Americanization of scholarly production and consumption in an age of academic corporatization.[61] Because of the multiracial and multinational character of the cadre of scholars who make up the "American" academy, it is important not to take this critique at face value, especially since many of those most influential in shaping the imperial turn have at best an angular relationship to American politics and culture. Although the most privileged of these (Said, Spivak, Homi Bhabha) have received the most press, the fact is that many less privileged nonwhite and non-American scholars make up the North American academy, even if it is still not as diverse as it should be. Nevertheless, complaints about the commodification and export of North American academic theory and practice do raise crucial questions about the function of

Americanization during an age when an accelerated neocolonial American politics is to be found in a variety of economic, cultural, and "virtual" domains.[62]

A similar critique has been raised to counter discourses of globalization in the academy — namely, that globalism allows a homogeneous "world" culture to be imagined and propagated in ways that serve the needs of transnational capital — that is, American capitalism and its liberalizing, neocolonial interests. Surely Hue-Tam Ho Tai articulates a crucial, if largely unremarked upon, point when she observes that "if imperialism is the nineteenth-century version of universalism, globalism is its twentieth-century reincarnation."[63] For some, these observations will seem far more obvious than they had been in the wake of 9/11; as one contributor to the *New York Times* wrote with a decided air of discovery in April 2002, "Today, America is no mere superpower or hegemon but a full-blown empire in the Roman and British sense."[64] Clearly, the stakes of Americanization and its critiques have been raised in the first few years of the new millennium. Far from being an incidental effect of market forces or even cataclysmic events, the so-called globalization of the planet is bound up with circuits of production and reproduction that appear to be organic and unmediated but that in fact are designed to erase their own histories and origins — with ties to a would-be hegemonic capitalism chief among them. So that even when the models of and rationales for globalization do not emerge directly or expressly from the West, they are always already imprinted with either a need or a desire for legibility by the West in such a way that their global character is arguably just another fiction, albeit a powerful one — especially in terms of market niches.

Contributors to *After the Imperial Turn* who engage with the question of globalism and its related categorical domains (transnationalism, localism, "area studies") are alive to these problematics, even as they try to think of ways to get beyond the box of globalization that is, in ways that still are not fully fathomed, also a legacy of the Enlightenment. How do we resist the seduction of national narratives and make sense of the violences they enact under the guise of patriotism, imperial and otherwise? How do we convince students that this is a valuable project, connected to the development of civic participation and responsibility in the twenty-first century in transformative and enduring ways? What is left to work with if the nation's role is diminished as a result of the imperial turn? What does that maneuver lead away from, exactly? What does it turn us toward, precisely? Do we, as inheritors of post-Enlightenment, postimperial thinking ourselves, even have the tools for undertaking such an enterprise? If Eurocentrism and "the planetary" together characterize modernity, (how) do new imperial histories rupture that binary?[65] What do accelerated discourses of globalization in institutions of higher education mean for the study of nation and empire? What erasures and glosses are thereby likely, and how do those differentially affect disciplines and area studies? Do challenges to the nation mean the end of history as we know it?

Readers of this volume should understand from the start that there is not always consensus herein about the possibility or even the desirability of pursuing the critique of the nation that can be entailed by the imperial turn, especially in the context of accelerating discourses on globalization. In fact, in contrast to the utopianism that has characterized the work of some scholars who have taken up multiculturalism and postcolonial theory as strategic weapons against disciplinary or national hegemonies, many of the authors here are cautious, if not skeptical, about the possibility of radical transformation after the imperial turn — in part because the disciplines have inherited nation-building models that are difficult to unthink. Rather than seeing this as some kind of "hip defeatism," I hope readers will take their skepticism as, among other things, an implicit critique of the triumphalism of imperial narratives and as recognition of the perilous, exhilarating contingency that informs politically engaged scholarship across the disciplines.[66] If not exactly a resource of hope, the "double bind" of necessity and impossibility that undergirds this collection signals a conviction about the need to think both with and through the nation in the shadow of colonialism and the penumbrae of postcolonialism and globalization.[67]

The call for papers for this collection emphasized my belief that academics are bound to understand what they do as an ideological act, as well as my conviction that there should be venues where they have the opportunity to think out loud about the politics of what they study, the methodological choices they make, and the analytical interventions they seek to stage. I was especially keen to see how those who use the resources of the so-called "new imperial history" remain self-conscious, in productive and usable ways, about the material and historical conditions that make such approaches possible and others unimaginable. The book that has resulted offers an opportunity for readers to work through the issues we all face as we attempt to account for the fact of empire in the "political constitution" of the postcolonial present.[68] Part 1 ("Nations, Empires, Disciplines: Thinking beyond the Boundaries") engages the question of how to think, teach, and work postnationally in all manner of geopolitical locations and from different disciplinary vantage points — from Washington State to the Antipodes, from history classrooms to the MLA job list to the colonial archive. The focus in this section is deliberately Anglocentric: for with Catherine Hall I believe that in order to interrogate fully the political and ideological power of any "nation," we must appreciate "the specificity of the national formation."[69] I hope readers will be able to track the centrifugal aspirations of British hegemony, as well as some of its centripetal effects, and ask, in the process, what is left of the empire as well as of the nation after the end of British imperialism in its formal, official incarnations. Part 2 ("Fortresses and Frontiers: Beyond and Within") opens up the discussion of empire, nation, and colony beyond the boundaries of British imperial history and scholarship, showcasing what other "national" scholarship has done, locating "area studies" in the context of national narratives and globalization, and underscoring the regulatory capacity of the state through citizenship machinery like the passport. The rubric "Fortresses and Frontiers" also highlights the ways in which convictions about the importance of space as well as of time have helped to shape historians' apprehensions of what counts as an empire, making clear how consequential newly visible imperial/colonial geographies have been for rethinking the nation. Part 3 ("Reorienting the Nation: Logics of Empire, Colony, Globe") features new directions in research that test the practicality and methodological limits of the imperial turn in all its complexity and interdisciplinarity, examining imperial/colonial politics from and about sites as disparate as New York, London, Paris, Hong Kong, the Caribbean, New Zealand, the Celtic fringe, and Ethiopia. Taken together the essays in this section illustrate that "going beyond the imperial turn is not necessarily synonymous with querying the nation" but may also "mean questioning some of the organizing logic of the new imperial history" itself.[70]

By reading historical writing as a narrative enterprise and literature as a rich source of historical evidence and knowledge, contributors to the volume track the ways in which disciplines have been constructed as nations, revealing the territorial investments of scholars and departmental curricula, as well as the imperial fantasies of "Self" and "Other" that have characterized the debates about the "new imperial studies." If canons of all kinds come under scrutiny thereby, it is not a given that the nation as such disappears from view; quite the contrary. The reprise of the nation in the wake of the imperial turn is, in the end, neither a paradox nor a surprise. As the essays collected here endeavor to illustrate, the nation's persistent reappearance is one fairly predictable effect of the cultural logic of post-Enlightenment political economies (both symbolic and "real"), which recommodify national subjects in new, and in the end not so unfamiliar, historical forms. Though their geographies, approaches, and conclusions are diverse, taken together, the authors included in the pages that follow are concerned with the wide variety of developments past and present that imperil—or in the end refashion—the nation as a subject of inquiry. Whether implicitly or explicitly, they represent the nation as an object of contest, negotiation, and, above all, struggle, both historically and in the contemporary moment. If, as a number of critics have suggested, the colonial age is not over "and is in fact still unfolding in the present global logic of modernity," the ramifications of this struggle cannot be ignored, either in our work or in those classroom contexts where we take up and presumably experiment with the ongoing problem of national time, nation-bounded histories, and the exigencies of a globalizing present.[71]

After the Imperial Turn seeks dialogue and critical companionship with a number of recent discussions about the directions of postmodern and postcolonial scholarship — discussions by which the conversation hoped for here has clearly been influenced. These include Gyan Prakash's *After Colonialism*, Terence J. MacDonald's *The Historic Turn in the Human Sciences*, and Victoria E. Bonnell and Lynn Hunt's *Beyond the Cultural Turn*.[72] On offer in this collection is not a sequel to these volumes, but rather an attempt to orient the debates therein around a specific set of questions about the project of national history and anxieties about its demise — questions that are implicit, but ultimately unacknowledged and underexamined, in all of them. How the nation and its fragments, the fragments of empire and their nations, bear on methodological procedures as well as conceptual reorientations in the humanities and the social sciences is more often than not a subject buried in much current work in ways that renaturalize the nation and realign it with all manner of turns, the cultural and the linguistic most celebrated among them.[73] Our contribution lies, I believe, in our determination to confront head on the anxieties engendered by the challenge to the nation that imperial histories have the capacity to mount not just to practitioners of national histories, but also to the ostensible critics of nation-building impulses and national/ist narratives, whether in the West or elsewhere. Above all, we wish to ask whether and how the nation remains central, possible, desirable, inadequate, and/or indispensable to history writing at century's end — and for whom — and what that means about the future of the disciplinary regimes in which we, our colleagues, and our students are implicated.

Notes

For their help in thinking through many of the premises of this introduction I am grateful to my colleagues in the 2001–2002 NEH Globalization Reading Group in the Department of History at the University of Illinois. Special thanks also go to Tony Ballantyne, Jim Barrett, Herman Bennett, Ian Fletcher, George Robb, Mrinalini Sinha, and Hsu-Ming Teo — careful readers and challenging interlocutors, each and every one. The comments and suggestions of three anonymous readers for Duke University Press were also exceedingly useful; they have helped to make the introduction more coherent and, I hope, more persuasive.

1 The title of this chapter reflects Dipesh Chakrabarty's take on the Enlightenment in rela-

tionship to the project of European colonialism; see his *Provincializing Europe: Postcolonial Thought and Historical Difference* (Princeton, N.J.: Princeton University Press, 2000). For themes of doubleness cast as im/possibility, see also Achille Mbembe, *On the Postcolony* (Berkeley: University of California Press, 2001), and Ien Ang, *On Not Speaking Chinese: Living between Asia and the West* (London: Routledge, 2001).

2   Etienne Balibar, *Race, Nation and Class: Ambiguous Identities* (London: Verso, 1992), p. 89. Fanon is quoted in Catherine Hall, "Introduction: Thinking the Postcolonial, Thinking the Empire," in her edited collection, *Cultures of Empire: Colonizers in Britain and the Empire in the Nineteenth and Twentieth Centuries: A Reader* (Manchester: Manchester University Press, 2000), p. 1

3   Prasenjit Duara, *Rescuing History from the Nation: Questioning Narratives of Modern China* (Chicago: University of Chicago Press, 1995), and Paul Gilroy, "Hatred of the Partially Familiar," *Times Higher Education Supplement*, June 25, 1999, p. 4.

4   See, for example, Warren I. Cohen, *East Asia at the Center: Four Thousand Years of Engagement with the World* (New York: Columbia University Press, 2000), and S. A. M. Adshead, *Material Culture in Europe and China, 1400–1800: The Rise of Consumerism* (New York: St. Martin's Press, 1997).

5   See Chakrabarty, *Provincializing Europe*; Uday Singh Mehta, *Liberalism and Empire: A Study in Nineteenth-Century British Thought* (Chicago: University of Chicago Press, 1999); and Ann Laura Stoler, *Race and the Education of Desire: Foucault's History of Sexuality and the Colonial Order of Things* (Durham, N.C.: Duke University Press, 1995).

6   See Chakrabarty, *Provincializing Europe*.

7   For one account of this postwar process, see Benjamin Lee, "Critical Internationalism," *Public Culture* 7 (1995): 559–592.

8   Paul Gilroy, *Against Race: Imagining Political Culture beyond the Color Line* (Cambridge, Mass.: Harvard University Press, 2000), p. 76.

9   See C. Hall, "Introduction," pp. 2ff.

10   Edward Said, *Culture and Imperialism* (New York: Knopf, 1993), p. 6

11   Peter Hulme, "Subversive Archipelagos: Colonial Discourse and the Break-Up of Continental Theory," *Dispositio* 14, 36–38 (1989): 3.

12   John M. MacKenzie's editorship of the multivolume series "Studies in Imperialism" is responsible for much of the wealth of historical material now available on the impact of empire on domestic British culture. See, for example, his *Imperialism and Popular Culture* (Manchester: Manchester University Press, 1986), and *Propaganda and Empire: The Manipulation of British Public Opinion, 1880–1960* (Manchester: Manchester University Press, 1984). Other early work includes Clare Midgley, *Women against Slavery: The British Campaign, 1780–1870* (London: Routledge, 1992); Jenny Sharpe, *Allegories of Empire: The Figure of Woman in the Colonial Text* (Minneapolis: University of Minnesota Press, 1993); Firdous Azim, *The Colonial Rise of the Novel* (London: Routledge, 1993); Catherine Hall: *White, Male and Middle Class: Explorations in Feminism and History* (London: Routledge, 1992), and "Rethinking Imperial Histories: The Reform Act of 1867," *New Left Review* 208 (1994): 3–29; Vron Ware, *Beyond the Pale: White Women, Racism and History* (London: Verso, 1992); Antoinette Burton: *Burdens of History: British Feminists, Indian Women, and Imperial Culture, 1865–1915* (Chapel Hill: University of North Carolina Press, 1994), and *At the Heart of the Empire: Indians and the Colonial Encounter in Late-Victorian Britain* (Berkeley: University of California Press, 1998); Annie E. Coombes, *Reinventing Africa: Museums, Material Culture, and Popular Imagination in Late Victorian and Edwardian England* (New Haven, Conn.: Yale University Press, 1994); Mrinalini Sinha, *Colonial*

Masculinity: The "Manly Englishman" and the "Effeminate Bengali" in the Late Nineteenth Century (Manchester: Manchester University Press, 1995); Anne McClintock, *Imperial Leather: Race, Gender and Sexuality in the Colonial Contexts* (New York: Routledge, 1995); Susan Zlotnick, "Domesticating Imperialism: Curry and Cookbooks in Victorian England," *Frontiers: A Journal of Women's Studies* 16, 2/3 (1996): 51–68; Shearer West, ed., *The Victorians and Race* (Aldershot: Scolar Press, 1996); James Walvin, *Fruits of Empire: Exotic Produce and British Taste, 1660–1800* (New York: New York University Press, 1997). For a fuller list of relevant citations see note 45.

13 Gretchen Gerzina, *Black London: Life before Emancipation* (New Brunswick, N.J.: Rutgers University Press, 1995), p. 204; see also Rozina Visram, *Ayahs, Lascars and Princes: Indians in Britain, 1700–1947* (London: Pluto Press, 1986); Peter Fryer, *Staying Power: The History of Black People in Britain* (London: Pluto Press, 1987); Colin Holmes, *John Bull's Island: Immigration and British Society 1871–1971* (London: Macmillan, 1988), pp. 1–85; and Shompa Lahiri, *Indians in Britain: Anglo-Indian Encounters, Race and Identity, 1880–1930* (London: Frank Cass, 2000).

14 Benita Parry, "Overlapping Territories and Intertwined Histories: Edward Said's Postcolonial Cosmopolitanism," in *Edward Said: A Critical Reader*, ed. Michael Sprinker (Oxford: Blackwell, 1993), p. 24. See also John M. MacKenzie, *Orientalism: History, Theory and the Arts* (Manchester: Manchester University Press, 1995).

15 Paul Gilroy, *The Black Atlantic: Modernity and Double Consciousness* (Cambridge, Mass.: Harvard University Press, 1993), p. 7

16 Olaudah Equiano was a slave from Benin who purchased his freedom in 1766 and wrote his life story (*The Interesting Narrative of the Life of Olaudah Equiano*) in 1789; Mary Seacole was a Jamaican nurse who served in the Crimean War and wrote an account of it (*The Wonderful Adventures of Mrs. Seacole in Many Lands*); see Paul Edwards and David Dabydeen, eds., *Black Writers in Britain, 1760–1890* (Edinburgh: Edinburgh University Press, 1991). For newspaper coverage of the Major government's response to their inclusion in British history texts, see "The 'Betrayal' of Britain's History," *Daily Telegraph*, September 19, 1995; "Heroic Virtues" and "History Fit for (Politically Correct) Heroes," *Sunday Telegraph*, September 24, 1995.

17 P. J. Marshall, "No Fatal Impact? The Elusive History of Imperial Britain," *Times Literary Supplement*, March 12, 1993, pp. 8–10; see also MacKenzie, *Orientalism*.

18 See Bill Schwarz, ed., *The Expansion of England: Race, Ethnicity and Cultural History* (New York: Routledge, 1996), and Catherine Hall, "Histories, Empires and the Post-Colonial Moment," in *The Post-Colonial Question: Common Skies, Divided Horizons*, ed. Iain Chambers and Lidia Curti (New York: Routledge, 1996), pp. 65–77; P. J. Marshall, *The Cambridge Illustrated History of the British Empire* (Cambridge: Cambridge University Press, 1996). Marshall agrees with two of the *Oxford English Dictionary's* (OED) definitions of "constitutive" as (1) "having the power of constituting; constructive" and (2) "that which goes to make up; constituent, component" but cannot agree with its third: "that which makes a thing what it is." Personal Communication, September 15, 1996.

19 See Marshall, "No Fatal Impact?"; David Cannadine, *Ornamentalism: How the British Saw Their Empire* (New York: Oxford University Press, 2001); and, to a lesser degree, Andrew S. Thompson, *Imperial Britain: The Empire in British Politics, c. 1880–1932* (London: Longman, 2000).

20 For two excellent discussions of colonial inscriptions on the Victorian metropole, see Ruth H. Lindeborg, "The 'Asiatic' and the Boundaries of Victorian Englishness," *Victorian Studies*, spring 1994: 381–404, and C. Hall, "Rethinking Imperial Histories."

21 See Sinha, *Colonial Masculinity*. For one example of how this false homogenization works

to obscure the role of the Celtic fringe in empire, see Dipesh Chakrabarty's discussion of how crucial Dundee was in the history of the jute mills in Calcutta: *Rethinking Working-Class History* (Princeton, N.J.: Princeton University Press, 1989), ch. 2.

22 This is Kathleen Wilson's definition of modernity. See her "Citizenship, Empire and Modernity in the English Provinces, c. 1720–1790," *Eighteenth Century Studies* 29, 1 (1995): 70.

23 McClintock, *Imperial Leather*, p. 36. For an example of someone who keeps the nation firmly in place, see Deirdre David, *Rule Britannia: Women, Empire and Victorian Writing* (Ithaca, N.Y.: Cornell University Press, 1995). For examples of strenuous resistance to this, see Gilroy, *Black Atlantic*, and Peter Linebaugh, "All the Atlantic Mountains Shook," *Labour/Le Travailleur* 10 (1982): 87–121.

24 I am aided in these observations by Prasenjit Duara's *Rescuing History from the Nation*.

25 See Elizabeth D. Ermarth, *Sequel to History: Postmodernism and the Crisis of Representational Time* (Princeton, N.J.: Princeton University Press, 1992), pp. 18, 21.

26 I am aided in this observation by Kim F. Hall's reading of Richard Hakluyt in *Things of Darkness: Economies of Race and Gender in Early Modern England* (Ithaca, N.Y.: Cornell University Press, 1995), p. 48.

27 See Judith Butler, "Contingent Foundations" and Joan Scott, "Experience," in *Feminists Theorize the Political*, ed. Judith Butler and Joan Scott (New York: Routledge, 1992), pp. 3–21 and 22–40 respectively, and Anna Marie Smith, *New Right Discourse on Race and Sexuality: Britain 1968–1990* (Cambridge: Cambridge University Press, 1994), p. 84.

28 See, for example, Elizabeth Buettner's review of C. Hall, ed., *Cultures of Empire*, for Reviews in History, February 4, 2002 (reviews-list@ihr.sas.ac.uk), and Susan Pedersen, "Introduction: Claims to Belong," *Journal of British Studies* 40 (2001): 450.

29 See Ann Laura Stoler and Frederic Cooper, "Introduction: Tensions of Empire: Colonial Control and Visions of Rule," *American Ethnologist* 16 (1989): 615, and Stoler, *Race and the Education of Desire*, p. 97.

30 Renata Salecl, "The Fantasy Structure of Nationalist Discourse," *Praxis International* 13, 3 (October 1993): 213–223.

31 Kobena Mercer, *Welcome to the Jungle: New Positions in Black Cultural Studies* (New York: Routledge, 1994), pp. 5 and 31.

32 For one account of the democratization phenomenon in the United States, see Joyce Appleby, Lynn Hunt, and Margaret Jacobs, *Telling the Truth about History* (New York: W. W. Norton, 1994).

33 Joanne Meyerowitz, ed., *Not June Cleaver: Women and Gender in Post-War America* (Philadelphia: Temple University Press, 1994).

34 Ann Curthoys and John Docker, "Is History Fiction?" *UTS Review: Cultural Studies and New Writing* 2, 2 (May 1996): esp. 18 and 29.

35 The term is Sudipta Kaviraj's. See his "The Imaginary Institution of India," in *Subaltern Studies VII: Writings on South Asian History and Society*, ed. Partha Chatterjee and Gyanendra Pandey (Delhi: Oxford University Press, 1993), p. 33.

36 David Harvey, *The Condition of Postmodernity* (Oxford: Blackwell, 1990), p. 238.

37 See Robert Carr, "Crossing the First World/Third World Divides: Testimonial Transnational Feminisms, and the Postmodern Condition," in *Scattered Hegemonies: Postmodernity and Transnational Feminist Practices*, ed. Inderpal Grewal and Caren Caplan (Minneapolis: University of Minnesota Press, 1994), p. 154.

38 Tom Nairn, *After Britain: New Labour and the Return of Scotland* (London: Granta, 1999); Peter Hitchens, *The Abolition of Britain: From Winston Churchill to Princess Diana* (San Francisco: Encounter Books, 2000).

39   Quoted in Clare E. Alexander, *The Art of Being Black: The Creation of Black British Youth Identities* (Oxford: Clarendon Press, 1996), p. 5.

40   Bhiku Parekh et al., *The Future of Multi-Ethnic Britain: Report of the Commission on the Future of Multi-Ethnic Britain* (London: Profile Books, 2000); Alan Travis, "'British' a Term of Coded Racism, Says Report," *Guardian Weekly*, October 19–25, 2000, p. 11.

41   Robin Cook, "Celebrating Britishness," June 20, 2001. London: Foreign and Commonwealth Office. http://www.fco.gov.uk/text_only/news/speechtext.asp4941.

42   See Carole Boyce Davies's discussion of how Latinos/Latinas have reconceptualized America in *Black Women, Writing, and Identity: Migratory Subjects* (London: Routledge, 1994), p. 10, and Arjun Appadurai, "The Heart of Whiteness," *Callaloo* 16, 4 (1993): 796.

43   See Peter Stansky et al., *North American Conference of British Studies Report on the State and Future of British Studies in North America* (November 1999).

44   Eric Williams, *Capitalism and Slavery* (Durham, N.C.: Duke University Press, 1944/1994); Christine Bolt, *Victorian Attitudes towards Race* (London: Routledge and Kegan Paul, 1971); Edward Scobie, *Black Britannia: A History of Blacks in Britain* (Chicago: Johnson Publishing, 1972); James Walvin, *Black and White: The Negro and English Society, 1555–1945* (London: Allen Lane, 1973); Douglas Lorimer, *Colour, Class and the Victorians: English Attitudes toward the Negro in the Mid-Nineteenth Century* (New York: Holmes and Meier, 1978); Anna Davin, "Imperialism and Motherhood," *History Workshop* 5 (1978): 9–65; Paul B. Rich, *Race and Empire in British Politics* (Cambridge: Cambridge University Press, 1986); Ron Ramdin, *The Making of the Black Working Class in Britain* (Aldershot: Gower Publishing, 1987); C. A. Bayly, *Imperial Meridian* (London: Longman, 1989); Susan Pedersen, "National Bodies, Unspeakable Acts: The Sexual Politics of Colonial Policy-Making," *Journal of Modern History* 63 (December 1991): 647–680; Nupur Chaudhuri, "Shawls, Curry, Jewelry, and Rice in Victorian Britain," in *Western Women and Imperialism: Complicity and Resistance*, ed. Nupur Chaudhuri and Margaret Strobel (Bloomington: Indiana University Press, 1992), pp. 231–246; Thomas C. Holt, *The Problem of Freedom* (Baltimore: Johns Hopkins University Press, 1992); Lynn Zastoupil, *John Stuart Mill and India* (Stanford, Calif.: Stanford University Press, 1994); Laura Tabili, *"We Ask for British Justice": Workers and Racial Difference in Late Imperial Britain* (Ithaca, N.Y.: Cornell University Press, 1994); C. Hall, "Rethinking Imperial Histories; Philippa Levine, "Re-Reading the 1890s: Venereal Disease as 'Constitutional Crisis' in Britain and British India," *Journal of Asian Studies* 55, 3 (August 1996): 585–612; Tim Fulton and Peter J. Kitson, eds., *Romanticism and Colonialism* (Cambridge: Cambridge University Press, 1998); Judith Walkowitz, "The Indian Woman, the Flower Girl, and the Jew: Photojournalism in Edwardian London," *Victorian Studies* 42 (fall 1998/99): 3–46; Jeffery A. Auerbach, *The Great Exhibition of 1851: A Nation on Display* (New Haven, Conn.: Yale University Press, 1999); Felix Driver and David Gilbert, eds., *Imperial Cities: Landscape, Display and Identity* (Manchester: Manchester University Press, 1999); Susan Thorne, *Congregational Missions and the Making of an Imperial Culture in Nineteenth-Century England* (Stanford, Calif.: Stanford University Press, 1999); Jonathan Schneer, *London 1900: The Imperial Metropolis* (New Haven, Conn.: Yale University Press, 1999); Catherine Hall, Keith McClelland, and Jane Rendall, *Defining the Victorian Nation: Class, Race, Gender and the Reform Act of 1867* (Cambridge, Cambridge University Press, 2000); Richard Drayton, *Nature's Government: Science, Imperial Britain and the "Improvement" of the World* (New Haven, Conn.: Yale University Press, 2000); Antoinette Burton, "Tongues Untied: Lord Salisbury's 'Black Man' and the Boundaries of Imperial Democracy," *Comparative Studies in Society and History* 43, 2 (2000): 632–659; Andrew S. Thompson, *Imperial Britain*; Peter H. Hoffenberg, *An Empire on Display: English, Indian, and*

Australian Exhibitions from the Crystal Palace to the Great War (Berkeley: University of California Press, 2001); Catherine Hall, *Civilising Subjects: Metropole and Colony in the English Imagination, 1830–1867* (London: Polity Press, 2002).

45 For continental Europe, see David Prochaska, "History as Literature, Literature as History: Cagayous of Algiers," *American Historical Review* 101 (1996); Tyler Stovall: *Paris Noir: African Americans in the City of Light* (Boston: Houghton Mifflin, 1996), and "The Color Line behind the Lines: Racial Violence in France during the Great War," *American Historical Review* 103 (1998): 737–769; Yaël Simpson Fletcher, "Unsettling Settlers: Colonial Migrants and Racialized Sexuality in Interwar Marseilles," in *Gender, Sexuality and Colonial Modernities*, ed. Antoinette Burton (London: Routledge, 1999), pp. 80–94; Gary Wilder, "Practicing Citizenship in Imperial Paris," in *Civil Society and the Political Imagination in Africa: Critical Perspectives*, ed. John L. and Jean Comaroff (Chicago: University of Chicago Press, 1999); Tina Campt, "'Afro-German': The Convergence of Race, Sexuality and Gender in the Formation of a German Ethnic Identity, 1919–1960," (ph.d. dissertation, Cornell University, 1996); Alice H. Conklin, *A Mission to Civilize: The Republican Idea of Empire in France and West Africa, 1895–1930* (Stanford, Calif.: Stanford University Press, 1997); Susanne Zantop, *Colonial Fantasies: Conquest, Family and Nation in Precolonial Germany, 1770–1870* (Durham, N.C.: Duke University Press, 1997); Lora Wildenthal: "Race, Gender and Citizenship in the German Colonial Empire," in *Tensions of Empire: Colonial Cultures in a Bourgeois World*, ed. Frederick Cooper and Ann Laura Stoler (Berkeley: University of California Press, 1996), pp. 263–283, and *German Women for Empire, 1884–1945* (Durham, N.C.: Duke University Press, 2001); Sara Friedrichsmeyer, Sara Lennox, and Susanne Zantop, eds., *The Imperialist Imagination: German Colonialism and Its Legacy* (Ann Arbor: University of Michigan Press, 1999); Frances Gouda, *Dutch Culture Overseas: Colonial Practice in the Netherland Indies, 1900–1942* (Amsterdam: Amsterdam University Press, 1995); Julia Clancy-Smith and Frances Gouda, eds., *Domesticating the Empire: Race, Gender, and Family Life in French and Dutch Colonialism* (Charlottesville: University Press of Virginia, 1998); Elsbeth Locher-Scholten, *Women and the Colonial State: Essays on Gender and Modernity in the Netherlands Indies, 1900–42* (Amsterdam: Amsterdam University Press, 2000). For a useful digest of the American literature, see *Pairing Empires: Britain and the United States, 1857–1947*, special issue of the *Journal of Colonialism and Colonial History*, guest ed. Paul Kramer and Jonathan Plotz (http://muse.jhu .edu/journals/journal_of_colonialism_and_colonial_history/toc/cch2.1.html); see also Amy Kaplan and Donald E. Pease, eds., *Cultures of United States Imperialism* (Durham, N.C.: Duke University Press, 1993); Kristin L. Hoganson, *Fighting for American Manhood: How Gender Politics Provoked the Spanish-American and Philippine-American Wars* (New Haven, Conn.: Yale University Press, 1999); Robert Gregg, *Inside Out, Outside In: Essays in Comparative History* (New York: St. Martin's Press, 1999); C. Richard King, ed., *Postcolonial America* (Urbana: University of Illinois Press, 2000); and Michael Adas, "From Settler Colony to Global Hegemon: Integrating the Exceptionalist Narrative of the American Experience into World History," *American Historical Review* 106, 5 (December 2001): 1692–1720.

46 Cannadine, *Ornamentalism*. See also the special issue of the *Journal of Colonialism and Colonial History*, April 2002, ed. Tony Ballantyne, which features a roundtable forum on the book: http://euterpe-muse.press.jhu.edu/journals/jcch/.

47 Nairn, *After Britain*; Hitchens, *The Abolition of Britain*; Catherine Hall, "The Rule of Difference: Gender, Class and Empire in the Making of the 1832 Reform Act," in *Gendered Nations: Nationalism and Gender Order in the Long Nineteenth Century*, ed. Ida Blom, Karen Hagemann, and Catherine Hall (New York: Berg, 2000). For the prehistory of this,

see Raphael Samuel: "Resurrectionism," in *Representing the Nation: A Reader* ed. David Boswell and Jessica Evans (London: Routledge, 1999), pp. 163–184, and *Theatres of Memory* (London: Verso, 1995).

48 Parekh et al., *The Future of Multi-Ethnic Britain.*

49 See Ien Ang, "Identity Blues," in *Without Guarantees: In Honour of Stuart Hall*, ed. Paul Gilroy, Lawrence Grossberg, and Angela McRobbie (London: Verso, 2000), p. 5; and Slavoj Žižek, "Enjoy Your Nation as Yourself!" *Tarrying with the Negative: Kant, Hegel and the Critique of Ideology* (Durham, N.C.: Duke University Press, 1993), pp. 200–237.

50 For the anticipation of such a history, see Michael Hardt and Antonio Negri, *Empire* (Cambridge, Mass.: Harvard University Press, 2000).

51 Gilroy, "Hatred of the Partially Familiar," p. 4; for immediate contemporary relevance, see David Slavin's "LePen's Race Card," posted to H-France@LISTS.AKRON.edu, May 3, 2002. Thanks to Clare Crowston for this reference.

52 See Craig Clunas, "Modernity Global and Local: Consumption and the Rise of the West," *American Historical Review* 104, 5 (December 1999): 1497–1511.

53 See J. Jorge Klor de Alva, "The Postcolonization of (Latin) American Experience: A Reconsideration of 'Colonialism,' 'Postcolonialism,' and 'Mestizaje,'" in *After Colonialism: Imperial Histories and Postcolonial Displacements*, ed. Gyan Prakash (Princeton, N.J.: Princeton University Press, 1995), pp. 241–278, and Walter D. Mignolo, *Local Histories, Global Designs: Coloniality, Subaltern Knowledges and Border Thinking* (Princeton: Princeton University Press, 2000). I am grateful to Elena Delgado for enouraging me to appreciate this point.

54 See Mbembe, *On the Postcolony*, and Partha Chatterjee, *Nationalist Thought and the Colonial World: A Derivative Discourse?* (London: Zed, 1986).

55 See Carol A. Breckenridge, "On the Transition," *Public Culture* 12, 3 (2000): ix.

56 I am grateful to Ian Fletcher for this observation.

57 Sinha, *Colonial Masculinity.*

58 See Ferdinand Coronil, "Beyond Occidentalism: Toward Non-Imperial Geohistorical Catgeories," *Cultural Anthropology* 11, 1 (1996); 51–87.

59 See Dipesh Chakrabarty, "The Death of History? Historical Consciousness and the Culture of Late Capitalism," *Public Culture* 4, 2 (1992): 47–65, and Ajay Skaria, *Hybrid Histories: Forests, Frontiers and Wildness in Western India* (Delhi: Oxford University Press, 1999).

60 For a discussion of postcolonialism's conservative effects, see Simon During, "Postcolonialism and Globalisation: A Dialectical Relation after All?" *Postcolonial Studies*, 1, 1 (1998): 31–47.

61 Bill Readings, *The University in Ruins* (Cambridge, Mass.: Harvard University Press, 1996). Lest we think this is a new phenomenon, we need only consult W. T. Stead's *The Americanization of the World* (New York: Horace Markely, 1901).

62 I am grateful to Hsu-Ming Teo for this observation. For a particularly smart discussion of postmodernist phenomena (like globalization) as an unacknowledged effect of postcolonial crisis and neocolonial management, see S. Shankar, *Textual Traffic: Colonialism, Modernity and the Economy of the Text* (Albany: State University of New York Press, 2001), pp. 33–37.

63 Hue-Tam Ho Tai, "Remembered Realms: Pierre Nora and French National Memory," *American Historical Review* 106, 3 (June 2001): 921.

64 Emily Eakin, "It Takes an Empire," *New York Times*, April 1, 2002; for two different responses, see Dinesh D'Souza, "Two Cheers for Colonialism," *Chronicle of Higher Educa-*

tion, May 10, 2002 (http:chronicle.com), and Amitav Ghosh, "Imperial Temptation," *The Nation*, May 27, 2002, p. 24.

65 See Enrique Dussel, "Beyond Eurocentrism: The World System and the Limits of Modernity," in *The Cultures of Globalization*, ed. Frederic Jameson and Masao Miyoshi (Durham, N.C.: Duke University Press, 1998), pp. 3–31.

66 "Hip defeatism" is Martha Nussbaum's rather glib critique of Judith Butler and of what she understands as postmodernism more generally. See Martha C. Nussbaum, "The Professor of Parody," *New Republic*, February 22, 1999, pp. 37–45.

67 See Ang, "Identity Blues," p. 2.

68 Hardt and Negri, *Empire*, pp. 1–66.

69 C. Hall, *Civilising Subjects*, p. 9.

70 E-mail correspondence with Lara Kriegel, February 20, 2001.

71 See David Bunn, "Comaroff Country," *Interventions* 31, 1 (2001): 6.

72 Prakash, ed., *After Colonialism*; Terence J. MacDonald, *The Historic Turn in the Social Sciences* (Ann Arbor: University of Michigan Press, 1996); Victoria E. Bonnell and Lynn Hunt, eds., *Beyond the Cultural Turn* (Berkeley: University of California Press, 1999).

73 I refer here to Partha Chatterjee's *The Nation and Its Fragments: Colonial and Postcolonial Histories* (Princeton, N.J.: Princeton University Press, 1993), and Madhavi Kale's *Fragments of Empire: Capital, Slavery, and Indian Indentured Labor Migration in the British Caribbean* (Philadelphia: University of Pennsylvania Press, 1998).

1

Nations, Empires, Disciplines:

Thinking beyond the Boundaries

SUSAN D. PENNYBACKER

Rethinking British Studies: Is There Life after Empire?

The elections of 1983 and 1987 pointed to yet another important social development: the growth of the immigrant population of peoples from Asia and the West Indies. . . . People of Asian and West Indian descent now make up a large part of the shopkeeping and public transportation work force in such cities [London, Leicester, Wolverhampton, and Bradford], with one result being that local shops stay open longer because the Asians are willing to work long and hard. Asian doctors have been essential to the National Health Service, since many homegrown British doctors prefer private practice. . . . It is clear, therefore, that the British Nationality Act of 1981 and its predecessors of the 1960s and 70s did not succeed in keeping Asians and West Indians from immigrating into Britain and that England, which for many hundreds of years had absorbed Celtic people from Ireland, Scotland, and Wales, is no longer exclusively white.
— Thomas William Heyck, *The Peoples of the British Isles*

Divisions were capable of being bridged in the light of a prevailing attachment to places, traditions and myths. The more ceremonial aspects, such as the enthusiasm for the Crown, masked a more fundamental kind of commitment, to which West Indian and other newer immigrant citizens could also respond. . . . The truth was, perhaps, that Britain in the years from 1914 to 1987 had not changed all that fundamentally.
— Kenneth Morgan, "The Twentieth Century"

The story cannot simply be told as one of decline. Though the laurels of international leadership passed to others during the twentieth century, Britain still had its moments of glory, not all of them illusory; and Britons nourished hopes, not all of them misguided. . . . [Decline of empire] could be represented, in a flattering but not wholly false light, as an enlightened transition to the creation of a multicultural Commonwealth.
— Peter Clarke, *The Penguin History of Britain*

The old American-centered specifications of black life as abjection, though tied to the immiseration of so many people, are incompatible with the new currency of black culture as commodity and cipher of vitality, fitness and health in a weightless global market that relies more than ever on blacks to supply some of its most alluring software. . . . Britain has been judged to be a relatively successful multicultural society.
— Paul Gilroy, "The Sugar You Stir"

No longer are lands outside the British isles the only theaters of racial and imperial conquest. In a reversal of fortune, the center of past empire has become a contested site for those who govern the history industry. How is Britain now captured; how is it understood in the work of the practitioners of our times? The quotations above suggest some notable directions. Thomas Heyck has written what is probably the most successful, "progressive" textbook presently used in the teaching of British history in American colleges and universities. Kenneth Morgan and Peter Clarke, both holders of prestigious chairs in Britain, have contributed two best-selling volumes to the Anglo-American canon of new, popular British histories. Paul Gilroy is a leading social theorist whose work on "race" has a wide academic following and whose voice is now highly influential among a multiracial, transatlantic intelligentsia. For different if frequently overlapping audiences, the few statements cited above mark out lines within which both "nation" and "empire" receive restorative treatment.

This essay asks a series of questions: How is the "nation" of Britain being construed within a popular interpretive literature? How do conflicting interpretations nevertheless reflect the omnipresence of the United States as the "negative example" of race relations and of a flawed "multiculturalism"? How do these issues, one of interpretation and one of political and demographic influence, affect the teaching of the subject still most often presented in its gut as "modern British history," fashionable packaging notwithstanding? Further, do new canons that include Hanif Kureishi, Michael Ondaatje, and Mary Prince transcend a past drill? Do new interrogations of old favorites like Austen, Roberts, and Orwell also assist American students and their overlords in negotiating that seductive pedagogic dance step, the "imperial turn"? How is the pursuit of modern British history faring in the "new era of globalization"? Are the cures working, the complaints subsiding, the patient rejuvenating?

The most explicitly racial narrative of English history is not that of empire per se but of slavery and antislavery. This story has altered considerably over time, and though William Wilberforce's triumph takes pride of place, the "economic" role of slavery has been increasingly emphasized in general works of history, even if slaves are afforded little agency. Before Heyck's work, R. K. Webb's *Modern England* was regarded as the textbook of choice in the United States. It explained:

Hence the importance of the west coast of Africa. There English merchants found buyers for printed cotton cloth from India and for English metal goods and gin; in return they got ivory and gold that could be sent to the Far East in exchange for cottons, silks, spices and tea, and they procured slaves for the West Indies and the southern colonies of North America, a trade on which much of the prosperity of Bristol, and to a lesser extent Liverpool, was based.[1]

Webb also wrote of "the one great legislative monument of the [Fox] ministry, the abolition of the slave trade . . . the first installment of a long campaign against slavery led by the Clapham Sect; Wilberforce had moved the bill."[2] But the Jamaican uprising of 1865, which led to the court-martial of Governor Eyre, found Webb more willing to judge character. He identified the anti-Eyre campaign in England as "a magnet for radical, progressive, and humanitarian sentiment":

The pro-Eyre forces were no mere cluster of reactionaries, although Kingsley had long shown his distaste for blacks, and Carlyle was by this time far gone in an unattractive, racist hatred of the world he had been unable to hector into his own image. . . . Eyre attracted as defenders many men who disliked what was happening around them; they were neither evil nor inhumane, but they believed sincerely that men of whatever breed should be kept in their places and ruled firmly — through natural deference where possible, by force if necessary.[3]

Heyck's discussion of slavery is more perfunctory, with white Englishmen occupying center stage in the context of economic imperative:

By 1700, the white population (overwhelmingly British) stood at a quarter of a million in the thirteen colonies; by 1750, it had grown to almost a million, and there were 250,000 African slaves as well. . . . The growth of slavery in the West Indies (and the simultaneous importation of slaves into some North American colonies) constituted a very important and new feature of life for some Britons.[4]

The passage from slavery to freedom is typically succeeded in historical narratives by the onset of the foreign policy of the mid- to late Victorian era. In Morgan's *Oxford History of Britain*, the late H. C. G. Matthew wrote of what Morgan termed "imperialist neuroses" at the fin de siècle, forebodings linked to the misgivings that surrounded the Boer War. Further, Morgan proclaimed the "forcible wrenching of Britain out of its place in the sun," insisting upon its enduring legacy: "Britain in many ways has been the cockpit of mankind."[5] The dissenters, from the Levelers to Orwell, remained "deeply committed to an almost religious sense of the civilized essence of their country and its people, their history and destiny."[6] The doubts revealed character — even the dissidents' exalted love of country. As empire faded, its aftermath became in some sense a reinvigorated subject, sustained precisely by the absence of what had ceased to be.

The indebtedness of twentieth-century histories to A. J. P. Taylor's *English History, 1914–45* is still visible. Though few American students would know his name, his candor remains unrivaled:

This book is about thirty years in the history of the English people, and others come in only if they made a stir in English politics or aroused English interest in other ways. Thus, I discuss the impact of events in India on English politics and do not attempt to narrate India's political history. Similarly, I have passed over developments in Africa which were significant for Africa, but not, at that time, for England.[7]

Taylor was fearless of the charge of exclusion, precise in his purpose, and confident in its rationale. Compare that assuredness with the tentative openings of both Morgan's panoramic *Oxford History of Britain* and Clarke's more discursive and ruminative *Hope and Glory*. Morgan begins by paying a kind of backhanded homage to Lord Trevelyan's masterpiece, his *History of England*:

Secure in itself, a vibrant, outward-looking island has proceeded to colonize and civilize the world. None of Trevelyan's themes can be dismissed. Equally, none can be accepted uncritically in the more tormented, doubt-ridden age of the late twentieth century, with its well-founded suspicion of racial and national stereotypes. The problem of trying to come to grips with the essential reality of British experience remains as pressing and as fascinating as ever.[8]

Clarke hesitates to affirm his subject, though he will soon find a way out of the bind, which he ascribes chiefly to others: "The main reason . . . why British history is no longer in thrall to triumphalist accounts is surely not just because of methodological enlightenment: it is because at the end of the twentieth century British historians lack confidence that there is much to celebrate."[9]

Whence the uncertainty, and how is it manifest in the imaginary journey from Blitz to Blair? It lies in part in the awkward pursuit of *racial narrative*, conjoined with the quest to salvage English *national character*. Taylor had provided an unsubtle, straightforward verdict on World War II and its aftermath: "Future historians may see the war as a last struggle for the European balance of power or for the maintenance of Empire. This was not how it appeared for those who lived through it. The British people had set out to destroy Hitler and National Socialism."[10] They had been through both wars, start to finish:

Yet they remained a peaceful and civilized people, tolerant, patient, and generous. Traditional values lost much of their force. Other values took their place. Imperial greatness was on the way out; the welfare state was on the way in. The British empire declined; the condition of the people improved. . . . 'British' here means, perhaps for the last time, the peoples of the Dominions and of the Empire as well as of the United Kingdom.[11]

But Taylor stopped in 1945. For those narrating the subsequent half century, the script changed drastically. Postwar immigration and its consequences had to be explained in order to confront national character. For Taylor, character appeared rock solid in the wake of the war, strengthened by the shared imperial experience, not stricken by it. Yet two decades later, Webb's rendering of the 1960s posited profound stresses on the national character:

The 1960's . . . saw . . . developments that, though they may have drawn on recessive traits in the nation's past, appeared as radical departures from settled and admired national traditions. . . . One of these new departures was the prominence assumed by racial tension and conflict. . . . Britain's prosperity served as a magnet to the poor and ambitious in colonies and former colonies. . . . The immigrants clustered in larger cities. . . . In 1958 there were race riots . . . serious as portents if not in damage to lives or property. . . . One can perhaps understand public hostility when strange, alien people were intruded into a situation of economic uncertainty, especially in communities that have been by tradition tightly knit and inward-turning — though to say that is not to deny the self-evident racial cast of thinking and feeling that underlie this phenomenon, a century after the Governor Eyre controversy.[12]

Heyck's more ostensibly liberal account of the century, fueled by its steady attention to the multiple histories of Scotland, Ireland, and Wales (hence *Peoples of the British Isles*), recorded new, seemingly unprecedented antagonisms:

Meanwhile, a new division was emerging in British society: race. . . . Labor was also idealistic about the Commonwealth: in 1948 the Labor government adopted the British Nationality Act, which allowed citizens of the Commonwealth to come to Britain with full rights of British citizenship. By 1951, the black population of Britain had doubled to 200,000, and in 1961 alone, 113,000 "colored" (including blacks, Indians and Pakistanis) immigrants arrived. The immigrants did not disperse evenly across the country but concentrated in a few urban areas. . . . Because the British were accustomed to a relatively homogeneous population, many of them did not readily accept the newcomers.[13]

The British accounts of Morgan and Clarke also struggle to make sense of this era of disruption. Enoch Powell's "Rivers of Blood" speech always appears. In Morgan's case, Welsh and Scots demands are contrasted favorably with those of the new arrivals, while nowhere are the interwar black and Asian communities acknowledged:

Less constitutional or placid were the demands of the black or brown minorities, over a million of whom had migrated to Britain from India, Pakistan, West Africa, and the West Indies since 1950. In addition to dilapidated housing and racial discrimination in employment and (sometimes) at the hands of the police, there was the added hazard of racial bigotry in older urban areas.[14]

Clarke attributes racist attitudes in the 1950s and 1960s to the uniqueness of the encounters: "It was the visible presence of 'dark strangers,' concentrated in some English towns and cities, which gave immigration statistics a racial edge. The newcomers had their own distinctive habits and conventions, from cooking to religion; and, of course, their own distinctive skin color."[15]

Thus, the convention of the recent literature on both sides of the Atlantic has been to acknowledge slavery and explain the mixed responses to it in terms of epistemological stances rather than approbations of repressive violence. Next follows the anxiety about empire fostered by the turn of the century, which still enjoyed, if rather more hesitatingly, the greatness of British imperial achievement. The era of the two wars culminated in a new perplexity prompted by a split response: if some knew of the need for racial harmony, many were simply bewildered by the foreignness of the invaders, curiously unused even to *seeing* them (seemingly even after years of colonial encounters, two wars in which they had participated, much travel by some to lands and territories peopled by "Others").

Still, proponents of national character were not perhaps wrong in exercising caution. Even Powell might be partially redeemed from the geopolitical vantage point of the 1990s, as Clarke admonishes: "Powell, however, had more of a point than his liberal critics allowed when he singled out the intractable difficulties in coming to terms with Islam. . . . Pakistani communities . . . presented an almost impenetrable cliff-face to the conventions of their host country."[16] Clarke reassuringly cites the *fatwah* issued against "profane" writer Salman Rushdie as a case in point.[17] One is reminded of the *Today Show* interview with the mild-mannered Asian milkman in outer West London in the first days of *l'affaire* Rushdie. When asked if he supported the *fatwah* against Rushdie, the man enthusiastically replied that he knew not who Rushdie was, but he certainly did support the *fatwah*. In light of September 11, 2001, Clarke's cautionary note takes on new vernacular meaning. Americans need not have laughed too heartily in hands-across-the-sea solidarity; they still continue to perform the ultimate role as validators of the rationality of British *character* by serving as the negative example of a society gone awry — the model of undesirable and endemic racial violence.

In the broadest sense, the "Americanization" of the postwar period left many in Britain, as well as their American British studies counterparts, in mourning for a *less colonized* society. England was more foreign to the English and too familiar to the Americans, who continued to travel there in great numbers. Lord Briggs explained in the early 1980s that it had become harder, and more distracting, to discern what really made an Englishman: "With immigration, membership of the European Community and increasing American influence through the media, identifying what was peculiarly English became an increasing national preoccupation."[18] Here he was almost certainly not referring to the Left's exchange of essays on "The Peculiarities."[19] Indeed, he had identified a major change in the motion of the country that was entirely new: "Until 1948 there had been only a trickle of black and colored immigrants into England, and it was in the 1950s that they became 'visible' ethnic minorities."[20]

When it came time to explain and to account for the racial violence of the Notting Hill and Nottingham era, historians uniformly also viewed these disorders as *unprecedented*; no brutal imperial image or prior instance of political violence was cited. Instead, the American case served as a warning of despair and, simultaneously, as the hope for what Britain had not, and would not, become. First was the better-than-others' approach to decolonization, with Algeria, but especially Vietnam, providing the negative cases. Perhaps in ignorance of his chosen authority's oft-cited prescription of "benign neglect" as the cure for American cities, Morgan leapt at the evidence for favorable comparisons, invoked without a trace of irony: "The American politician, Daniel Moynihan, could write of the new prestige of Britain in the Afro-Asian Third World for having liberated so large a proportion of the world's population without the bitterness of the French in Algeria, the Dutch in Indonesia, or the Belgians in the Congo."[21] Clarke repeated the argument: "British decolonization was to prove relatively successful, leaving few of the scars suffered by other ex-colonial powers in their own extrication from empire."[22]

Similarly, Britain came out well when its record on race was compared to that of the Americans. Morgan noted Powell's use of the American example: "'Rivers of blood' were forecast in British cities on the lines of the race riots of the United States."[23] Only Northern Ireland was more "disturbing" in its levels of violence.[24] Sked and Cook also made the analogy: "The experience of almost American-style riots alarmed the British public, particularly since they raised awkward questions concerning the police. Traditionally the public had been proud of their policemen who still enjoyed enormous respect."[25]

Six years ago, Arthur Marwick's more ersatz quantitative approach yielded "comprehensive results" affirming a comparative trend in Britain's favor. He asked what the aftermath of the "appalling episodes of violence" of the 1980s had been for Britain, chastising its former critics, turning the tables on the arrogant American contentions that Britain was more racially backward than its larger and more powerful ally:

It was common ground among social commentators, and perhaps, above all, among American observers, black and white, of the British scene . . . that Britain had been slow and feeble in facing up to problems of racial prejudice and tension. . . . My conclusion will be that, given that racism is manifest in every advanced country, the levels of integration achieved by Britain in the mid nineties were better than might well have been predicted ten years earlier; at the bottom of the scale black youths were still suffering disproportionately, but this (as in America) was becoming more a class, rather than a purely racial, issue — in the "enterprise culture" all of the poorest were getting poorer (while some small businessmen, particularly Asian — and Chinese — were doing quite well).[26]

This mantra of racial success seemed to intensify in the accounts published during the first Blair era, prior to the disturbances that occurred in Bradford and other cities during the summer of 2001. Until these events, a fresh sigh of relief was not fazed by the unsolved Stephen Lawrence murder case or the more recent death of a Nigerian youth on his way back from computer class at the local library in a housing estate in Peckham, south London.[27] In the second case, as the assailants were reportedly other black youth, the attack was placed in the category of black-on-black crime. It would have been, in that sense, presumably irrelevant to Marwick's calculations or perhaps an example of the "underclass" behavior, American-style, as diagnosed above.

Britain seemed to have escaped the American dilemma, but why? Morgan bemoaned the recent racial past: "There were sporadic troubles in the Notting Hill area of London and the St. Paul district of Bristol. In the summer of 1981 it seemed for a time that Britain was experiencing the full horrors of race riots on the American pattern, as black youths in the Toxteth area of Liverpool and the Brixton district of south London engaged in prolonged rioting, all faithfully recorded (and perhaps whipped up) by television reporting."[28] But when he came to write his more recent short introduction to the twentieth century, Morgan proclaimed stability, a new harmony recognizable to anyone reading the early Blair rhetoric or the American press coverage of his first election and its aftermath. Notting Hill had found its place in the sun, the recent debate as to whether to continue the Carnival at all entirely absent from the revised record:

The population remained intensely various, distinct, individual. In a largely ur-
banized society, the countryside retained a fierce (perhaps exaggerated) sense of its
own needs and identity. Much of Britain in the late nineties was still the same
relatively neighborly society where people pursued their hobbies, cherished their
gardens, and entertained in their own homes. Most powerfully of all, despite the
rhetoric about 'a young country,' the British retained a pride in their collective
past — even if "British history" (largely ignored in the Millennium Dome) might
have to be redefined in a pluralist, polycultural sense to take account variously of
Celtic devolution, Americanized popular culture, Commonwealth immigration,
and membership of Europe. . . . Debates over the significance of Diana's death and
of the meaning of the millennium offered insights into this abiding folk memory. An
awareness of the past shone through in innumerable local festivals . . . even in the
multi-ethnic Notting Hill carnival, now over thirty years old.[29]

This palpable transition in spirit did not have its unconditional adherents among
American practitioners of British studies. The Webb textbook only made it
through early Thatcher, and its verdict had the glumness of those years about it.
Webb had taken the low road instead of the high, but he still got there in the end:

Some of that admired reasonableness has dissipated. There have been bursts of
violence through the postwar years, particularly in cities — Teddy Boys and Skin-
heads, racial violence, hooliganism among football crowds . . . more instances of
sullenness and rudeness. . . . [But] reasonableness, grace, and even a sense of style in
an age not much given to it have survived wars, social conflict, loss of prestige,
economic problems that will not go away, and a tide of criticism at home and abroad
that would swamp a less secure or more sensitive people. . . . Greatness is to be
found in the refusal to pursue it.[30]

This was not Taylor, nor the reincarnated Morgan, but it was a backhanded,
doleful affirmation. Writing from an ostensibly more progressive vantage
point during the twilight of the John Major government, the late Roy Porter
had similarly reassured his wide popular readership:

Some might look to apocalyptic collapse, but one thing that London's history shows
time and again is that the millennial mode is premature: London's crack-up has a
long way to go before it bears mentioning in the same breath as many North
American cities — Newark, Chicago, Detroit, Los Angeles, Washington and maybe
these days Miami — where poverty, homelessness, hopelessness and appalling levels
of violence have created anti-cities at the city's heart; where those who can have fled
the inner-city. By contrast, much of London . . . still radiates the deeply livable
quality evoked by Betjeman.[31]

In 2001 the Bradford and other "riots," as well as controversies over the Notting Hill Carnival, threatened complacent comparison. September 11 further altered the comparative landscape, with its revival of an Anglo-American collusion in a military and diplomatic mission. In the lead-up to this changed political climate, the cultural studies community did not abjure the comparative framework and perhaps surprisingly clung rather tenaciously to nationally derived arguments about racial harmony and the hopes for racial progress, even in the face of the theoretical obliteration of "race" as a category of endeavor and experience altogether. Thus, ordinary Europeans could transcend and live on beyond the prejudices of the colonized world. Benedict Anderson's *Imagined Communities* posited the weight of memory on the elites. He wrote of the "equanimity with which metropolitan popular classes eventually shrugged off the 'losses' of the colonies. . . . In the end, it is always the ruling classes, bourgeois certainly, but above all aristocratic, that long mourn the empires, and their grief always has a stagey quality to it."[32]

Paul Gilroy offered a forthright comparative language for judging aspirations and assessing achievement between the two nations, *imagined* though they may be. The new era of post-postwar offered new opportunities for Europeans to free race from a notion of victimhood that Gilroy associates with American discursive conventions and prejudice, "black life as abjection."[33] Not a Blairite new dawn per se, but what still appeared to him very recently as a new era in geopolitics offered new possibilities: "We must also note that — to oversimplify somewhat — the period of decolonizing struggles is basically over."[34] This is a European language at heart, and it is counterposed to the ways in which many describe the American conundra. Gilroy proposed a process to which the American version of British studies in its mainstream, and (more important) civil society, was not then and is not now committed. He was in many ways heartened by what he discerned as "a chaotic pattern of ongoing struggles which aim at nothing short of making Europeans more comfortable with their continent's irreversibly heterocultural character and at breaking the vicious circles of their phobic responses to alterity."[35]

Not entirely unlike the historians surveyed above, Gilroy recognized this shift in purpose as related not only to the move beyond decolonization, but also the concomitant end of the era of immigration — surely again *not* what was, at that time, the American condition. He is emphatic: "*This* version of multiculturalism ceases to be about the problems of administering the lives of 'immigrants.' "[36] As he did in the *Black Atlantic*, he battled notions of "ethnic absolutism," decrying forms of identity politics that could not withstand the challenges of globalization, characterizing the pursuit of essences as "the arcane desires of the butterfly collectors of alterity who prefer their cultures integral and like their differences to remain absolute. Their power is going as people seek antidotes to the perils of globalization."[37] This may have been meant as a description of some Americans, from Afrocentrics to the Christian Right. Certainly it was a hopeful note sounded for Britain, and more so for a wider Europe, a pre-September 11 postcolonial, postimmigrant, authentically multicultural continent. But its applicability to the United States qua United States was neither advocated nor presumed by Gilroy. In fact, this intellectual and political project implies that this dream seemed least possible in America.

Yet in the multicultural United States, even with its "ethnic absolutisms," the engagement of "race" as an academic category — of hiring and firing, of research and rhetoric, of curriculum, and of institutional practice — has been so pervasive that even British studies has more than its toes wet. The awkward fit between racial suggestions that emanate from the mainstream Americanist influence in history departments and the antiquarian soul of British studies has elicited much recent commentary.[38] Still, few have asked what the resulting pedagogy looks like, and so this essay takes as its concluding effort a short and rather abashed glance at the modern British history classroom in the elite northeastern liberal arts college milieu.

Many calls for racial content have preceded the small steps taken by British historians who work in the United States. Many modern British studies instructors who profess multiculturalism by night are stuck in the cold light of day with the standard kinds of narrative texts cited above, perhaps by now trading Webb for Heyck, Morgan for Clarke, Briggs for the new slim and chic syntheses like Christopher Harvie and H. C. G. Matthew's *Nineteenth-Century Britain: A Very Short Introduction*.[39] And yet these students are *also* simultaneously being taught by colleagues from other fields whose training and preoccupations affect their charges' youthful responses to and representations of "British history." Unorthodox perceptions of Britain are inspired by trips to a diverse London, by press coverage of events like the Irish peace negotiations (and, now, by Blair's alliance with Bush). The rapid rise in the numbers of postcolonial and ethnic studies appointments has its own impact on what students bring with them to the classroom. The market in ideas and impressions is large. Affirmative action and its critics; the demography of the American nation; the very, very different notions of higher education and of teaching that mark out Britain from America result in a very different student perception of Britain on the U.S. side of the waters. This perception is decisively influenced, on the one hand, by the written image of an idealized U.K., described so convincingly and unhesitatingly by the historians cited above and, on the other hand, by the deeply racialized languages of the academy and media in the United States, of which they partake daily.

This imaginary Britain is a Britain thus interpreted through the mediating lens of American racial categories. And it is a perception that, perforce, just cannot seem to give up the nation — not least because students are so strongly urged to reject the racist superpower, on one side, and asked to see a better nation, a leaner and kinder nation, an alternative nation, on the other. Ironically, this is also the role that the old, WASPy Britain has played for earlier generations of ethnically and racially stressed out white Americans. Britain has indeed risen again to soothe the MTV generation's anxieties. Much mischief ensues in the classroom.

Contrast the cry for inclusion of the non-Western, uttered by the now retro Eric Wolf, with the "island people" concepts articulated above. As his elders in anthropology had done before him, Wolf called for the abrogation of "the boundaries between Western and non-Western history . . . in the belief that a better understanding of our human condition is now within our grasp."[40] Simplistic perhaps, but a popular U.S. forerunner of the more highly theorized, nuanced, and "multicultural" approaches that followed and as distant from "imperial history" in Britain as A-levels are from the requirements for an American high school diploma. While the British student of British history attends a university where many subaltern studies practitioners may lurk, he or she is far less likely to encounter them in history departments per se than are American students who take a multidisciplinary curriculum.[41] At the very least, American students will have encountered American historians whose work has undergone successive racial alterations of direction, characterized by a massive rethinking of the weight of a passionate racial consciousness in their study of national or "transnational" histories. Thus David Roediger introduced *Wages of Whiteness* with a personal testament to the "nonacademic" origins of his commitment to racial issues:

Until very recently, I would have skipped all this autobiographical material, sure that my ideas on race and the white working class grew out of conscious reflection based on historical research. But much of that reflection led me back to what my early years may have taught me: the role of race in defining how white workers look not only at Blacks but at themselves; the pervasiveness of race; the complex mixture of hate, sadness and longing.[42]

This kind of approach can be unforgettable for students in one respect or another; they take it with them into their own cognitive world. They filter what they hear or read about Britain through the mesh that American racial discourses provide.

Confronted with a very complicated menu of options, ill equipped to absorb much of the terminology of debate, carrying with them the lessons learned in secondary school or earlier, usually exclusively drawn from American history, students spend a few hours a week within the British studies classroom, desperately trying to connect a reading of Austen's *Sense and Sensibility* with the Napoleonic *imperial* wars; finding a place for race within Robert Roberts's *Classic Slum*; or figuring out which borders the *English Patient* transgressed and why he is not English.[43] Is Kureishi's *My Beautiful Laundrette* about homophobia, or Asian shopkeepers, or Pakistani politics, or Hindu ritual, or hooliganism, or racism, or all of the above?[44] Was Orwell a racist? Is *Road to Wigan Pier* patronizing of poor people and *Burmese Days* a cynical apologia for imperial agents and *compradors*?[45] The politically correct British studies approach is a demanding one.

Not surprisingly, the anxiety of a bluebook exam *sans* computer can sometimes be best resolved with recourse to another kind of cognitive space, a grafting of American presumptions onto a particular question of British history; suddenly the narratives of race and national character appear in strange, morphed guises. Here is an excerpt from an examination essay on the Caribbean slave narrative, *The History of Mary Prince*.[46] Of Prince, the student states:

She would only aspire to being a servant, she makes no case that free blacks could do professions, and to educate them would give society a much higher potential. I only bring this up, because they are the sort of arguments that Mill makes for women. Both slaves and women have been historical [*sic*] subjugated in the Empire. Perhaps that [*sic*] such rhetoric would have been too radical coming from a slave, or perhaps slavery did some damage to the psyche, that it was beyond a slave to think that they or their children might be a professional or that they might contribute to the betterment of society. . . . Clearly the damage had been done psychologically. Many slaves may have shared the attitude of Mary Prince that black people belonged as hardworking servants, and that could help explain many of the problems of following generations rising beyond that station. Of course, this is coupled with attitudes of white supremacy and some legal subjugation.[47]

Thus, slaves did not aspire to rise up in the social hierarchy; the link between race and "gender" is one of abjection. The slave was incapable of agency, damaged in psychological terms. As in Nicholas Lemann's imaginary journey from Clarksville to Chicago, the seeds of virtually genetically transferred attitudes were already sown, long before Prince recited her narrative to the antislavery folks.[48] And there were also some structural impediments along the way.

This thoughtful reply assumes a clear concept of mobility and the absence of desire; it is straight out of the motivational language that every glib study of the American "inner city" deploys. The American model is thus transposed to the 1830s British Caribbean. More typical are essays that look for a rationale for brutal physical violence, always assuming that there ought to have been one, morally, in order to explain white behavior. "She is flogged for the smallest of mistakes whether it is her fault or not."[49] Hyperbole also intrudes: "In 1833 slavery was abolished in the colonies due mainly to the publication of Mary Prince's narrative."[50] Or homage accrues to the omnipotent white, antislavery editor: "This passage reflects the constant attempts that [the editor] makes in an effort to humanize Prince so that the masses will view her as just another person, and not a slave and sub-Human [*sic*] form of life."[51] Not unlike the tenor of student essays written about Primo Levi's *Survival in Auschwitz*,[52] the emphasis flows inexorably toward the thesis of dehumanization: "Yet, as her masters began to change, due to her being sold, Prince lost all of her humanity. The masters were able to take everything away from her except her strong will. . . . Prince undergoes some very sinful acts during her time as a slave. She has intercourse with one of the sailors while she is in Antigua and she also gets married while being a slave. . . . As a slave, humanity was lost and brutality gained. . . . It was an era that lasted way too long."[53]

Another kind of "dehumanization" is perceived by American students confronting a strong literary treatment of working-class life; arguably, the highly racialized paradigms of American poverty, or indeed the myths of American national superiority, influence the ways that texts like Roberts's *Classic Slum* and Sillitoe's *Saturday Night and Sunday Morning*,[54] are currently read:

The quotation . . . from . . . Alan Sillitoe . . . is a direct comment on the deterioration of British working class society despite the continuation of the idea that Britain is the model nation that all other countries should look to for inspiration. . . . The society in which Arthur lives has deteriorated into essentially one of monotonous work with dangerous, illegal or immoral activities thrown in sporadically. Despite this slow breakdown of society, the people of Britain still view themselves as leaders in the international community.[55]

The fantastic quality of such a depiction flows from a sense that to be "working class" is to be English, to be immoral, to be deteriorating, un-American, unbefitting of the qualities of the people whose country is *a true world leader*. It is as if England's "primitive" postwar working class were a by-product of empire's decline, with lives so unlike those enjoyed by "most Americans." These notions emanate from sources other than Sillitoe's story, if from it at all. There are also certainly rival responses, other ways in which English national character is thought about. Students' sources differ even as their takes differ. But the drift toward a rejection of a politically correct rendition of British history, a strong tone of moral censorship — toward values that are unmistakably American, including a kind of liberal but white sense of race, a strong tone of moral censorship, and white entitlement — very often typify unbridled prose written in the few moments when the Web and the prepared paper are absent.

As a reminder that hints at the multiplicity of appropriations made more possible by the global links of the present-day academy, we close with two countervailing and yet related expressions of race and character. The first is the summary statement on Roberts's *Classic Slum*, offered in a bluebook essay by an Asian student resident in the United States. In describing the transition of Salford from the late Victorian period to the 1920s, he states, delightfully, "There emerged a better class of people by status, standing class, [*sic*] and people began to get more educated and westernized." Second is the alert sounded by Mike and Trevor Phillips in their highly successful and massive oral histories of the Caribbean presence in Britain in the postwar world: *Windrush: The Irresistible Rise of Multi-Racial Britain*. In it appears a sweet, cautionary disclaimer that provides students with a rejoinder to the pervasive portrait of the immigrant; a different vantage point introduces a collection that they love to read. Referring to the arrival of the ship that brought the first large postwar group of Jamaicans to Britain, the Phillips remark:

In much the same way, as the *Windrush* people recede into myth they also seemed to have been transformed into objects, a block whose sole distinguishing characteristic is the color of their skins. The result being that in many contemporary histories they turn up as a sort of sudden infestation whose number account for various social problems. At the other end of the scale, we are offered selective descriptions which identify them as an isolated, ghettoized unit of an African diaspora, whose "blackness" makes them interchangeable with people in Africa or the USA. . . . Listening . . . reminds us that they and their successors are a diverse group of individuals, shaped by a specific and a peculiar history.[56]

No single racial narrative or statement of national character survives close scrutiny. Yet many have hold of a popular readership, be they the British reading public or American liberal arts students. In the competing claims on the intellects of readers lies the new context for postimperial interpretation. Assumptions about national destiny, racial disorder, equilibrium, and multiculturalism can be historicized. We can discern the fault lines of a contest for keeping "Britain" functional. We can map out the desire for a new cosmopolitanism, perceive the breakpoints among national political cultures, and look for life after empire or even, perhaps now, "new empire" and the opponents thereof. No successful popular history is likely to fail to confront imperial loss or superpower gain. No history, no imaginative landscape, will accomplish in and of itself the abrogation of racial identity or the transcendence of national boundaries. No student is likely to read even the ostensibly "fairest" text with an uninflected glance. Still, we are better critics and sharper historians if we are mindful of the unstoppable will to narrate, of the desire to use history itself as an element of national character — as a means of racial uplift and reassurance, as a metaphorical life preserver.

Notes

1 R. K. Webb, *Modern England: From the Eighteenth Century to the Present*, 2d ed. (New York: Harper and Row, 1980), p. 15.

2 Ibid., p. 145.

3 Ibid., p. 321.

4 Thomas William Heyck, *The Peoples of the British Isles: A New History, from 1688 to 1870* (Belmont, Calif.: Wadsworth, 1992), pp. 150, 149.

5 Kenneth Morgan, "Editor's Foreword," in *The Oxford History of Britain*, ed. Kenneth Morgan (Oxford: Oxford University Press, 1988), pp. viii–ix.

6 Ibid., p. x.

7 A. J. P. Taylor, *English History, 1914–45* (Oxford: Oxford University Press, 1985), p. vi.

8 Morgan, "Editor's Foreword," p. vii.

9 Peter Clarke, *Hope and Glory: Britain 1900–90* (London: Penguin, 1996), p. 2.

10 Taylor, *English History*, p. 600.

11 Ibid., p. 600 n. 1.

12 Webb, *Modern England*, pp. 616–617.

13 Heyck, *The Peoples of the British Isles*, pp. 274–75.

14 Morgan, "The Twentieth Century (1914–87)," in Morgan, ed., *Oxford History of Britain*, p. 647.

15 Clarke, *Hope and Glory*, p. 324.

16 Ibid., p. 329.

17 Ibid.

18 Asa Briggs, *A Social History of England* (New York: Viking, 1983), p. 312.

19 See Edward P. Thompson, "The Peculiarities of the English," in *The Poverty of Theory and Other Essays* (New York: Monthly Review Press, 1978), pp. 35–91.

20 Briggs, *A Social History*, p. 310.

21 Morgan, "The Twentieth Century," p. 641.

22 Clarke, *Hope and Glory*, p. 403.

23 Morgan, "The Twentieth Century," p. 647.

24 Ibid.

25 Alan Sked and Chris Cook, *Postwar Britain: A Political History, 1945–1992*, 4th ed. (London: Penguin, 1993), p. 353.

26 Arthur Marwick, *British Society since 1945*, 3d ed. (London: Penguin, 1996), p. 457. Penguin Social History of Britain.

27 See, for example, "Condon Tells of Shame Over Failures," *Times* (London), February 25, 1999, and "Police Take Damilola Appeal on the Road," *Independent*, January 1, 2001, p. 7.

28 Morgan, "The Twentieth Century," pp. 651–652.

29 Kenneth Morgan, *Twentieth-Century Britain: A Very Short Introduction* (Oxford: Oxford University Press, 2000), p. 108.

30 Webb, *Modern England*, p. 626.

31 Roy Porter, *London: A Social History* (Cambridge, Mass.: Harvard University Press, 1995), p. 387.

32 Benedict Anderson, *Imagined Communities: Reflections on the Origin and Spread of Nationalism*, 2d ed. (London: Verso, 1991), p. 111.

33 Paul Gilroy, Lawrence Grossberg, and Angela McRobbie, eds., *Without Guarantees: In Honour of Stuart Hall* (London: Verso, 2000), p. 126.

34 Ibid.

35 Ibid., p. 129.

36 Ibid., p. 132.

37 See Paul Gilroy: *The Black Atlantic: Modernity and Double-Consciousness* (London: Verso, 1993), pp. 1–2, and in Gilroy, Grossberg, and McRobbie, eds., *Without Guarantees*, and "The Sugar You Stir," p. 133.

38 For an evaluation of the state of the field from the point of view of the professional organization of British historians in the United States and Canada, see Peter Stansky et al., *National Conference on British Studies Report on the State and Future of British Studies in North America* (November 1999), passim.

39 Christopher Harvie amd H. C. G. Matthew, *Nineteenth-Century Britain: A Very Short Introduction* (Oxford: Oxford University Press, 2000).

40 Eric Wolf, *The People without History* (Berkeley: University of California Press, 1982), p. x.

41 For example, Gayatri Chakravarty Spivak, *In Other Worlds: Essays in Cultural Politics* (New York: Routledge, 1988), p. 197.

42 David Roediger, *The Wages of Whiteness: Race and the Making of the American Working Class* (London: Verso, 1991), p. 5.

43 Jane Austen, *Sense and Sensibility* (New York: Modern Library, 2000); Robert Roberts, *The Classic Slum: Salford Life in the First Quarter of the Century* (New York: Viking Penguin, 1973); Michael Ondaatje, *The English Patient* (New York: Knopf, 1993).

44 Hanif Kureishi, *My Beautiful Laundrette and Other Writings* (London: Faber and Faber, 1996).

45 George Orwell: *Road to Wigan Pier* (New York: Harcourt, 1972); *Burmese Days* (London: Harcourt, 1950).

46 Moira Ferguson, ed., *The History of Mary Prince, a West Indian Slave, Related by Herself* (Ann Arbor: University of Michigan Press, 1977).

47 Examination essay, 2000.

48 Nicholas Lemann, *The Promised Land* (New York: Random House, 1995).

49 Examination essay, 2000.

50 Ibid.

51 Ibid.

52 Primo Levi, *Survival in Auschwitz* (New York: Simon and Schuster, 1995).

53 Examination essay, 2000.

54 Alan Sillitoe, *Saturday Night and Sunday Morning* (New York: HarperCollins, 1978).

55 Examination essay.

56 Mike and Trevor Phillips, *Windrush: The Irresistible Rise of Multi-Racial Britain* (London: HarperCollins, 1998), pp. 400–401.

STUART WARD

Transcending the Nation: A Global Imperial History?

The writing of the British imperial past has long been harnessed to the conceptual and methodological pull of the nation. From the earliest forays into imperial history in the late nineteenth century to more recent attempts at self-consciously "transnational" studies, historians have invariably fallen back on national paradigms in order to generate meaningful questions and themes. Ronald Robinson and John Gallagher once famously observed that the imperial historian "is very much at the mercy of his own particular concept of empire."[1] But it is equally true that the writing of the imperial past has been at the mercy of the national idea. This is not to cast a blanket of scorn over a rich and variegated tradition — it is the very nature of historical scholarship to study problems rooted in the contemporary condition, and national paradigms have seemed perfectly logical in a world conceived in terms of distinctive nationalities. Rather, by examining recent attempts to elude the confines of national frameworks, I wish to explore the implications of a historiography where the nation is stripped of its determining role. Although the idea of nationalism has had a profound influence on the ways in which people have made sense of the imperial experience, the central task of a transnational history of imperialism is to interrogate this phenomenon rather than to replicate it. At the same time, it is worth considering the kinds of ideological positions that may be undermined by the transnational project (as well as who the beneficiaries might be).

John Seeley's *Expansion of England*, first published in 1883, is often regarded as the founding text of British imperial historiography.[2] Seeley's overriding theme was the need to breathe new life into British history by linking it to that of empire, but he unwittingly pioneered a distinct offshoot of British historiography that evolved its own preoccupations and themes, running in parallel to, but rarely intersecting with, the history of the British Isles. The timing of Seeley's work is significant, situated as it was in the context of late Victorian political culture, where the empire was becoming increasingly implicated in ideas about British national identity and British national interest. The evolution of a transnational Britishness in the eighteenth and early nineteenth centuries had been powerfully reinforced by a "nascent imperialist sensibility."[3]

But the position of colonists within this wider British community was highly ambiguous. On the one hand, these transplanted Britons laid claim to the identity implicit in British culture, but they were often regarded from a metropolitan perspective as somehow less than full Britons (or as Ben Franklin bitterly complained, "a different Species from the English of Britain").[4] Toward the end of the nineteenth century, however, improvements in transport and communications, the mounting commercial rivalry among the European nation-states, and the political evolution of the self-governing "Dominions" led to a new emphasis on the worldwide community of the British race. This took its most concrete form in the various schemes for imperial federation, where leading figures in British politics such as Joseph Chamberlain and Leo Amery appealed to their kinsmen to promote a "wider patriotism, blended with and yet transcending our several national patriotisms." As Andrew Thompson has argued, from the late 1870s and early 1880s "imperial language came to signify a feeling of solidarity between English society at home and the overseas British societies in the Empire."[5]

The late Victorian imperial ideal has been given a variety of labels: a "community of Britishness," a "British world," "British race patriotism," a "fraternity of British communities," and so on. Douglas Cole termed it "Britannic nationalism" on the grounds that it conveyed all of the central features of the national idea — far more so than the several more localized forms of patriotism that resided within its ambit.[6] But whatever the term, it is clear that the idea of a greater Britain lay at the core of Seeley's initial foray into the history of the British Empire. Indeed, "Greater Britain" was the term he himself preferred to that of "British Empire," as it served to convey his deep sense of the organic links uniting a single imperial nation. In his *Expansion of England* he underlined that "our Empire is not an Empire at all in the ordinary sense of the word. It does not consist of a congeries of nations held together by force, but in the main one nation, as much as if it were no Empire but an ordinary state."[7] Little wonder that Seeley so urgently called for the incorporation of empire into British historiography — a more parochial focus on the British Isles simply failed to do justice to the scope and organic unity of the greater British nation.[8]

The paradigm of Britannic nationalism was to inform the work of several generations of historians, ranging from the imperial federalism of "Round Table" scholars like Alfred Milner and Lionel Curtis to the "dominion ideal" espoused by Richard Jebb and W. K. Hancock. Even a gentle critic of empire such as J. A. Hobson could conceive of British colonies as a "natural overflow of nationality," establishing "local self-government in close conformity with the political customs of the mother country."[9] For imperial scholars of the interwar generation, historical debate tended to revolve around the appropriate constitutional form of imperial cooperation. On the one hand were those who, like Curtis, believed that some form of imperial federation was vital to the ongoing unity and vitality of the British peoples of the world. The opposing view, most clearly articulated by Richard Jebb, held that "such phrases as 'the Expansion of England' or 'Greater Britain,'" which were used to promote the ideal of imperial federation, were simply inappropriate to the political temper in the Dominions.[10] Jebb based his observations on an extensive tour of the "British world" around the turn of the century, reaching the conclusion that Dominion nationalism posed no threat whatsoever to imperial cohesion so long as British countries like Australia, Canada, New Zealand, and South Africa were never presented with a stark choice between federation or separatism. Thus Jebb could champion vigorously the "separate national aspirations" of the Dominions while at the same time celebrating the "Soul of the Empire."[11]

Jebb's conviction that Dominion nationalism need not be in conflict with a wider sense of British community was taken up in the interwar years by one of the foremost imperial historians of the age, W. K. Hancock. Although he conceded that in his native Australia, "pride of race counted for more than love of country," this did not imply any fundamental clash of sentiments.[12] On the contrary, in his passionate wartime defense of the imperial ideal (designed mainly for American consumption), he depicted imperial and national sentiments as mutually reinforcing. "Each member of the family declares its independence; each proclaims its interdependence. Here, in this sundered world of snarling nationalism, it is a true political miracle. . . . Monarchy grows into democracy, Empire grows into Commonwealth, the tradition of a splendid past is carried forward into an adventurous future."[13] Thus Hancock made a clear distinction between the "snarling nationalism" of the Axis powers, on the one hand, and the more harmonious and beneficial ties of the British "family." Like Seeley, he had difficulty incorporating Indians into his familial framework, and despite his two-volume biography of Jan Smuts, he rarely placed black Africans in the foreground of his narrative. As Roger Louis has noted, Hancock never "saw the full force of the initiative of the Africans themselves in shaping their own history. In the biography, Africans are conspicuous by their absence."[14]

The work of Hancock and his generation was characterized by a teleology of constitutional progress — of British countries moving ever closer to the British ideal of good governance. Constitutional history figured largely in the history of the empire in the interwar years because it raised issues that went to the very heart of the problem of reconciling a pan-British identity with the practicalities of separate statehood. This was the central object of imperial historiography as it was originally conceived—the expansion and evolution of the Britannic nation. The often heated historical debates of the first half of the twentieth century were contained within a shared teleology of linear national progress and a common "British" destiny. From the early 1950s, fundamental changes in the political and ideological context rendered the Britannic nationalist paradigm increasingly obsolete. The empire itself was on the wane, together with the political and economic capacity of the British state to influence events abroad. The idea of greater Britain had always rested as much on an imagined community of interest as it did on ideas of cultural affinity, but this could hardly be sustained in a world of greatly diminished British power and authority.[15] As a consequence, there evolved more exclusive nationalities in places like Canada and Australia and, increasingly, in the United Kingdom itself.[16] Even more problematically, Britain's decision to enter the European Economic Community in 1961 proved to be a traumatic exercise for all parties concerned. The symbolism of Britain joining a new community of "foreigners" undermined the idea of greater Britain as a focus of civic identification and raised new conceptual barriers among the countries that once comprised the British world. Although the transition from empire to multiracial commonwealth was passed off to the British electorate as the culmination of Britain's imperial achievement, this late imperial hubris failed to survive long enough to make any impression on imperial historiography.[17] Seeley's *Expansion of England* went out of print on the eve of the Suez crisis, and entirely new ways of conceptualizing the imperial past emerged.[18]

Of particular significance was the publication in 1953 of Robinson and Gallagher's article, "The Imperialism of Free Trade," in which they pointed out how the emphasis on constitutional history had fostered a conception of the imperial subject coterminous with the areas colored red on the map. "All imperial history," they observed, "has been written on the assumption that the empire of formal dominion is historically comprehensible in itself and can be cut out of its context in British expansion and world politics."[19] In a similar vein, R. W. Southern argued in 1961 that the constitutional foundations of imperial history had become increasingly irrelevant. Oxford graduates could no longer aspire to the administration of some far-flung outpost of greater Britain, and constitutional history should therefore be replaced by the study of the remaining sources of British influence in the world—namely, culture and ideas.[20] In shifting the focus to the more nebulous aspects of "informal empire" and "cultural imperialism," historians began to blur the boundaries of the Britannic nationalist paradigm and opened up the possibility of studying the interactions between imperial and indigenous cultures.

But the allure of nationalism continued to determine the contours of imperial scholarship. In particular, the colonial nationalist liberation movements of the 1950s and 1960s provided the ideological framework for the emergence of "area studies." J. W. Davidson's pioneering work in "Pacific studies" in the 1960s stemmed from much the same impulse as the founding of the *Journal of African History* in that same era. The "discovery" of Australian history by Russell Ward, Manning Clark, and others in the 1950s was prompted by the sense that the British historical tradition was no longer adequate in the light of the dissolving material bases of the British connection.[21] Scholarly interest turned away from the ideal of organic imperial community and toward new teleologies of national self-determination. Within this new paradigm, the forces of imperialism and nationalism, far from being mutually reinforcing, were posited as direct antagonists. Not surprisingly therefore, the proliferation of area studies was hotly resisted by the old school constitutionalists such as Vincent T. Harlow and Geoffrey Elton—or Hugh Trevor Roper, who infamously condemned the study of African history as offering little more than the "unrewarding gyrations of barbarous tribes." Area studies could hardly appeal to a mind-set still rooted in the "expansion of England." More moderately, historians in the 1980s pondered the question whether the rise of "area studies" had entirely undermined the rationale of "imperial history" as a discrete subdiscipline of historical inquiry.[22]

Literary studies, too, responded to the "wind of change" with the emergence of "Commonwealth literature" in the early 1960s. The field was initially inspired by the prevailing optimism for the "new Commonwealth" and emphasized the common cultural characteristics of writing in English of "British" origin. But by the early 1970s, national exceptionalism was winning out over the unifying elements of the English literary tradition. This paved the way for the emergence of "postcolonial studies," which posited the English literary heritage in stark opposition to colonial literatures of resistance. Despite its postmodern theoretical foundations, the self-consciously political function of much of this work demanded a (selectively) positivist view of national culture. The rigid distinction between colonizer and colonized was challenged by Homi Bhahba in his attempt to "provide a form of the writing of cultural difference . . . that is inimical to binary boundaries." Yet much of his work on "hybridity" and "in-betweenness" presupposed discrete national cultures from which colonial hybrids were composed. In anticipation of this problem, Bhabha asserted that "all forms of culture are continually in a process of hybridity."[23] But this merely undermined the conceptual purchase of hybridity as a form of agency specific to the colonial encounter. Or as Arif Dirlik more bluntly put it: "So we are all hybrids—so what?"[24] It was the paradigm of colonial nationalist resistance that invested postcolonial theory with meaning and purpose.[25] Indeed, the clearest indication of the national preoccupations of colonial discourse analysts was their deep-seated unwillingness "to pay the full price which comes with discourse theory's avowed epistemology of extreme cultural relativism."[26] To do so would have defeated the underlying colonial nationalist teleology that informed the entire "postcolonial project." Thus for all its "deconstruction" of colonial discourse, postcolonial theory was bound to leave the nation firmly intact.[27]

Clearly, then, the idea of the nation provided a ready framework whereby the multifaceted political, economic, and cultural exchanges between the British Isles and the wider world were rendered comprehensible. So much so, in fact, that the very language of imperial scholarship has become implicated in the linear narratives of the nation. But this problem has been fully recognized in more recent times, and there have been various attempts to erode the centrality of the nation in the depiction of the imperial world. The most common approach has been to focus on the intersection between the histories of "metropole" and "periphery" — toward the progressive dismantling of the traditional distinction between "empire" and the "home front."[28] John M. MacKenzie's "Studies in Imperialism" series has been particularly influential in knitting the imperial experience into the fabric of British social history more generally, thereby extending the traditional parameters of the subject. The new cultural history of imperialism has explored a wide array of social and cultural themes, from propaganda to children's literature, education, sport, travel, cinema, and other popular entertainments, compiling a picture of the multifarious ways in which, to use Mary Louise Pratt's phrase, the "periphery determined the metropolis."[29] MacKenzie's emphasis on what he terms the "sheer porousness" of metropolitan culture holds out the possibility of transcending nationalist teleologies without necessarily abandoning the practice of "history" altogether.[30]

There is, however, some debate about the validity of claims that the imperial context calls for the reconstitution of the "British" historical subject. P. J. Marshall, for example, argues that the imperial experience did not really have much of a formative influence on British institutions and social structures. Rather, he contends, it was the other way around: the empire could serve as a useful legitimating field that "reflected and reinforced certain trends in British history, but rarely seems to have pushed it in radically new directions."[31] The debate remains wide open, but it is worth noting that the power to "reinforce" certain historical trends is surely, in itself, a formidable legacy of empire.[32] It is a legacy that becomes even more apparent in the era of imperial decline, when powerful social and political institutions became stripped of their legitimacy.[33]

A more vexing problem has been posed by Antoinette Burton, who warns that the whole "empire and metropolitan culture" paradigm may be merely another way of shoring up the nation-state as the "sovereign ontological subject" of historical enquiry.[34] Just as John Seeley turned to the empire as a way of reinvigorating British history, there remains an undeniable hint of "what do they know of England who only England know" in the more recent appeals for integrating the histories of periphery and metropole. Mrinalini Sinha has commented on how, in much of this work, the colonial context is seldom developed, appearing either as a backdrop against which metropolitan culture is defined, or else the arena where discrete national culture is projected outward for the purpose of imperial domination. "Typically" she argues, "the 'imperial' gets conceptualized simply as an extension of the 'national,' or at best a shadowy presence in the making of the 'national.'"[35] In order to escape this simple conflation of the metropolitan with the colonial, Sinha has put forward the transnational paradigm of "imperial social formation." This model, she argues, allows for the "different trajectories of metropolitan and colonial histories" but at the same time conveys the sense that "metropolitan and colonial histories were both constituted by the history of imperialism."[36] Sinha's work, together with Catherine Hall's study of Caribbean influences on British intellectual culture in the nineteenth century and Antoinette Burton's work on Indians "at the heart of Empire" in late Victorian Britain, represents the most self-conscious attempt to integrate the historical experiences of metropole and periphery and thereby (as Burton puts it) "denaturalize the easy association of Britain with home."[37]

The environmental historian Richard Drayton has adopted a similar approach, likening the imperial experience to an "engine" that brings "human communities, once separated by distance and culture, into systems of exchange and interdependence." It is these "systems" that form the object of his study, rather than the national cultures that were forged by them. For Drayton, the process inexactly labeled as "the expansion of Europe" is better understood as the "contraction of the world."[38] This may be a convenient stance for a work that seeks to encompass "the world" from the confines of Kew Gardens, but there are broader reasons for this new emphasis on the "global." Drayton's work is clearly influenced by the emergence in recent decades of the new discipline of "World History," with its ardent conviction that the various thematic and geographical subdisciplines of historical scholarship are only fully intelligible in relation to the whole. For the world historian, no historical problem is too big, nor any chronological time span too vast—a perspective that throws out important methodological clues and raises new political dilemmas in extracting the nationalist paradigm from deep roots in Western historiography.

Yet while the methodologies of "world history" can provide a means of evading the conceptual framework of nationalism, its practitioners remain equally at the mercy of their "particular concept of empire." Take, for example, the recent spate of "world history" offerings in explaining the "rise of the West." What these works share in common is the broad chronological brush and sweeping spatial range of the world historian. But their conclusions hint at some of the perhaps unforeseen implications of a transnational imperial history. At one extreme is André Gunder Frank's *ReOrient: Global Economy in the Asian Age,* which dismisses the idea of Western global ascendancy as a Eurocentric myth.[39] Taking a global view over several millennia, Frank sees the recent successes of Western imperialism and mercantilism as a mere blip on the screen that is already being reversed by the onset of a new, expansive cycle centered on East Asia. Thus, by situating his work outside of the determinants of the nation, Frank denies that the history of European expansion is worth dwelling on as a phenomenon in its own right.

Further difficulties arise in the work of David Landes and Thomas Sowell, each of whom finds the key to Western material prosperity in certain attributes inherent in European cultures. Sowell occupies the opposite extreme to the macroeconomy of André Gunder Frank. While Frank's world history is conceived almost solely in global economic and mercantile terms, Sowell asserts the primacy of the "cultural capital" that lies at the heart of all economic development.[40] David Landes's *The Wealth and Poverty of Nations* takes a more wide-ranging approach but nonetheless comes down heavily in favor of cultural determinism. While he acknowledges Europe's prior advantages in terms of geography and environment, he regards these advantages as only a small part of the explanation. "If we learn anything from the history of economic development," he argues, "it is that culture makes all the difference." Hard work, thrift, patience, curiosity, tenacity, ingenuity, and free markets are among the qualities listed as fundamental to the accumulation of the wealth and technical know-how essential to European expansion. Landes consistently asserts the theme that "people made all the difference," but when it comes to explaining the impulse behind the expansion of Europe, Landes suddenly appears as a universalist. He puts forward his "law of social and political relationships" in typically direct fashion: "Where one group is strong enough to push another around and stands to gain by it, it will do so." Imperialism then, in Landes's world view, "is the expression of a deep human drive."[41]

Again, this raises questions about the kinds of political and ethical positions that may be undermined by attempts to subvert the nationalist historiographical agenda. It is rare among world historians, for example, to hear demands, implicit or explicit, for correcting the past misdeeds of imperialism, whether in relation to issues of slavery, indigenous land rights, or other postimperial controversies. John Hirst, for example, underlines that "the expansion of Europe was a phenomenon of such magnitude with such a profound and irreversible effect on humankind that it might be thought that our moralising tendency would be silenced in the face of it."[42] Even a relatively sympathetic voice like Jared Diamond's can offer the inheritors of past injustice little more than a logical explanation and the reassurance that their misfortune was no fault of their own.[43] Equally typical is the studiously noncommittal conclusion of Philip Curtin's study, *The World and the West*: "Globalization has some benefits, but it also has costs."[44] But this reluctance to make ethical judgments about the imperial past is no less political in its ramifications, even if only by default. In silencing the "moralising tendency" of left-wing critics, the macrohistorical perspective of the world historian lends itself to an alternative morality of laissez-faire liberalism.

Nonetheless, the intervention of "world history" in an area that has traditionally been the preserve of imperial history suggests a more general paradigmatic shift. As the national determinants of imperial scholarship give way to the transnational preoccupations of globalization, the field of "imperial history" may be set to stage a major comeback, reclaiming ground that had been lost during the proliferation of area studies. The recent five-volume *Oxford History of the British Empire* appears paradoxically as both the last of its kind (in terms of offering a synthesis of the five-hundred-year trajectory of British imperialism set firmly within a national framework) and a sign of things to come (in terms of equating British expansion with the globalization of the modern world). The authors of the earlier volumes are well aware of the problems inherent in applying the term "British" (or even "Empire") to the era prior to the mid-eighteenth century but are unable to reconcile this with the national requirements of the collections as a whole. And in the later volumes, chapters focusing on national case studies are often light on "imperial" content (or as Stephen Howe comments, some might have been subtitled "Trying to Escape the History of Empire").[45] Yet other areas that engage more directly with the "British Empire," deriving from literary or discursive analytical perspectives, are either completely overlooked or subjected to scorn. A process of staking out and defending the terrain of the imperial historian is clearly in evidence, particularly in the final volume on *Historiography*. An underlying anxiety about "what constitutes imperial history" pervades all five volumes.

But the *Oxford History* is also concerned with extending the rubric of imperial history, as a means of investing the subject with new relevance for contemporary readers. It is significant that Robin Winks singles out David Landes's

Wealth and Poverty of Nations as a text that might "centre the debate" on empire and economics into the new century.[46] Other contributors equally point to the global context as a fruitful area of future inquiry. A. G. Hopkins, in his reflections on the "future of the imperial past," calls for a renewed focus on the transnational deployments of "material forces" as a means of eluding the constraints of the nation and thereby rejuvenating scholarly interest in imperial history.[47] Stephen Howe endorses this "optimistic" approach, surmising that "if the great historiographical shift of the twentieth century's second half was from Imperial to national history, there are good reasons to think that in coming decades the pendulum can and should swing back."[48] But is the pendulum the appropriate metaphor? Howe himself notes that imperial history, from the earnest pleadings of Seeley and Curtis to the emancipatory drive of the postcolonialists, has long been characterized by political and ethical engagement. If the above sample of "world history" is anything to go by, the new investment in global imperial history promises a self-conscious distancing from ethical standpoints, becoming ever "disentangled from questions of morality," as Hopkins terms it.[49] Far from representing the return arc of the pendulum, the move toward a global footing for imperial history may serve to undermine the remaining ethical barriers to the unchecked dissemination of global capital.

At the very least, it remains clear that the "globalization" paradigm is the front runner in the race for alternatives to national perspectives on empire. But it is worth bearing in mind that the search for a global framework for the imperial past is no less a reflection of the preoccupations of our own age than were the national paradigms of preceding eras. A. G. Hopkins made this explicit in his remark: "Imperial history provides a means of understanding some of the large problems facing today's world. . . . The imperial power promoted a form of cosmopolitanism that strengthened its own sense of national identity, whereas the global forces that impinge on the world today have challenged and often weakened national institutions and identities. . . . The issues raised by these momentous developments call for a reappraisal of their antecedents."[50] Or as Stephen Howe more succinctly puts it, "Globalization today impresses on us the need to reappraise the global systems of the past."[51] We need to ask the question, therefore, whether transcending the nation in imperial scholarship represents the emancipation of the imperial experience from the distorting prism of national ideologies, or whether it merely entails a re-viewing of the past according to the prerogatives of the present—by predating "globalization" to an age where the term embodied a quite different set of meanings. On the basis of recent historiographical trends, we might confidently predict that the study of history is not, after all, irretrievably bound up in the discourse of nation. But it does seem destined to be ever rooted in our own self-image. From that, there would seem to be no escape.

Notes

1   John Gallagher and Ronald Robinson, "The Imperialism of Free Trade," *Economic History Review* 6, 1 (1953): 1.
2   See, for example, Catherine Hall, ed., *Cultures of Empire: Colonizers in Britain and the Empire in the Nineteenth and Twentieth Centuries: A Reader* (Manchester: Manchester University Press, 2000), p. 1. This view of Seeley's place in imperial historiography is emphatically disputed by Andrew Porter in his review of Hall's volume. See *Journal of Imperial and Commonwealth History* 29, 3 (September 2001): 138.
3   Kathleen Wilson, *The Sense of the People: Politics, Culture and Imperialism in England, 1715–1785* (Cambridge: Cambridge University Press, 1995), p. 157.
4   See discussion in Jack P. Greene, "Empire and Identity from the Glorious Revolution to the American Revolution," in *The Oxford History of the British Empire*, vol. 3: *The Eighteenth Century*, ed. P. J. Marshall (Oxford: Oxford University Press, 1998), pp. 220–227.
5   Andrew S. Thompson, *Imperial Britain: The Empire in British Politics, c. 1880–1932* (London: Longman, 2000), p. 187.
6   Douglas Cole, "The Problem of 'Nationalism' and 'Imperialism' in British Settlement Colonies," *Journal of British Studies* 10, 2 (May 1971): 160–182.
7   John Seeley, *The Expansion of England: Two Courses of Lectures* (London: Macmillan, 1883 [1899 ed.]), pp. 10, 13.
8   See Peter Burroughs, "John Robert Seeley and Imperial History," *Journal of Imperial and Commonwealth History* 2 (January 1973): 191–211.
9   Quoted in Thompson, *Imperial Britain*, p. 18.
10   Richard Jebb, *Studies in Colonial Nationalism* (London: Edward Arnold, 1905), p. viii.
11   Ibid., pp. vii, 327.
12   W. K. Hancock, *Australia* (London: Benn, 1930), pp. 56–57.
13   W. K. Hancock, *Argument of Empire* (Harmondsworth: Penguin, 1943), p. 12.
14   W. M. Roger Louis, "Introduction," in *The Oxford History of the British Empire*, vol. 5: *Historiography*, ed. R. W. Winks (Oxford: Oxford University Press, 1999), p. 30.
15   See Neville Meaney, "Britishness and the Problem of Australian Nationalism," and Stuart Ward, "Sentiment and Self-Interest: The Imperial Ideal in Anglo-Australian Commercial Culture," both in *Australian Historical Studies* 116 (April 2001): 74–91 and 91–108.
16   See Kathleen Paul, *Whitewashing Britain: Race and Citizenship in the Postwar Era* (Ithaca, N.Y.: Cornell University Press, 1997).
17   See John Darwin, "Fear of Falling: British Politics and Imperial Decline since 1900," *Transactions of the Royal Historical Society* 36 (1986): 27–43.
18   In 1961, Enoch Powell lamented that Seeley's study was "now almost forgotten." See Simon Heffer, *Like the Roman: The Life of Enoch Powell* (London: Weidenfeld and Nicolson, 1998), p. 335.
19   Robinson and Gallagher, "The Imperialism of Free Trade," p. 1.
20   R. W. Southern, *The Shapes and Substance of Academic History*, cited in Geoffrey Elton, *The Practice of History* (London: Fontana, 1969), p. 185.
21   J. W. Davidson, *Samoa mo Samoa: The Emergence of the Independent State of Western Samoa*

(Melbourne: Oxford University Press, 1967); Russell Ward, *The Australian Legend* (Melbourne: Oxford University Press, 1958). See also Ann Curthoys's essay in this volume.

22 See, for example, D. K. Fieldhouse, "Can Humpty-Dumpty Be Put Together Again? Imperial History in the 1980s," *Journal of Imperial and Commonwealth History* 12, 2 (1984): 9–23.

23 Homi Bhabha: *The Location of Culture* (London: Routledge, 1994), p. 251, and "The Third Space," in *Identity: Community, Culture, Difference*, ed. Jonathan Rutherford (London: Lawrence and Wishart, 1990), p. 211.

24 Arif Dirlik, panel commentary at the opening of the Center for Postcolonial Studies, Copenhagen University, April 1999.

25 Stephen Slemon made this explicit in his assertion that postcolonial studies needed "to become more tolerant of methodological difference, at least when that difference is articulated towards emancipatory anti-colonialist ends." See Slemon, "The Scramble for Postcolonialism," in *The Post-Colonial Studies Reader*, ed. Bill Ashcroft, Gareth Griffiths, and Helen Tiffin (London: Routledge, 1995), p. 51.

26 D. A. Washbrook, "Orients and Occidents: Colonial Discourse Theory and the Historiography of the British Empire," in Winks, ed., *Historiography*, p. 606.

27 See generally Partha Chatterjee, *Nationalist Thought and the Colonial World: A Derivative Discourse?* (London: Zed, 1986).

28 John M. MacKenzie, *Propaganda and Empire: The Manipulation of British Public Opinion, 1880–1960* (Manchester: Manchester University Press, 1984); S. Marks, "History, the Nation and the Empire: Sniping from the Periphery," *History Workshop Journal* (1990); Hall, ed., *Cultures of Empire*; Antoinette Burton, "Rules of Thumb: British History and 'Imperial Culture' in Nineteenth- and Twentieth-Century Britain," *Women's History Review* 3 (1994): 483–500.

29 Mary Louise Pratt, *Imperial Eyes: Travel Writing and Transculturation* (London: Routledge, 1992), p. 6.

30 John M. MacKenzie, *Orientalism: History, Theory and the Arts* (Manchester: Manchester University Press, 1995), p. 208.

31 P. J. Marshall: "No Fatal Impact? The Elusive History of Imperial Britain," *Times Literary Supplement*, March 12, 1993, p. 10; "Imperial Britain," *Journal of Imperial and Commonwealth History* 23 (1995).

32 For dissenting views, see Thompson, *Imperial Britain*, and Antoinette Burton, "Who Needs the Nation? Interrogating 'British' History," *Journal of Historical Sociology* 10 (September 1997).

33 See Stuart Ward, ed., *British Culture and the End of Empire* (Manchester: Manchester University Press, 2001).

34 Burton, "Who Needs the Nation?," p. 232.

35 Mrinalini Sinha, *Colonial Masculinity: The "Manly Englishman" and the "Effeminate Bengali" in the Late Nineteenth Century* (Manchester: Manchester University Press, 1995), p. 10.

36 Ibid., p. 182.

37 Antoinette Burton, "Some Trajectories of 'Feminism' and 'Imperialism,'" in *Feminism and Internationalism*, ed. M. Sinha, D. Guy, and A. Woollacott (Oxford: Blackwell, 1999), p. 217; Catherine Hall, *White, Male and Middle Class: Explorations in Feminism and History* (London: Routledge, 1992). See also Antoinette Burton, *At the Heart of the Empire: Indians and the Colonial Encounter in Late-Victorian Britain* (Berkeley: University of California Press, 1998).

38 Richard Drayton, *Nature's Government: Science, Imperial Britain, and the "Improvement" of the World* (New Haven, Conn.: Yale University Press, 2000), p. xiv.

39 André Gunder Frank, *ReOrient: Global Economy in the Asian Age* (Berkeley: University of California Press, 1998).

40 Thomas Sowell, *Conquests and Cultures: An International History* (New York: Basic Books, 1998).

41 David Landes, *The Wealth and Poverty of Nations: Why Some Are So Rich and Some So Poor* (London: Little, Brown, 1998), p. 63.

42 John Hirst, "Australian History and European Civilisation," *Quadrant* 37, 5 (1993): 32.

43 Jared Diamond, *Guns, Germs and Steel: The Fates of Human Societies* (New York: W. W. Norton, 1997). While Diamond is not inclined to apologize for the past five hundred years of European imperialism, he is at pains to absolve the downtrodden from any attribution of innate inferiority (and perhaps more to the point, to refute populist assumptions about an innately superior West).

44 Philip D. Curtin, *The World and the West: The European Challenge and the Overseas Response in the Age of Empire* (Cambridge: Cambridge University Press, 2000).

45 Stephen Howe, "The Slow Death and Strange Rebirths of Imperial History," *Journal of Imperial and Commonwealth History* 29, 2 (2001): 138.

46 Robin W. Winks, "The Future of Imperial History," in Winks, ed., *Historiography*, p. 661.

47 See Hopkins's "Development and the Utopian Ideal," in Winks, ed., *Historiography*, pp. 651–652. His thoughts are elucidated in more detail in "Back to the Future: From National History to Imperial History," *Past and Present* 164 (1999): 198–243.

48 Howe, "Slow Death," p. 138.

49 Hopkins, "Development and the Utopian Ideal," p. 637.

50 Hopkins, "Back to the Future," pp. 240–243.

51 Howe, "Slow Death," p. 138.

HEATHER STREETS

Empire and "the Nation": Institutional Practice, Pedagogy, and Nation in the Classroom

This essay seeks to engage the question "Who needs the nation?" and to interrogate the relationship of "the nation" to both institutional practice and pedagogy.[1] It draws from my experience as a recent PH.D. hired to teach (among other things) the history of imperialism at a large state university in the Pacific Northwest, Washington State University (WSU). My aims are twofold. First, I want to suggest the need to consider the future of national histories as both an intellectual and an institutional problem whose fate can be shaped by the practical demands of departmental structure and curriculum design as much as by scholarly debate and discourse. Second, I want to draw attention to the potential for imperial history courses influenced by "the imperial turn" to underscore the "all-pervasive, unavoidable imperial setting," in which the contemporary United States is enmeshed.[2] By focusing on a heated conflict in my "Imperialism and the Modern World" course, I reflect on the ways that imperial history can potentially destabilize powerful national imaginaries of white, middle-class America — in particular, assumptions about the superiority of Western culture and technology and "white" American prerogatives to speak for non-Western "Others."

I begin with institutional practice because, whether we like it or not, our employing institutions can be instrumental in opening up or foreclosing intellectual and pedagogical projects regarding "the nation." In short, practical demands matter. Issues like job security, territorial jealousies, departmental expectations, university culture, and enrollment quotas help to determine the courses we can offer and play a role in conditioning our future directions in academia. Gayatri Spivak has observed that the "*kind* of teaching machine" people from "the margin" enter "will determine [the margin's] contours."[3] Her remark, though referring to "outsiders" entering academia, is also relevant in a much wider context, for surely the question of who can afford to refigure national histories in pedagogical practice will be part of understanding better who "needs" the nation, "who manufactures the 'need' for it, and whose interests it serves."[4]

I offer my own case here both as a way of underscoring the importance of university environments for the future of national histories and as a preface for locating my "Imperialism and the Modern World" course in its wider institutional context. My research in exploring the constructedness of racial and gendered identities within a comparative imperial framework, though already in progress at the time I was hired, has been stimulated and shaped by an environment that both values and demands interdisciplinary, transnational teaching. For nearly the past decade, WSU has administered an extensive, interdisciplinary World Civilizations Program, in which every undergraduate is required to take two semester-long courses. Many history faculty, including me, teach a section of World Civilizations every year. While the course presents obvious difficulties in terms of methodology, teaching it has nevertheless required me to read far afield from my areas of specialization in Britain and the British Empire.[5] In the process, I have been forced to think, for the practical reasons of constructing a meaningful and useful course, about where the nation "fits" in a world history framework, and by implication where the nation "fits" in the way I "do" history. Although this is an ongoing intellectual project, teaching World Civilizations has highlighted for me the problematic nature of using "nations" as the building blocks of history, for such an approach obscures both complex connections that defy state boundaries and the contingent historical nature of "national" formations themselves. Instead, with the help of a variety of texts, as well as practical advice from colleagues, I have been increasingly interested in exploring world history thematically.

Aiding this project is the structure of WSU's core curriculum, for its requirements encourage history faculty to offer courses outside strictly defined national boundaries. In particular, upper-division undergraduates are required to take a course whose purpose is to integrate various disciplinary fields of knowledge and to permit advanced study outside a student's major. In the humanities and social sciences, these courses — known as "capstones" — are meant to address global or comparative "topics of permanent or perennial interest."[6] By implication, history capstones, which include my "Imperialism and the Modern World," are generally transnational in nature, by which I mean that they seek to illuminate particular themes (such as imperialism, world trade, or urbanization) through comparative case studies that transcend national boundaries.

For those of us inclined or expected to offer such courses, they have the double attraction of virtually ensuring high enrollments. From my perspective as a junior faculty in a department with a small contingent of European historians, this attraction has been difficult to resist. For the last decade, history enrollments at WSU have been in steady decline, and in no field more precipitously than European history. Courses in European history often have difficulty attaining critical mass, which in turn has resulted in an alarming number of class cancellations. As a result, I have felt the need to increase the number and frequency of course offerings that fulfill capstone or other general education requirements.[7] In turn, my teaching has become markedly less "nationally oriented" in the three years since I was hired, and my investment in national histories — or even in calling myself a "British historian" — has diminished correspondingly.

Perhaps ironically, the practical demands of my institutional environment have influenced, to a large degree, my "need" for the nation and the way I "manufacture" it in my teaching and research. While this may at one level appear problematic, in my case it is also certain that such practical demands have yielded new spaces for transnational study. The point, therefore, is that any project of rethinking "the nation" in historical practice and scholarship needs to take seriously the obstacles or opportunities that institutional practices can present.

I want now to address the problem of "who needs the nation" in our "teaching machines" in quite a different way. Since my arrival at WSU, I have taught my "Imperialism and the Modern World" course three times. Each year, I have dramatically changed the readings to reflect new scholarship, and each year I have a new group of students from a wide variety of majors and backgrounds. Nevertheless, every time I teach the course, ideas about and conflicts over American national mythologies form one of the primary subtexts of our class discussions. In what follows, I explore the stakes in just one of the many ideological conflicts this class has engendered among my students: in this case, a clash over the effects of the "civilizing mission." I have chosen this conflict, which occurred the first time I taught the course, because of its particular explosiveness and because the students involved articulated their concerns so clearly. At the same time, I want to emphasize that this conflict was unusual only in terms of the vehemence with which it was pursued. Similar conflicts have regularly ensued each semester over similar issues, although space does not allow me to develop them here. Moreover, class size, gender divisions, and racial/ethnic makeup each semester has remained fairly constant. My goal, then, is not to single out this conflict as exceptional, but instead to use it as a means of exploring in some depth the ways imperial history informed by "the imperial turn" can both expose unacknowledged assumptions of racial difference and subvert powerful ideas about America's place as a champion of global progress.

That so many conflicts develop in these classes is due, in large part, to the course design, which itself is deeply influenced by my ideological investment in historical scholarship influenced by "the imperial turn." Thus, despite class

sizes of thirty-five to forty students each semester, I remain philosophically opposed to teaching in traditional lecture form. As a student of feminist theory as
well as of the history of imperialism, I remain dissatisfied with academic efforts
to impose totalizing, "objective" narratives on the historical past. Within the
field of imperial history, it is exactly the power of dominant groups to "know"
and "possess" the truth of the past and its peoples that my own research
contests. To teach the history of imperialism as a series of lectures, I believe,
might replicate — albeit in a different way — the tidy process of "knowledge
production" that has so often gone hand in hand with imperial domination.

Moreover, to teach the history of imperialism as a chronological narrative
ending with European decolonization allows American students to shore up
their beliefs that imperialism is not a subject that involves their own society. It
is far too easy, when presented with such a structure, for students to claim that
"we" did not have an empire like the Europeans, and "we" have always fought
for freedom and democracy whenever it was endangered. By presenting imperial history as a set of thematic problems open to discussion, analysis, and
interpretation, I aimed to challenge this strategy of distancing by opening a
dialogue between the past and the present.

In light of these concerns, I chose readings that sampled a wide variety of
theoretical and methodological approaches to the history of imperialism as a
global phenomenon since 1800. My selections, therefore, included "classic"
theoretical approaches to imperialism from the late nineteenth and early twentieth centuries, as well as path-breaking approaches to colonial resistance, economic imperialism, postcolonial criticism, and the "new imperial history." To
eliminate the possibility of narrative "coverage," as well as to get away from
"national" explanations for imperialism, reading selections spanned more than
two centuries and a wide geographical range.[8] Finally, readings reached beyond the "discipline" of history to consider approaches inspired by literary
criticism, contemporary journalism, fiction, economics, and anthropology.

The class itself was based almost entirely around written analysis and discussion of the readings. There were no exams or quizzes. As a way of ensuring
preparation for discussion, 35 percent of the grade was based on an e-mail
discussion group, to which students posted responses to the readings each
evening before class. I used these responses to plan the following day's discussion, to gauge student comprehension, to identify areas needing further expli-
cation, and to draw out the comments of students who were reluctant to speak
during class time. A further 20 percent of the grade was devoted to participation and attendance. The final 45 percent of the grade was allocated equally to
individual research papers and to group projects designed to bring together
common themes in the papers.

The results of this experiment in class design have been both exciting and problematic. On the one hand, the e-mail discussion group and attendance requirement accomplished the goals for which they were intended: students came prepared to class and critically engaged with assigned readings. Class discussions have been frequently animated. On the other hand, the intensive dialogue in which we found ourselves created a high level of classroom conflict. The necessity for all students to respond to the readings via e-mail exposed oppositional perspectives and ideologies where they would otherwise have remained both unspoken and unacknowledged. This, in turn, revealed sensitive divisions within the class that often revolved around a conservative white majority and an outspoken, more racially diverse minority.

That "race" and racial ideologies can play an important role in these conflicts was certainly borne out by the conflict under question. Typically for WSU, in this semester all but four members of the class identified themselves as "whites" of European ancestry; of the four, one was African American and three were Asian/Pacific American.[9] Two of the students of color—the African American, "James," and a Filipino American, "Daniel"—formed the backbone of the opposition to the conservative white majority. These men, both seniors majoring in English, were extremely articulate and well versed in critical race theory. Although they were frequently silent in class, their e-mail responses were highly critical of both the legacies of imperialism and the unexamined racial and cultural assumptions that undergirded many of their fellow students' responses. While they were by no means the only students to offer critical interpretations of the readings and of class discussions, the fact that they were students of color seemed to threaten many white students in the class far more deeply than identical criticisms made by other whites, male or female. This racially specific defensiveness, I believe, was a result of the discomfort many white students felt from being openly challenged by men who seemed to embody a much larger critique of white American culture on a national scale.[10]

The character of the conservative majority was also clearly outlined by some of the most vocal personalities in the class. Seven white men in the class were seniors on ROTC scholarships. They had enrolled together and thus frequently formed a coordinated bloc of opinion in class discussions. All were articulate, hard working, and highly confident in both their speaking abilities and their opinions. Their tendency was to attempt to see the positive side of imperial expansion, or at least to challenge overwhelmingly negative interpretations.[11] In the e-mail discussion and in class, their opinions frequently clashed with those of James and Daniel.

The most explosive conflict of the semester, touched off by a debate over the nature of the "civilizing mission," proved to be particularly revealing about both the political divisions in the class and the contemporary subtexts from which they drew. The class had just read and discussed, without marked contention, Michael Adas's chapter on the civilizing mission in his *Machines as the Measure of Men*, Rudyard Kipling's *White Man's Burden*, Alice Conklin's "The French Republican Civilizing Mission," and Adrian Hastings's "Christianity, Civilization, and Commerce." In the e-mail discussion for that night, most of the class had come to a consensus about the arrogance and self-serving nature of European "civilizing" rhetoric and had criticized such rhetoric as deeply hypocritical. Yet during class discussion the next day, a majority of students registered the qualified opinion that some aspects of European expansion may have, in the long run, been beneficial for colonized peoples. Their examples included the creation of infrastructure such as railroads, roads, and canals; the outlawing of certain practices such as *suttee* (widow immolation); improved hygiene; and, most unanimously, the spread of Western medicine.

Had I chosen the next readings purposefully to challenge our previous class discussion, I could not have done so more carefully, for these included David Arnold's "Medicine and the Colonization of the Body in India" and Timothy Burke's "Colonialism, Cleanliness, and Civilization in Colonial Rhodesia." Both selections challenge the benevolence of "civilizing" imperialism by exposing the arrogance, anxieties, and self-serving nature of even the most apparently "humanitarian" aims of improved hygiene and medical care. Arnold's essay is an indictment of British efforts to control a massive outbreak of plague in India between 1896 and 1930, arguing that fear of economic losses motivated the British to take extreme measures that violated Indian cultural codes as well as basic human dignity. Burke, in turn, explores British efforts to promote the use of soap in the "civilization" of what they perceived to be dirty African bodies and the ways these efforts were fundamentally tied to European notions of racial hierarchies. Thus, in their online responses to the readings, I asked the students to address Arnold's perspective on the benefits of Western medicine in light of our previous class discussion and to reflect more generally on the ways control over individual colonized bodies was linked to the civilizing mission.

In spite of what I believed to be Arnold's unambiguous presentation of plague control as both ineffective and insensitive, a number of students in the class insisted that British efforts — though not as effective as they might have been — had been carried out with good intentions and had at least been "better than nothing." "David," a key member of the ROTC group, offered the following interpretation:

The English went in and took over administration of aid to the Indians during their plague. Arnold seemed to view this as positive. While the Indians lost their autonomy, they were cured and the British were able to ensure their economic success. He also explained that the British tried to respect the caste system whenever possible. I suppose the British should get credit for helping people from the lower castes because the higher castes would have left them to die if they couldn't care for themselves. . . . I think that both pieces showed that control over bodies was necessary to the sanitation [*sic*] on disease prevention. The Africans most likely did not understand western medicine and were therefore scared of it. Like taking a little child to the doctor to get a vaccination you must hold them down and make them get a shot. The same was necessary for Africans.

In addition to his stunning misreading and inaccurate conflation of both pieces, David's response was problematic on a number of other levels. He clearly accepted British assertions that they were in a position to know what was best for the colonial people under their control and characterized colonial peoples — like many colonial officials had done before him — as children. Though he acknowledged that British disease-control measures resulted in a loss of autonomy for colonial subjects, he assumed such measures were justified without considering their effects on individual men and women. Indeed, his response implicitly denied the importance of individual subjectivity for colonial peoples.

David's response — like that of so many of his classmates — revealed his own unexamined assumptions about the superiority of Western "civilization," the right of Europeans to act in the name of colonized peoples, and the unimportance of individual colonial subjectivities in the face of Western technology. In some ways, it is true, Arnold's piece invites this type of response. Indeed, because Arnold fails to acknowledge the reality of preexisting Indian medical traditions, it was easy for students like David to assume that the British were importing Western medicine into an area wholly devoid of medical practices. In their eyes, any intervention — even if ultimately harmful — was better than none at all.

Yet Daniel and James offered radically different interpretations than most of the class. Daniel's response confronted the confidence of our previous discussion about the benefits of Western medicine:

Now here's an article for all the people who thought Western medicine was a benefit of imperialism. . . . Western medicine was applied in a penal fashion, declaring that plague-ridden patients were to be hospitalized forcefully if required, that any building or object even suspected of carrying the plague was to be destroyed, and that, in essence, Indians were some sort of sub-humans whose medical treatment was to be treated only as a way to perpetuate British hegemony and profit maximization. Some benefit to the colonized.

James's response was also directed to the previous class discussion about the "benefits" of Western medicine. His anger focused on what he accurately sensed was an eagerness in the class to brush over the more unpleasant aspects of imperial expansion on native peoples and to focus on positive "end results." This, he believed, was a result of the fact that virtually no one in the class identified with the position of colonized peoples:

The Arnold essay points to a theme which I believe has been running throughout the semester. That is that a problem isn't really a problem unless a person sees it directly or it affects that person directly. The British were only primarily concerned with the health of the colonizers and the shift to "concern" for the Indians didn't come about until the plague threatened the viability and success of British markets. . . . It is too simple to just say that "oh I can't really blame them for thinking this" or "things could have gotten out of hand if they hadn't done anything" [much of the class had responded in this way]. The issues are not that easy and go much deeper. I suppose if it was left up to most of the class, they would not blame anybody for anything unless the treatment somehow affected non–people of color.

According to James, students in the class easily assumed the good intentions of European imperialists, and even when those good intentions were not realized, felt little remorse over the results because those who suffered had not been of European descent.

James's anger intensified when he read David's response to the readings. In a second e-mail that evening, he directly challenged David's characterization of Africans as children and argued that such an analogy was deeply interwoven with ideologies of racial superiority: "[David's] posting comparing Africans to little kids is not only demeaning but it also reiterates the racist beliefs of the past and how they manifest themselves in the future. Making such sweeping comments that the Africans were probably scared of Western medicine is not only a broad generalization but that was not even the point of the chapter."

David's immediate response indicated bewilderment and anger at James's criticisms. His subsequent attempts to clarify his meaning and restate his comments in a less offensive manner, however, only reiterated his misreading of the articles, his assumption that Western medical technology was superior, his view of African natives as unsophisticated, and his failure to understand James's criticisms:

I think it is safe to say that people are scared of the unknown. I may be wrong but I hardly think that qualifies me as a racist. I was trying to make a point that while the Europeans may have introduced problems they thought they were doing right by trying to fix them. I made the child analogy because I thought that the western medicine would be as foreign to them as it is to a child now-a-days. . . . I figured that if they didn't have the medicine themselves, then they wouldn't understand it. . . . Now let me make it clear I do not think that the Africans were incapable of comprehension, I just don't think they understood it when it first showed up. I may have used a poor analogy and for that I apologize. I also don't believe that because I thought the Europeans were trying to help makes me a racist either. . . . In the future I suggest that you talk to me if you have a problem with me instead of suggesting to everyone that I am racist. It just may be that you misunderstood what I was implying.

James's response was unequivocal: "I stand by my earlier comments. While they may have been suggestive in implying you are a racist that was not the intent. My point was that what you said is an illustration of how the racial and racist ideologies of the past are manifested in the present day. If I misunderstood what you meant, then that is my fault. However, given our previous class discussions, I saw very little ambiguity in your comments."

What was revealing about the conflict, as James clearly saw, is that although the grounds over which it was fought were historical, its significance lay in the present. The stakes were much higher than an academic disagreement over how Africans (or Indians) were treated. Instead, David's interpretation signaled continuities — as well as identification — with the arrogant, ethnocentric, racist approaches of European imperialists in non-European areas. And these continuities, of course, suggested difficulties in the present, for if David and his like-minded classmates interpreted the past this way, it implied also their extension into matters of race and culture in contemporary society. David's response highlighted how deeply rooted are ideas of Western technological, scientific, and medical superiority within our culture and how complexly intertwined these ideas are with unexamined ideologies of racial difference. Thus, even when Arnold clearly demonstrated the ineffectiveness of British efforts to combat the plague, students had difficulty seeing the destructiveness of such interventions and were quick to make light of the consequences for colonial subjects.

Indeed, conflicts over the meaning of both Arnold and Burke, borne out by the e-mail and class discussions, challenged and exposed the ease with which many white, middle-class students in the class identified with European efforts to bring "civilization" to non-Europeans throughout the world. These students, I believe, saw such efforts as analogous to an honorable "American" tradition of aiding peoples everywhere in the fight against hunger, disease, poverty, and tyranny. As such, it is not much of a stretch for these students to assume that European imperialists were at least acting out of morally defensible motivations to "help" colonial peoples. To challenge these assumptions, as James did, is to challenge a core piece of American national mythology.[12]

The issue of identification also goes to the heart of concerns with "the nation." Over the course of the semester, it became increasingly clear that many white students, without knowing it, identified their own sense of self and "nation" as exclusively European in origin.[13] They felt most drawn to, and most sympathetic toward, the Europeans from whom they believed they were descended and had difficulty imagining the struggles of non-European colonial subjects. The personal terror experienced by colonial subjects during imperialism seemed incomprehensible to them because they could not imagine—as James and Daniel could—a world in which their origins or their color might be used to regulate their activities, limit their freedoms, or silence their protests.

This conflict, however, proved to be a catalyst for some students, as the destabilizing effects of James's criticisms spurred a heightened awareness of their own racial and national assumptions. Many wondered aloud whether or not, in light of our readings, the United States might also qualify as an imperial power or commented on their surprise at the enduring legacy of racial and gendered hierarchies in our own society. The myth of the United States as the paragon of democracy, justice, and peace in the post–World War II and (more recently) the post-Communist world can be, admittedly, difficult to penetrate. Most of my students have been saturated in a culture of American exceptionalism since elementary school, the basic tenets of which are reified daily in political speeches, advertisements, and popular culture. American global dominance is rarely analyzed as an imperial phenomenon outside academia, and even within the field of U.S. history much remains to be done.[14] Yet in response to class readings, discussion, and the e-mail responses, some students became increasingly adept at making connections between the imperialisms of the past and the current dominant position of the United States in global politics.

On the other hand, other students grew increasingly resistant to our project of critical engagement with both the readings and each other. Some, indeed, became aggressively defensive and registered unease about the benefits of revisiting such sensitive historical issues. Their comments in class and in the e-mail discussion grew impatient and embattled, as though our subject matter was a personal attack on "their" culture. In response to Michael Adas's chapter on the origins of scientific racism, for example, several students felt it necessary to point out that racism and the oppression of colonial peoples was not their fault. Two students (both white women) asked why we had to pick on their

(European) ancestors as "the bad guys." In response to Catherine Hall's article on the Morant Bay rising and Scott Cook's chapter on "Women as Colonizers and Colonized," one of the ROTC seniors asked if we had not done enough "bashing of white men." In response to Edward Said's *Orientalism*, a significant minority of the class responded that this was just one more reading about how "bad" Europeans were for looking down on non-Europeans. One student was so disgusted by our attention to ideology and representation that he dropped the class in midsemester.

In addition, much of this growing defensiveness seemed to be directed, in a personal way, at James. Perhaps because he was African American, his consistent challenges to conservative interpretations of the readings seemed to function as a symbolic indictment of "white" culture.[15] Even though other white and nonwhite students were frequently as outspoken as James, the students who had gone on the defensive seemed to hold him primarily responsible for creating discord in the class. On two occasions, white students privately e-mailed James after his online responses to censure him for carrying too large a racial "chip" on his shoulder. In James's view, such defensiveness signaled guilty consciences. In response to a particularly defensive set of responses to Said's *Orientalism*, James asked: "Why does it seem to bother people in class that the other side of history is being told? Up until the past 30 years, most of what would have been taught would have been almost all positive in regards to the U.S. and Britain. Is it a sense of guilt that makes people want to avoid the atrocities and focus on the positives?" My sense, however, was that in addition to issues of guilt, student defensiveness stemmed also from resistance to the destabilizing potential of the issues at hand. Students who argued they were not responsible for the actions of their European "ancestors" were clearly struggling with the problem of how far their own complicity in contemporary global inequalities extends. Students uncomfortable with "bashing white men" correctly sensed that revisiting history with the concerns of the present holds a real potential for upsetting their own complacence with both global affairs and intimate personal relations. Their resistance, then, seemed at least partly an attempt to avoid facing the political and ideological challenges articulated both by the readings and, much more threateningly, by James.

As I have watched, facilitated, and negotiated such struggles during this and subsequent semesters, I have come to believe that conflict *itself*—in spite of, or perhaps because of, the discomfort it causes—is among the most valuable products of this kind of discussion-based course. In a conventional lecture class, students with radically different interpretations would never have the chance to challenge one another, and contemporary issues raised by the historical issues under study would remain unexplored. In this class, though, students are repeatedly confronted with perspectives different from their own, as well as with their own assumptions about the past and the present. Although some become alienated and aggressive, many come to understand that managed conflict can be more productive and inspiring than enforced consensus or silence.

End-of-semester course evaluations have seemed to bear this out. Indeed, over subsequent semesters the majority of students indicated that our often contentious discussions were by far the most effective aspect of the class.[16] While some feel that discussions are "touchy feely junk," many more echo the student who wrote that "We've had great class discussions and addressed difficult/controversial issues." Even more encouraging are those students who say the course has "given me a new perspective on life" or that "I had never really thought too much on issues of imperialism, but now I see and understand its impact."

Moreover, the fact that serious, important conflicts did (and continue to) arise in response to both readings and discussion is testament to the potential for historical approaches influenced by "the imperial turn" to subvert powerful, yet often unspoken, national imaginaries in the present. As the conflict under question demonstrated, anxieties about the stability of "the nation" need not be produced by specific references to one's own nation. Indeed, none of our readings that semester were "about" the United States, and our discussions — though frequently using the United States as an unspoken referent — primarily focused on historical issues brought out by the readings. Clearly, the history of imperialism, particularly when its practitioners challenge conventional boundaries (whether they be racial, gendered, or geographic), can destabilize much of what we know (or think we know) about the present as well. In the British context, Antoinette Burton has argued that recent historical efforts insisting on remapping Britain as an "imperial landscape" have "met with an opposition so determined that it would be easy to imagine that they pose some kind of threat to national security."[17] This, I think, is only partly hyperbole, for in teaching about the history of imperialism "after the turn," what is at stake — for students as well as scholars — is not so much national security, but the security of "the nation" and with it, the necessity of remapping the self.

Notes

1   See Antoinette Burton, "Who Needs the Nation? Interrogating 'British' History," *Journal of Historical Sociology* 10, 3 (September 1997): 227–248.

2   Edward Said, "Secular Interpretation, the Geographical Element, and the Methodology of Imperialism," in *After Colonialism: Imperial Histories and Postcolonial Displacements*, ed. Gyan Prakash (Princeton, N.J.: Princeton University Press, 1995), p. 34.

3 Spivak refers here to particular "national" contexts of U.S., Canadian, or British "teaching machines." Gayatri Spivak, *Outside in the Teaching Machine* (New York: Routledge, 1993), p. ix.

4 Burton, "Who Needs the Nation?," p. 234.

5 This issue of faculty development is one of the principal benefits advocates of world history consistently cite. See, for example, Jeffrey Wasserstrom, "Eurocentrism and Its Discontents," *Perspectives* (January 2001).

6 *WSU Catalog*, Tier III Courses, *http://134.121.31.99/default.asp?page=/catalog/*.

7 Three out of the five courses I will teach in the 2001–2002 academic year are general education requirements, including "World Civilizations since 1500" and two capstone courses, "Imperialism in the Modern World" and "Historical Geography."

8 For the advantages of taking a "long view" in teaching imperial history, see Doug Peers, "British Imperialism and the Dynamics of Race, Gender, and Class in the Long Nineteenth Century," *Radical History Review* 71 (1998): 169.

9 WSU is 87 percent white. See the data on WSU Institutional Research, Ethnic Enrollment WSU Pullman, since 1968. *http://www.ir.wsu.edu/default.asp?page=Data&Cat=1*.

10 Indeed, a 1997 study, partially conducted at WSU, concluded that white college students maintain a high degree of racial discomfort and fear toward nonwhites. See Eduardo Bonilla-Silva and Tyrone Forman, "'I Am Not a Racist But . . ?': Mapping White College Students' Racial Ideology in the USA," *Discourse and Society* 11, 1 (2000): 50–85. Many of the essays in David Schoem, Linda Frankel, Ximena Zuniga, and Edith A. Lewis, eds., *Multicultural Teaching in the University* (Westport, Conn.: Praeger, 1993), explore the problems and issues related to racial, ethnic, and/or sexual orientation differences in American university classrooms.

11 Indeed, every time I have taught the class white ROTC men have been the center of articulate conservatism in class discussions and in e-mail responses.

12 Stuart Creighton Miller, *"Benevolent Assimilation": The American Conquest of the Philippines, 1899–1903* (New Haven, Conn.: Yale University Press, 1982), discusses this in the context of the Philippine-American war. See especially chs. 1 and 13.

13 For a recent published articulation of this tendency, see Peter Brimelow, *Alien Nation: Common Sense about America's Immigration Disaster* (New York: Random House, 1995). Brimelow contends that "the American nation has always had a specific ethnic core. And that core has been white" (p. 10). This was often an unspoken assumption in my class.

14 Although space constraints do not allow me to explore this issue fully, some recent works that explore U.S. policy in terms of global imperialism include Peter Hahn and Mary Ann Heiss, eds., *Empire and Revolution: The United States and the Third World since 1945* (Columbus: Ohio State University Press, 2000), and Amy Kaplan and Donald E. Pease, eds., *Cultures of United States Imperialism* (Durham, N.C.: Duke University Press, 1993).

15 For the often tense dynamics between African American and white students on college campuses, see Shelby Steele, "The Recoloring of Campus Life: Student Racism, Academic Pluralism, and the End of a Dream," in *Campus Wars: Multi-Culturalism and the Politics of Difference*, ed. John Arthur and Amy Shapiro (Boulder, Colo.: Westview Press, 1995).

16 In the semester during which this conflict occurred, in response to the question "What aspects of the professor's instructional techniques did you consider to be effective?," sixteen out of thirty-three students who handed in end-of-semester evaluations specifically wrote about the value of the class discussions. One student wrote that class discussions were not helpful.

17 Burton, "Who Needs the Nation?," p. 230.

ANN CURTHOYS

We've Just Started Making National Histories, and You Want Us to Stop Already?

The yearning to escape the national boundaries that mark history-writing seems to be shared by historians in many places. Influenced by an international language of cultural theory, we seek to write postcolonial, diasporic, and world histories that help us understand historical experiences and processes in both depth and breadth. Intellectual trends that support this beyond-the-nation approach include not only postcolonial and diasporic theory, but also the study of religion, gender, class, and environmental change. Our yearnings are not, however, purely the product of changing theoretical paradigms for history. Another reason (is it not?) is a desire among us historians to communicate our craft beyond our national boundaries. We are chafing at the national bit, wanting international readers to engage with our ideas and dilemmas, to praise us for our achievements, and to criticize our failures. At least I am. Too often, the national frameworks of history mean that international scholarly communication does not happen among historians. While some national histories are taught extensively beyond their national borders — British, U.S., German, French, Russian, Chinese — a great many others — that is, most — are not. To take the examples I know best, Australian, New Zealand, and Canadian histories still have little purchase or audience outside their home countries.

The reasons lie partly in the institutions of international circulation of knowledge and power but mainly within the histories themselves. Historians write national histories for national audiences, and there is something about our mode of address that confines most of us to that audience. This was brought home to me recently when reviewing a book on new New Zealand histories. It was a fine book, well crafted, well written, and conceptually rigorous. Yet I found it hard to get truly engaged. The factual details were unfamiliar, yet the stories were very like those I know from Australian history. It was both too different and too similar to the histories I read and write myself. In a flash, I suddenly saw my own work as non-Australians might see it — esoteric, familiar, and unnecessary. In rejecting older imperial history frameworks, where Australian (and other settler society) histories appeared purely as effects of metropolitan imperial history, and opting for a more independent, nationally focused history, we have surely lost as well as gained. This essay traces some of the processes whereby a national history was built and an autonomous but narrow history developed from a derivative yet broader one, and it ponders these gains and losses.

*   *   *

For Australian historians, the nation, far from being a tired old concept, is still relatively new. As a national project, Australian history is only decades old.[1] Though there were some key school history texts such as Ernest Scott's immensely popular *A Short History of Australia*, published in 1916 and reprinted for decades afterward, and a slowly growing number of specialist studies and collections of documents, only a modest amount of Australian national history was written before World War II.[2] Early national histories included Keith Hancock's *Australia* (1930), to which I return below. The first academic history journal specializing in Australian history started as late as 1940; there was no separate organization for historians until the Australian Historical Association was formed in 1974, though historians did meet annually before that as a distinct section of the Australian Association for the Advancement of Science (AAAS). When I was searching for a Ph.D. topic in 1967, it was still a radical act to choose an Australian topic studied in Australia. Bright history students went generally to Oxford or Cambridge and studied British or European history or, less often, to the United States to study U.S. history.

While a major reason for this slow development was the small size and number of universities until the 1950s, an associated cultural reason was a middle-class anxiety that Australia lacked a worthy intellectual national culture and was merely a second-rate derivation of Britain. Australia, many thought, was mediocre, philistine, contemptible, forever doomed by location and distance and by its fraught penal and colonial origins. D. H. Lawrence had said influentially on his visit to Australia in 1922, "That's what the life in a new country does to you: makes you so material, so outward, that your real inner life and your inner self dies out and you clatter around like so many mechanical animals," and many intellectuals agreed with him.[3]

The question of whether or not Australia was a second-rate society was felt most keenly in relation to Britain, the place of origin of the vast majority of the population. For many Australians, Britain remained Home (my grandmother always spoke of England as Home, though she and her parents had been born in the Australian colonies and had never been to England). When young journalist Margaret MacPherson explained to George Bernard Shaw, who visited New Zealand in 1935 at the age of eighty, that in the Dominions there was no culture, "no drama, no music, no art," Shaw replied: "You Australasians are extraordinary, really. Every year, thousands of you take that long, uncomfortable journey to see an inferior country, which you persist in calling Home in spite of the fact that its people ignore you and are scarcely aware of your existence. I wish I could persuade you that THIS is your home, that these lands should be the center of your art, your culture, your drama."[4]

Historian W. K. Hancock articulated this psychological attachment to Britain and sense of Australian cultural inferiority in his extremely popular book, *Australia* (1930). He described Australians as transplanted Britons who had set down only shallow roots. The great mass of Australian writing, he said, did not express an affinity of place. The best Australian novels dealt with "individuals and families uprooted from England, and unacclimatized to Australia," flitting uneasily between two hemispheres. He observed, however, that Australians were gradually developing an attachment to the soil, which is why they "were quick to resent the suggestion of patronage in the word colonial."[5] Later in the book, he said in a notably but not unusually masculinist creation story of Australian history: "Our fathers were homesick Englishmen, or Irishmen, or Scots; and their sons, who have made themselves at home in a continent, have not yet forgotten those tiny islands in the North Sea." In a flurry of gendered and sexualized metaphors, he went on: "A country is a jealous mistress and patriotism is commonly an exclusive passion; but it is not impossible for Australians, nourished by a glorious literature and haunted by old memories, to be in love with two soils."[6] Australians saw British history as *their* history. Nation and empire were not alternatives; one was a part of the other. Until 1948 Australians were Australian citizens *and* British subjects. High school texts emphasized the importance of the fact that most Australians were the descendants of British immigrants and were European in culture and inheritance. Scott's *Short History*, for example, stressed the British imperial link, ending with fulsome praise of the British Commonwealth.

The disjunction between Australia's geography and cultural heritage was responsible for another major area of uneasiness in pre–World War II Australian historiography. "Asia" had long been a subject for fear in the white Australian imaginary — fear of being swamped by much larger populations to the north, invaded by China or Japan, and drawn away from a European and into an Asian cultural sphere. Historians before the war, like the vast majority of the population, supported the White Australia Policy, Keith Hancock's *Australia* in 1930 asserting with approval that "among the Australians pride of race counted for more than love of country."[7] Australia, he wrote, had a great deal to fear from Asia: "Facing her northern doors were vast reservoirs of yellow humanity, whose outpourings, if unchecked, would ruin what she held most precious — the economic and racial foundations of her homogenous egalitarian society."[8] Ernest Scott had similarly felt no embarrassment in supporting racial immigration policies as necessary to Australian economic well-being.

Concomitant with this sense of Australian history as part of British imperial history and Australian society as protecting itself from "Asia" went an avoidance of the history of colonization itself — that is, of the processes whereby one group of societies — those of the Indigenous peoples inhabiting the continent before the British settlers arrived — was largely dispossessed so that British colonization might be established and developed. In the nineteenth century, these processes were part of public discussion and represented in popular histories, sometimes revealing an anxiety about the morality of the brutal processes involved in taking other people's land by force and often reflecting on the "inevitability" of colonization and the destruction it brought. These anxieties faded in the early twentieth century, so that the story of dispossession largely disappeared from public consciousness, memorializing, and published histories. So great had the silence become that in 1924 Stephen Roberts's impressively researched *History of Australian Land Settlement* barely mentioned prior Indigenous occupation of the land and the struggles between the Indigenous peoples and the incoming settlers for control of the land, instead analyzing and sympathizing with the squatters who overcame difficulties presented by "the blacks, floods, fires, drought, accidents."[9] Six years later, Hancock's *Australia* described the Australian Aborigines as "pathetically helpless when assailed by the acquisitive society of Europe." The advance of British civilization, he said in a tone made popular in the nineteenth century and continuing well into the twentieth, made inevitable "the natural progress of the aboriginal race towards extinction." Though Hancock saw the replacement of one society by another as inevitable, he did not condone the process by which it had happened: "sometimes the invading British did their wrecker's work with the unnecessary brutality of stupid children."[10]

Very gradually, Australian historiography fashioned for itself a national, nonimperial identity. This development of a professional, academic, national history was part of a broader intellectual project. While many Australian intellectuals in the postwar period thought Australian society and culture derivative and second-rate and felt restive and isolated as a result, some began to argue that social and cultural life in Australia was much more interesting than mere philistine externality. Australians, they said, must discard the notion that they lived in a society lacking in talent and ingenuity. Australian *history*, some historians began to argue, was fascinating, distinctive, and national rather than imperial. One historian, Manning Clark, remarked in a celebrated intervention in 1954: "Let up drop the idea that our past has irrevocably condemned us to the role of cultural barbarians." He opposed the idea that Australians were indifferent to things of the mind and the concomitant idea that there were no engrossing differences, no great issues, no epic dramas of conflicting principles and historical personalities. Clark found particularly offensive Lawrence's sweeping claim that Australians possessed no inner life. Australian history for him was one expression of a major human struggle between opposing life philosophies and religions, notably Protestantism and Catholicism. His interest in Australia was not a nationalistic emphasis on exclusive virtues or characteristics, but rather an opportunity to observe the playing out of major European and Enlightenment conflicts, dilemmas, and dramas in salient, distinctive, and interesting ways. The inner life erupted into public actions and contests among men — and he meant men — in a history so profound that it required a novelistic kind of historical writing to do it justice. It should, he demanded, be "great as literature," have something to say about "human nature," and return to "the great themes they [historians] abandoned when they joined in the vain search for a science of society."[11]

This prewar "diasporic" consciousness of being both British and Australian continued well into the postwar period. Lloyd Evans's 1957 school text, *Australia and the Modern World*, pointed to the importance of British descent and said: "That is one reason for studying British and European history in our schools. We are, in fact, studying the sources of our own way of life."[12] John M. Ward, Challis Professor of History at the University of Sydney when I was a student, was a specialist in British colonial policy and Australian colonial history and belonged to a school of history that sought to illuminate the Australian aspects of imperial history.[13] In a review of the state of Australian history in his presidential address to Section E of AAAS in 1959, J. A. La Nauze described Australia as "at least until recently, a notably derivative and dependent society in its culture and institutions. Until the present generation, nearly everything came from Britain." As a result, he insisted on the importance of knowing British in order to understand Australian history.[14]

Ambivalence about the status and importance of Australian history was evident in some of the new general histories being produced in the 1950s and 1960s to meet the rapid growth in the university study of Australian history.[15] Douglas Pike's 1962 *Australia: The Quiet Continent*, for example, saw Australian history as relatively uneventful and undramatic, as his title implies. "Compared with old-world glories it seems to give the young continent scarcely any history worthy of the name. Here was no cradle of civilization. No enemies invaded these shores to quicken fervent nationalism. No colonizing crusade ever left this land to conquer and rule other countries. No local battles or revolutions disturbed this peaceful isolation."[16] This quiet history was best explained by emphasizing Australian history as a product of British history. To this day, he observed in 1962 with some irony, "Britain still supplies Australia with money and migrants, and the British tie still saves many Australians from thinking for themselves about international affairs."[17]

Australian historiography began to detach itself not only from British imperial historiography, but also from its former alliance with the White Australia Policy. After World War II, historians could rarely defend racially based immigration policies. The world had changed in the wake of the Holocaust and of the emergence of the opposition to racial discrimination now embodied in the United Nations. More materially, government and business wanted to trade with Asia as never before, and Australian travelers went to Asian countries in increasing numbers. The processes of decolonization and the growth of trade and investment in Asia led to both a greater interest in Asia and the Pacific and a growing diffidence about the White Australia Policy. History syllabuses in schools and universities were revised to place more emphasis on Asia and its future relations with Australia. Evans's *Australia and the Modern World*, to take just one example, stressed that Australians had once thought of Asia as "a distant region with which Australians have little in common."[18] What had been a threat for Hancock in 1930 was now welcomed: "Australia is being drawn into a much closer relationship with Asian people." Asian government officials come to study forms of government, and students come to gain qualifications. "We, in return, have much to learn from Asia, and in years to come civilization in Australia will undoubtedly reflect Eastern influences."[19] School texts also set about explaining Asian nationalism to Australian schoolchildren. *Australia and the Modern World* told its high school readers that Asian peoples believed that Europeans gained far more wealth from their colonies than they put back in the development of services and that they exploited Asians as a cheap source of labor, employing them in mines and plantations. These peoples had the right to govern themselves. "It is important for us to realize that Asian people have a strong sense of tradition. . . . Asians resented the patronizing manner and rudeness of many foreign visitors to their countries. Asians were frequently excluded from European clubs and hotels, and were often displayed in novels, written by second-rate authors, as lacking courage in time of war and danger."[20]

In this climate of new awareness that Australia's economic future depended on Asia and a growing discomfort with Australia's own openly racist immigration policy, the general Australian histories of the 1950s and 1960s were more critical of such policies than their predecessors. Most gave some attention to the conflicts between Chinese and Europeans on the gold fields in the nineteenth century and the erection of laws restricting immigration, leading to the White Australia Policy. Marjorie Barnard's popular book, *A History of Australia*

(1962), spent many pages explaining the origins of the White Australia Policy and the difficulties it had caused Australia in the past. Manning Clark's *Short History* in 1963 was noticeably unsympathetic in its account of the anti-Chinese riots. "The diggers," he wrote, "had found a scapegoat for their subterranean passions; in time the minds of large sections of the community would be moved by the same emotions." He saw the anti-Chinese movement as infected by "the poison of race hatred."[21]

Coming to terms with a history of dispossession, exploitation, and institutionalization of Indigenous people, however, took historians somewhat longer. Despite the completion of three specialist studies of Indigenous policy in the 1940s, the general Australian histories of the 1950s and 1960s had even less Indigenous material than their predecessors.[22] Whatever their political complexion and whether they saw Australian history as a clash among different philosophies or settlers battling a harsh unknown environment, none of them gave serious recognition to dispossession. Pike's *Australia: The Quiet Continent* was typical in speaking on its first page of a "native people in stone-age bondage" and painting a story of a thorough and inevitable dispossession. "Primitive food-gatherers," he commented a little later, "were no match for the white invader. The native had to change his ways or fight for his sacred lands. Whether he chose dependence or clash, the end was death, lingering or sudden."[23] Much further to the left of the political spectrum, Russell Ward remarked in his 1965 book, *Australia*, written for the American market, that one "difficulty that Australian pioneers — unlike those of North America, South Africa, and New Zealand — did not have to contend with was a warlike native race" and went on to describe the lives of Indigenous peoples as "nasty, brutish, and short," redeemed perhaps by the lack of territorial conflict and ambition.[24] Even those historians who were troubled by the White Australia Policy had little to say on Indigenous history. Manning Clark in his *Short History* evoked quite sympathetically the point of view of the settlers: "They were angered by the indolence of the aborigine, by his inability and absence of desire to exert himself to raise himself out of his material squalor."[25] (In later years he was to publicly bemoan his own blindness in this area.)

Several developments led to a new interest in Indigenous history in the 1960s. With the growth of demands for full citizenship by the early Indigenous rights (or "Aboriginal Advancement") movement in Australia in the 1950s came a new interest in Indigenous peoples and cultures, expressed in novels, film, art, and design. Political concern with racism in its local and international manifestations increased, along with a growing protest movement seeking equality and social justice for Indigenous people. Very slowly these political changes had an impact on historiography, and a public rethinking of Australian history emerged. Writers, activists in the Indigenous rights movement, and scholars working in related disciplines such as archaeology, anthropology, and art history were the first to incorporate some recognition of dispossession in their work.

Freelance writers influenced by the movement for Indigenous rights wrote two of the most interesting books of this period. One was also an early and rare example of women's history. Eve Pownall's *Mary of Maranoa*, first published in 1959, began with a chapter titled "Stone Age Women" and subtitled "Australia's First Housekeeper." It noted the exploitation of Indigenous women by sealers and drew attention to the ways in which immigrant and white Australian-born women had little understanding of Indigenous cultures. It emphasized the importance of traditional medicines in the outback and Indigenous women's role as emergency midwives and nursemaids to white children and as domestic servants and stock workers.[26] Signaling the impact of the growing movement for Indigenous citizenship and human rights, Pownall concluded that the real pioneers of today were the white women who realized the importance of "the task of building new lives and better relationships among the dark people of their district." Pownall expressed the paternalistic but energetic desire to seek human rights for Indigenous people when she spoke of these women's "sense of urgency to improve their lot and give them back some of the dignity as human beings of which loss of their tribal life has bereft them."[27]

Another early sign of this new historiography was E. G. Docker's 1964 book, *Simply Human Beings*. This was a detailed history by a freelance writer of Indigenous-white relations from first contact to the policies of protection, laissez-faire, and assimilation. "In Australia," he noted, "the modern school child is taught merely to believe that . . . the black man is backward, though through no fault of his own."[28] Docker urged a new respect: for Indigenous physical prowess. "Man for man he is incomparably a better fighter, hunter, swimmer, fisherman." It seemed to him odd that a society that admired masculine values as much as did the Australian society did not admire Indigenous people more. He pointed to the irony of a situation where successive generations of Indigenous schoolchildren "have sat through their history lessons listening patiently to the recital of how the white race has conquered the Earth. History has nothing to offer them, describing the world and values of the white man."[29] *Simply Human Beings* mounted a thorough attack on the prevailing policy of assimilation and urged instead an approach that emphasized "everything that is still valuable in aboriginal life, particularly its communal features."[30] It opposed those do-gooders who wanted to incorporate Indigenous people into white Australian society and asked how many thought they had anything to learn from the Aboriginal. The book ended by urging acknowledgment of the Aborigine not as an imitation white man but as "a full-fledged man" and recognition of Indigenous rights, in particular the restoration of Indigenous lands.[31]

In both these books Indigenous claims and history were understood in new ways, albeit through gendered lenses. Where Pownall urged white women to recognize their debts to Indigenous women, Docker urged white men to respect Indigenous men's physical prowess. In the context of their time, a sense of gender solidarity could work to overcome racial exclusion and ignorance. Books such as these were precursors to a revolution in attitudes to Indigenous history that took off, like so many other social, cultural, and political changes, from the late 1960s.

Historians in the 1970s and 1980s moved from laggards to leaders in the investigation of histories of Indigenous colonization, dispossession, and institutionalization. Charles Rowley was commissioned in 1964 by the Social Sciences Research Council to undertake a major study of Indigenous history, policy, and practice, and his first volume, *The Destruction of Aboriginal Society* (1970), put Indigenous history on a new footing. Exhibiting a strong emphasis on policy issues and drawing attention to social and economic effects of dispossession, discriminatory government policies, and institutionalized racism, it helped provide a sound chronological and analytical structure for the histories that followed. A younger generation of historians now entered the field. One history with a Marxist flavor, emphasizing especially the use of violence in the recruitment and management of Indigenous labor, was Evans, Saunders, and Cronin, *Exclusion, Exploitation and Extermination: Race Relations in Colonial Queensland* (1975). The journal *Aboriginal History* was initiated at the Australian National University in 1977, with Diane Barwick as its first editor, and ever since has supported the growth of scholarship in the field. The new scholarship was synthesized in Richard Broome's *Aboriginal Australians* (1982), a survey history much used in university history teaching, reprinted every year, and selling over twenty-five thousand copies, with an updated edition appearing in 1994. Henry Reynolds in *The Other Side of the Frontier* (1981), which read colonial sources against the grain to explore Indigenous responses to European invasion, was the first in an impressive series of books on different aspects of Indigenous history. Indigenous history came into national public consciousness in an unprecedented way in the context of the bicentennial commemoration of 1988. The general histories produced specifically for the commemoration of British settlement placed considerable emphasis on Indigenous history, though John Molony's one-volume history remained in an earlier national mold, and the individual volumes in each of the multivolume general histories varied considerably in their focus and coverage.[32]

From the run-up to the Bicentennial, in the mid-1980s onward, Indigenous people's accounts of the colonial past were increasingly heard. Indigenous women and men stressed in public debate their prior occupation, direct experience of invasion and racism, and struggles for survival. This counterhistory was told especially through Indigenous narratives—autobiographies, life stories, biographies, oral histories—the best known internationally being one of the earliest, Sally Morgan's *My Place*, written in the newly emerging mixed-genre life-writing tradition, about her discovery and recognition of Indigenous identity.[33] Indigenous history had entered public consciousness to an even greater extent with landmark legal decisions recognizing native title in 1992, in which Henry Reynolds's work was influential, and a public inquiry (reported in 1997) into the history of the removal of Indigenous children from their communities. In this heightened political atmosphere, history became a subject for public debate to an unprecedented degree. Support for Pauline Hanson's populist One Nation Party brought to light a popular backlash against histories that emphasized the devastating effects of the invasion, dispossession, segregation, exploitation, institutionalization, and child removal policies of the past. Many non-Indigenous Australians openly expressed a preference for returning to a historiography that assumed the rightful colonization of the land and emphasized colonists' struggles and difficulties; processes of "pioneering" and settlement; and hard-won achievement of economic development, political freedoms, and social harmony. In such a highly charged and divided atmosphere, it seemed that historians had lost their ability to provide apparently unifying national narratives.

It was not only Indigenous history that grew in these last three decades of the twentieth century; Australian history of all kinds developed rapidly. Along with a dramatic growth in the numbers of universities and colleges, university students, and professional academic historians (from less than twenty before World War II to over four hundred by 1973) came a large and lively national historiography.[34] This national history covered a wide variety of types and styles, similar to that elsewhere—political, labor, social, feminist, and cultural histories.[35] Labor history had a special strength, as it did also in Canada and New Zealand, as historians with political affinities with the Left sought to uncover a history of the working class in the Australian context. Some, like Robin Gollan, had been trained in England, been influenced by the Communist Historians Group there, and returned home determined to develop histories of class and class struggle for Australia. Others, like Eric Fry, undertook some of the first PH.D.s in Australia and developed a school of history with its own journal, *Labor History*, which investigated the histories of trade unions, major conflicts between capital and labor, and (later on) working-class communities. Historians of a range of political persuasions developed a national political history, with biographies of leading political figures, political histories of the various colonies and later states, and histories of the processes of federation that underpinned the formation of the Australian nation in 1901.

Increasingly powerful in the formation of Australian national histories from the early 1970s were the feminist histories. Historians were disproportionately well represented among the students and young academics involved in the women's movement of the 1970s and were in the forefront of the development of women's studies programs. We also wrote manifestos, theses, essays, and books setting out to revolutionize Australian history, to understand the Australian past as gendered, and to connect Australian history to a worldwide story of power struggles between women and men. Anne Summers promoted the new Australian feminist history in 1975 in her book, *Damned Whores and God's Police*, with an argument that the way in which Australian history, culture, and society were generally conceptualized and understood has been based on images of male Australians only.[36] Since then, feminist history has been remarkably successful in challenging and changing the historical profession in Australia.[37] Feminist historians, using a variety of forms from scholarly journal articles to museum exhibitions and film, researched the lives of women of various social classes, women's activity at different levels of politics, the cultural meanings of sexual difference, the nature of sexual ideology and discourse, the interconnections between family and work, and notions of the public and the private.

The two revolutions — Indigenous history and feminist history — went in parallel through the 1970s and 1980s. They took a while to connect, in large part because most white Australian feminists for a long time had considerable difficulty in placing themselves on the side of the oppressors rather than the oppressed. Part of the problem is indicated in the subtitle to *Damned Whores and God's Police*: "The Colonisation of Women in Australia." The analogy of colonial invasion, exploitation, and dispossession was used metaphorically, theoretically, and rhetorically to describe the experience of white women, thus minimizing the possibility of recognizing that white women were themselves colonizers, part of the invading society that dispossessed and exploited Indigenous women and men. The breakthrough came with Ann McGrath's book, *Born in the Cattle* (1987), which gave a gendered analysis of Indigenous labor and focused on the sexual dynamics of race relations on the cattle stations. In the 1990s, influenced by developments within feminist theory internationally and a heightened attention to Indigenous demands at home, questions of race and gender came closer together.[38]

The national history that developed in the post–World War II era has, of course, been highly diverse. It has been differentiated, as national histories always are, by political attachments, theoretical approaches, and variations in historical method. The ever-popular historiographical theme of "convict women" helps us pinpoint both its diversity and commonalities. Here is a theme that has longevity and that has intrigued historians of very different persuasions. In tracking the convict woman through Australian historiography, perhaps we gain a clue to its deepest obsessions and concerns. Given her iconic aura, the figure of the convict woman has witnessed multiple transformations and reversals. Is she Medusa, ever untamable and always outside, or can she be brought back in? As the historiography of convict women has grown, we create and inherit a palimpsest of historiographical debates: about her sexual morality, degree of criminality, and general character; her value as a worker and as a mother; her experiences of transportation and life as a convict and ex-convict; her relations with state authority and especially her transgression and rebelliousness, individual and collective; her relationships with officers, employers, and convict men; and her influence on subsequent gender relations in Australia. Through contested allegorical images of the convict woman, national history is made and remade in moral, economic, and cultural terms, implying the eternally recurrent question: Is Australian history a cause for shame or pride?

The convict woman emerged as a historical figure in the 1950s. Convict men had been given a history rather longer, from the evocation of extreme punishments in Australia's most famous nineteenth-century novel, Marcus Clark's *For the Term of His Natural Life*, to the development of the popular idea that the mass of convicts were unjustly transported. In 1922 historian George Arnold Wood famously asked: "Is it not clearly a fact that the atrocious criminals remained in England, while their victims, innocent and manly, founded the Australian democracy?"[39] This belief in relatively innocent convicts caught in an evil, inhuman system continued to have, and indeed still has, popular resonance. In the 1950s, however, some leading academic historians—Manning Clark, Lloyd Robson, and A. G. L. Shaw—revised this judgment on the basis of new and extensive archival research, instead emphasizing the convicts' criminality.[40] It is only at this point that the convict woman enters the historiography. In the hands of these historians the convict woman was drawn as a professional prostitute, degraded, debauched, and drunken—a picture drawn from a range of documents written during the convict period by officers, surgeons, and other middle-class observers. From such sources an enduring lurid portrait emerged of the convict colonies as each constituting one large brothel, which, contemporary observers urged, should be closed immediately. Deborah Oxley argues that the 1950s historians were especially influenced by Henry Mayhew, whose *London Labor and the London Poor* had been recently reissued and who drew a sharp distinction between honest worker and member of a special criminal class. The convicts generally were placed in the latter category, and convict women accordingly designated as the abandoned and degraded prostitutes who served them.[41]

Enter the feminist historians, especially Anne Summers's best-selling *Damned Whores and God's Police*, mentioned above. Speaking from the perspective of early 1970s women's liberation, Summers accepted the verdict that the women were all prostitutes but argued this was the fault of an evil order that permitted them no alternatives. The colonies were a place of debauchery and sexual coercion of various kinds; early New South Wales was a giant brothel run by the "imperial whoremaster." The convict women, though, could offer resistance and did so in the female factories established to house those unable to work on assignment.[42]

Meanwhile, a different historiography was developing, some of it rethinking the convict system as a whole. John Hirst, in *Convict Society and Its Enemies*, warned against uncritical use of nineteenth-century descriptions of convict society. He pointed out how often the picture of corrupt masters, a brutal system, and degraded convicts was drawn by opponents of transportation setting out to discredit the entire system in a continuing battle for prison reform rather than transportation.[43] It is from these opponents of transportation that we gain the image of New South Wales as a giant brothel. Michael Sturma suggested that all this historiography, men's and women's, was based on a misunderstanding of the use of the term "prostitute" in the original sources, for it meant simply unmarried sexual relations, including monogamous cohabitation as well as sex for sale.[44] A group of women historians began to rehabilitate the convict woman, emphasizing her effectiveness as a worker, wife, companion, and mother, so that the first generation of non-Indigenous native-born were generally agreed to be healthy, noncriminal, and hard working. Portia Robinson and others wanted to rescue the convict woman from the epithets of harlot, strumpet, and whore that the male commentators and historians had allocated her. The convict woman, they insisted, conformed rather better to middle-class norms and values than had been generally recognized. Whatever her life in Britain, she became a more or less reformed character in the colonies.[45]

Robert Hughes's *The Fatal Shore* (1987) combined elements of all previous scholarship. Unlike the others, his imagined (and achieved) audience was

British and American rather than Australian. *The Fatal Shore* combines the moral condemnation of the twentieth-century male historians, an older popular tradition that saw the convict system as entirely evil, and a feminist sympathy for the powerless and exploited convict woman. Hughes paints a picture of hell, a drama of lust, drunkenness, and degradation. On the voyage out, as he depicts it, the women had frequent intercourse with the seamen and marines. When the women landed at Sydney Cove, two weeks after the men, and the convict men and women could get together for the first time, there were scenes of riot and debauchery all night. This was accompanied by a storm, the women floundering through a "rain-lashed bog," pursued by male convicts. He goes luridly on: "And as the couples rutted between the rocks, guts burning from the harsh Brazilian aguardiente, their clothes slimy with red clay, the sexual history of colonial Australia may fairly be said to have begun."[46]

Hughes described the shipboard selection of women convicts to be servants as a "slave market." The Parramatta Female Factory was a scene of "disgusting squalor"; women were subject to degrading language, such that "the pervasive belief in their whorishness and worthlessness must have struck deep into the souls of these women." He paid special attention to Norfolk Island, a place of secondary punishment: "In such an amoral environment, although male convicts had some rights (however attenuated), the women had none except the right to be fed; they had to fend for themselves against both guards and male prisoners." While flogging of women was rare in New South Wales and Tasmania, it was common on Norfolk Island, and Hughes devotes time describing the chief jailer's "love of watching women in their agony while receiving a punishment on the Triangle."[47]

The convict woman continued to fascinate historians in the 1990s. In her poststructuralist history, *Depraved and Disorderly*, Joy Damousi detects in the nineteenth-century male observers various sexual and other anxieties, a mixture of repulsion, fear, and fascination. Damousi also cites examples of transgression and resistance through song, dance, joke, laughter, rude language, and sometimes organized riot and rebellion. In her 1998 *Convict Women*, Kay Daniels also focuses on convict women's engagement with the state, emphasizing the practical limitations on the vision and power of the convict administration; the means convict women used to combat state authority; and the women's substantial economic, sexual, legal, and domestic vulnerability.[48] Deborah Oxley's *Convict Maids* argued that in terms of occupational skills and experience, the female convicts were ordinary working-class and rural women whose crimes emerged directly from their situation.

All these histories tell stories about the past as a way of pondering the present. All create the emblematic convict woman to suit their own times. The debauched whore of the 1950s and 1960s may be a figure of the imagination of male historians, newly confident enough to say unpleasant things about the convicts. The sexual slaves of the feminist imagination of the 1970s hinted at the anger of young feminist historians at their own treatment in their society, searching for a reason and a history for that inequality. The good wives and mothers of the women's historians of the 1980s sought for Australian women a history of which not to be ashamed, incorporating convict women within a popular pioneer legend, the mothers of the nation. All these convict women are ultimately allegorical figures of any uneasy nation and an uneasy historiography, haunted by origins, by creation stories that rarely provide the promise of a reassuring future or comforting tropes, metaphors, and images.

*   *   *

The desire to escape the nation must surely, then, be ambivalent. As a relatively recent phenomenon in Australian historical scholarship, the "nation" still constitutes a central organizing concept for historians of all political and theoretical persuasions and is likely to continue to do so in the foreseeable future. It is important to recognize that the pleasures of national historiography are immense. A national focus ensures us a large and interested audience and enables our historical work to count in current debate and contemporary local culture. Manning Clark's funeral in 1991 was attended by the prime minister and many leading government ministers, while the work of Henry Reynolds has been subject to huge amounts of public contestation and debate. Australian historiography has influenced many of the debates and movements of the postwar period — the labor movement, feminism, Indigenous rights, immigration policy, environmental concerns, and much else. Historians continue to be frequently called to speak on issues of the day, such as immigration, republicanism, and the constitution. The past has become central to debates over Indigenous policy — for example, the question of a national apology for the child removal policies of the past. It is a force in the heritage and tourist industry, public celebrations, and war commemoration. It is also important in popular culture; the role of history in the opening ceremony of the 2000 Olympics, for example, was profound, acting as a basis for staging a dynamic multicultural society aware of its pasts, present, and futures be they Indigenous, colonial, or postcolonial. While outsiders tend to find the importance accorded to history and historians in public debate in Australia rather curious, seeing Australia as a "new" country without a history to speak of, it is precisely because the sense of a distinctive Australian past is indeed rather fragile, still in the making, that historians achieve such high profile.

Hence my title. We've just started making national histories, and you want us to stop already? I feel just a little like the feminist women of color who said in the 1980s: now we are finally in the academy sufficiently to enable us to write black women's history, and you tell us the subject is dead and there is no such thing as "woman." Are the critiques of national history strongest in those national intellectual cultures where "the nation" has been relatively secure and where interest in that nation's history has long extended beyond its borders? Is the rejection of "nation" a luxury, mainly for those intellectuals who inhabit powerful or at least populous nations? Is the desire to go beyond national history only possible when there is little—in terms of historians' influence on national politics and policy—to lose?

Yet there *is* ambivalence, and the nation as a framework for historical understanding has severe limits. National histories generally tend to focus on what is distinctive about the history of the nation, what seems to hold it together, and Australian histories have been no exception. There is an implicit assumption that this—the discovery of what makes a nation, a people, distinctive—is the task of national history, rather than a focus on what is shared with histories and societies elsewhere. Australian national history has seen, relatively speaking, a decline of interest in Australia's place in the British Empire and later Commonwealth and a decline of interest overall in international and regional contexts and referents. In some ways, while Australian history has become more independent, complex, diverse, autonomous, and self-critical, it has also become more insular, isolated, defensive, and inward-looking. One result is that it continues to be of interest mainly to Australians and to have relatively little purchase or relevance abroad. The more it matters to us, it seems, the less it matters to anyone else. Just as Australian history has become influential in and subject to local public debate, it has also, with some honorable exceptions, begun to look a little old-fashioned, rather isolationist in a globalizing world.[49] Our deep concern with the nation and national history—our focus on local anxieties and debates—runs counter to the growing interest in transnational frameworks in recent scholarship and commentary.

Many Australian historians in fact do share with their counterparts elsewhere a desire to escape the national boundaries that mark so much historical work. We are all becoming increasingly interested in trying to understand growing world cultural interaction, world history, international flows of people, ideas, cultures, and internationalization of the economy. We wish to understand a world in which the powers of national governments seem to diminish and the exchange of people, goods, ideas, and culture continues to expand. We want to know what the long-term historical trends are that make this possible.

This growing attention to non-national frameworks is already refiguring

Australian historical work. Let us take just one example, migration, a major phenomenon in Australian history and society. Past models of migration history have tended to focus on the movement of people to Australia from somewhere else and on their experiences in their new country. There has been an emphasis on the contribution of migrants to the Australian economy and cultural life; the society of origin forms a kind of background to the story, represented in the kinds of objects and cultural practices that migrants bring with them. The history of migration and the history of colonization tend to be two separate fields of historical endeavor. A transnational approach helps us to see that migration of all kinds, however desperate the circumstances of particular groups of immigrants, has in settler societies been part of the processes of colonization and conversely that the continuing processes of colonization have influenced the experiences of immigrants. Such an approach also places more emphasis on the country of departure and situates the history of those who migrate in the context of other national histories. Chinese migrants to Australia, for example, are understood in terms of Chinese history, Vietnamese in terms of Vietnamese history, British in terms of British history, and so forth. Most obviously, a global or transnational approach places heavier emphasis on the notion of diaspora, which recognizes that migration does not always mean the transfer of a sense of belonging from one society to another, but rather to the formation of a diaspora of people who maintain a sense of identity and practical links across national boundaries. Vast numbers of people — African, Jewish, Indian, Armenian, Chinese, or whatever — now constitute groups with this diasporic sense of the world. This is what British migrants have done in Australia for over two centuries, as older histories recognized and some newer ones have tended to forget. Thus diasporic histories return us to an older interest in British identities and connections in the Australian colonies and later the Australian nation.

I want to conclude on this note. Australian like any national history can be represented as something autonomous or as part of worldwide history and cultural exchange. We have surely isolated ourselves long enough. It is time for historians generally, and Australian historians specifically, to (re)join a world historical community. We can *both* help refigure the meanings of Australian culture *and* contribute to the creation of a transnational historical culture that does not forget the power of the local, the specific, and, indeed, the national.

Notes

I wish to acknowledge the assistance of the Australian Research Council and Stephanie Liau and John Docker in the preparation of this essay.

1   For a discussion of pre–World War II Australian historiography, see Chris Healy, *From the Ruins of Colonialism: History as Social Memory* (Melbourne: Cambridge University Press, 1997); Stuart Macintyre: "The Writing of Australian History," in *Australians: A Guide to Sources*, ed. D. H. Borchardt (Sydney: Fairfax, Syme, and Weldon, 1987), pp. 1–29, and *History, the University and the Nation* (London: Sir Robert Menzies Centre for Australian Studies, Institute of Commonwealth Studies, University of London, 1992; Stuart Macintyre and Julian Thomas, eds., *The Discovery of Australian History 1890–1939* (Carlton: Melbourne University Press, 1995); G. Walsh, *Australia: History & Historians* (Canberra: Australian Defence Force Academy, 1997).

2   Stuart Macintyre, *A History for a Nation: Ernest Scott and the Making of Australian History* (Carlton: Melbourne University Press, 1994); R. M. Crawford, M. Clark, and G. Blainey, *Making History* (Ringwood: Penguin, 1985).

3   Quoted in C. M. H. Clark, "Rewriting Australian History," in his *Occasional Lectures and Speeches* (Melbourne: Fontana, 1980), p. 5.

4   Quoted in Margaret MacPherson, *I Heard the Anzacs Singing* (New York: Creative Age Press, 1942).

5   W. K. Hancock, *Australia* (Melbourne: Jacaranda Press, 1961), pp. 42–47; first published 1930.

6   Ibid., p. 51. Compare A. Curthoys and J. Docker, "The Two Histories: Metaphor in English Historiographical Writing," *Rethinking History* 1, 3 (1997): 259–273; B. G. Smith, *The Gender of History: Men, Women, and Historical Practice* (Cambridge, Mass: Harvard University Press, 1998), esp. ch. 4.

7   Hancock, *Australia*, p. 49.

8   Ibid., p. 50.

9   Stephen Roberts, *History of Australian Land Settlement, 1788–1920* (Melbourne: Macmillan, in association with Melbourne University Press, 1924), p. 181.

10 Hancock, *Australia*, p. 21.

11 Clark, "Rewriting Australian History," p. 5.

12 Lloyd Evans, *Australia and the Modern World* (Melbourne: Cheshire, 1957), p. 1.

13 John M. Ward: *Earl Grey and the Australian Colonies, 1846–1857: A Study of Self-Government and Self-Interest* (Carlton: Melbourne University Press, 1958), and *James Macarthur, Colonial Conservative, 1798–1867* (Sydney: Sydney University Press, 1981).

14 J. A. La Nauze, "The Study of Australian History, 1929–1959," *Historical Studies: Australia and New Zealand* 9, 33 (November 1959): 10.

15 For example, R. M. Crawford, *Australia* (London: Hutchinson University Library, 1952); G. Greenwood, ed., *Australia: A Social and Political History* (Sydney: Angus and Robertson, 1955); A. G. L. Shaw, *The Story of Australia* (London: Faber, 1955); M. Barnard, *A History of Australia* (Sydney: Angus and Robertson, 1962); C. M. H. Clark, *A Short History of Australia* (New York: New American Library, 1963); Russell Ward, *Australia* (Sydney: Horwitz, 1965).

16 Douglas Pike, *Australia: The Quiet Continent* (London: Cambridge University Press, 1962), p. 223.

17 Ibid., p. 225.

18 Evans, *Australia and the Modern World*, p. 1.

19 Ibid.

20 Ibid., p. 321.

21 Clark, *Short History*, pp. 133–134.

22 E. Foxcroft, *Australian Native Policy: Its History, Especially in Victoria* (Melbourne: Mel-

bourne University Press, 1941); Paul Hasluck, *Black Australians: A Survey of Native Policy in Western Australia, 1829–1897* (Melbourne: Melbourne University Press, 1942); C. Turnbull, *Black War: The Extermination of the Tasmanian Aborigines* (Melbourne: Cheshire, 1948).

23 Pike, *Australia: The Quiet Continent*, p. 36.

24 R. Ward, *Australia*, p. 21.

25 Clark, *Short History*, p. 40.

26 Eve Pownall, *Mary of Maranoa: Tales of Australian Pioneer Women* (Sydney: F. H. Johnston, 1959).

27 Ibid., p. 267.

28 E. G. Docker, *Simply Human Beings* (Melbourne: Jacaranda Press, 1964).

29 Ibid., p. 237.

30 Ibid., p. 248.

31 Ibid., p. 254.

32 V. Burgmann and J. Lee, eds., *A People's History of Australia*, 4 vols. (Ringwood: Penguin, 1988); Geoffrey Bolton, gen. ed., *The Oxford History of Australia*, 4 vols. (Melbourne: Oxford University Press, 1987–1994); K. Inglis and A. Gilbert, eds., *Australians: An Historical Library*, 10 vols. (Sydney: Fairfax, Syme, and Weldon, 1987); John Molony, *A History of Australia* (Ringwood: Penguin, 1988).

33 Sally Morgan, *My Place* (Fremantle: Fremantle Arts Centre Press, 1988).

34 Macintyre, "The Writing of Australian History," p. 22.

35 For a series of surveys on developments in Australian historiography, see Graeme Davison, John Hirst, and Stuart Macintyre, eds., *The Oxford Companion to Australian History* (Melbourne: Oxford University Press, 1998).

36 Anne Summers, *Damned Whores and God's Police: The Colonisation of Women in Australia* (Ringwood: Penguin, 1975).

37 For discussion and commentary on this literature, see Ann Curthoys, *For and against Feminism: A Personal Journey into Feminist Theory and History* (Sydney: Allen and Unwin, 1988).

38 Patricia Grimshaw, Marilyn Lake, Ann McGrath, and Marian Quartly, *Creating a Nation* (Melbourne: McPhee Gribble, 1994); F. Paisley, *Loving Protection? Australian Feminism and Aboriginal Women's Rights, 1919–1939* (Carlton: Melbourne University Press, 2000); M. Lake, *Getting Equal: The History of Australian Feminism* (Sydney: Allen and Unwin, 1999).

39 G. A. Wood, "Convicts," *Journal of the Royal Australian Historical Society* 8, 4 (1922): 187; quoted in Robert Hughes, *The Fatal Shore: A History of Transportation of Convicts to Australia, 1787–1868* (Sydney: Collins Harvill, 1987), p. 159.

40 C. M. H. Clark, *A History of Australia*, vol. 1 (Melbourne: Melbourne University Press, 1963); Lloyd Robson, *The Convict Settlers of Australia: An Enquiry into the Origin and Character of the Convicts Transported to New South Wales and Van Diemen's Land, 1787–1852* (Melbourne: Melbourne University Press, 1965); A. G. L. Shaw, *Convicts and the Colonies: A Study of Penal Transportation from Great Britain and Ireland to Australia and Other Parts of the British Empire* (London: Faber, 1966).

41 Deborah Oxley, *Convict Maids: The Forced Migration of Women to Australia* (Melbourne: Cambridge University Press, 1996).

42 Summers, *Damned Whores and God's Police*.

43 John Hirst, *Convict Society and Its Enemies: A History of Early New South Wales* (Sydney: Allen and Unwin, 1983).

44 Michael Sturma, "'Eye of the Beholder': The Stereotype of Women Convicts 1788–1852," *Labour History*, no. 34 (May 1978).

45 Portia Robinson, *The Women of Botany Bay: A Reinterpretation of the Role of Women in the Origins of Australian Society* (Ringwood: Penguin, 1988).

46 Hughes, *The Fatal Shore*, p. 89.

47 Ibid., pp. 258, 261.

48 Joy Damousi, *Depraved and Disorderly: Female Convicts, Sexuality and Gender in Colonial Australia* (Melbourne: Cambridge University Press, 1997); Kay Daniels, *Convict Women* (Sydney: Allen and Unwin, 1998).

49 One of the exceptions is Marilyn Lake, whose work frequently appears in international and comparative history collections.

TERRI A. HASSELER AND PAULA M. KREBS

Losing Our Way after the Imperial Turn:
Charting Academic Uses of the Postcolonial

The academic specialization called postcolonial studies arose in the field of English literature in the 1980s with the publication of key works that linked the study of literature to the politics of critically examining British colonialism and its aftermath. As debates about the new field developed, U.S. English departments recognized that study of the postcolonial had become an important element of an education in English, whether postcolonialism entailed studying texts from postcolonial nations, texts by postcolonial subjects, or theories of what constituted the postcolonial. As the specialization of postcolonial literature and culture developed, English departments had decisions to make: what kinds of new courses to offer to graduate and undergraduate students, how much to invest in the future of the new subfield, whether to offer courses as "special topics" or to introduce them as regular offerings, and, most significant, how to staff the new courses. This essay offers a case study of the incorporation of postcolonial studies into the field of a "national" literature like English by focusing on hiring patterns. We start where all job candidates in English start—with the Modern Language Association (MLA) *Job Information List*, which appears four times a year and lists essentially all openings in English departments. In this job list, all the forces that shape the discipline come together: hiring practices, graduate curricula, and emerging fields of research. The intersection of these forces in the job list indicates the value placed on a specialization, highlighting where funding and intellectual energy go. We believe that the creation of positions in English departments is a central part of the institutionalization of postcolonial studies, to be reckoned alongside the establishment of an MLA division on the topic, the creation of large collections of essays and introductory guides for students, and the less tangible but no less important "buzz" in the profession as a whole that accompanies the rise of a new area of expertise—especially when that buzz involves a transnational phenomenon like postcolonial studies.

In our study of the last ten years of MLA job listings that included reference to the term "postcolonial," we started with the assumption that postcolonialism would be paired with twentieth-century British specializations. We thought that the discipline might associate the postcolonial with such canonical modernists as Forster and Conrad, whose novels on colonial themes have received so much critical attention. For example, early studies of colonialism and postcolonialism, such as the work of Jenny Sharpe, Patrick Brantlinger, and Sara Suleri, inevitably turn to *A Passage to India* or *Heart of Darkness*.[1] And, of course, decolonization itself is understood as a twentieth-century phenomenon, particularly associated with the breakup of the British Empire. We wondered whether, in job descriptions, "postcolonial" would be synonymous with theory; whether literary applications would be less important than a grounding in the critical approaches of people such as Homi Bhabha and Gayatri Chakravorty Spivak; whether a larger transnational sense of postcolonialism had given way to an area studies focus or, even more narrowly, a focus on South Asia. What effect had the tightening of the job market had on the nascent field of postcolonial studies? More simply, were there more jobs or fewer in postcolonialism, and what could that mean for graduate programs?

The hiring process plays a fundamental role in shaping the nature of any discipline: graduate schools begin to offer courses to train students to fit the parameters of the job descriptions; departments begin jockeying to hire "name" postcolonialists from other schools in order to legitimize a postcolonial specialization at their own institutions; small schools struggle to keep up with the changes in the discipline, trying to hire postcolonialists without, sometimes, a clear sense of what the discipline might be. This uncertainty is not surprising, as there appears to be little consensus even among major research institutions.

The definition of postcolonialism in the United States exists in a market context. Departments, especially smaller ones, need faculty who can cover several fields; all schools have budget limitations; and many schools are scrambling to make up for years of neglect in hiring people of color. Our examination of job descriptions confirmed many of our concerns about the shaping of the postcolonial, but what we found was less sinister than what we might have suspected at first glance. The trends we observed clearly reflect market forces, but they also appear to acknowledge a potential shift in the politics of the larger field of English studies. Nevertheless, we remain cautious about these changes within the discipline.

The postcolonial is a debated term, of course, with a range of definitions that can emphasize area studies, identity politics, border issues, the influence of postmodernism, or even U.S. domestic race theory. When "postcolonial" is used to refer to the national literatures or culture of a region that is a former British colony, we often find an interdisciplinary emphasis on history, politics, and literature. This is the postcolonial of, for example, the Subaltern Studies group, working very specifically on aspects of Indian history, or of the writer and critic Ngùgì wa Thiong'o, who abandoned English to write in his native Gikuyu. This is not to say, of course, that the Subaltern Studies group and others do not use concepts of the postmodern or identity politics or other aspects of the definition of postcolonialism. But other definitions of postcolonialism are less likely than, for example, the work of Jenny Sharpe to call for an understanding of the history, politics, and language that produced a particular cultural text.[2]

Identity politics, growing out of the feminist and civil rights movements, focused on location, drawing attention to a field of study wider than traditional periods and genres, including feminist criticism, race theory, and queer studies. Identity politics argued that who the scholar is affects how she operates in academic culture, including what texts she chooses to teach, how she works with her colleagues, and how she is treated within the discipline. As the term itself suggests, identity is political, and the scholar has a responsibility to a larger political struggle. However, with the advent of postmodernism and the death of the unified subject, locational politics lost its cachet within academic discourse. The shift to postmodernism resulted in a backlash against identity politics as "untheorized," at best, and "navel gazing," at worst. We can see this, for example, in Sara Suleri's critique of bell hooks: "hooks' study is predicated on the anecdotes of lived experience and their capacity to provide an alternative to the discourse of what she terms patriarchal rationalism. Here the unmediated quality of a local voice serves as a substitute for any theoretical agenda that can make more than a cursory connection between the condition of postcolonialism and the question of gendered race." Suleri concludes that hooks's strategy "registers as black feminism's failure to move beyond the proprietary rights that can be claimed by any oppressed discourse."[3]

Suleri represents a fairly vocal critique of identity politics within the academy; however, others, shaped by postmodernism yet acknowledging political commitment, are bringing to identity politics a more nuanced theoretical position. Cornell University's Laura Donaldson (Cherokee) asserts, "Coming from a postcolonial nation—and I realize that's a problematic formulation when you're talking about native peoples—I think it's important to talk about culture and identity and to assert core values that might carry over from nation to nation or generation to generation. I don't think of that as essentialism."[4] In *Feminist Genealogies, Colonial Legacies, Democratic Futures*, Chandra Mohanty and M. Jacqui Alexander similarly critique the effect of postmodernism on colonialism: "Thus, for instance, localized questions of experience, identity, culture, and history, which enable us to understand specific processes of domination and subordination, are often dismissed by postmodern theories as reiterations of cultural 'essence' or unified, stable identity."[5] They acknowledge, however, that postmodernism has forced us to reconsider the parameters of the postcolonial: "What kind of racialized, gendered selves get produced at the conjuncture of the transnational and the postcolonial? Are there selves which are formed outside of the hegemonic heterosexual contract that defy dominant (Western) understanding of identity construction? Are they commensurate with the multiple self constructed under (American) postmodernism?"[6] When postmodernism and postcolonialism collide, we are faced with questions not only about the self and identity construction, but also about the transnational and the construction of the nation itself.

Even the earliest imperial/colonial studies produced challenges to the concept of a national history, forcing historians to recognize the permeability of national boundaries. The postcolonial pushes these boundaries even further, recognizing the effects of diaspora, migration, and slave trading on culture. Moreover, it brings to attention the mixed racial, national, and cultural identities formed from these dislocations. Yet because of the complexity of the boundary breaking involved in the concept of the postcolonial, disciplines face a significant problem in attempting to define postcolonial. Because of what appears to be a return to traditional periods in the field of English studies, it has been especially difficult for postcolonial studies to gain a foothold. Postcolonialism not only asks English literature to expand the national borders of what is appropriate for study, but also challenges the epistemology that undergirds the discipline itself. Departments that have funneled all their resources into British and American literature are suddenly asked to teach Asian and African writing, when many have not yet come to terms with ethnic literatures within Britain and the United States. The postcolonial depends on terms that violate the boundaries within which English departments have always operated—terms such as "Black Atlantic," "transnational," or "diaspora." Moreover, the postcolonial also calls for a new focus on area studies. Many English departments seem to have a pattern of resolving this dilemma by discarding the specifics of history and location required for a course in diasporic or area studies in favor of the general—a course or two in postcolonial theory rather than a series of courses in South Asian, Caribbean, or African literatures, for instance, across historical time periods. Perhaps this is a product of the newness of the discipline. Berkeley's Priya Joshi points out, "When new methodologies emerge, academics mistake the methodology for the discipline. Teaching a class in East African drama is not a bad idea. Specifically enables greater depth."[7] It is a lament we heard over and over from postcolonialists, who are asked to teach a course in theory but discouraged from pursuing more specific courses on literature.

However, postcolonial studies has made some fairly dramatic shifts in the last few years, and we argue that these shifts reflect market forces in English studies, especially the pressures of hiring on recent ph.d.s. Our study of job openings in "postcolonial" since 1990 reveals an increase in the number of openings for ph.d.s with specializations in postcolonial studies, but this increase is not an unqualified acknowledgement of some triumph of the postcolonial. As we will show, jobs in postcolonial are increasing as enrollments in graduate courses in postcolonial appear to be decreasing. In addition, jobs in postcolonial seem to have evolved into positions in which postcolonial is one of a range of specialties expected from a recent ph.d. rather than a legitimate single concentration. As Donaldson puts it, "This structure of hiring is domesticating the postcolonial, producing jobs in which you wouldn't have time or support to pursue a more radical critique." Donaldson sees institutions dealing with the postcolonial as they have dealt with the "multicultural" — "as an add-on, guaranteed never to disrupt."[8] For Priya Joshi, the domestication of the postcolonial produces "breadth rather depth" in the courses that are taught, as well as the scholarship that is done, in postcolonialism. For Joshi, the radical critique in postcolonialism comes in "getting your hands dirty" in the archives, applying theory to texts. However, she also noted that departments often do not provide the funding or support for such an approach.[9]

How, then, are graduate students in English departments trained to do postcolonial critique? Some graduate programs that are strong in postcolonialism consciously avoid treating the postcolonial as a single concentration. Does the University of Illinois, with at least four members of the graduate faculty who work in postcolonial studies, train postcolonialists? "I really hope not," Ania Loomba responded. "Postcolonial perspectives in relation to a field [are] much more of what I am interested in."[10] In this model, the ideal department becomes one in which postcolonial scholarship has a significant presence on everyone's syllabus. Such an approach mirrors the effect of feminism on the discipline. It is a rare graduate student who does not have access to the language of gender critique. Is the goal of postcolonialism to change the culture of English so that all graduate students can apply postcolonial critique to any period or text?

Some of our findings were predictable: the largest proportion of jobs was concentrated in states such as California, New York, and Massachusetts; the majority of jobs were at the assistant professor level; and the number of jobs increased over the course of the 1990s. Some of our findings were surprising: a huge proportion of jobs was linked to African American literature; when postcolonial was linked to a literary period, it was almost as likely to be paired with the Renaissance as with the twentieth century; and small liberal arts schools were searching as seriously for postcolonialists as were major research universities. However, we learned very quickly not to take any of these results at face value. For example, while small liberal arts colleges may have placed many of the ads, it was often because their previous hire had moved to a different position. Thus, we found schools advertising the same position three times in our ten-year study.

When considering our findings on disciplinary areas, we were surprised to find that postcolonialism was linked with almost every historical field in the English department canon, starting with the Renaissance. Our first concern, as we already noted, had been that postcolonialism would be linked almost exclusively with the twentieth-century British field, first as a result of the historical time period of decolonization, but even more so because literary and cultural theory tends to be associated with a twentieth-century focus. Victorianists, for instance, can rest easy knowing that our study revealed that postcolonialism was indeed associated with the nineteenth century and even the eighteenth. Upon closer examination of the job listings, however, we found that postcolonial jobs seemed somewhat haphazardly put together, which raised a number of other questions, such as how do departments formulate their job descriptions? The story of the postcolonial that we see in the narrative of the MLA job listings is not coherent; it reads as a bit of floundering. One year a position is listed for an Afro-Caribbeanist, and another year, after the original hire has moved elsewhere, it is listed for an African Americanist who can do postcolonial theory. Yet another year it is for a postcolonialist with grounding in American ethnic literature. This results in what Priya Joshi calls a very "expensive" process of defining the field: "They are flailing around with what they want to hire in postcolonial." As Joshi notes, we would not see this in eighteenth-century literature because hiring institutions know what the field is and what they are looking for.[11] On a political level, Jenny Sharpe notes that these jobs might also reveal a conflict within the search committee — some want one field and others another, and all get lumped together, resulting in the grocery-list job descriptions that are often standard in postcolonial studies.[12]

Priya Joshi has termed what some have claimed to be the profession's ignorance about the field of postcolonialism "not an ignorance [but] an indifference."[13] That indifference might be because the discipline has already decided that the location of postcolonial studies is "theory." The ruling principle appears to be that if a department can hire a theorist, then it has its obligatory postcolonialist, and nothing more need be done. Indeed, references to theory did appear in the job listings with tremendous frequency; thus, a Victorianist rooted in postcolonialism was asked to demonstrate a basis in theory. This is a reasonable requirement. But whose theory, the reader wonders, and how is it applied? In the graduate classroom, Ania Loomba notes, students' expectations are that postcolonial materials are always paired with theory. At many schools there is a resistance to a course that asks one to spend a semester on a region, and yet both Loomba and Joshi observed that that is where the most important work in postcolonial studies is occurring.[14] Rather, graduate students want access to theory and are often shocked to find how historicized the courses are. Loomba stated that in the 1980s there was more overlap between postcolonialism and high theory. Jenny Sharpe claimed, however, that interest in postcolonial theory is also on the downslide in recent years, perhaps reflecting the general decline in status of theory in English departments.[15] So has postcolonial theory really taken over postcolonial studies? Or have area studies and historical periods become the newly desired focuses? In either case, the battle between the two segments has resulted in a failure to appreciate fully what a merged relationship between theory and location might look like.

Postcolonialism, we argue, is political. To call oneself a postcolonialist is (or should be) an inherently political act, as is calling oneself a feminist, for example. Like feminism, and indeed with feminism in some of its best work, postcolonialism has been an approach that foregrounds politics — the politics of nationalism, race, and identity formation. Literature is an essential aspect of such cultural struggle, of course. But so, too, is history. Postcolonial theory has never been strictly literary theory, as it has always included anthropology, sociology, and political science, grounded in the experience of real people in particular geographic locations. When postcolonial studies in English foregrounds theory, that theory is often divorced from political action. When, however, postcolonial studies in English places the emphasis on area studies, focusing narrowly on a particular geographic or ethnic entity, the study can lack a larger theorization. What we have been able to discern from the hiring process is that departments do not consciously recognize the activist nature of postcolonialism — that when hiring a postcolonialist, they are hiring someone of a specific political position. This is unlike feminism, in which activism has never been fully stripped from the term, despite the efforts of many theoretical movements in feminism. When a department hires a feminist, it generally recognizes that some political agenda accompanies the hire. Postcolonialism, too, is political, but many departments do not appear to see it as a politics of activism; rather they manipulate it at the "local" level of identity. Thus, one political direction, activism, is replaced by the political thrust of deans and administrators who are looking to fulfill expectations about hirings of color. Though there is a shared agenda here — the postcolonialist political agenda would similarly be to hire people of color — the philosophy that propels the hiring is very different. Jenny Sharpe outlines the history of relations between and critiques of postcolonialism and U.S. multicultural studies in her essay,

"Postcolonial Studies in the House of U.S. Multiculturalism." She sees the two concentrations as existing in a kind of uneasy alliance, and she criticizes studies of postcolonialism that subsume the African American under the rubric of the postcolonial. The field of postcolonial studies today, she indicates, "is pulled between questions of ethnicity and those of globalization, although they may be two sides of the same coin."[16] Sharpe points out that the postcolonial can never be seen as entirely separate from, say, African American or Latino/a studies in the United States: "The term 'postcolonial' has greater currency in imperial centers like Britain and the United States, as well as former settler colonies like Australia, New Zealand, and Canada, than in Third World Nations," she writes. "As such, it is bound up with multicultural education, which is a concern of racially diversified First World Nations alone."[17]

Karen Chow of the University of Connecticut, however, notes that in ethnic American studies, postcolonialism is viewed with a somewhat suspicious eye. Though postcolonialism provides a language for critiquing the "international connections between exploitations of people of color in the United States and those outside the United States," [the] ethnic studies [field] fears that "the vogue for postcolonialism would subsume ethnic studies." Conservative departments see postcolonialism as "a little less reactionary and antagonistic than ethnic studies." Chow asserts that "some departments might be more comfortable hiring a minority person who does postcolonialism and is more likely to talk about a different country" than they would be hiring "someone who does African American [studies] with a more Marxist perspective." Thus hiring a postcolonialist could be seen as an attempt to "diffuse the impact of the political aspects of ethnic American studies."[18]

In fact, almost 40 percent of the jobs we saw advertised linked postcolonial with African American studies or African American literature. What are the implications of this finding? Is "postcolonial" being defined as "African diaspora"? Many postcolonialists would be surprised by this, given the recent assumption that postcolonial has come to be synonymous with South Asia. But is it South Asian literature or South Asian ph.d.s that make up postcolonialism? Jenny Sharpe chaired the division on literatures other than British and American and a discussion group on postcolonial studies at the MLA's 2000 convention and noted that both meetings were largely dominated by South Asians. Our study shows that only a handful of postcolonial jobs in the last ten years cited South Asian or Indian as an area of concentration. Many of the recent jobs in postcolonial studies have tied that field to literatures of the African diaspora, so we wondered whether training in postcolonial in general, or training in South Asian, was seen as substituting for training in literatures of the African diaspora when it came to hiring. Were new hires expected to teach the literatures of all former British colonies? What did a South Asian racial or ethnic identity mean in the job hunt in postcolonial?

One of our interviewees talked about what she described as the practicalities of the job search. She said that she counseled white graduate students not to specialize in postcolonial, as the jobs that were out there were earmarked, for all intents and purposes, for candidates of color. When we saw the large percentage of jobs in postcolonial paired with African American, we were surprised by the pairing and assumed that it could only mean that departments were simply trying to hire a person of color. Otherwise, we wondered, why would fields as different as African American and postcolonial be yoked? After the initial turn to the postcolonial in the late 1980s, ethnic studies in the United States began to assume a new significance. Researchers working on Latino/a literatures and Asian American literatures, in addition to African American literature, began to use some of the theoretical constructs of postcolonialism, and postcolonialism began taking seriously some of the frameworks used by U.S. studies. The notion of the Black Atlantic, for example, is a postcolonial concept that enables us to consider slave narratives from the Caribbean alongside those from the United States, in the context of Phillis Wheatley and even Crimean War heroine Mary Seacole.

Given that the overlap between U.S. ethnic studies and postcolonial studies has been extremely fruitful for U.S. studies, as indicated in Amritjit Singh and Peter Schmidt's *Postcolonial Theory and the United States*, perhaps the running together of the two fields in so many new positions makes sense.[19] The development of organizations like the United States Association of Commonwealth Literature and Language Studies (USACLALS) marks an institutionalization of that link, and Singh indicates in the organization's newsletter that it intends to "generate and join . . . dialogue between Postcolonial Studies and American Studies. . . . Regardless of whether we work in Commonwealth literatures or American Studies in its broadest meaning, the postcolonial and the neo-colonial intersect and collide in fascinating and complex ways."[20] Still, with much resistance to the use of the term "Commonwealth" in many postcolonial circles and in light of the narrow areas of specialization permitted in many graduate programs, it is difficult for us to see ethnic U.S. literatures and postcolonial as being as popular a combination as our job list numbers would seem to indicate. The politics of hiring may simply mean that departments are trying to get the most for their money when administrations are unwilling to offer more than one postcolonial theory course or South Asian literature course. While postcolonial searches conducted with an emphasis on the African American may, in some cases, have been attempts simply to diversify the faculty or to ghettoize all the disciplines of difference into one person, they may also be the result of search committees being unable to decide in what field to hire. What-ever the reason for these ads, they do reflect a change in the scholarship on postcolonial studies, where African American literature is now often seen in a diasporic connection to Afro-Caribbean and even African literature. Despite the fact that much early work in postcolonial literature focused on African literature, few postcolonial jobs in the last ten years mention African literature on its own; African always appears in conjunction with African American and Caribbean. It appears that African diasporic literatures have replaced African literatures in postcolonial specializations, the assumption being that the litera-ture of the diasporas can replace the literature of the African continent.

We observed a few other trends worth mentioning, for they reflect changes in English departments and their relations to other departments. For example, we found that "world literature," once a course in literature in translation that ran, perhaps, from Greek tragedy through Goethe to Dostoyevsky, has become a euphemism for the area covered by postcolonial: "world literatures in En-glish." A significant proportion (of the MLA job list) of the postcolonial jobs — about fifty of the seven hundred or so ads — were in film studies or mentioned film studies, while comparative literature positions (about forty) and creative writing positions (closer to fifty) appeared more frequently than we had ex-pected as well. We thought we would see more emphasis on the Antipodes than we did; just a handful of jobs mentioned Australia or New Zealand. And, finally, very few jobs spoke of Africa in any terms other than the totalizing, as if all literatures in English in Africa fell easily under the same heading.

Have we lost our way after the imperial turn? The turn to postcolonialism may show up in places besides those job listings that foreground the postcolo-nial: in our recent searches within our own departments, we interviewed can-didates whose work ranged from examinations of East European border issues to the Middle East's role in the definition of Europe to Asian American film studies. All these candidates identified themselves as postcolonialists, yet nei-ther of our job listings named postcolonial as one of the specializations we sought. While this indicates the extent to which postcolonialism has become part of the common language of literature departments, there are nevertheless many dialects within this language. We all read Spivak and Said, but that can get us only so far. The more specialized postcolonialists become, the deeper into area studies or U.S. ethnic studies or what Joshi described as the "grunt work" of *applying* postcolonial theory, the less easy it is for them to talk to each other. This increasing specialization in postcolonial studies results in a kind of language where translation is incomplete because the Asian American film specialist does not necessarily share the same reference points as the person working on South African literature. But we see this incomplete translation as evidence of the breadth of postcolonialism in the twenty-first century, of the recognition that the postcolonial of one region is not the same as the postcolonial of another.

The job market in postcolonial studies in English reveals a dynamic field, in which "postcolonial" can mean many different things. This variety is a positive development, although anecdotal reports of declining enrollments in graduate postcolonial courses are worrying. In this time of retrenchment and what is seen as a general return to more traditional period and genre courses, college catalogs nevertheless include more courses in postcolonial theory, as well as the literatures and cultures of many different areas. Of course, the status of postcolonial studies varies from department to department and state to state as well (the states with the highest number of jobs in postcolonial in the period of our study were California, New York, and Massachusetts, perhaps predictably). But to judge from the increase of jobs listed, the number of publications in the area (especially such teaching texts as *Dangerous Liaisons*, *Colonialism/Postcolonialism*, *Colonial Discourse and Postcolonial Theory*, and *The Post-Colonial Studies Reader*), and the wide variety of other specializations now being paired with postcolonial, the field is pretty healthy.[21] However, things are not ideal for the field: jobs too often constrain postcolonialists from being able to teach a range of courses in their area, as fiscal considerations lead departments to allow just one slot for a course that does not fit the traditional curriculum. Doubts still remain as to whether some postcolonial hires are aimed not at changing traditional department curricula but at simply adding a person of color to the staff who is then not given the space to teach the range of courses that go with a postcolonial specialization. Is English the only field within postcolonialism in which we are in danger of losing a sense of the political implications of globalization on everyday lives? Scheduling a course in postcolonial theory is not the same as recognizing the national and transnational implications of decolonization and globalization. Postcolonialism is as much a political position as ethnic American studies. What our research reveals is that postcolonialism has infiltrated many aspects of English studies. Our hope is that its presence will, in time, radically transform disciplinary boundaries, approaches to texts, and even the politics of institutions.

Notes

The authors owe a great debt to Gillian Sutton, who compiled our database of job listings, and to the postcolonial scholars who generously gave us their time during their busy semesters: Karen Chow, Laura Donaldson, Priya Joshi, Ania Loomba, Lavina Shankar, Jenny Sharpe, and Amritjit Singh.

1 Jenny Sharpe, *Allegories of Empire: The Figure of Woman in the Colonial Text* (Minneapolis: University of Minnesota Press, 1993); Patrick Brantlinger, *Rule of Darkness: British Literature and Imperialism, 1830–1914* (Ithaca, N.Y.: Cornell University Press, 1988); Sara Suleri, "Woman Skin Deep: Feminism and the Postcolonial Condition," *Critical Inquiry* 18, 4 (Summer 1992): 756–769.

2 See Sharpe, *Allegories of Empire*, esp. introduction and ch. 1.

3 Suleri, "Woman Skin Deep," p. 764.

4 Telephone interview, January 2001.

5 M. Jacqui Alexander and Chandra Mohanty, eds., *Feminist Genealogies, Colonial Legacies, Democratic Futures* (New York: Routledge, 1997), p. xvii.

6 Ibid.

7 Telephone interview, January 2001.

8 Telephone interview, January 2001.

9 Telephone interview, January 2001.

10 Telephone interview, January 2001.

11 Telephone interview, January 2001.

12 Telephone interview, January 2001.

13 Telephone interview, January 2001.

14 Telephone interviews, January 2001.

15 Telephone interview, January 2001.

16 Jenny Sharpe, "Postcolonial Studies in the House of U.S. Multiculturalism," in *A Companion to Postcolonial Studies*, ed. Henry Schwartz and Sangeeta Ray (London: Blackwell, 2000), p. 123.

17 Sharpe, "Postcolonial Studies," p. 114.

18 Telephone interview, January 2001.

19 Amritjit Singh and Peter Schmidt, "Introduction," in their *Postcolonial Theory of the United States: Race, Ethnicity, and Literature* (Jackson: University of Mississippi Press, 2000).

20 *USACLALS Newsletter* 1, 1 (December 2000): 1.

21 Anne M. McClintock, Aamir Mufti, and Ella Shohat, eds., *Dangerous Liaisons: Gender, Nation, and Postcolonial Perspectives* (Minneapolis: University of Minnesota Press, 1997); Ania Loomba, *Colonialism/Postcolonialism* (New York: Routledge, 1998); Patrick Williams and Laura Chrisman, eds., *Colonial Discourse and Postcolonial Theory* (New York: Columbia University Press, 1994); Bill Ashcroft, Gareth Griffiths, and Helen Tiffin, eds., *The Post-Colonial Studies Reader* (London: Routledge, 1995).

TONY BALLANTYNE

Rereading the Archive and Opening up the Nation-State:
Colonial Knowledge in South Asia (and Beyond)

The relationship between the imperial-colonial state and its archives — repositories of cartographic, linguistic, ethnological, ethnographic, religious, economic, and historical knowledge in all their various forms — has come to provide a crucial window into the construction of British dominance in South
Asia. In light of the "linguistic turn" and the Foucauldian inflection of many of
the essays in the later volumes of *Subaltern Studies*, it is increasingly difficult to
view the archive as a store of transparent sources from which histories that
recover a total image of the South Asian past might be assembled; rather the
archive has been reimagined as a site saturated by power, a dense but uneven
body of knowledge scarred by the cultural struggles and violence of the colonial past. As Gayatri Chakravorty Spivak emphasized some fifteen years ago,
the archive of colonialism was itself the product of the "commercial/territorial
interest of the East India Company."[1] This shift in understanding of the archive
also reflects a growing awareness of its power, as we are increasingly sensitive
to not only its central role in the day-to-day function of empire, but also the
symbolic weight it carried in the broader cultural and political projects of
imperialism. As Thomas Richards has recently demonstrated, the "total archive" was a seductive and powerful imperial fantasy, as a diverse array of
Britons, from colonial administrators to Theosophists enchanted with the "oc-
cult knowledges" of the "East," dreamed that world mastery might come about
through documentation and the construction of an empire of knowledge
based on the pen rather than the sword.[2] Most important, we are increasingly
aware that the archive itself was the site where the transformative power of
colonialism was enacted and contested. Drawing on indigenous sources, land
revenue and census records, ethnographic essays, and a multiplicity of other
sources, historians of empire explained British power and made sense of the
diverse peoples over which the British Empire exercised authority. Simultaneously, however, these new forms of colonial knowledge, frequently conveyed
in print, were reworked as revivalist leaders, indigenous reformers, urban literati, and nationalist ideologues redefined the boundaries of their communities,

fashioning powerful interpretations of the past and constructing new visions for the future.[3]

Thus, the colonial state's archives of geographical, ethnological, and scientific knowledge have been at the center of the "cultural turn" within the context of South Asian historiography. South Asia has, of course, become the privileged site for both postcolonial studies and the elaboration of new models of historical analysis. The debates stimulated by the work of the subaltern studies collective and the global interdisciplinary impact of theorists such as Homi Bhabha, Gayatri Spivak, Dipesh Chakrabarty, and Ashis Nandy have not only radically transformed approaches to the South Asian past over the last two decades, but have also invested South Asian studies with the problematic tag of "exemplar" and "model."[4] If the study of South Asia has played a significant role in driving the "cultural turn," or at least the postcolonial component of that turn, it is important to note the uneven development of South Asian historiography. Although the neutrality of the term "South Asia" escapes the nationalist overtones and reductive effect of "India," it cannot mask the fact that these new approaches to the region's past have largely been driven from within India and overwhelmingly focus on cultural locations within the territorial boundaries of that modern nation-state. Equally important, even within India, this scholarship is inconsistent in depth and quality: Bengal, and especially Calcutta, remains the exemplary site for much work on intellectual and cultural history, but significant bodies of work of comparable sophistication are hard to find for other regions such as Punjab, Rajasthan, or Gujarat. Thematically as well, the development of the historiography has been patchy: communalism remains a central concern, while gender and the environment have both emerged over the last two decades as important and productive problematics, but other forms of the new cultural history — histories of material culture, emotions, and leisure — remain in their early stages.

This essay explores the main features of this historiographical terrain in an attempt to reconnect interrogatives of the nation with the problem of the state. It begins by tracing the divergent intellectual currents that have highlighted knowledge as a problematic for the study of colonial South Asia. The newfound prominence of knowledge cannot simply be read as a product of the growing influence of Foucault's work on power/knowledge on the Subaltern Studies collective or as the inevitable outcome of the reception of Said's *Orientalism* within the South Asian context. Rather, I suggest that the centrality of knowledge is also born out of a "statist turn" in South Asian historical writing, a foregrounding of the state in historical writing that must be located against intellectual shifts and political crises within both South Asia and the United Kingdom. While this statist turn has undercut inherited traditions of liberal historiography that celebrated the relative weakness of the British state at home and in the colonies, it has also reaffirmed the nation-state's primacy in historical practice. The chapter concludes by suggesting that one way in which we can open up both the nation-state and the discipline of history is to move toward a more mobile approach to the colonial past. Such an approach eschews either the metropolitan focus of the British imperial tradition or the national focus of the colonial histories, to conceive of the empire as a series of historically contingent networks that connected disparate locations into circuits of exchange and debate. By tracing the emergence, consolidation, and eventual atrophy of these "webs of empire," we not only reveal particular forms of what we might term "imperial globalization," but also initiate a further reappraisal of the production of colonial knowledge. This new model is grounded in the recognition of the porousness of national boundaries and what Peter Hulme terms the "constant, intricate, but mostly unacknowledged traffic" that not only linked Europe and its colonies, but also forged important ties between disparate colonies as well.[5]

*   *   *

A central concern in South Asian history over the past two decades has been to reveal the various ways in which "India" has been imagined, constituted, and finally realized as a territorially bounded nation-state. While the distant origins of this process can be traced to an important and diverse body of Arabic, Turkic, and Persian texts that framed the northwest portions of South Asia as "Hind" and its inhabitants as "Hindus," the rise of the British East India Company initiated a rapid intensification of this process. Matthew H. Edney's *Mapping an Empire* provides rich insights into the construction of a new understanding of the region as the company emerged a political force after its assumption of the *diwan* of Bengal, Bihar and Orissa in 1765. Edney's spatial history documents the Company state's use of cartography to frame a new and increasingly coherent image of "India." As the Company's commercial and territorial ambitions expanded, as it hoped to extend its power beyond coastal entrepôts to encompass as much of South Asia as possible, the British moved away from older conceptualizations of Asia inherited from the cosmopolitan discourses of Ptolemic and Renaissance geography. European notions of the "East Indies," structured by the long-established distinction between *India intra gangem* — the Indies this (i.e., Europe's) side of the Ganges delta — and *India extra gangem* — India beyond the Ganges (which included much of modern mainland Southeast Asia and Indonesia), were increasingly modified as company mapmakers excised much of Southeast and Central Asia from their maps and narrowed their focus on a tightly defined "India."[6] This new conceptual geography was consolidated, elaborated, and endlessly reproduced by the Company state, prizing as it did both the pragmatic and ideological value of cartography. It is in this shift in representational practice, Edney suggests, that "modern India was born."[7] Thus, in the construction of an increasingly bounded and coherent image of "India," the region was reimagined within the emerging framework of the nation-state.[8]

Edney's arguments about the power of state-generated cartography can be read as an extensive exploration of the "survey modality," one of the six "investigative modalities" (along with the historiographic, observational/travel, enumerative, museological, and surveillance) identified by Bernard Cohn as being fundamental in the framing of "India" under colonialism. For Cohn, the power of these modalities marked a fundamental rupture within the South Asian past; the rise of the Company state enacted a shift from a premodern and indigenous "theater of power" to a series of "officializing' procedures" that European states and their colonial projections used to extend their power over their new domains.[9] In a series of wide-ranging essays, Cohn's *Colonialism and Its Forms of Knowledge* highlights the increasingly organized and rigid view that the colonial states developed of South Asian culture and history. In numerous domains, from diplomatic ritual to the composition of grammars, from the working of the colonial legal system to curatorial practice, Cohn argues that the British "constantly followed the same logic; they reduced vastly complex codes and their associated meanings to a few metonyms."[10] For Cohn, this simplification and essentialization was the key play of imperial power: in short, British dominance was enacted through the intellectual and cultural objectification of "India."

C. A. Bayly's monograph, *Empire and Information*, offered a very different image of both the construction of colonial knowledge and the development of the colonial state. Where both Foucault and the Subaltern Studies project imprint Cohn's later work, Manuel Castells's model of the "informational city" and Harold Innis's pioneering work on empire and communications led Bayly to cast his study as a work on "social communication" rather than a post-Foucauldian analysis of "knowledge."[11] As a result and in contrast to Cohn, who emphasizes the hegemonic power of the colonial state, Bayly insists on the ability of South Asian groups, especially scribal elites, to negotiate positions for themselves within this increasingly commercialized colonial "information-order," and he highlights important elements of continuity between the precolonial and the colonial periods. *Empire and Information* presents an image of South Asia where knowledge, or at least "information," remains at the center of our understandings of the colonial period, but its position, like the authority of the colonial state itself, was much more fragile and open to contestation.[12]

Unlike Cohn's investigative modalities, which are grounded in European learned traditions, Bayly emphasizes the "dialogic" construction of colonial knowledge, reinforcing the central analytical thrust of Eugene Irschick's work on land tenure in the Madras hinterland. In light of Mikhail Bakhtin's stress on the dialogic construction of texts, Irschick's *Dialogue and History* stresses the hybrid nature of colonial knowledge. Irschick argues that social meaning was composed through "a negotiated, heteroglot construction shaped by both weak and strong, the colonized and colonizer, from the present to the past."[13] He warns that "we can no longer presume" that British understandings of India were the "product of an 'imposition' by the hegemonic colonial power onto a mindless and subordinate society."[14] This insistence on the agency of indigenous groups and the importance of indigenous mentalities undercuts Said's insistence on the hegemonic power of European representations, locating instead the emergence of new social formations at the cultural interstices of colonialism. Local aspirations and British policy were in a constant dialogue, a dynamic process of exchange where claim and counterclaim led each interest group to modify its position almost constantly.[15]

*   *   *

Of course, it is important to recognize the material, cultural, and political constraints that increasingly impinged on the ability of South Asians to shape such dialogic processes; caste identities, material conditions, gender, and literacy were crucial forces in determining the ability of individuals and communities to mold the outcomes of these cross-cultural encounters. In light of these discrepancies in power and the centrality of knowledge in the consolidation of colonial authority, the archive has become deeply problematic; the manuscript collections, parliamentary papers, court records, periodicals, and newspapers used by historians of South Asia are not simply documents that allow us to access the colonial past, but rather themselves were constitutive of the multiple inequalities of that past. This recognition of the archive as both the product of the uneven dialogics of the colonial encounter and a space where the conceptual schemas of colonialism were worked out raises fundamental questions about historical scholarship. If this is the nature of the archive of colonialism, how must it be read? Given its centrality to the colonial project, what colonial perspectives are foregrounded? What groups are privileged? More important, what are its exclusions? Whose voices are silenced? What groups and individuals are reduced to fleeting traces and isolated textual fragments?

These questions are particularly pressing for historians exploring gendered subjectivities and the dynamics of gender construction and performance in South Asia. The colonial archive itself was heavily gendered; not only was the bureaucratic machinery of empire overwhelmingly male, but also most of the texts produced by South Asians were written by those male indigenous experts, scribal professionals, and textbook authors recognized and supported by the colonial state. In effect, the dialogic construction of colonial archives was the product of the negotiations between British and indigenous males; the most striking disparity within the archives of empire is their gendered nature and the relative absence of female-produced texts. Thus female voices, restricted within the cultural terrain of precolonial social systems, stifled by both the colonial state and the power of patriarchy, are difficult, and some would say even impossible, to recover. As Spivak has argued, the search for South Asian women's subjectivities in the archive is analogous to being "in the shadow of shadows."[16] In her important essay, "The Rani of Sirmur," Spivak is critical of Foucault's belief that oppressed subjects were able to speak and articulate their subjectivity; she asserts that this position is untenable within a context of colonialism and especially in colonial South Asia, where masculinized ideologies saturated a heavily gendered political economy. As Spivak shows, the Rani of Sirmur (a small hill state in what is now Himachal Pradesh) emerges in the colonial archives "only when she is needed in the space of imperial production." As the Company state attempted to consolidate its northern frontier in the Shimla hills, it exhibited a strong interest in the political structure and courtly politics of the states on its borders. It is within this political and diplomatic framework that the rani appears so briefly in the Company's archives as "a king's wife and a weaker vessel."[17] Spivak extended this vision of the "shadowy" nature of the archive in her seminal article, "Can the Subaltern Speak?," where she rejected the possibility of recovering subaltern mentalities in general, but especially those of the "female subalterns."[18]

While Spivak's work was crucial in highlighting the primacy of gender in determining the texture of the colonial archives, her vision of colonial authority and subaltern agency has been contested.[19] Lata Mani's exploration of gendered forms of alterity in discourses surrounding suttee presents a more nuanced view of agency and the archive. Mani acknowledges the importance of Spivak's intervention but warns against seeing Spivak's argument as "conclusions about colonial discourse in general," instead using it as a starting point for an extensive rereading of contemporary accounts of suttee.[20] Mani reveals the highly disparate texture of the dense archive of materials generated by evangelical missionaries, state functionaries, and indigenous male reformers surrounding this most contentious tradition. She stresses that these elite debates over the "scriptural" basis of the practice and its meaning within high-caste Hindu "tradition" generally erased female subjectivity, as women became instead the "ground" for debates about the nature of custom and modernity.

Although Mani's analysis follows Spivak to the extent that she makes it clear that any desire to effect a full recovery of female subjectivity is misplaced, it also suggests that a nuanced reading of colonial texts can unsettle the fundamental assumptions of male-produced eyewitness accounts of suttee. Mani traces acts of resistance to the coercive techniques that often enabled the performance of suttee and highlights the occasional accounts that disrupt official discourses by focusing on the physical and emotional pain inflicted upon women; these accounts compromise and even rupture key "fictions" about suttee, especially the dominant representation of it as a "religiously inspired act of devotion to the deceased husband."[21] Equally important, Mani delineates the ways in which members of learned male indigenous elites were authorized as experts within the colonial system through debates on suttee: pandits employed in the company's legal system and Brahmanical experts were subjected to "continual and instinctive questioning" by British authorities, and out of their competing opinions and interpretations a new, synthesized vision of "custom" was textualized and ensconced as the bedrock of colonial policy. This "incitement to discourse" directed toward male "authorities" must be set in contradistinction to the muffling of female voices, revealing the fundamentally gendered dynamic of British knowledge construction and policy making in relation to suttee.[22]

If the figure of the suttee embodies the disempowering work of elite discourse, whether produced by Britons or South Asians, texts written by women have not generally enjoyed the same authority as male authors working in well-established literary and nationalist traditions. As Susie Tharu and K. Lalita observe in the preface to their momentous two-volume collection, *Women Writing in India*, compiling a body of texts by women was a battle against both the elitist and transitory nature of archives, where female-produced texts were dispersed or damaged or even sold as "junk." The key repositories for the reconstruction of South Asian women's writing lay, and no doubt continue to lie, not in the records generated by the colonial and postcolonial state, but rather in family archives and personal collections. Accessing female literary production requires not only an active "reading against the grain of literary histories," but also the interrogation of the "imagined communities" and "new citizens" sculpted by nationalist literary traditions.[23]

Although the members of the subaltern studies collective have expressed limited interest in questions of gendered subjectivity, Ranajit Guha has framed a discussion of gender and the archive within a larger exploration of the "small voice" of the South Asian past.[24] In reflecting on the archival base for the reconstruction of the colonial period, Guha advocates the construction of a multivocal history grounded in the "listening to and conversing with the myriad voices in civil society."[25] Guha's realization of both the multivocality of the past and the ways in which women's voices have been elided calls the very future of "History" into question. Gender cannot simply be accommodated into "History," as the reconstitution of women's voices and the analytical weight attached to gender exceed the limits of a liberal inclusionist tradition, fundamentally transforming the conventions and purpose of history writing itself.[26]

Leading historians of Dalits (oppressed people) and Adivasis (aboriginal people) have also underlined the analytical and ideological limitations of "traditional" history. Ajay Skaria's history of the frontiers of western India places a critical examination of historical practice at its very core. Not only does Skaria contest the equation of history with Europe, the Enlightenment, and modernity, but also his analysis offers a radically different vision of how history might be written. In exploring the *goths* (narrative, account) of the Dangi people, he exposes the limits of the analytical categories inherited from the colonial archives that so often structure analyses of the South Asian past and probes the complex relationships between writing and orality, colonialism and resistance.

Most important, Skaria's work eschews the linear temporality of most professional history, adopting its structure from the temporal logic of Dangi *goths* that divide the past into two distinct epochs: the *moglai* — an age of freedom and mobility — and the *mandini* — a subsequent age of restricted mobility and disempowerment. Skaria orders his text according to these cultural and temporal logics but also suggests that his book can be actively reread to explore the tensions among his key sources: the Dangi oral narratives and supplementary written texts produced by the Dangis' rivals, the British, and later nationalists. In providing this alternative trajectory through his text (suggesting that the reader should in fact begin with chapter 3, followed by chapter 10, and culminate with chapter 20), Skaria forcibly reminds us of the contrivance of history and emphasizes the multiplicity of narratives that communicate the Dangi past.[27] History, in the end, becomes a series of different (and frequently competing) epistemological and narrative strategies for making sense of the past.

*   *   *

Such attempts to radically reimagine the production and function of historical narratives have been met with a hostile response. An unlikely coalition of British imperial historians, American South Asians wedded to the "new social history," and historians uncomfortable with the turn toward new reading strategies (such as "discourse analysis") have moved to shore up disciplinary boundaries through an appeal to the disciplinary power of "History."[28] Despite playing a pivotal role in formulating a new approach to British history that has revealed the constitutive role of the empire in metropolitan culture, John

MacKenzie has led the resistance against disciplinary interlopers. Although the second half of MacKenzie's *Orientalism: History, Theory and the Arts* provides important insights into the productive engagement between European artistic traditions and the "Orient," it opens with a stinging critique of those literary critics, art historians, and postcolonial theorists who have embraced historical analysis without, in MacKenzie's view, following the cherished norms of disciplined practice.[29] More recently, in a generally favorable review of Skaria's *Hybrid Histories*, MacKenzie casts doubt upon Skaria's efforts to "cast aside the modernist thrust of most history writing." In response to Skaria's exploration and juxtaposition of divergent narratives, MacKenzie observes that "complex though the narratives are, there remain gaps"; Skaria's inability (or, at a fundamental level, unwillingness) to fashion a *comprehensive* history is presented as a significant failure.[30]

What is striking about these exchanges over the "cultural turn" in the South Asian context is that they leave the centrality of the nation-state unquestioned. Despite the radically different epistemological positions and divergent forms of analytical practice that have energized the conflicted terrain of South Asian historiography since the 1980s, we can identify a common interest in the state resulting from a historiographical confluence within both revisionist studies of the British past and reappraisals of colonialism within South Asia. A fundamental reevaluation of the development of the state, initiated largely by the work of John Brewer, has been crucial to molding a new understanding of the British past. Attacking long-established liberal historiographical traditions that depicted the metropolitan state as weak and the United Kingdom as a lightly governed society, Brewer highlighted the rise of the military-fiscal state from the seventeenth century onward. Drawing on new apparatuses for domestic surveillance, an increasingly professionalized bureaucracy, and a range of enumerative projects, in addition to greatly expanded military power, the "Janus-faced" British state consolidated its authority within the kingdom's borders, as well as projecting its authority out into the Celtic "fringes" and beyond.[31] Brewer's *Sinews of Power* was written from the perspective of Westminster and Whitehall, "the center of the core," but his arguments have proven suggestive for historians of South Asia. Recent studies have recast the colonial state fashioned by the East India Company as a "military-fiscal state," albeit one that was influenced by the "Prussian model" grounded in the "subsidiary alliance" and that remained heavily dependent on South Asian capital, bureaucrats, and soldiers.[32] These reassessments of the Company state have undermined an older view of the rise of the British in South Asia that emphasized the "collapse" of Mughal authority and the Company's opportunism, demonstrating the ways in which the rapid expansion of the Company's military establishment, together with the emergence of new and virulent strains of racial thought, drove a long and violent process of expansion, culminating in the annexation of Punjab, the last major independent South Asian polity, in 1849.[33]

If it is tempting to read the "statist turn" in British history (and, by extension, British imperial history) as being born out of debates over Britain's relationship with Europe and the search for solutions to the ongoing conflict in Northern Ireland, we can also locate an analogous "statist turn" within the South Asian context. The centrality of the state in the work of the Subaltern Studies collective is not surprising given that the collective was formed in the wake of the "Emergency" of 1975. Indeed, at one level, the collective's work can be read as a series of interventions in debates over the "crisis of the state" in South Asia.[34] The growing influence of Foucault's studies of biopower, knowledge production, and governmentality on the collective (especially David Arnold, Gyan Prakash, and Partha Chatterjee) has further cemented the primacy of the state: the prison, the asylum, the police station, and the hospital have emerged as key sites for historical analysis.[35]

This deep investment in the state has spilled over into an equally deep investment in the nation. Of course, this is not surprising given that Ranajit Guha's programmatic essay, "On Some Aspects of the Historiography of Colonial India," which opened the first volume of *Subaltern Studies*, began by asserting that the "historiography of Indian nationalism has for a long time been dominated by elitism — colonialist elitism and bourgeois-nationalist elitism." For Guha, the project of the collective was not only to deconstruct these elitisms and to recover the subaltern pasts, but also to study the *"historic failure of the nation to come to its own."*[36] In one sense the nation provides an integrative element for *Subaltern Studies*; although many of the essays in the subsequent volumes focus on particular forms of economic production and clearly defined segments of South Asian society, these fragmentary histories are invested with meaning because they are part of a project to construct what Partha Chatterjee has termed an "Indian history" of peasant and subaltern politics.[37]

Of course, in evoking the nation and a notion of national culture, Chatterjee replicates what Sudipta Kaviraj has termed the "narrative contract" between history and the nation-state.[38] Unpicking the relationship between the nation-state and history has proven difficult for a discipline where the nation structures so much of our professional training and classroom experience; it is not surprising that the key works that have mapped theoretical and methodological approaches to the study of transnational cultural formations have been produced by anthropologists and sociologists rather than historians.[39] Historians of South Asia have been remarkably slow to interrogate the privileged status of the nation and to engage with the push toward "history beyond the nation." Certainly, the well-established historiography on the early modern Indian Ocean has highlighted the pivotal role of merchant diasporas, shipping routes, and commercial practices that linked South Asia to East Africa, the Islamic world, and East and Southeast Asia, but this literature is deeply wedded to the quantitative spirit of social history and offers little in the way of cultural analysis.[40]

For a later period, Mrinalini Sinha's *Colonial Masculinity*, a richly textured study of the interface between colonialism and gender ideologies, suggests an important heuristic model that was attuned to the importance of culture, offering one way out of the straitjacket of nation-focused history. Undercutting both the "metrocentric" tradition of imperial history (where the empire is viewed from London or Oxbridge but seen only to have effects "out there" in the colonies) and the narrowly national focus of much colonial history, Sinha elaborates the notion of an "imperial social formation."[41] This formulation recognizes the crucial conjunction between metropolitan culture and the colonial project but—mindful of Gauri Viswanathan's warning against the easy conflation of the "national" and the "imperial"—also emphasizes "the essentially uneven and contradictory impact" of this intersection.[42] As Sinha explains, historians need to be sensitive "on the one hand, to the different trajectories of metropolitan and colonial histories and, on the other, the mutual implication of both these histories in the 'uneven and combined development' of the global political economy."[43] This suggestive model reinforces the thrust of earlier works by John MacKenzie, Rozina Visram, Peter Fryer, and Gretchen Gerzina, while important recent works by Antoinette Burton, Michael Fisher, James Walvin, Susan Thorne, and James Schneer have revealed much about the contours and fault lines of this "imperial social formation."[44]

＊　＊　＊

These works have punctured the fiction that Britain was somehow insulated from the effects of imperialism, reminding us of the important cultural traffic between the metropole and the periphery. But these reorientations can be pushed further still. It is important to recognize not only that the empire was comprised of networks and exchanges that linked the various colonies to the metropole, but also that its very structure was dependent upon a series of crucial horizontal linkages among colonies. I believe it is productive to conceive of the empire not in terms of a spoked wheel with London as the "hub," where the various "spokes" (whether flows of finance, lines of communication, or the movement of people and objects) from the periphery meet, but rather in terms of a complex web consisting of "horizontal" filaments that run among various colonies in addition to "vertical" connections between the metropole and individual colonies.

This metaphor of the web has several advantages for conceptualizing the imperial past. At a general level, it underscores that the empire was a *structure*, a complex system of overlapping and interwoven institutions, organizations, ideologies, and discourses. The web captures the integrative nature of this cultural traffic, the ways in which the empire connected disparate points in space into a complex mesh of networks. Archives of various types — the libraries of learned societies, the records produced by missionary organizations and reform movements, private libraries assembled by colonial intellectuals, and the official archives of colonial government — can be understood as crucial nodes in these webs. Identifying archives as nodes within a larger system of imperial knowledge production recognizes the double function of the archive. At one level, archives are the product of centripetal processes, as various webs of correspondence, institutional exchanges, and publication networks draw material together into the archival space where it is collected, organized, and stored. But archives also have a centrifugal function: they are centers from which knowledge was distributed, whether through the act of reading, correspondence, the intertextual nature of print culture, or the exchange of manuscript or printed material.

Unfortunately we have a very limited understanding of the circulation of ideas and the movement of information across the empire, largely because of the ways in which historians imagine the spatial significance of the archive. Even after the cultural turn, most historians view the archive as providing the materials for studying a carefully delimited space, whether it is a city, a district, or the nation; effectively, the archive comes to stand as a proxy for the unit of analysis.[45] Even those historians sensitive to the occlusions of the imperial archive typically view archives as enclosed, static, and discreet, rather than the product of the constant circulation of information and the heavy intertextuality of many forms of knowledge.[46] By emphasizing the mobility of colonial knowledge and the interweaving of the archives of empire, we can place greater emphasis on the transnational cultural and intellectual traffic that was the very lifeblood of empire.

What are the effects of this web model for our understanding of colonial knowledge, particularly in relation to South Asia? At a fundamental level, it might return the region to the broader "bundles of relationships" that underpinned the development of South Asian knowledge communities and learned traditions.[47] Just as works by Sanjay Subrahmanyam, C. A. Bayly, and Francis Robinson have unraveled some of the crucial knowledge networks that linked

South Asia to a wider Islamic world of learning from the early modern period through the mid-nineteenth century, recent work by Richard Grove on environmental thought and S. B. Cook on understandings of custom and land tenure have hinted at the significance of such exchanges under the British as well.[48]

Here, for example, we might reevaluate the broader imperial and transnational contexts that framed the Company's projection of a systematized image of "India." From the early 1830s the Ordnance Survey of Ireland served as a key reference point for the Great Trigonometrical Survey of India. While Captain Henry Kater, an influential assistant on the East India Company's early surveys, played a pivotal role in the debates in the late 1820s that fixed the eventual scale and organization of the Ordnance Survey, the flow of ideas was generally from Ireland to India. George Everest, the surveyor-general of India, established an important relationship with Thomas Frederick Colby, director general of the Ordnance Survey (1820–1847), visiting the Irish survey on Colby's invitation. Everest believed that the Irish model, especially its technologies and institutional structure, should be transplanted to India in order to put the colonial state's intellectual and ideological project on a sound footing. The other leading figure in colonial surveying in India, Thomas Best Jervis, extended these arguments, stressing that the division of labor employed in Ireland would be even more advantageous in India. The dull repetitive work at the heart of the survey would be delegated to local workers trained in a limited range of simple tasks, while the officers would be able to focus on the computations and scientific issues. This system would expose Indians to the usefulness of science and inculcate disciplined and conscientious work patterns among the indigenous population. These links between the Ordnance Survey and the Great Trigonometrical Survey of India were further cemented by the exchange of personnel, as all of the company's engineer cadets were sent to the Ordnance Survey for training prior to being sent to India.[49] This series of personnel movements and intellectual exchanges was just one part of a dense cluster of military, economic, and political networks that wove Ireland and India together in the nineteenth century.

Following on from this, the image of the web underlines the inherently relational nature of the empire, as it reinforces the multiple positions that any given colony, city, community, or archive might occupy. If colonial administrators in South Asia drew heavily on Irish precedents and models, we must also recognize that India was a subimperial center in its own right. While John Cell and Robert Tignor traced the impact of India-derived models in the political economy of colonial African states, the ethnological models developed in colonial India also had a global impact.[50] If the Irish Ordnance Survey provided an important blueprint for the Company's cartographic project in South Asia, Anglo-Irish antiquarians wove Celticism and Orientalism together in their discussions of the "Eastern origins" of Irish culture, elaborating arguments that were reworked by a later generation of Irish cultural nationalists.[51] The work of British Orientalists (such as Sir William Jones) was also influential in molding the development of the Scottish tradition of "philosophical history." Between the 1770s and the mid-nineteenth century, this tradition was particularly influential in shaping British understandings of non-European societies, as Scottish historians fixed the position of various indigenous populations within their developmental schema. The Scottish tradition was especially powerful in Southeast Asia, where an important group of Edinburgh-educated company administrators produced the seminal studies of the region's cultures, languages, and history, viewing the region as "Further India" or the "Indian archipelago," a cultural and geographic extension of India.[52]

These Indocentric visions of Southeast Asia can be read as part of a wider process of "intellectual regionalization": the creation of a zone of ethnological exchange and analysis that focused on South Asia but that reached out into Southeast Asia, the Pacific islands, and Australasia. European linguists, colonial administrators, and settler ethnologists interpreted the peoples of the Pacific against the backdrop of South Asian ethnology. In this sense, we can speak of an "Oriental Renaissance in the Pacific," revising Raymond Schwab's Eurocentric view of the impact of South Asia on late eighteenth- and nineteenth-century cultural, artistic, and political traditions. The interweaving of orientalism and the ethnology of the Pacific was facilitated by the ethnographic and linguistic data assembled by Joseph Banks, James Cook, and Georg and Johann Forster, which suggested that the Pacific islands were peopled from the coast of Asia rather than America or the fabled southern continent.[53] The Scottish orientalist William Marsden lent philological support to this diffusionist theory in a 1781 paper that established the deep-seated affinities that underpin the languages of the Malay peninsula and central and eastern Polynesia.[54] A later generation of missionary ethnologists placed even more emphasis on the Indian (rather than Southeast Asian) origins of Polynesian culture, as they scribbled word lists that compared Maori and Sanskrit, explored analogies between Polynesian and South Asian material culture, and identified parallels between caste and *tapu*, Hindu deities and Polynesian *atua*.[55] These early Indocentric researches fashioned a basic framework for Pacific ethnology until the 1930s; despite intense debates over the precise origins of the cultures of the Pacific (were they Malay, Dravidian, Aryan or tribal?), leading European and settler authorities alike subscribed to diffusion-ist models focused on a distant Asian homeland.[56]

*   *   *

These debates at the distant margins of the empire over the debt of Polynesian culture to South Asian traditions are a potent example of the complex exchanges that facilitated the transplantation and adaptation of ethnological paradigms from one part of the empire to another. The importance of such cultural traffic within the empire means that we need to revisit the spatial basis of our analytical models. Certainly, we must recognize that one of the central projects of empire was the construction of a new world of territorially bounded nation-states, but we must also recover the deep structures of empire that integrated each colony into a larger imperial system, albeit a system both fluid and fragile. An important starting point for such a project is to reconceptualize the archive. If the last twenty years of historical writing on South Asia has underlined the power struggles that molded the colonial archive and has mapped the archive's occlusions and silences, it has also reinstantiated the primacy of the nation-state. A critical rereading of the archive that is sensitive to the mobility of ideas, traces the dissemination of information and ideologies across time and space, and highlights the intertextuality of colonial knowledge will allow us to explore the role of knowledge production in the globalized political economy of empire and to reevaluate the production of difference under colonialism. Such a project will not only fashion a more nuanced understanding of the construction of colonial knowledge, but will also enable us to adopt a more mobile and transnational approach to the imperial past while recognizing the power of the nation-state and the "national knowledges" produced by colonialism.

Notes

1 Gayatri Chakravorty Spivak, "The Rani of Sirmur: An Essay in Reading the Archives," *History and Theory* 24 (1985): 263.
2 Thomas Richards, *The Imperial Archive: Knowledge and the Fantasy of Empire* (London: Verso, 1993).
3 Some of these themes have been explored in Vasudha Dalmia, *The Nationalization of Hindu Traditions: Bharatendu Harishchandra and Nineteenth-Century Banaras* (Delhi: Oxford University Press, 1997); Gyan Prakash, *Another Reason: Science and the Imagination in Modern India* (Princeton, N.J.: Princeton University Press, 1998); Tapan Raychaudhuri, *Europe Reconsidered: Perceptions of the West in Nineteenth Century Bengal* (Delhi: Oxford University Press, 1988); Thomas R. Trautmann, *Aryans and British India* (Berkeley: University of California Press, 1997).
4 Dipesh Chakrabarty, "Historiadores de las minorías, pasados subalternos," *Historia y Grafía* 12

(1999): 87–111; Vinayak Chaturvedi, *Mapping Subaltern Studies and the Postcolonial* (London: Verso, 2000); Frederick Cooper, "Conflict and Connection: Rethinking Colonial African History," *American Historical Review* 99 (1994): 1516–1545; Florencia E. Mallon, "The Promise and Dilemma of Subaltern Studies: Perspectives from Latin American History," *American Historical Review* 99 (1994): 1491–1515; Sabra J. Webber, "Middle East Studies and Subaltern Studies," *Middle East Studies Association Bulletin* 31 (1997): 11–16.

5 Peter Hulme, "Subversive Archipelagos: Colonial Discourse and the Break-Up of Continental Theory," *Dispositio* 14 (1989): 3.

6 Edney points out that this process was also facilitated by expansion and consolidation of Mughal authority over the bulk of South Asia under Aurangzeb (1658–1707). Matthew H. Edney, *Mapping an Empire: The Geographical Construction of British India, 1765–1843* (Chicago: University of Chicago Press, 1997), pp. 4–9. Changing cartographic representations of South Asia can be traced over the *longue durée* in Susan Gole, *Early Maps of India* (Edinburgh: Skilton, 1978), and J. B. Hartley and David Woodward, eds., *The History of Cartography*, vol. 2, Book 1: *Cartography in the Traditional Islamic and South Asian Societies* (Chicago: University of Chicago Press, 1992).

7 Edney, *Mapping an Empire*, p. 9.

8 As Chandra Mukerji has argued, cartographic and surveying practices played a central role in the process of state definition, as they "were also expressions of a politico-economic order that made the state seem the natural unit of geographical analysis." *From Graven Images: Patterns of Modern Materialism* (New York: Columbia University Press, 1983), p. 128.

9 Bernard S. Cohn, *Colonialism and Its Forms of Knowledge: The British in India* (Princeton, N.J.: Princeton University Press, 1996), p. 3. The importance of Cohn's work on colonial knowledge is explored in Saloni Mathur's thoughtful review essay: "History and Anthropology in South Asia: Rereading the Archive," *Annual Review of Anthropology* 29 (2000): 89–106.

10 Cohn, *Colonialism and Its Forms of Knowledge*, p. 162.

11 C. A. Bayly, *Empire and Information: Intelligence Gathering and Social Communication in India, 1780–1870* (Cambridge: Cambridge University Press, 1996); Harold Innis, *Empire and Communications* (Oxford: Clarendon Press, 1950); Manuel Castells, *The Informational City: Information Technology, Economic Restructuring, and the Urban-Regional Process* (Oxford: Basil Blackwell, 1989).

12 This is in stark contrast to the arguments elaborated about the connections between social communication and nation building in Karl W. Deutsch, *Nationalism and Social Communication: An Inquiry into the Foundations of Nationality* (London: Chapman and Hall, 1953).

13 Eugene F. Irschick, *Dialogue and History: Constructing South India, 1795–1895* (Berkeley: University of California Press, 1994), p. 10; Mikhail Bakhtin, *The Dialogic Imagination: Four Essays*, ed. Michael Holquist (Austin: University of Texas Press, 1981).

14 Irschick, *Dialogue and History*, p. 8.

15 Saurabh Dube's study of the Satnamis of central India affirms this approach, stressing the dynamism and fluidity of identity within a colonial context. Dube argues that the Satnami past cannot be read as a simple clash between "timeless tradition" and colonial modernity. Rather, he argues that "the symbols and practices of imperial rule offered a pool of resources that were deployed in selective, diverse, and even conflicting ways by the Satnamis to redefine identities, construct traditions, fashion legalities, and define pathologies within the community, and to thus participate in the construction of a colonial modernity." *Untouchable Pasts: Religion, Identity, and Power among a Central Indian Community, 1780–1950* (Albany, N.Y.: State University of New York Press, 1998), pp. 17–18.

16 Spivak, "The Rani of Sirmur," p. 265.

17 Ibid., pp. 266, 270.

18 Gayatri Chakravorty Spivak, "Can the Subaltern Speak?" in *Marxism and the Interpretation of Culture*, ed. Cary Nelson and Lawrence Grossberg (Urbana: University of Illinois Press, 1988), pp. 271–313.

19 For example, Benita Parry, "Problems in Current Theories of Colonial Discourse," *Oxford Literary Review* 9 (1987): 27–58; Ania Loomba: "Dead Women Tell No Tales: Issues of Female Subjectivity, Subaltern Agency and Tradition in Colonial and Post-Colonial Writing on Widow Immolation in India," *History Workshop Journal* 36 (1993): 209–227, and *Colonialism/Postcolonialism* (London: Routledge, 1998), pp. 231–244

20 Lata Mani, "Cultural Theory, Colonial Texts: Reading Eyewitness Accounts of Widow Burning," *History Workshop Journal* 36 (1993): 396. These arguments are elaborated more fully in Lata Mani, *Contentious Traditions: The Debate on Sati in Colonial India* (Berkeley: University of California Press, 1998).

21 Mani, "Cultural Theory, Colonial Texts," p. 403.

22 Lata Mani, "Production of an Official Discourse on *Sati* in Early Nineteenth Century Bengal," *Economic and Political Weekly* (1986): WS-37.

23 Susie Tharu and K. Lalita, eds., *Women Writing in India: 600 B.C. to the Early 20th Century* (London: Pandora Press, 1991), pp. xviii–xxi.

24 Kamala Visweswaran, "Small Speeches, Subaltern Gender: Nationalist Ideology and Its Historiography," *Subaltern Studies* 9: 88.

25 Ranajit Guha, "The Small Voice of History," *Subaltern Studies* 9: 3–6. Of course, Guha's use of the adjective "small" reveals the ways in which the categories and assumptions of the state are reproduced, as it reinforces pernicious divisions between the "big" history of the state and the public sphere and the "small" history of women and other subordinate groups.

26 Although Guha's essay stands as an important affirmation of gender as a central site for the reimagining of the relationship between the archive and historical practice, it is somewhat belated in recognizing the fundamental challenge of gender history, effacing important models that were already in print by the mid-1990s, including: Alice W. Clark, ed., *Gender and Political Economy: Explorations of South Asian Systems* (Delhi: Oxford University Press, 1993); J. Krishnamurty, ed., *Women in Colonial India: Essays on Survival, Work, and the State* (Delhi: Oxford University Press, 1989); Rosalind O'Hanlon, *A Comparison between Women and Men: Tarabai Shinde and the Critique of Gender Relations in Colonial India* (Oxford: Oxford University Press, 1994); Bharati Ray, ed., *From the Seams of History: Essays on Indian Women* (Delhi: Oxford University Press, 1995); Kumkum Sangari and Sudesh Vaid, eds., *Recasting Women: Essays in Colonial History* (Delhi: Kali for Women, 1989).

27 Ajay Skaria, *Hybrid Histories: Forests, Frontiers, and Wildness in Western India* (Delhi: Oxford University Press, 1999), pp. 17–18.

28 For example, David Washbrook, "Colonial Discourse Theory and the Historiography of the British Empire," in *The Oxford History of the British Empire*, vol. 5: *Historiography*, ed. Robin Winks (Oxford: Oxford University Press, 1999); Peter Heehs, "Shaped like Themselves," *History and Theory* 39 (2000): 417–428.

29 John M. MacKenzie, *Orientalism: History, Theory and the Arts* (Manchester: Manchester University Press, 1995). MacKenzie was responding in particular to Sara Suleri, *The Rhetoric of English India* (Chicago: University of Chicago Press, 1992), and Gauri Viswanathan, *Masks of Conquest: Literary Study and British Rule in India* (London: Faber, 1990).

30   John M. MacKenzie, "Review of Ajay Skaria, *Hybrid Histories: Forests, Frontiers and Wild-ness in Western India*," *American Historical Review* 106 (2001): 153–154.

31   John Brewer, *The Sinews of Power: War, Money, and the English State, 1688–1783* (New York: Knopf, 1989), p. xvii.

32   C. A. Bayly, "The British Military-Fiscal State and Indigenous Resistance: India 1750–1820," in *An Imperial State at War: Britain from 1689 to 1815*, ed. Lawrence Stone (London: Routledge, 1994), pp. 322–354, esp. p. 333. Also see Nancy G. Cassels, ed., *Orientalism, Evangelicalism, and the Military Cantonment in Early Nineteenth-Century India: A Histo-riographical Overview* (Lampeter: Edwin Mellen Press, 1991); Douglas M. Peers, *Between Mars and Mammon: Colonial Armies and the Garrison State in India 1819–1835* (London: Tauris Academic Studies, 1995).

33   These arguments must also be read against the backdrop of revisionist work on the Mogul state. Key entry points into this literature are Muzaffar Alam, *The Crisis of Empire in Mughal North India, Awadh and the Punjab, 1707–1748* (Delhi: Oxford University Press, 1993); C. A. Bayly: *Indian Society and the Making of the British Empire* (Cambridge: Cambridge University Press, 1988), and *Imperial Meridian: The British Empire and the World* (London: Longman, 1989), pp. 16–74.

34   Ranajit Guha, "Introduction," in *The Subaltern Studies Reader, 1986–1995* (Minneapolis: University of Minnesota Press, 1997), p. xi; C. A. Bayly, "Rallying around the Subaltern," *Journal of Peasant Studies* 16 (1988): 110–120.

35   This Foucauldian imprint is most evident in David Arnold, *Colonizing the Body: State Medicine and Epidemic Disease in Nineteenth-Century India* (Berkeley: University of Cal-ifornia Press, 1993), and Prakash, *Another Reason*. For post-Foucauldian studies of bio-power produced outside the collective, see: Waltraud Ernst, "Asylum Provision and the East India Company in the Nineteenth Century," *Medical History* 42 (1998): 476–502; James H. Mills, "Reforming the Indian: Treatment Regimes in the Lunatic Asylums of British India, 1857–1880," *Indian Economic and Social History Review* 36 (1999): 407–429; Satadru Sen, "Policing the Savage: Segregation, Labor and State Medicine in the Anda-mans," *Journal of Asian Studies* 58: 753–773; Anand A. Yang, "The Voice of Colonial Discipline and Punishment: Knowledge, Power and the Penological Discourse in Early Nineteenth Century India," *Indo-British Review* 21 (1993): 62–71.

36   Emphasis in original; *Subaltern Studies* 1: 1, 7.

37   Chatterjee distinguishes this "Indian history of peasant struggles" from a "history of peasant struggles in India." Where the latter approach transplants a model of universal history into the framework of India, "the task is to ground one's historical consciousness in the immanent forms of social development that run through Indian history and from that standpoint to engage our colonial experience in a process of struggle." Here, it seems to me, Chatterjee fails to problematize what constitutes "Indian" and replicates the *natural-ness* of the nation as a site for historical inquiry. Chatterjee, "Nation and Its Fragments," p. 18.

38   Ironically this was in *Subaltern Studies* 7. Sudipta Kaviraj, "The Imaginary Institution of India," *Subaltern Studies* 7: 1–39. Also see Antoinette Burton, "Who Needs the Nation? Interrogating British History," *Journal of Historical Sociology* 10 (1997): 227–248.

39   Paul Gilroy, *The Black Atlantic: Modernity and Double Consciousness* (Cambridge, Mass.: Harvard University Press, 1993); Aihwa Ong, *Flexible Citizenship: The Cultural Logics of Transnationality* (Durham, N.C.: Duke University Press, 1998).

40   Amitav Ghosh's essay, "The Slave of MS. H.6," *Subaltern Studies* 7: 159–220, is a notable exception and stands as the only significant contribution that *Subaltern Studies* has made to this literature. Key entry points into this literature are: S. Arasaratnam, "Recent Trends in

the Historiography of the Indian Ocean, 1500–1880," *Journal of World History* 1 (1990): 225–248; Satish Chandra, ed., *The Indian Ocean: Explorations in History, Commerce, and Politics* (New Delhi: Sage, 1987); K. N. Chaudhuri, *Asia before Europe: Economy and Civilisation of the Indian Ocean from the Rise of Islam to 1750* (Cambridge: Cambridge University Press, 1990); Kenneth McPherson, *The Indian Ocean: A History of People and the Sea* (New York: Oxford University Press, 1993); Rudrangshu Mukherjee and Lakshmi Subramanian, eds., *Politics and Trade in the Indian Ocean World: Essays in Honour of Ashin Das Gupta* (New York: Oxford University Press, 1998).

41 Mrinalini Sinha, *Colonial Masculinity: The "Manly Englishman" and the "Effeminate Bengali" in the Late Nineteenth Century* (Manchester: Manchester University Press, 1995). An early diagnosis of the centrifugal interpretation of the empire and a call for a centripetal analysis was John M. MacKenzie, *Propaganda and Empire: The Manipulation of British Public Opinion 1880–1960* (Manchester: Manchester University Press, 1984).

42 Sinha, *Colonial Masculinity*, p. 10; Gauri Viswanathan, "Raymond Williams and British Colonialism," *Yale Journal of Criticism* 4 (1991): 47–66.

43 Sinha, *Colonial Masculinity*, p. 182.

44 Gretchen Gerzina, *Black London: Life before Emancipation* (London: John Murray, 1995); Rozina Visram, *Ayahs, Lascars and Princes: Indians in Britain 1700–1947* (London: Pluto Press, 1986); and Peter Fryer, *Staying Power: The History of Black People in Britain* (London: Pluto Press, 1984); Michael H. Fisher, *The First Indian Author in English: Dean Mahomed (1759–1851) in India, Ireland and England* (Delhi: Oxford University Press, 1996); James Walvin, *Fruits of Empire: Exotic Produce and British Taste, 1660–1800* (Basingstoke: Macmillan, 1997); Antoinette Burton, *At the Heart of the Empire: Indians and the Colonial Encounter in Late-Victorian Britain* (Berkeley: University of California Press, 1998); Susan Thorne, *Congregational Missions and the Making of an Imperial Culture in Nineteenth-Century England* (Stanford, Calif.: Stanford University Press, 1999); Jonathan Schneer, *London 1900: The Imperial Metropolis* (New Haven, Conn.: Yale University Press, 1999).

45 See, for example, Richard M. Eaton's valorization of "local knowledge," found in "district archives, local libraries, private collections, zamindari records": "(Re)imag(in)ing Other²ness: A Postmortem for the Postmodern in India," *Journal of World History* 11 (2000): 72.

46 These arguments are developed in a fuller form in Tony Ballantyne, *Orientalism and Race: Aryanism in the British Empire* (London: Palgrave, 2001).

47 This formulation draws from Eric R. Wolf, *Europe and the People without History* (Berkeley: University of California Press, 1982), p. 3.

48 Bayly: *Imperial Meridian*, pp. 16–74, and "India and West Asia, c. 1700–1830," *Asian Affairs* 19 (1988): 3–19; Francis Robinson, "Technology and Religious Change: Islam and the Impact of Print," *Modern Asian Studies* 27 (1993): 229–251. Sanjay Subrahmanyam: "Connected Histories: Notes towards a Reconfiguration of Early Modern Eurasia," *Modern Asian Studies* 31 (1997): 735–762, and "Iranians abroad: Intra-Asian Elite Migration and Early Modern State Formation," *Journal of Asian Studies* 51 (1992): 340–363.

49 J. H. Andrews, *A Paper Landscape: The Ordnance Survey in Nineteenth-Century Ireland* (Oxford: Clarendon Press, 1975); Edney, *Mapping an Empire*, pp. 276–277, 281–285.

50 John W. Cell, "Anglo-Indian Medical Theory and the Origins of Segregation in West Africa," *American Historical Review* 91 (1986): 307–335; Robert L. Tignor, "The 'Indianization' of the Egyptian Administration under British Rule," *American Historical Review* 68 (1963): 636–661.

51 For example, L. C. Beaufort, "An Essay upon the State of Architecture and Antiquities, Previous to the Landing of the Anglo-Normans in Ireland," *Transactions of the Royal Irish Academy* 25 (1828): 101–241; Ulick J. Bourke, *The Aryan Origin of the Gaelic Race and Language, Showing the Present and Past Literary Position of Irish Gaelic* (London, 1875); Charles Vallancey: *An Essay on the Antiquity of the Irish Language: Being a Collation of the Irish with the Punic Language* (Dublin: S. Powell, 1792), and *The Ancient History of Ireland, Proved from the Sanscrit Books of the Bramins of India* (Dublin, 1797).

52 For example, John Crawfurd, *History of the Indian Archipelago: Containing an Account of the Manners, Arts, Languages, Religions, Institutions, and Commerce of Its Inhabitants*, 3 vols. (Edinburgh, 1820), and William Marsden, *Bibliotheca Marsdeniana Philologica et Orientalis* (London, 1827). Such texts are carefully contextualized in Jane Rendall, "Scottish Orientalism: From Robertson to James Mill," *Historical Journal* 25 (1982): 43–69.

53 These developments are reviewed in Tony Ballantyne, "The 'Oriental Renaissance' in the Pacific: Orientalism, Language and Ethnogenesis in the British Pacific," *Migracijske Teme: A Journal of Ethnic and Migration Studies* 15 (1999): 423–449.

54 William Marsden, "Remarks on the Sumatran Languages," *Archaelogia: Or, Miscellaneous Tracts Relating to Antiquity* 7 (1782): 154–158.

55 For example, Richard Taylor: *Our Race and Its Origin* (Auckland, 1867), and *Te ika a Maui: Or, New Zealand and Its Inhabitants*, 2d ed. (London, 1870); Octavius Hadfield, GNZ MMSS 39, Auckland Public Library.

56 See Ballantyne, *Orientalism and Race*.

2

Fortresses and Frontiers:

Beyond and Within

GARY WILDER

Unthinking French History:
Colonial Studies beyond National Identity

A proliferation of conference papers at professional meetings, journal articles, and job listings indicates that the colonial empire is consolidating as a sub-specialty of French history. Not since the feminist rewriting of the revolution has it seemed possible to undertake so much new work in a field that appears to be so thoroughly worked over.[1] But the opportunity to tell novel stories about French history also entails a responsibility to deliberate about the terms in which these stories are told. I hope in the following to provoke discussion on various existing and possible frameworks for engaging French colonial history.

Schematically, we can isolate two positions among many that are concerned with the disciplinary implications of this new interest in French colonialism. One is professionally defensive and conservative; it fears that the rise of colonial history will somehow be at the expense of traditional French history. A prominent scholar expressed this viewpoint in an invited public address to French historians delivered at a recent meeting last year.[2] Collapsing imperialism, immigration, and transnationalism, the speech warns that the academic preoccupation with "globalization" will likely mark the end of "a scholars' paradise" (whose high point was the 1970s and 1980s) in which conventional French history occupied a prominent place in U.S. colleges and universities.[3] We are told to expect diminished material resources (fewer job openings and research grants, university presses no longer interested in monographs) and new research agendas that foster "revivals . . . of older styles of historiography," such as international relations, and "a return to the historiographical general-ism that preceded the era of in-depth archivally based specialization that began around 1970."[4] In short, "the global perspective" may mean the end of French history as we know it.

This intervention does not distinguish between material processes of eco-nomic globalization and their corresponding neoliberal ideologies, on the one hand, and scholarly attempts to analyze and historicize them, on the other. While the former are indeed undermining liberal education and humanities scholarship, the latter may produce accounts that challenge the new common sense that identifies the global market with peace, prosperity, and democracy. But such work will also destabilize many key categories around which disciplinary history has been organized, such as nationality and national identity. The question then becomes whether we resist such scholarship as arriving at the expense of traditional (French) history or welcome it for refiguring the very meaning of French history. Two assumptions are contained within this defensive position. The first is that the French nation and its colonial empire are distinct entities; one makes an agonistic choice between studying one or the other. The second is that the proper object of French history is a normative nation-state in which territory, population, and state are isomorphic and where race, nationality, and citizenship entail one another.

The growing interest in the empire indicates that most French historians are not defensive about traditional French history being displaced by colonial history. On the contrary, the second position I would like heuristically to isolate embraces the colonial turn as the very future and salvation of a French history that risks becoming marginal in the American university. Witness the rising number of graduate students who enter ph.d. programs in French history with the intention of studying the imperial past. This openness to renovating French history from a colonial perspective was exemplified in a special forum published in 2000 by *French Historical Studies* (the same journal that published the address discussed above) devoted to "Teaching National and Regional History in a Global Age." It included valuable articles by colonial scholars proposing concrete ways French historians could integrate primary and secondary sources on the empire into their European history courses. Serving as literature reviews for nonspecialists and implying a methodological claim about the centrality of colonialism to French history, these essays sought to open and expand the field of national history in innovative ways.[5]

One of the pieces, by an established scholar whose work has contributed greatly to introducing colonial issues to French historians, focuses on "teaching French history as colonial history and colonial history as French history."[6] The author discusses several courses in which she sought to transform canonical narratives by integrating metropolitan and colonial history; her pedagogy thematized the way that European nations and their overseas territories intersected with and influenced each other during the modern period. In short, this revisionist approach differs markedly from the defensive position's will to treat the French nation as a strictly European entity that existed prior to and stood apart from colonialism and other "global" phenomena.

But closer attention to the objectives of these courses also reveals a danger of "teaching French history as colonial history and colonial history as French history." Core course questions included "Did those who learned French in the colonies consider themselves French? How did the French view them? What did it mean to be French during the colonial era, and what does it mean today?" The point of another course was "to explore the process of French identity formation in the modern era and so find better answers to these questions about how "Others" have historically fit into France's sense of self, home, and nation."[7] Here the desire to bring French and colonial history into conversation with one another risks domesticating the latter, whose analytic possibilities are restricted to the contours of the former. I am not making a facile accusation here about Eurocentrism; I think that it is enormously useful to rethink French history from a colonial perspective. My point rather is that the embrace of colonial history as French history often shares with the defensive position an attachment to the normative nation-state. In this case we are presented with a more complex understanding of French nationality as forged through a difficult relationship with non-European colonial subjects and postcolonial immigrants. But national identity remains the undisturbed condition and goal of historical interpretation.

In this essay I would like to address the limitations of this narrow national paradigm for analyzing French colonialism. One set of questions about national history concerns *how* we treat the relationship between the republican nation and the colonial empire. Another concerns *whether* the nation itself is an adequate category for grasping imperial history. But first I need to outline a brief genealogy of the consolidation of nation as the privileged subject of French history and colonial studies.

*   *   *

There are many ways to account for the dominance of nation-based (colonial) history in the U.S. academy until now; space does not allow me to pursue them here. These would include the way nationalist (and republican — namely, French) norms have become our intellectual common sense, as well as the historical formation of disciplinary history and its corresponding professional institutions. I would like to suggest that it is also possible to relate the current preeminence of the national paradigm to the eclipse of academic Marxism in both French history and colonial studies beginning in the 1980s. Since that time, scholarship on nations, nationality, and nationalism has exploded.[8]

There are good reasons that historians today do not often turn to Marx for a theoretical standpoint. We are familiar with the historiographical revision of a traditional Marxist interpretation of the French Revolution.[9] Accounts organized around the revolution as a transition to capitalism often depended on an anachronistic and fetishized conception of class.[10] By the 1980s, the most influential French history shifted its focus to the socially constitutive character of discourses.[11] Even the *Annales* school had redirected its analysis from material structures to *mentalités*.[12] One strand of historiography treated politics, or political culture, as an autonomous domain that had to be analyzed on its own terms.[13] Another shifted our attention to everyday practices, cultural processes, and marginalized social actors.[14]

These transformations in French historiography converged with parallel developments in colonial studies. Marxist theories of imperialism had dominated scholarship in the 1960s and 1970s.[15] Following the national independence of former colonial territories and in response to transhistorical modernization theory, there was a proliferation of research on capitalism as a world system, the development of underdevelopment, and unequal exchange leading to dependency.[16] These global-Marxist perspectives were challenged for their loose periodizations and imprecise definitions of capitalism. Critics defined world systems theory as a simple inversion of development economics that remained Eurocentric, totalizing, and functionalist. Historians challenged the idea that African, Asian, and Caribbean histories were simply effects of an inexorable global capitalism. They emphasized the contingency of capitalism outside of Europe. By showing that its features were selectively appropriated and reordered in local settings, their work also sought to restore historical agency to non-Western peoples.[17]

At the same time a new field of non-Marxist colonial studies developed in the opening provided by Said's *Orientalism*. Informed by poststructuralist theories of language and power, scholars since the 1980s have studied colonial discourses and the politics of knowledge production. They have drawn our attention to *epistemic* violence, as well as to the imbrication of colonialism and culture.[18] Another strand of colonial historiography demonstrated that "the colonizer" is not a monolithic category. These scholars studied contradictions within colonial projects and conflicts among different fractions of Europeans, often divided by class and gender.[19] Others have focused on the strategies and technologies of colonial government in local contexts or on the ways they are undermined by indigenous practices of resistance.[20] Much of this work is anxious about overgeneralization; critical of homogenizing discussions of "colonialism" as such, it demands that we pay attention to national specificity. Different national empires, we learn, had different colonial policies that led to distinct colonial societies.[21] Another important move among historians has been to focus on the formative intersections between metropolitan and colonial societies.[22] Despite their differences, these various movements away from Marxism in both French history and colonial studies have affirmed the nation as a privileged unit of analysis.

We need to ask what implications the presumptive national paradigm might have for colonial historiography now that it is being written by scholars trained in French history. Historians of France who study the empire can usefully complement the work long done by African, Asian, and Caribbean historians. By challenging clear distinctions between European and non-European history, French historians are well placed to explore the intersections between continental and colonial societies. Our work seeks to demonstrate that French national history cannot be grasped apart from the imperial context through which it was forged. But does an expanded conception of "French" history itself compel us to rethink national historiography rather than reproduce it on a wider scale?

Important research has focused on the production and circulation of colonial ideologies in metropolitan and overseas France.[23] Some of these studies have sought to link such ideology to projects of colonial rule, paying special attention to French attempts to refashion colonial societies.[24] Much of this work seeks to identify the gap between official rhetoric and colonial realities; it challenges France for failing to follow through on its own improving, civilizing, and republican promises. Valuable as such accounts surely are, they risk treating republican universalism and colonial racism as opposed to each other in order to criticize the former from the standpoint of the latter (and vice versa).[25] By accepting republicanism's own claim to be a universalism, colonial racism is then explained as the absence or failure of republicanism. Criticism is therefore directed either at a "false" universalism that is designed to mask or rationalize "real" racializing practices. Or the problem is construed in terms of a limited universalism that has not been sufficiently extended to all social groups.

This perspective thus tends to focus on contradictions *between* republicanism and colonialism or racism rather than *within* the French nation-state itself. By identifying the problem as a lack or absence of republicanism or as the failure of the nation to realize its own promises, the normative French nation remains the ultimate and untroubled referent of historical analysis. Colonial historiography then becomes a matter of examining either the way republicanism is played out in the colonies or the role of colonialism in shaping French national identity. An alternative approach would analyze the colonial context in order to reconceptualize our very understanding of universalism, republicanism, and the French nation-state. It would do so through more integrated accounts that demonstrate the intrinsic relationship among the republican nation, its universalist politics, and colonial racism. Rather than ask whether republicanism was sufficiently extended in the colonies or what impact colonialism had on national identity, colonial history could illuminate the fundamentally disjunctive relationship among race, nationality, and citizenship. It would thereby challenge, rather than reproduce, republican ideologies of the nation. Historical intersections between the nation and the empire would then not simply show the way they influenced one another but would decisively alter the meaning of each and compel us to think of them together.

I believe that these are some of the lessons we learn from the valuable work by Laurent Dubois on "republican racism" in postemancipation Guadeloupe, Elizabeth Thompson on the "colonial civic order" of Syria and Lebanon under the mandate, and Maxim Silverman on racialization and criminalization of immigration by the postcolonial republican state.[26] I too have tried to indicate these very connections in my work on "colonial humanism," "subject-citizens," and "the imperial nation-state."[27]

Colonial histories that have gone the furthest in transforming rather than simply extending national epistemologies have addressed the fluid and reciprocal relationship between metropolitan and colonial politics.[28] For example, works on the late eighteenth and early nineteenth centuries have helped us rethink the republican legacy of the French Revolution itself (including the periods immediately before and after) from an imperial perspective.[29] We could look also to Patricia Lorcin's account of the mutually constitutive relationship among colonial politics, colonial science, and metropolitan scholarship in producing the racial categories that organized nineteenth-century French Algeria.[30] Or to Alice Bullard's inquiry into the French republic's simultaneous production of political radicals and non-European natives as "savage" in New Caledonia after the Paris Commune.[31] Research on the centrality of gender and sexuality to French colonial policies has also been especially attentive to intersections between metropole and empire.[32]

In short, colonial history has the opportunity to alter our core understanding of the republican nation in the same way that feminist history did by showing us that the French republic was created not without women, but against them.[33] We learned that the postrevolutionary political order required a gendered private sphere in which citizens would be produced by republican mothers. But can we similarly claim that republican politics *required* a colonial empire and racialized subjects? I am not convinced by formulas about a society's foundational need for others. It is one thing to understand the empire and republic as mutually constitutive or to foreground the contradictions that unfold once the national state becomes imperial. It is another to say that racism and imperialism were functional necessities of republicanism. Sexism and racism occupy formally similar positions in French republican history; these differentiating processes even often work together. Yet the two should not be collapsed; they entail distinct logics and technics of domination. A critical history of republicanism is indeed indispensable if we want to understand the dynamic and dilemmas of French imperialism. But I would argue that neither nation nor republic can in themselves fully account for sustained overseas expansion, the structural links between metropole and empire, or the simultaneity and interconnections that we find across colonial empires in the modern period.

I have thus far asked whether colonial historiography refigures or simply expands a normative conception of the French nation. Here I would like to add a second and related question: What are the limitations of the national paradigm itself for grasping some of the central features of French colonial history? Is there any reason to assume that the French nation, national identity, and republicanism provide the most fruitful grids of intelligibility when studying colonialism? Perhaps an earlier emphasis on colonial political economy reduced the French civilizing mission and governing practices to a crude logic of capital.[34] But it would be at least as limiting to reduce French colonialism to nationalist desire.[35]

Take for example the period between 1789 and 1848. Important revisionist histories have demonstrated that the dynamic of the French Revolution itself was inseparable from Antillean slave labor insurrections and that the very content of republican citizenship was forged through these colonial struggles over emancipation. But do these issues also not require a regional or Atlantic understanding of the Caribbean as a network of plantation slave societies linked to each other, the United States, and Europe through a political economy with its own structure, rhythms, and tensions? Or perhaps they become intelligible only within the framework of abolitionism as a transnational social movement or the interconnected Atlantic revolutions? Alternatively, as Wallerstein argues, maybe this moment of national and colonial crisis should be folded into a story about the struggle between Britain and France for hegemony over the capitalist world system following the decline of Amsterdam's leadership.[36] Recent scholarship has demonstrated the central role non-national processes and actors — such as sailors and maritime trading networks, pan-African slave diasporas, and the formation of a transnational laboring class — have played in shaping early modern empires.[37]

The goal here is not simply to contextualize national history in terms of broader dynamics but to question the national paradigm itself. I am not only suggesting that a consideration of non-national factors will yield a fuller understanding of French colonial history (although this is certainly true). My point is that colonial analysis may mean confronting and representing processes that are not themselves national. The relevant historical units might be regional economies, diasporic communities, transnational social movements and religious formations, or even a world system, each with its own structure, contradictions, and historicity.

Here we might look to Julia Clancy-Smith's social history of populist colonial rebellions in nineteenth-century French North Africa.[38] It demonstrates that the cyclical Saharan *jihads* against an expansionist colonial state can be understood only in terms of a regional political economy and transnational Islamic ecumene in a context of imperial social transformations. Through such categories Clancy-Smith elaborates the border-crossing circuits of commodities, information, and actors that sustained these politics. Frederick Cooper's massive history of labor politics in French and British Africa leading up to decolonization is more comparative than transnational.[39] His account shows, nevertheless, that decolonization was not simply a French or British national affair. The end of empire, we learn, is intelligible only in the context of international labor policies and politics, the formation of a supranational ideology of development, and ongoing intersections not only between metropoles and their colonies, but also across French and British colonial empires.[40]

Another example with which I am more familiar is that of French West Africa after World War I. Historians have explained the emergence of an overseas reform movement in terms of the French state's new commitment to the doctrine of colonial association or the integration of the colonial administration into the broader republican civil service and the better training received by a new generation of French officials.[41] But can a French national optic account for the uncanny resemblance among new governing projects instituted in the British, French, Belgian, and Dutch empires at roughly the same time? Despite different political and economic contexts, there were new emphases across empires on native policies that promoted some combination of economic development, social welfare, and administrative knowledge of indigenous societies. Likewise, how would a republican-national framework account for the simultaneous emergence of various forms of anticolonial nativism and nationalism across the colonial empires (including the United States) at precisely this moment? What about the fact that many of these oppositional movements developed through their relationships to working-class internationalism and transnational movements such as pan-Africanism?

These examples suggest that we have no reason to invest French republicanism and national identity a priori with privileged explanatory power. We need ways to grasp the distinct spatial and temporal coordinates of these other histories as they intersect with national histories in order to study imperialism on its own terms rather than as the predicate of French history. I am not arguing that colonial scholars abandon national history. Much recent research demonstrates that French republicanism and national identity were indeed formed in relation to the colonial empire. Recent writing on the historical geography of capitalism shows that the global is often embedded in or produced through the national.[42] Fernando Coronil's recent book on the Venezuelan state, for example, shows us how a modern nation can be constructed on the material and symbolic foundation of multinational corporations and transnational capitalism.[43] But I am suggesting that writing French colonial history may require us to begin *unthinking* national historiography.[44] It is possible, as Charles Maier has recently argued, that the national history paradigm is an expression of a historically specific sociospatial configuration centered on the sovereign territorial nation-state.[45] It is not clear that we can or should simply extend established narratives, periodizations, and analytic frameworks to the colonial field without modification. Such unthinking would perhaps leave us free to wonder what it would mean to approach colonial documents from a properly imperial rather than a French national standpoint.

The Marxian tradition may provide insight into how we might develop such an analytic standpoint. In both French history and colonial studies the shift away from Marxist history has been compounded by the antifoundational critique of a universalizing social science. We have thus inherited a healthy skepticism of grand theory, structural explanations, and long-term perspectives in historical analysis.[46] This suspicion is shared by empirical microhistory, self-reflexive metahistory, and subaltern history alike. But how then are we to account, as I asked above, for nation-states' systematic overseas expansion and the structural resemblances that we find across colonial empires at certain historical conjunctures?

It would be misguided to call for the pendulum to swing back to a determinist Marxism that treats politics and culture reductively and is unable, for example, to recognize the struggles around gendering and racialization as social constitutive. We may not accept Marx's critique of political economy as an adequate description of colonial social relations. But his analysis of the immanent contradictions of capital accumulation and the crisis-prone tendencies of the system does seek to account for the expansive, globalizing dynamic of modern European societies. Likewise world systems theory may fetishize the global scale of analysis, flatten the heterogeneity of colonial societies, and diminish their impact on regional and world history.[47] And the new Marxist geography may not be able to address the specificity of metropolitan and colonial government.[48] But these currents of thought, through concepts such as international division of labor, uneven development, and spatial fix, do seek to account for the historical simultaneity and interconnections that exceed national specificity and characterize imperial formations.

I believe we can recognize the analytic power of the Marxian tradition while avoiding the traditional Marxist temptation to produce total explanations. For the interwar period, this would mean relating the emergence of similar governing projects across empires to new regimes of capital accumulation that develop simultaneously within a global framework of monopoly capitalism, state planning, economic depression, interstate rivalry, neomercantilist protectionism following World War I, and the worldwide crisis of labor discipline following the Russian Revolution.[49] This approach has its explanatory limitations. But if we choose not to recuperate the dimensions of Marxian analysis that provide global and imperial standpoints for colonial history, we then need to develop other frameworks that do equivalent analytic work.

One such alternative, or complementary approach, would draw insights from Marx's methodology but focus less on *political economy* than on the long-term characteristics of *political modernity*. Extending Marx's understanding of capitalism as producing structured social formations subject to rounds of crisis and reconfiguration, we can shift analysis away from the commodity form to the nation-state form. Without reifying "the political" or reducing it in the French case to republicanism, we can inquire into political *form*. Do tensions within the nation-state between universality and particularity, the civil and the political, democracy and rationality, parliament and administration, create a historical dynamic driven by immanent contradictions?[50] Just as scholars have identified (and debated) a series of phases within the development of capitalism, we too can trace conjunctural transformations in political rationality. Mercantilism, liberalism, welfare, and post-Fordist neoliberalism are all articulated with the form of the nation-state. But each order has its own governmental strategies, technologies, knowledge, and targets that must be studied.[51]

A long-term structural conception of the nation-state as a modern political form may help us account for the supranational simultaneity of governing projects across colonial empires during the interwar period. This would mean locating common transformations in colonial government within a more pervasive reconfiguration of the form and rationality of Western states that began in the late nineteenth century. National-state politics became increasingly oriented toward social welfare, population management, and a circular relationship among knowledge, planning, and administration.[52]

But if a world systems framework risks moving us too far from a specifically political field, this focus on the nation-state form may not be able to make subtle enough distinctions between the metropolitan and specifically colonial aspects of modern politics. We might then imagine a third possibility that would conceptualize France as an *imperial* nation-state in which the parliamentary republic and administrative empire are articulated within a single political formation. From this perspective the opposition between nation and colony or the national and transnational is refigured. Processes that often appear to us as transnational can be grasped as already national once the nation is considered on an imperial scale. Thus the formation of pan-African identifications among cultural nationalists in Paris between the wars can be seen as a civic practice through which to claim citizenship rights. Alternatively, seemingly national politics, like colonial subjects' participation in the republican public sphere between the wars, might have imperial implications, such as creating networks of pan-African solidarity that will mobilize against colonial rule.[53] This perspective would also allow us to analyze interwar colonial reforms in West Africa within the framework of an imperial nation-state seeking to reconcile republican welfare with colonial paternalism at a moment of growing material and ideological interpenetration of continental and overseas France.[54]

A final approach would entail elaborating fields and structures of modern *coloniality* that cannot be reduced to metropolitan nations.[55] It is possible that at a given time Dutch, French, and British colonial societies and forms of government had more in common with each other than they did with their respective national societies and states. Perhaps colonial history requires us to develop ways to analyze these common features of modern imperial formations in their systemic specificity. Mahmood Mamdani attempts to do this with his theory of "decentralized despotism" as a general type of African colonial government.[56] Ann Stoler offers another perspective on this issue when she points out the ways that practices of comparison between and borrowings across empires were themselves features of colonial policy making.[57]

This last perspective would help us address the emergence between the wars of an international reform movement among administrators across colonial empires. The institutional and ideological formation created through a web of organizations, journals, readerships, conferences, and colonial expositions focused on new practices of colonial administration in British, French, Dutch, and Belgian colonies; it would have to be analyzed in its own right. Likewise we would treat the international communist and transnational pan-Africanist networks spanning Europe, the United States, and the colonial empires — not restricted to national political spaces — as the matrix out of which anticolonial movements developed after World War I. Poststructuralism has taught us to reinterpret capitalism through non-Marxist categories such as discourse, culture, and desire. In contrast, I propose that modified Marxian frameworks can help us understand the noncapitalist dimensions of our political modernity through an imperial optic.

Of course such broad non-national frameworks risk obscuring qualitative differences among national colonial policies and flattening incommensurable historical cases. Overgeneralization can be dangerous. These approaches would have to complement, locate, and modify national histories, not replace them. This is neither an apocalyptic prediction about the end of the nation-state nor a call to purge our intellectual vocabulary of national terms. As I have suggested above, fruitful research on the intersections between metropole and empire are just beginning. But I would argue that non-national analytic frameworks may allow us to recognize those intersections more clearly and represent them in ways that disrupt rather than affirm a normative relationship among territory, population, and state or race, nationality, and citizenship.

Nor am I calling here for a new multinational comparative history. Such comparisons may of course be invaluable for the kind of work I am imagining here. But it is also possible to produce thorough comparative histories without challenging the national paradigm at all. By questioning the limits of nation-based history, I am not implying that we need to add more nations as cases to our monographs. I have tried here to outline a qualitative limitation concerning the analytic framework and object of analysis, not a quantitative limitation concerning the number of national cases one needs to study before drawing more general conclusions. These remarks are less focused on what nations we study than on how we approach and understand any one of them. It would thus be possible to write non-national histories focused on a single nation-state.

It is important for us to draw on insights from other fields in order to write colonial history and revise French national history. But there is no reason that our historical research on the French empire should not contribute directly to methodological and theoretical debates on colonialism and globalization. A French colonial historiography less focused on republicanism and national identity can begin to historicize our current round of globalization by relating it to an earlier global formation of high imperialism. I believe that the short-term future of colonial studies will rest in part on this task of deepening our understanding of current globalization by relating it to imperialism.

The goal of these manifold reflections has been to suggest that *unthinking* national history may help us identify other historical optics. Colonial history written from a global or imperial perspective may enable us to *rethink* dominant narratives of French national history. Our project then would be not only to expand the field of French history to include the empire, but also to destabilize and reorder that field itself. By studying the French empire on its own terms, we can recognize the French nation as *a feature, not a container*, of imperial history.

Notes

Earlier versions of this paper were presented at the Western Society for French History meetings in Los Angeles, November 2000, and the conference on Post-Colonial Studies: Regards croisés France/États Unis in Paris, May 2001. For their helpful comments on this paper I would like to thank Andrew Aisenberg, Antoinette Burton, Rachel Lindheim, Kevin Platt, Ann Stoler, and, for the numerous conversations about French colonialism that we have had over the years, Laurent Dubois.

1 Joan Landes, *Women and the Public Sphere in the Age of the French Revolution* (Ithaca, N.Y.: Cornell University Press, 1988); Christine Fauré, *Democracy without Women: Feminism and the Rise of Liberal Individualism in France* (Bloomington: Indiana University Press, 1991); Geneviève Fraisse, *Reason's Muse: Sexual Difference and the Birth of Democracy* (Chicago: University of Chicago Press, 1994); Dorinda Outram, *The Body and the French Revolution: Sex, Class, and Political Culture* (New Haven, Conn.: Yale University Press, 1989); Lynn Hunt, *The Family Romance of the French Revolution* (Berkeley: University of California Press, 1993); Joan Wallach Scott, "French Feminists and the Rights of 'Man,'" *History Workshop* 28 (1989): 1–21; Sean Reynolds, ed., *Women, State, and Revolution: Essays on Power and Gender in Europe since 1789* (Brighton: Wheatsheaf Books, 1986). See also Carole Pateman, *The Sexual Contract* (Stanford, Calif.: Stanford University Press, 1988).

2 Jan Goldstein, "The Future of French History in the United States: Unapocalyptic Thoughts for the New Millennium," *French Historical Studies* 24, 1 (winter 2001): 1–10.

3 Ibid., p. 7.

4 Ibid., pp. 7, 8.

5 "Forum: Teaching National and Regional History in a Global Age," *French Historical Studies* 23, 2 (spring 2000): 215–238.

6 Alice L. Conklin, "Boundaries Unbound: Teaching French History as Colonial History and Colonial History as French History," *French Historical Studies* 23, 2 (spring 2000): 215–238.

7 Ibid., p. 224.

8 Obvious touchstones amid the voluminous literature include Benedict Anderson, *Imagined Communities: Reflections on the Origin and Spread of Nationalism*, 2d ed. (London: Verso, 1991); Rogers Brubaker, *Citizenship and Nationhood in France and Germany* (Cambridge, Mass.: Harvard University Press, 1992); Ernest Gellner, *Nations and Nationalism* (Ithaca, N.Y.: Cornell University Press, 1983); Anthony Giddens, *The Nation-State and Violence* (Berkeley: University of California Press, 1987); Eric Hobsbawm, *Nations and Nationalism since 1780* (Cambridge: Cambridge University Press, 1990); Anthony D. Smith, *National Identity (Ethnonationalism in Comparative Perspective)* (London: Penguin, 1991). See also the essays collected in Gopal Balakrishnan, ed., *Mapping the Nation* (London: Verso, 1996), and Geoff Eley and Ronald Grigor Suny, eds., *Becoming National: A Reader* (London: Oxford University Press, 1996).

9 For examples of standard Marxist interpretations, see Georges Lefebvre, *The Coming of the French Revolution* (Princeton, N.J.: Princeton University Press, 1947), and Albert Soboul, *A Short History of the French Revolution, 1789–1899* (Berkeley: University of California Press, 1977). For an overview of revisionist historiography of the revolution, see Gary Kates, "Introduction," in *The French Revolution: Recent Debates and New Controversies*, ed. Gary Kates (London: Routledge, 1998). For an elaboration of the idea of "traditional Marxism," see Moishe Postone, *Time, Labor, and Social Domination: A Reinterpretation of Marx's Critical Theory* (Cambridge: Cambridge University Press, 1993).

10 For an expanded understanding of class that rejects the revolution as a conflict between bougeoisie and nobility, see Colin Lucas, "Nobles, Bourgeois, and the Origins of the French Revolution," *Past and Present* 60 (August 1973): 84–126.

11 See, for example, *François Furet, Interpreting the French Revolution* (London: Cambridge University Press, 1981); Lynn Hunt, *Politics, Culture, and Class in the French Revolution* (Berkeley: University of California Press, 1984); William H. Sewell Jr., *Work and Revolution in France: The Language of Labor from the Old Regime to 1848* (Cambridge: Cambridge University Press, 1980).

12 Immanuel Wallerstein, "Fernand Braudel, Historian, '*homme de la conjoncture,*'" in Immanuel Wallerstein, *Unthinking Social Science: The Limits of Nineteenth-Century Paradigms* (Cambridge: Polity Press, 1991). See also the historiographical essays collected in Jacques Revel and Lynn Hunt, eds., *Histories: French Constructions of the Past* (New York: New Press, 1995).

13 Keith Michael Baker, ed., *The French Revolution and the Creation of Modern Political Culture,* vol. 1: *The Political Culture of the Old Regime* (London: Oxford University Press, 1987); Colin Lucas, ed., *The French Revolution and the Creation of Modern Political Culture,* vol. 2: *The Political Culture of the French Revolution* (London: Oxford University Press, 1988); Mona Ozouf, *Festivals and the French Revolution* (Cambridge: Cambridge University Press, 1988); Keith Michael Baker, *Inventing the French Revolution: Essays on French Political Culture in the Eighteenth Century* (London: Cambridge University Press, 1990); Roger Chartier, *The Cultural Origins of the French Revolution* (Durham, N.C.: Duke University Press, 1991).

14 Louise A. Tilly and Joan W. Scott, *Women, Work, and Family* (New York: Holt, Rinehart, and Winston, 1978); Joan Wallach Scott: *Glassworkers of Carmaux: French Craftsmen and Political Action in a Nineteenth-Century City* (Cambridge, Mass.: Harvard University Press, 1980), and *Gender and the Politics of History* (New York: Columbia University Press, 1988); Bonnie G. Smith, *Ladies of the Leisure Class* (Princeton, N.J.: Princeton University Press, 1981); Natalie Zemon Davis, *Society and Culture in Early Modern France* (Stanford, Calif.: Stanford University Press, 1987); Katherine A. Lynch, *Family, Class, and Ideology in Early Industrial France: Social Policy and the Working-Class Family, 1825–1848* (Madison: University of Wisconsin Press, 1988); Lynn Hunt, *The New Cultural History* (Berkeley: University of California Press, 1989); Rachel Fuchs, *Poor and Pregnant in Paris: Strategies for Survival in the Nineteenth Century* (New Brunswick, N.J.: Rutgers University Press, 1992); Mary Louise Roberts, *Civilization without Sexes: Reconstructing Gender in Postwar France, 1917–1927* (Chicago: University of Chicago Press, 1994); Laura Lee Downs, *Manufacturing Inequality: Gender Division in the French and British Metalworking Industries, 1914–1939* (Ithaca, N.Y.: Cornell University Press,1995); Leora Auslander, *Taste and Power: Furnishing Modern France* (Berkeley: University of California Press, 1996); Judith Coffin, *The Politics of Women's Work: The Paris Garment Trades, 1750–1915* (Princeton, N.J.: Princeton University Press, 1996).

15 For an overview, see Anthony Brewer, *Marxist Theories of Imperialism: A Critical Survey* (London: Routledge, 1980).

16 André Gunder Frank, *Capitalism and Underdevelopment in Latin America* (New York: Monthly Review Press, 1969); Immanuel Wallerstein: *The Modern World System,* vol. 1: *Capitalist Agriculture and the Origins of the European World-Economy in the Sixteenth Century* (New York: Academic Press, 1974), and *The Capitalist World Economy: Essays* (Cambridge: Cambridge University Press, 1979); Samir Amin, *Accumulation on a World Scale: A Critique of the Theory of Underdevelopment* (New York: Monthly Review Press, 1974); Arrighi Emmanuel, *Unequal Exchange: A Study of the Imperialism of Trade* (New York:

Monthly Review Press, 1972); Fernand Braudel, *Capitalism and Civilization*, vol. 3: *The Perspective of the World* (New York: Harper and Row, 1984).

17 See Frederick Cooper's extensive review and critique of world systems scholarship: "Africa and the World Economy," in *Confronting Historical Paradigms: Peasants, Labor, and the Capitalist World System in Africa and Latin America*, ed. Frederick Cooper, Allen Isaacman, Florencia Mallon, and William Roseberry (Madison: University of Wisconsin Press, 1993), and "Conflict and Connection: Rethinking Colonial African History," *American Historical Review* 99 (1994): 1516–1545. On the agency of the colonized, see James C. Scott, *Weapons of the Weak: Everyday Forms of Peasant Resistance* (New Haven, Conn.: Yale University Press, 1985); Jean Comaroff, *Body of Power, Spirit of Resistance: The Culture and History of a South African People* (Chicago: University of Chicago Press, 1985); Ranajit Guha and Gayatri Chakravorty Spivak, eds. *Selected Subaltern Studies* (New York: Oxford University Press, 1988); Dipesh Chakrabarty, *Rethinking Working Class History: Bengal 1890–1940* (Princeton, N.J.: Princeton University Press, 1989). For attempts to articulate the analysis of global capitalism and local social anthropology within a world systems perspective, see Eric Wolf, *Europe and the People without History* (Berkeley: University of California Press, 1982); Sidney Mintz, *Sweetness and Power: The Place of Sugar in Modern History* (New York: Penguin, 1985).

18 Examples include Edward Said: *Orientalism* (New York: Vintatge, 1978), and *Culture and Imperialism* (New York: Knopf, 1993); Michael Taussig, *Shamanism, Colonialism, and the Wild Man: A Study in Terror and Healing* (Chicago: University of Chicago Press, 1987); Timothy Mitchell, *Colonizing Egypt* (Cambridge: Cambridge University Press,1988); Bernard S. Cohn: *An Anthropologist among the Historians and Other Essays* (Delhi: Oxford University Press, 1990), and *Colonialism and Its Forms of Knowledge: The British in India* (Princeton, N.J.: Princeton University Press, 1996); Nicholas B. Dirks, ed., *Colonialism and Culture* (Ann Arbor: University of Michigan Press, 1992); Partha Chatterjee: *Nationalist Thought in the Colonial World: A Derivative Discourse?* (Minneapolis: University of Minnesota Press, 1993), and *The Nation and Its Fragments: Colonial and Postcolonial Histories* (Princeton, N.J.: Princeton University Press, 1993); Nicholas Thomas, *Colonialism's Culture: Anthropology, Travel and Government* (Princeton, N.J.: Princeton University Press, 1994); Ann Laura Stoler, *Race and the Education of Desire: Foucault's History of Sexuality and the Colonial Order of Things* (Durham, N.C.: Duke University Press, 1995).

19 Frederick Cooper and Ann Laura Stoler, "Between Metropole and Colony: Rethinking a Research Agenda," in *Tensions of Empire: Colonial Cultures in a Bourgeois World*, ed. Frederick Cooper and Ann Laura Stoler (Berkeley: University of California Press, 1997); Ann Laura Stoler: "Sexual Affronts and Racial Frontiers: European Identities and the Cultural Politics of Exclusion in Colonial Southeast Asia," in Cooper and Stoler, eds., *Tensions of Empire*, and "Carnal Knowledge and Imperial Power: Gender, Race, and Morality in Colonial Asia," in *Gender at the Crossroads of Knowledge: Feminist Anthropology in the Postmodern Era*, Micaela de Leonardo (Berkeley: University of California Press, 1991).

20 Paul Rabinow, *French Modern: Norms and Forms of the Social Environment* (Chicago: University of Chicago Press, 1989); John L. and Jean Comaroff, *Of Revelation and Revolution*, vol. 1: *Christianity, Colonialism, and Consciousness in South Africa*, and vol. 2: *The Dialectics of Modernity on a South African Frontier* (Chicago: University of Chicago Press, 1991, 1997); Guha and Spivak, eds., *Selected Subaltern Studies*; Cohn, *An Anthropologist among the Historians*.

21 Cooper and Stoler, "Between Metropole and Colony"; Rabinow, *French Modern*; Frederick Cooper, *Decolonization and African Society: The Labor Question in French and British Africa* (Cambridge: Cambridge University Press, 1996).

22 See, for example, Wolf, *Europe and the People without History*; Mintz, *Sweetness and Power*; Rabinow, *French Modern*; Thomas C. Holt, *The Problem of Freedom: Race, Labor, and Politics in Jamaica and Britain, 1832–1938* (Baltimore: Johns Hopkins University Press, 1992); Ranajit Guha, *A Rule of Property for Bengal: An Essay on the Idea of Permanent Settlement* (Durham, N.C.: Duke University Press, 1996); Cooper and Stoler, "Between Metropole and Colony"; Stoler, *Race and the Education of Desire*; Comaroff and Comaroff, eds., *Of Revelation and Revolution*, vol. 2; John and Jean Comaroff, "Homemade Hegemony," in their collection, *Ethnography and the Historical Imagination* (Boulder, Colo.: Westview Press, 1992); Said, *Culture and Imperialism*; Nicholas B. Dirks, "Introduction: Colonialism and Culture," in Dirks, ed., *Colonialism and Culture*; Antoinette Burton, *Burdens of History: British Feminists, Indian Women, and Imperial Culture, 1865–1915* (Chapel Hill: University of North Carolina Press, 1994).

23 Earlier touchstones include Raymond Betts, *Assimilation and Association in French Colonial Theory* (New York: Columbia University Press, 1961); Raoul Girardet, *L'Idée coloniale en France de 1781 à 1962* (Paris: La Table Ronde, 1972); Charles-Robert Ageron, *France coloniale ou parti colonial?* (Paris: PUF, 1978); William B. Cohen, *The French Encounter with Africans: White Response to Blacks 1530–1880* (Bloomington: Indiana University Press, 1980); William Schneider, *An Empire for the Masses: The French Popular Image of Africa, 1870–1900* (Westport, Conn.: Greenwood Press, 1982).

24 Michael Crowder, *Senegal: A Study of French Assimilation Policy* (London: Methuen, 1967); William B. Cohen, *Rulers of Empire: The French Colonial Service in Africa* (Stanford, Calif.: Hoover Institution/Stanford University Press, 1971). More recent work includes David Prochaska, *Making Algeria French: Colonialism in Bône, 1870–1920* (Cambridge: Cambridge University Press, 1990); Gwendolyn Wright, *The Politics of Design in French Colonial Urbanism* (Chicago: University of Chicago Press, 1991); Herman Lebovics, *True France: The Wars over Cultural Identity, 1900–1945* (Ithaca, N.Y.: Cornell University Press, 1992); Alice Conklin, *A Mission to Civilize: The Republican Idea of Empire in France and West Africa, 1895–1930* (Stanford, Calif.: Stanford University Press, 1997).

25 A good example of this tendency would be the recent book by Africanist Bernard Mouralis: *République et colonies: Entre histoire et mémoire: La République française et l'Afrique* (Paris: Présence Africaine, 1999).

26 Laurent Dubois: *Les Esclaves de la République* (Paris: Calman-Lévy, 1998), and "'The Price of Liberty': Victor Hugues and the Administration of Freedom in Guadeloupe, 1794–1798," *William and Mary Quarterly* 56, 2 (April 1999): 363–392; Elizabeth Thompson, *Colonial Citizens: Republican Rights, Paternal Privilege, and Gender in French Syria and Lebanon* (New York: Columbia University Press, 2000); Maxim Silverman, *Deconstructing the Nation: Immigration, Racism, and Citizenship in Modern France* (London: Routledge, 1992).

27 Gary Wilder: "Practicing Citizenship in Imperial Paris," in *Civil Society and the Political Imagination in Africa: Critical Perspectives*, ed. John L. and Jean Comaroff (Chicago: University of Chicago Press, 1999); "The Politics of Failure: Historicizing Popular Front Colonial Policy in French West Africa," in *French Colonial Empire and the Popular Front: Hope and Disillusion*, ed. Tony Chafer and Amanda Sackur (New York: St. Martin's Press, 1999); "Framing Greater France between the Wars," *Journal of Historical Sociology* 14, 2 (June 2001): 198–225.

28 Rabinow, *French Modern*; Lebovics, *True France*; Conklin, *A Mission to Civilize*; Cooper, *Decolonization and African Society*.

29 Besides the classic C. L. R. James, *The Black Jacobins: Toussaint L'Ouverture and the San Domingo Revolution* (New York: Vintage, 1989 [1938]), see also Robin Blackburn, *The*

Overthrow of Colonial Slavery, 1776–1848 (London: Verso, 1988); Sue Peabody, *"There Are No Slaves in France": The Political Culture of Race and Slavery in the Ancien Régime* (London: Oxford University Press, 1996); Carolyn E. Fick, "The French Revolution in Saint Domingue: A Triumph or a Failure?" in *A Turbulent Time: The French Revolution and the Greater Caribbean*, ed. David Barry Gaspar and David Patrick Geggus (Bloomington: Indiana University Press, 1997); Dubois: *Les Esclaves de la République*, and "'The Price of Liberty'"; John Garrigus, "White Jacobins, Black Jacobins: Bringing the Haitian and French Revolutions Together in the Classroom," *French Historical Studies* 23, 2 (spring 2000): 259–275.

30 Patricia Lorcin, *Imperial Identities: Stereotyping, Prejudice, and Race in Colonial Algeria* (London: I. B. Tauris, 1995).

31 Alice Bullard, *Exile to Paradise: Savagery and Civilization in Paris and the South Pacific, 1790–1900* (Stanford, Calif.: Stanford University Press, 2000).

32 Stoler: "Carnal Knowledge and Imperial Power," and "Sexual Affronts and Racial Frontiers"; the French essays in Julia Clancy-Smith and Frances Gouda, eds., *Domesticating the Empire: Race, Gender, and Family Life in French and Dutch Colonialism* (Charlottesville: University Press of Virginia, 1998); Françoise Vergès, *Monsters and Revolutionaries: Colonial Family Romance and Métissage* (Durham, N.C.: Duke University Press, 1999); Owen White, *Children of the French Empire: Miscegenation and Colonial Society in French West Africa, 1895–1960* (London: Oxford University Press, 2000).

33 Landes, *Women and the Public Sphere.*

34 See, for example, Jean Suret-Canal, *Afrique noire: L'Ère colonial, 1900–1945* (Paris: Éditions Sociales, 1962); Catherine Coquery-Vidrovitch, *Le Congo au temps des grandes compagnies concessionaires, 1898–1930* (Paris: Mouton, 1972).

35 See Henri Brunshwig, *French Colonialism, 1870–1914: Myths and Realities* (London: Pall Mall, 1966). Notable exceptions that are not Marxist but thematize political economy include Jacques Marseille, *Empire colonial et capitalisme français: Histoire d'un divorce* (Paris: Albin Michel, 1984), and Cooper, *Decolonization and African Society.*

36 Wallerstein, "The French Revolution as a World Historical Event," in Wallerstein, *Unthinking Social Science.*

37 See, for example, Paul Gilroy, *The Black Atlantic: Modernity and Double Consciousness* (Cambridge, Mass.: Harvard University Press, 1993); Marcus Rediker, *Between the Devil and the Deep Blue Sea: Merchant Seamen, Pirates, and the Anglo-American Maritime World, 1700–1750* (Cambridge: Cambridge University Press, 1987); Peter Linebaugh and Marcus Rediker, *The Many-Headed Hydra: Sailors, Slaves, Commoners, and the Hidden History of the Revolutionary Atlantic* (Boston: Beacon Press, 2000); Jacqueline Nassy Brown: "Enslaving History: Narratives on Local Whiteness in a Black Atlantic Port," *American Ethnologist* 27, 2 (May 2000); "Black Liverpool, Black America and the Gendering of Diasporic Space," *Cultural Anthropology* 13, 3 (August 1998); Julius Sherrard Scott III, "The Common Wind: Currents of Afro-African Communications in the Era of the Haitian Revolution" (Ph.D. dissertation, Duke University, 1986). For comparison, see also Robin Blackburn, *The Making of New World Slavery: From the Baroque to the Modern 1492–1800* (London: Verso, 1997).

38 Julia Clancy-Smith, *Rebel and Saint: Muslim Notables, Populist Protest, Colonial Encounters: Algeria and Tunisia, 1800–1904* (Berkeley: University of California Press, 1994).

39 Cooper, *Decolonization and African Society.*

40 See also the essays in Frederick Cooper and Randall Packard, eds., *International Development and the Social Sciences: Essays on the History and Politics of Knowledge* (Berkeley: University of California Press, 1997).

41 Conklin, *A Mission to Civilize*; Cohen, *Rulers of Empire*.

42 Saskia Sassen: "Spatialities and Temporalities of the Global," *Public Culture* 12, 1 (2000); "Embedding the Global in the National: Implications for the Role of the State," in *States and Sovereignty in the Global Economy*, ed. David A. Smith, Dorothy J. Solinger, and Steven C. Topik (London: Routledge, 1999); Neil Brenner, "Global, Fragmented, Hierarchical: Henri Lefebvre's Geographies of Globalization," *Public Culture* 10, 1 (1997): 135–167.

43 Fernando Coronil, *The Magical State: Nature, Money, and Modernity in Venezuela* (Chicago: University of Chicago Press, 1997). See also Walter D. Mignolo, *Local Histories, Global Designs: Coloniality, Subaltern Knowledges, and Border Thinking* (Princeton: Princeton University Press, 2000).

44 I borrow "unthinking" from Wallerstein, *Unthinking Social Science*, pp. 1–4.

45 Charles Maier, "Consigning the Twentieth Century to History: Alternative Narratives for the Modern Era," *American Historical Review*, 105, 3 (June 2000): 807–831. Maier's provocative argument rightly asks us to recognize the relationship between intellectual paradigms and sociospatial structures. But his account is one-sided, focused exclusively on recent processes of deterritorialization rather than their relationship with simultaneous processes of reterritorialization. For a more integrated approach, see Neil Brenner, "Beyond State-Centrism? Space, Territoriality, and Geographical Scale in Globalization Studies," *Theory and Society* 28 (1999): 39–78.

46 For defenses of this approach, see Charles Tilly, *Big Structures, Large Processes, Huge Comparisons* (New York: Russell Sage Foundation, 1984), and Immanuel Wallerstein, *The Essential Wallerstein* (New York: New Press, 2000).

47 Giovanni Arrighi, *The Long Twentieth Century: Money, Power, and the Origins of Our Times* (London: Verso, 1994); Giovanni Arrighi and Beverly J. Silver, *Chaos and Governance in the Modern World-System* (Minneapolis: University of Minnesota Press, 1999).

48 Henri Lefebvre, *The Production of Space* (London: Blackwell, 1991); David Harvey: *The Urban Experience* (Baltimore: Johns Hopkins University Press, 1989), and *Limits to Capital* (London: Verso, 1999).

49 For analyses of the historical interconnections among state forms, accumulation strategies, and hegemonic projects, see Bob Jessop, *State Theory: Putting Capitalist States in Their Place* (University Park: Pennsylvania State University Press, 1990). David Harvey summarizes theorists who relate regimes of accumulation to modes of political regulation in *The Condition of Postmodernity* (Cambridge: Blackwell, 1989). For the use of "entwinement" to describe nonreductive interconnections between the economic and political levels of society in modern European history, see Michael Mann, *The Sources of Social Power*, vol. 2: *The Rise of Classes and Nation-States 1760–1914* (Cambridge: Cambridge University Press, 1993). On the labor indiscipline and the capitalist state during this period, see Antonio Negri, "Keynes and the Capitalist Theory of the State," in Antonio Negri and Michael Hardt, eds., *Labor of Dionysus: A Critique of the State-Form* (Minneapolis: University of Minnesota Press, 1994).

50 On these tensions, see Hannah Arendt, *Origins of Totalitarianism* (New York: Harcourt, Brace, Jovanovich, 1951); Pierre Rosanvallon: *L'État en France de 1789 à nos jours* (Paris: Éditions du Seuil, 1990), and *Le Sacre du citoyen: L'Histoire du suffrage universel en France* (Paris: Gallimard, 1992); Etienne Balibar and Immanuel Wallerstein, *Race, Nation, Class: Ambiguous Identities* (London: Verso, 1992); Etienne Balibar: *Les Frontières de la démocratie* (Paris: Éditions de la Découverte, 1992), and *Masses, Classes, Ideas: Studies on Politics and Philosophy before and after Marx* (New York: Routledge, 1994).

51 This approach would entail reading people like Arendt, Balibar, Ewald, Foucault, Lefort, and Rosanvallon alongside Marxist state theorists like Jessop, Offe, Negri, and Poulantzas.

52 For this kind of approach, see Gary Wilder, "The French Imperial Nation-State: Colonial Humanism, Negritude, and Interwar Political Rationality" (book mauscript in progress). On political rationality, see Michel Foucault: "The Subject and Power," in *Michel Foucault: Beyond Structuralism and Hermeneutics*, ed. Hubert Dreyfus and Paul Rabinow (Chicago: University of Chicago Press, 1982); his course descriptions in *Résumé des cours, 1970–1982* (Paris: Julliard, 1989); "The Political Technologies of Individuals," in *Technologies of the Self*, ed. Luther H. Martin, Huck Gutman, and Patrick H. Hutton (Amherst: University of Massachusetts Press, 1988); "Omnes et Singulatim: Towards a Criticism of 'Political Reason,'" in *The Tanner Lectures on Human Values*, vol. 2 (Salt Lake City: University of Utah Press, 1981); "Governmentality," in *The Foucault Effect: Studies in Governmentality*, ed. Graham Burchell, Colin Gordon, and Peter Miller (Chicago: University of Chicago Press, 1991); "Faire vivre et laisser mourir: La Naissance du racisme," *Les Temps Modernes*, February 1991: 37–61. For explicit or implicit accounts of French political rationalities, see Rosanvallon, *L'État en France;* François Ewald, *L'État providence* (Paris: Grasset, 1986); Jacques Donzelot, *L'Invention du social: Essai sur le déclin des passions politiques* (Paris: Éditions du Seuil, 1984); Giovanna Procacci, *Gouverner la misère: La Question sociale en France, 1789–1848* (Paris: Éditions du Seuil, 1993); Sylvia Schafer, *Children in Moral Danger and the Problem of Government in Third Republic France* (Princeton, N.J.: Princeton University Press, 1997); Andrew Aisenberg, *Contagion: Disease, Government, and the "Social Question" in Nineteenth-Century France* (Stanford, Calif.: Stanford University Press, 1999).

53 See Wilder: "Practicing Citizenship in Imperial Paris"; and "Panafricanism and the Republican Political Sphere," in *The Color of Liberty: Histories of Race in France*, ed. Tyler Stovall and Sue Peabody (Durham, N.C.: Duke University Press, forthcoming).

54 Wilder, "The French Imperial Nation-State."

55 For a differently inflected discussion of "coloniality," see Walter Mignolo: *Local Histories, Global Designs*, and "The Many Faces of Cosmopolis: Border Thinking and Critical Cosmopolitanism," *Public Culture* 12, 3 (fall 2000): 721–748.

56 Mahmood Mamdani, *Citizen and Subject: Contemporary Africa and the Legacy of Late Colonialism* (Princeton, N.J.: Princeton University Press, 1996).

57 Ann Laura Stoler: "Carnal Knowledge and Imperial Power"; "Colonial Aphasia and the Place of Race in France: The Politics of Comparison," keynote address at 1951–2001: Transatlantic Perspectives on the Colonial Situation conference, New York University, April 27–28, 2001; and "Tense and Tender Ties: Intimacies of Empire in North American History and (Post) Colonial Studies," *Journal of American History*, December 2001.

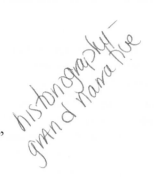

LORA WILDENTHAL

Notes on a History of "Imperial Turns" in Modern Germany

Overseas empire was a part of German national identity and popular imagination in imperial Germany, or the *Kaiserreich* (1871–1918). In fact, even a hundred years before that, "colonial fantasies" enlivened the imagination of German speakers.[1] Nevertheless, since 1918 and more clearly since 1945, colonialism's supposed absence from the German past has become a quiet but stubborn part of German identity. German postcolonial identity — that is, Germans' self-identification as actors in the global capitalist world of colonialism, then development — has been insular, even self-consciously provincial, since 1945. This is surprising given that Germans have traveled and lived all over the world and that people from all over the world have traveled to and lived in Germany. There are provincial parts of the world, but twentieth- and twenty-first-century Germany is not one of them.

Some of the most eloquent descriptions of this insular or provincial postcolonial identity have been formulated by Afro-Germans responding to white German's bafflement that Germans of color exist. In a recent documentary film on the poet May Ayim, who was born in Germany, Ayim says: "The first question is always, 'Where did you come from?' and the second question is, 'When are you leaving?'"[2] One of the uncounted tendrils of German and world history — in Ayim's case, the post–World War II circulation of African intelligentsia through German universities — had placed her and her interlocutor in the same room, the same country, and the same culture. The surprise Ayim and so many other Germans of color have encountered on the part of white or "majority Germans" (*Mehrheitsdeutsche*) itself has historical roots.[3] Two episodes in particular — the defeat of conventional overseas empire in 1918 and the defeat of the Nazi racial state in 1945 — have produced a postcolonial and post-Nazi German identity with two key features. First, from 1919 on, the colonial project of assimilating "Others" to a second-tier German status (and being faced, as European colonizers were, with individuals who demanded first-tier German status) was over. Second, from 1945 on, Germanness was no longer ideologically connected to a supranational permanent German identity that might lend global reach to German culture. In other words, the old nineteenth- and early twentieth-century nationalist dream of mobilizing overseas white Germans around the world into ambassadors for German state power was dead, and no one has wished to revive it. The postcolonial, post-Nazi German identity includes a repudiation or at least a forgetting of Germans' older imperial reach or ambition—a repudiation or amnesia so strong that it can posit a provincial twenty-first-century Germany. From a number of political standpoints, it has been easier to minimize the history of German interactions with people around the world and to be surprised when confronted with evidence of Germany's economic and cultural reach.

While the contours of this postcolonial, post-Nazi identity can be explored through many different sources, this essay will focus on successive eras in the memory of German colonialism and on the historiographical treatment of German colonialism by historians in Germany and in English-speaking countries. Given that national and racial identities have been shaped historically to a great extent by state rule and bureaucratic practice, formal empire offers a good context for examining them. The context of formal colonialism also offers a way to anchor racist ideas in a specific legal, social, and economic setting, which helps prevent them from appearing as free-floating, decontextualized essences in their own right. In and out of colonial projects, who has held racist ideas and what kind of power they had to implement their ideas has made all the difference to persons' lives and liberties. The historiography of German colonialism not only offers us valuable analyses of questions of race, power, and economic inequality, but also has itself been shaped by the different phases of German postcolonial and post-Nazi identity.

Between 1884 and 1900, Germany gained a colonial empire of about 1 million square miles and about 12 million inhabitants in Africa and the Pacific. It was the third largest in territory and fifth largest in population among the British, French, Dutch, Belgian, U.S., Portuguese, Italian, and Spanish overseas empires.[4] States today whose lands were wholly or partly under German colonial rule include Namibia, Tanzania, Togo, Cameroon, Nigeria, Ghana, Rwanda, Burundi, Papua New Guinea, the Republic of the Marshall Islands, the Republic of Nauru, China, the Northern Mariana Islands, Palau, the Federated State of Micronesia, and Western Samoa. It is true that German investment and settlement in other lands, such as Southeastern Europe or the United States, far overshadowed those in the German colonial empire. Rather than turning our attention away from the German colonial empire, however, this observation ought to make us ask more questions, such as why such non-colonial overseas social and economic ties have *also* never been really integrated into the main historiography on Germany. That is, history writing remains overwhelmingly defined by the nation-state.

In fact, there is a rich historical literature on German colonialism, produced during and since the colonial era—richer than even many historians of Germany suspect. It is not always easy to find; a lot of German history is to be found under the rubric of Pacific history or in Africana collections or has been written by geographers, anthropologists, literary scholars, and feminist scholars, as well as by historians. This work can be frustrating for historians of Germany to use because much of it does not weave together the colony and metropole in the analysis of its chosen themes. In spite of that rich literature, German history textbooks show an overwhelming consensus. They dismiss Germany's formal empire as a brief episode with an at most superficial impact on Germany both at the time and over the long term. In fact, eight well-known English-language textbooks on modern Germany that are in print or recently were in print reveal a trend: the newer the textbook, the more sweeping the dismissal of German colonialism in the German past.[5] If we compare Hajo Holborn's 1969 account, *A History of Modern Germany 1840–1945*, with Volker Berghahn's 1994 account, for example, we see that while Holborn's account is brief and lacks the concepts of race and gender that many people interested in colonial studies these days would look for, Holborn supplies information and arguments that readers can pursue. In the case of Berghahn's and indeed most recent textbooks, the reader would have to contradict directly what the textbook says in order to raise any questions about German colonialism. It may be that the increasing prominence of social history and the decreasing prominence of the history of foreign policy and high politics have helped produce a more provincial view of German society—even though social historians have brought us a sophisticated literature on gender, race, and class that is now being applied to work on intercultural contact and imperial domination.

Who among historians of Germany has been writing about German colonialism? The literature can be (very) roughly grouped into five categories. One is the historiography produced in the German Democratic Republic (GDR). These historians took German colonialism very seriously as part of the history of capitalist and "imperialist" (used in the largest, indeed overinflated, sense) Germany, and they enjoyed years of privileged access to the best set of archival holdings in either German state (primarily the files of the German Colonial Office).[6] For all the shortcomings of their interpretations, their knowledge of the archival sources is perhaps even now unmatched, and Western scholars have been drawing on, not to say recycling, East German historians' archival research for years. A second category comprises the basic monographs on each

German colony and on the colonial administration and agitation movement in Germany, all produced in West Germany and other Western academic settings.[7] A third category is the work produced by historians who have taken up Aimé Césaire's and Hannah Arendt's suggestions that German colonialism was a totalitarian predecessor to Nazism. These historians have often focused on the anticolonial uprising in Namibia between 1904 and 1907 that resulted in a military goal and near realization of the annihilation of all Herero, as well as extremely high fatalities among other Namibian combatant groups. They have also focused on the post-1907 expropriation, forced labor, and compulsory identification there as examples of totalitarian thinking in a colonial context.[8] A fourth, overlapping category has taken up German colonialism as a means of analyzing the cultural and political importance of race in German history, including the history of German women.[9]

None of these four categories of work on German colonialism has had remotely the same impact on the dominant narratives of German history as has a fifth category: the history of German colonialism in its guise of social imperialism. This kind of work has not only entered the dominant historiography of Germany, but has even decisively shaped it since the 1960s. Two pathbreaking books, Fritz Fischer's *Germany's Aims in the First World War*, published in Germany in 1961, and Hans-Ulrich Wehler's *Bismark and German Imperialism*, published in Germany in 1969, launched social imperialism as a paradigm for understanding German politics in the late nineteenth and early twentieth centuries.[10] The social imperialism thesis held that German politicians used imperial ambitions to gain and manipulate domestic popular consent to policies that in fact went against the interests of most Germans, especially working-class Germans. These two books used sources from the German colonial empire. Later books took up Fischer's and Wehler's arguments but no longer included material on the German colonial empire.[11] The literature on social imperialism soon gained a consistently domestic, internal focus on party-political coalitions and struggles over industrialization inside Germany. While German colonialism was, on this social imperialist model, described as insignificant, the effect of social imperialist politics within Germany was described as very great. As a result, colonialism, by way of social imperialism, became a central part of German history—but in a way that obviated reference to actual colonial affairs or to any people besides white German speakers living in Central Europe.[12] The possibility of discussing contact and exchange was thereby lost in the most widely received aspect of German colonialism.

What, historically, has produced the stubbornly non-postcolonial postcolonial German identity and, by extension, a historiography that, where it has discussed German colonialism, has stressed its insignificance, left out people of color, and turned it into a domestic political affair? These identities and perceptions themselves have a history, and scholars of German colonialism today stand within that history. Looking back from the vantage point of 2002, we view German colonialism through accreted layers of German history. Each of these layers, or eras, has lent its own meaning to German colonialism.

By 1914, and especially between 1907 and 1914, the idea of Germany as a colonial power had become a normal part of German national identity. There were many controversies within Germany about how to run the overseas empire, but no one expected it to disappear. Many people sensed that war was imminent in the early 1900s, but neither Germans nor the people living under German colonial rule foresaw that a war would mean the end of Germany's colonial empire. The Versailles Treaty of 1919, in that mixture of power politics and moralizing that was typical of the overall postwar settlement, distributed Germany's colonies as League of Nations mandates to the victors: Britain, South Africa, Portugal, Belgium, France, Australia, and Japan (Italy was otherwise compensated). Germany lost its colonial empire on the official grounds that it had been cruel to Africans, Pacific Islanders, and Chinese and that "dereliction in the sphere of colonial civilisation" made it impossible for the Allied powers to "again abandon" millions of "natives" to it.[13]

In 1919, Germany became a postcolonial society — yet not in the way that, for example, Britain and France are. Germany became a postcolonial society at the hands of other colonial powers and not primarily at the hands of colonial subjects, who had tried and failed to shake off German rule. The divergences that one may find between the German and other overseas colonial empires can often be traced, oddly, to *this* moment of the end of German colonial empire. At this moment, Germany's colonial history gained commonalities with, for instance, Spain in the wake of the Spanish-American War of 1898 or Italy during and after World War II.[14] Not only were Germany's historical experiences different from that moment onward, but the questions that historians asked and around which the historiography developed were different from those of Britain, France, or the Netherlands, for example.

The history of placing colonialism as a finished chapter in the larger German past started in 1919. Among the first actors in that history were stubbornly procolonial Germans who were committed inflexibly to revising the Versailles Treaty. Along with those who resented the displacement of ethnic Germans from the newly independent Central European states, they drifted in the late 1920s and early 1930s with a greater or lesser degree of enthusiasm for the most insistently revisionist party, the Nazis. That was not the only reaction to Versailles among colonialists, however. More flexible, pragmatic revisionists had another response that had greater importance over the long run for a lastingly white German identity and a provincial view of Germany's relationships to other peoples in the world. Even though this pragmatic response to forced decolonization in 1919 did not prevail in the early 1930s, it came again to the fore during the next period of defeat and crisis, after 1945.

The flexible revisionists put forward two ideas. One was that colonizers were white, Germans were white, and white people should stick together. The idea was not new, for both rivalry and solidarity had characterized the modern European colonial powers. Already during the negotiations over the Versailles Treaty, proposals appeared for the inclusion of Germany in the oversight commissions for the former German colonies and even in projected commissions to oversee all European-ruled colonies. Even if Germany were to lose its own overseas empire, these flexible revisionists argued, Germans as whites and civilized people ought to share in a pan-European alliance of colonizers against the nonwhite rest. In 1920 the former governor of German Samoa and former colonial secretary Wilhelm Solf expressed this idea as he called for European cooperation in the development of Africa. Solf argued that since abuses had existed in all the European overseas empires, all colonies and not just the formerly German ones ought to be placed under boards of international oversight.[15] Later in the decade, as the idea of German participation in international monitoring groups gained ground, some Germans questioned the need for individual states' overseas possessions, as previously conceived of, at all. Instead, they proposed a collective European colonialist and economic exploitation of non-European areas.[16]

The second response of the pragmatic revisionists to forced decolonization was that Germans, having suffered humiliating defeat, had a special knowledge of what it meant to be victims and even a sort of moral virtue deriving from that victim status. For example, the feminist and social imperialist Else Lüders conceded in a 1920 brochure aimed at newly enfranchised German women that defeat in World War I had shattered the "beautiful dreams of a greater Germany with a strong, well-rounded colonial empire."[17] Yet, she claimed, "Germany is called upon, precisely by virtue of its suffering and its tragic fate, to become the leader in the struggle for a new moral and social order in national and international life."[18] Lüders envisioned this role of international moral leadership as a unifying experience for Germans. She urged that all Germans, from western and eastern Germany as well as from the former colonies, stick together, and she alluded to a century-old worry that Germans living abroad were too ready to assimilate to other cultures:

Now we too have to *pass the test of our Germanness*. All too often through the centuries, the German has suffered from losing his Germanness much too rapidly, from always fertilizing lands with culture but only on behalf of foreign states. Now at this time of need we must prove more than ever our loyalty to Germandom. Then one day again — God grant by the peaceful path of an agreement — that will come together which belongs to Germany as *one* people [das zusammenfinden, was als *ein* Volk zu Deutschland gehört].[19]

Lüders, like Solf, supported the restoration of Germany's colonies to German rule and the simultaneous placement of all colonies under League of Nations oversight. Germany would then administer its colonies as "deputy" of the League of Nations.[20]

The proposals of Solf, Lüders, and others were symptomatic of a new white colonizing role to be mediated by "international" (but de facto European or neo-European) institutions.[21] At the same time, social scientists in the Weimar Republic produced scholarship that positioned Germans as partners in a larger "white" civilizational mission over "black" people supposedly needing guidance.[22] This white or pan-European colonizing identity might have replaced the German colonizing identity of the pre–World War I imperial German era. Although inspired by very different political goals, it was not so different from a proposal by members of the Pan-African Congress of 1919 for direct League of Nations administration of the former German colonies.[23] And the German proposals were couched in the language of humanitarianism and welfare that was typical of interwar colonial discourse in all the European empires. However, the joint white colonizing identity did not prevail in the 1930s; imperial metropoles remained states and not interstate organizations.

In addition to the moment of German decolonization imposed by other colonial powers in 1919, it was the advent of Nazism that has most strongly shaped retrospective perceptions of German colonialism. Germany's forced decolonization was not a high priority of Hitler's, but neither did he ignore it.[24] In one sense, Nazism can be understood as a rejection of colonialism as a project of white international cooperation and a choice for competition with other colonial powers over which metropole or nation-state would be the most internally racially pure and disciplined. The question of how to relate German colonial empire to Nazism has shaped the historiography of German colonialism, while the very different question of how to relate overseas empire to liberalism has shaped the historiographies of British and French colonialism. Seeing German colonialism through the lens of Nazism and the Holocaust has led to two general approaches to the history of German racism. One of these approaches is to ignore, for example, anti-African racism in exploring the history of racism that led up to the Holocaust. That carries the implication that while anti-Semitism does need explanation, racism against Africans and other non-Europeans does not. The other of these approaches is to collapse all forms of racism together. To do so, however, assumes that racism against Africans, Pacific Islanders, or Chinese, for example, necessarily sheds light on anti-Semitism. But that is something to be established through contextualized research and not taken as given, as if forms of racism exist as abstract essences amenable to neat typologies. Collapsing forms of racism together analytically also raises the problem of why, for example, anti-African racism is related to genocide when expressed and implemented by Germany but not when it is expressed and implemented by Britain, Belgium, France, or Italy.

It is so difficult (and also so interesting) to analyze relationships between colonialism and Nazism precisely because of the differences between the two. Colonialism was (and is) much more eclectic in the political views that it encompassed than Nazism or fascism.[25] Indeed, colonialism is probably better compared to capitalism or racism than to fascism. Colonialism, capitalism, and racism are all large, complex, flexible systems within which we live, whether we live in democracies or dictatorships and whether we live in the nineteenth, twentieth, or twenty-first centuries. Colonialism has flourished under all kinds of regimes, as fascism could not. The history of colonialism, like capitalism, does not deliver simple lessons. There is no single interpretation of colonialism that can be the key to German history; German colonialism is not a mirror we can hold up to a putative German national character. German colonialism provided instances both like and unlike Nazism and the Holocaust, and it was both like and unlike other modern European empires and the United States of its day.

After World War II, the European metropoles began to lose their grip on the colonies. During that same era, the idea of Germans as whites survived its Nazi appropriation and became stabilized in a post-Nazi, democratic West Germany. The GDR, meanwhile, posited its own discontinuity from the German bourgeois imperialist and fascist past (and the history of racism against people of color in the GDR is just now beginning to be written). In one post-1945 manifestation of that stubborn white identity, the children of African American GIs and white West German mothers were deemed permanently unassimilable to German society and were, where possible, sent for adoption to the United States. At the same time, other West Germans saw these children's continued presence in the Federal Republic as a means of proving the absence of racism there.[26] Even as the Holocaust became a global symbol for the importance of antiracism, Hitler's legacy was a Germany that was ideologically, if not absolutely de facto, "without Jews" and "white."[27] Contact, mixing, and assimilation were thought to be elsewhere or, at worst, making threatening incursions into Germany, as the key word "Americanization" suggested.[28]

More recently, a lasting wave of racist violence against people of color and people from poor countries in West Germany and post-1990 Germany has shaped the perception of German colonialism and its legacies. Discussion of connections between racism in the Federal Republic and Germany's colonial past extends back at least to 1984, the centenary of the first German colonial annexations. Since that time, a number of valuable books have appeared that analyze current racism against people of color in Germany through histories of colonial and postcolonial encounters.[29] Through these books and through occasional press articles about Kiao Chow, Namibia, and other places once under German colonial rule, Germans have discovered and rediscovered their colonial past and the history of German contacts all over the world.[30]

Yet the stubbornly white German identity remains. It seems to draw upon an odd assortment of sources: insularity, victim status, and the desire for the moral high ground—or its opposite, the special guilt of an exceptional and extraordinary German racism, which comprises the analysis of some of the oppositional histories of German colonialism.[31] The questions posed during various eras of memory (or amnesia) about German colonialism are not likely to go away; rather, they will continue to accrete. The challenge for both readers and writers of the historiography of German colonialism is to work against making German colonialism stand in for things it cannot explain and yet at the same time discern how it has affected, through silences as well as loud statements, other aspects of German history.

Notes

1 Susanne Zantop, *Colonial Fantasies: Conquest, Family, and Nation in Precolonial Germany, 1770–1870* (Durham, N.C.: Duke University Press, 1997).
2 *Hope in My Heart: The Maria Ayim Story*, dir. Mrais Binder; dist. Third World Newsreel (Germany, 1997).
3 I have borrowed the term "majority Germans" from Gotlinde Magariba Lwanga, who uses it to refer to white, Christian, or secularized Christian Germans in her article "Deutsche, nein danke? Anmerkungen zu Staatsangehörigkeit, BürgerInnenrechten und Verfassung," in *Entfernte Verbindungen: Rassismus, Antisemitismus, Klassenunterdrückung*, ed. Ika Hügel et al. (Berlin: Orlanda Frauenverlag, 1993), pp. 260–272.
4 Wolfgang J. Mommsen, *Imperialismus: Seine geistigen, politischen und wirtschaftlichen Grundlagen; Ein Quellen- und Arbeitsbuch* (Hamburg: Hoffmann und Campe, 1977), pp. 37–38.
5 Textbooks surveyed, with the dates of the newest editions, are the following: Volker Berghahn, *Imperial Germany* (Providence, R.I.: Berghahn, 1994); Holger H. Herwig, *Hammer or Anvil? Modern Germany, 1648–Present* (Lexington, Mass.: D. C. Heath, 1994) (Herwig has written elsewhere on Germans in Venezuela); Hajo Holborn, *A History of Modern Germany 1840–1945* (Princeton, N.J.: Princeton University Press, 1969); Wolfgang J. Mommsen, *Imperial Germany 1867–1918: Politics, Culture, and Society in an Authoritarian State*, trans. Richard Deveson (New York: St. Martin's Press, 1995); Dietrich

Orlow, *A History of Modern Germany: 1871 to Present* (Englewood Cliffs, N.J.: Prentice Hall, 1999) (which contains a useful map of the colonial empire); Koppel S. Pinson, *Modern Germany: Its History and Civilization*, 2d ed. (New York: Macmillan, 1989); Peter Pulzer, *Germany 1870–1945: Politics, State Formation, and War* (New York: Oxford University Press, 1997); A. J. Ryder, *Twentieth-Century Germany from Bismarck to Brandt* (New York: Columbia University Press, 1973). Given that Mommsen is a leading historian of German imperialism, it is not surprising that his discussion is more sophisticated than the others; it is, however, focused on the domestic effects of social imperialist manipulation.

6 Some of the most important are Fritz Ferdinand Müller, *Deutschland–Zanzibar–Ostafrika* (Berlin: Rutten and Loening, 1959); Horst Drechsler, *"Let Us Die Fighting": The Struggle of the Herero and Nama against German Imperialism (1884–1915)* (London: Zed, 1980); Helmuth Stoecker, ed., *German Imperialism in Africa: From the Beginnings until the Second World War*, trans. Bernd Zöllner (Atlantic Highlands, N.J.: Humanities Press, 1986) (there is a 1991 revised German edition); and Peter Sebald, *Togo 1884–1914: Eine Geschichte der deutschen "Musterkolonie" auf der Grundlage amtlicher Quellen* (Berlin: Akademie, 1988).

7 For example, Karin Hausen, *Deutsche Kolonialherrschaft in Afrika: Wirtschaftsinteressen und Kolonialverwaltung in Kamerun vor 1914* (Freiburg i.B.: Atlantis, 1970); Peter J. Hempenstall, *Pacific Islanders under German Rule: A Study in the Meaning of Colonial Resistance* (Canberra: Australian National University Press, 1978); John Iliffe, *Tanganyika under German Rule, 1905–1912* (London: Cambridge University Press, 1969); Juhani Koponen, *Development for Exploitation: German Colonial Policies in Mainland Tanzania, 1884–1914* (Münster: Lit, 1994); John Schrecker, *Imperialism and Chinese Nationalism: Germany in Shantung* (Cambridge, Mass.: Harvard University Press, 1971); L. H. Gann and Peter Duignan, *The Rulers of German Africa, 1884–1914* (Stanford, Calif.: Stanford University Press, 1977); Horst Gründer, *Geschichte der deutschen Kolonien*, 3d rev. ed. (Paderborn: Ferdinand Schöningh, 1995). This last book has a useful, if now slightly dated, bibliography on German colonialism.

8 Aimé Césaire, *Discourse on Colonialism*, trans. Joan Pinkham (New York: Monthly Review Press, 1972), p. 14; Hannah Arendt, *The Origins of Totalitarianism*, new ed. (New York: Harcourt, Brace, Jovanovich, 1979); Helmut Bley, *Namibia under German Rule*, trans. Hugh Ridley (Hamburg: Lit, 1996); Henning Melber, "Kontinuitäten totaler Herrschaft: Völkermord und Apartheid in 'Deutsch-Südwestafrika': Zur kolonialen Herrschaftspraxis im Deutschen Kaiserreich," *Jahrbuch für Antisemitismusforschung* 1, ed. Wolfgang Benz (Frankfurt a.M.: Campus, 1992), pp. 91–116; Robert J. Gordon and Stuart Sholto Douglas, *The Bushman Myth: The Making of a Namibian Underclass*, 2d ed. (Boulder, Colo.: Westview Press, 2000), esp. p. 241; Robert J. Gordon, "The Rise of the Bushman Penis: Germans, Genitalia and Genocide," *African Studies* 57 (1998): 27–54.

9 For example, Marcia Klotz: "Global Visions: From the Colonial to the National Socialist World," *European Studies Journal* 16 (1999): 37–68, and "Memoirs from a German Colony: What Do White Women Want?" in *Eroticism and Containment: Notes from the Flood Plain*, ed. Carol Siegel and Ann Kibbey (New York: New York University Press, 1994), pp. 154–187; Pascal Grosse, *Kolonialismus: Eugenik und bürgerliche Gesellschaft in Deutschland 1850–1918* (Frankfurt a.M.: Campus, 2000); Sara Friedrichsmeyer, Sara Lennox, and Susanne Zantop, eds., *The Imperialist Imagination: German Colonialism and Its Legacy* (Ann Arbor: University of Michigan Press, 1999); Russell A. Berman, *Enlightenment or Empire: Colonial Discourse in German Culture* (Lincoln: University of Nebraska Press, 1998); Lora Wildenthal, *German Women for Empire, 1884–1945* (Durham, N.C.: Duke

University Press, 2001). The history of German anthropology has been pursuing these questions also; see, for example, H. Glenn Penny and Matti Bunzl, *Worldly Provincialism: German Anthropology in the Age of Empire* (Ann Arbor: University of Michigan Press, forthcoming).

10 Fritz Fischer, *Germany's Aims in the First World War* (New York: W. W. Norton, 1967); Hans-Ulrich Wehler, *Bismarck und der deutsche Imperialismus* (Frankfurt a.M.: Suhrkamp, 1984; reprint).

11 This literature is too vast to list. A typical example is Karl Holl and Gunther List, eds., *Liberalismus und imperialistischer Staat: Der Imperialismus als Problem liberaler Parteien in Deutschland 1890–1914* (Göttingen: Vandenhoeck and Ruprecht, 1975).

12 Two historians of social imperialism turned their work in new directions that avoided this uncoupling of actual empire from social imperialism. One is Woodruff D. Smith, who wrote the basic English-language survey of the German colonial empire, *The German Colonial Empire* (Chapel Hill: University of North Carolina Press, 1978), as well as a history of German imperialist ideology, *The Ideological Origins of Nazi Imperialism* (New York: Oxford University Press, 1986). Smith brought his knowledge of colonial science to bear in his more recent *Politics and the Sciences of Culture in Germany, 1840–1920* (New York: Oxford University Press, 1991). The other major exception is Klaus J. Bade, who wrote an important early social imperialism study, *Friedrich Fabri und der Imperialismus in der Bismarckzeit: Revolution–Depression–Expansion* (Freiburg i.B.: Atlantis, 1975); he has since written a great deal about migration, labor, and racial politics in twentieth-century Germany. See *Deutsche im Ausland — Fremde in Deutschland: Migration in Geschichte und Gegenwart* (Munich: C. H. Beck, 1992); *Ausländer–Aussiedler–Asyl: Eine Bestandsaufnahme* (Munich: C. H. Beck, 1994); and *Das Manifest der 60: Deutschland und die Einwanderung* (Munich: C. H. Beck, 1994), all authored or edited by Bade.

13 "Reply to the Allied and Associated Powers to the Observations of the German Delegation on the Conditions of Peace," June 16, 1919, in *Urkunden zum Friedensvertrage von Versailles vom 28, Juni 1919*, ed. Erster Teil, Herbert Kraus, and Gustav Rödiger (Berlin: Franz Vahlen / Hans Robert Engelmann, 1920), p. 604.

14 On Spain, see Sebastian Balfour, "The Loss of Empire, Regenerationism, and the Forging of a Myth of National Identity," in *Spanish Cultural Studies: An Introduction; The Struggle for Modernity*, ed. Helen Graham and Jo Labanyi (Oxford: Oxford University Press, 1995), pp. 25–31, and references cited therein; on Italy, see the unfortunately untranslated work of Angelo Del Boca, esp. *L'Africa nella coscienza degli Italiani: Miti, memorie, errori, sconfitte* (Rome: Laterza, 1992). I thank Mia Fuller for this and other references on Italian colonialism.

15 Wilhelm Solf, *Afrika für Europa: Der koloniale Gedanke des XX. Jahrhunderts* (Neumünster i.H.: Theodor Dittmann Verlag, 1920). Others advocating German participation in a European colonial administration included Hjalmar Schacht, who spoke of a pan-European "communal" exploitation of areas with natural resources, including Russia and Africa, to be carried out in self-conscious opposition to communism, and Kurt Weigelt, who suggested that an area from Cameroon to the Rio de Oro be administered by the United States, France, Britain, and Germany. See Adolf Rüger, "Das Streben nach kolonialer Restitution in den ersten Nachkriegsjahren," in *Drang nach Afrika: Die deutsche koloniale Expansionspolitik und Herrschaft in Afrika von den Anfängen bis zum Verlust der Kolonien*, ed. Helmuth Stoecker, rev. ed. (Berlin: Akademie, 1991), p. 271; Franz Ansprenger, *The Dissolution of the Colonial Empires* (New York: Routledge, 1989), pp. 125–126.

16 For example, "Braucht Deutschland Kolonien?" *Hamburger Monatschefte für Auswärtige Politik* 5 (1927): 609–676, and *Für oder gegen Kolonien* (Berlin, 1928). The secret German

memorandum to the council of the League of Nations on September 20, 1924, stated a willingness to join and included a request to be active in a mandate system; on September 9, 1927, a German representative joined the standing mandate commission of the League of Nations. Gründer, *Geschichte der deutschen Kolonien*, p. 223.

17 Else Lüders, *Frauengedanken zum Weltgeschehen: Bekenntnisschrift einer demokratischen Frau* (Gotha: Verlag Friedrich Andreas Perthes, 1920), p. 29; Lüders translations are mine.

18 Ibid., p. iv; see also p. 29.

19 Ibid., p. 30; emphasis in original.

20 Ibid., pp. 30–31.

21 Paul Gordon Lauren, *Power and Prejudice: The Politics and Diplomacy of Racial Discrimination*, 2d ed. (Boulder, Colo.: Westview Press, 1996), pp. 82–126.

22 For example, Manfred Sell, "Die schwarze Völkerwanderung," *Preussische Jahrbücher* 224 (1931): 157–181; this was published in book form during the Nazi period as *Die schwarze Völkerwanderung: Der Einbruch des Negers in die Kulturwelt* (Vienna: Wilhelm Frick, 1940). See also Richard Thurnwald, *Black and White in East Africa: The Fabric of a New Civilization; A Study in Social Contact and Adaptation of Life in East Africa* (New York: Humanities Press, 1950), p. 2. The book was completed in 1933.

23 W. E. B. Du Bois, *The World and Africa*, rev. ed. (New York: International Publishers, 1992), pp. 8–11. See also Adolf Rüger, "Imperialismus, Sozialreformismus und antikoloniale demokratische Alternative: Zielvorstellungen von Afrikanern in Deutschland im Jahre 1919," *Zeitschrift für Geschichtswissenschaft* 23 (1975): 1293–1308.

24 See Alexandre Kum'a N'dumbe, *Was wollte Hitler in Afrika? NS-Planungen für eine faschistische Neugestaltung Afrikas* (Frankfurt a.M.: IKO Verlag für Interkulturelle Kommunikation, 1993), and Klaus Hildebrand, *Vom Reich zum Weltreich: Hitler, NSDAP und koloniale Frage, 1919–1945* (Munich: W. Fink, 1969), for two divergent and closely documented interpretations of that relationship.

25 See Robert Aldrich and John Connell, *The Last Colonies* (New York: Cambridge University Press, 1998).

26 Tina Campt, Pascal Grosse, and Yara-Colette Lemke-Muniz de Faria, "Blacks, Germans, and the Politics of the Imperial Imagination, 1920–60," in Friedrichsmeyer, Lennox, and Zantop, eds., *The Imperialist Imagination*, pp. 205–232; Yara-Colette Lemke-Muniz de Faria: "Afrodeutsche Kinder und Jugendfürsorge 1945–1960: Absonderung oder Eingliederung" (Ph.D. dissertation, Technical University of Berlin, 2000), and "Germany's 'Brown Babies' Must Be Helped: U.S. American Adoption Plans for Afro-German Children, 1950–1955," in *Black Voices against Social Exclusion*, Tina Campt and Anette Wierschke (Oxford: Berghahn, 2001).

27 Bernt Engelmann, *Deutschland ohne Juden: Eine Bilanz* (Munich: Franz Schneekluth, 1970).

28 Uta Poiger, *Jazz, Rock, and Rebels: Cold War Politics and American Culture in a Divided Germany* (Berkeley: University of California Press, 2000).

29 Wilfried Westphal, *Geschichte der deutschen Kolonien* (Munich: Bertelsmann, 1984); Marie Lorbeer and Beate Wild, eds., *Menschenfresser, Negerküsse: Das Bild vom Fremden im deutschen Alltag* (Berlin: Elefanten Press, 1991); Detlef Bald, ed., *Die Liebe zum Imperium: Deutschlands dunkle Vergangenheit in Afrika; Zu Legende und Wirklichkeit von Tanzanias deutscher Kolonialvergangenheit; Eine Lesebuch zum Film* (Bremen: Übersee Museum, 1978).

30 On surprise at German traits in regions formerly colonized by Germany, see, for example, Harald Maass and Michael Wolf, "Das deutsche Hong Kong," *Zeit-Magazin*, June 6, 1997,

pp. 26–34, and Brigitta Schmidt-Lauber, *Die abhängigen Herren: Deutsche Identität in Namibia* (Hamburg: Lit, 1993), for comments on Federal Republic of Germany tourists' reactions to the Germanness of Namibia.

31 See Omer Bartov, "Defining Enemies, Making Victims: Germans, Jews, and the Holocaust," *American Historical Review* 103 (1998): 771–816, and Anson Rabinbach, "The German as Pariah: Karl Jaspers and *The Question of German Guilt*," *Radical Philosophy*, no. 75 (January–February 1996): 15–25.

CHRISTOPHER SCHMIDT-NOWARA

After "Spain": A Dialogue with Josep M. Fradera on Spanish Colonial Historiography

The last twenty years of scholarship on Spain's nineteenth-century empire have turned conventional wisdom on its head. For decades after the Spanish-Cuban-American War of 1898, scholars and intellectuals from various countries represented the Spanish defeat and loss of Cuba, Puerto Rico, and the Philippines as confirmation of Spain's chronic inability to keep pace with the modern world. The "Disaster" of 1898 was an inevitable conclusion to the Spanish American revolutions of the 1810s and 1820s, when Spain had lost the majority of its American colonies. Indeed, in most surveys of modern Spanish history, the colonies make their appearance only in 1898 and only as one more piece of evidence of Spain's failed transition to modernity.

Of late, however, historians from Spain and the former colonies, especially Cuba and Puerto Rico, have found compelling evidence that the nineteenth-century colonial project fundamentally transformed both colonial and metropolitan societies. Cuba, for instance, grew to be the largest slave society in Spanish American history during the nineteenth century. Between the later eighteenth century and the closing of the Cuban slave trade in 1867, Cuba imported more slaves — approximately 780,000 — than all of Spanish America combined did from the early sixteenth to the late eighteenth centuries.[1] Puerto Rico, too, saw the most dramatic transformation of its economy and society since the conquest in the early sixteenth century, like Cuba through the dramatic growth of its sugar and slave economy.[2] Numerous local studies in Spain have demonstrated that the colonial project was central not only to the consolidation of the liberal regime in the nineteenth century, but also that the colonial connection was instrumental in the development of Spanish capitalism in its myriad regional manifestations.[3] Finally, the wars with Cuba in the last third of the nineteenth century (1868–1878, 1879–1880, 1895–1898) represented massive efforts on both sides. Most scholars would now agree that 1898 was not a whimper but a bang.[4]

To date there is no synthetic treatment of modern Spanish history that takes into account the colonial project and these revisions. The structure of Spanish historiography makes such a reevaluation difficult. Regional history is predominant, and few historians are willing to make broad generalizations that cut across the peculiarities of Spain's many regions and "nations." "Spanish" history not only faces a challenge from the perspective of colonial history, but it has also been virtually eroded from within by the decentralization of historical research and publication. As regional governments have assumed more power in the twenty-five years since Franco's death, they have enthusiastically patronized local universities and research institutions and subsidized the publication of monographic studies of local history. In terms of colonial historiography, Galicians write about Galicians in Cuba, Mallorcans about Mallorcans in Puerto Rico, and Catalans about Catalans in the Philippines. In Madrid, the state remains central to historiography but usually at the cost of local particularity and variation. Thus, the revisionist works on empire in many ways mirror the changing institutional and political nature of Spanish academia under the constitutional monarchy. Moreover, as the discussion below makes abundantly clear, more than thirty years of dictatorship in the name of national unity and imperial greatness have made most contemporary historians wary of "Spain" as an ideological and political project.

Some historians, however, have chosen to research and write on multiple levels despite the institutional and political complexity of doing so. Josep M. Fradera has few peers in this regard.[5] Professor of history at the Pompeu Fabra University in Barcelona, Fradera has written major works on Catalan economic, political, and intellectual history; Spanish state formation; and, of particular relevance for this essay, the recasting of the Spanish colonial project between the mid-eighteenth and late nineteenth centuries. The breadth of his research, as well as his knowledge of various national historiographies of empire from the early modern to the modern period, puts him in a unique position to reflect on the state of contemporary Spanish historiography after its own peculiar turn from, and then back to, empire.[6]

Questions and Answers

1. QUESTION: Catalonia has long been an important site of research on Spanish colonialism and colonialism's role in Spain's uneven transition to modernity. When I was first learning about Spain and its empire in Cuba, Puerto Rico, and the Philippines, I turned to Catalan historians such as Jordi Maluquer de Motes, Miquel Izard, and Jaume Vicens i Vives, as well as to your work and that of numerous young Catalan historians. Why has Catalonia, and Barcelona in particular, been such an important center of colonial historiography?

ANSWER: The place of colonial relations, or better said, the place of the empire in the development of early modern Spain—which was not a homogeneous political entity, as John H. Elliott has recently reminded us, but a complex system built around the monarchy, one of the best examples of the "composite state"—was radically absent from historical studies in the widest sense. The reasons for this absence are historical. The Spanish metropolis lost two bloody colonial wars, the first at the beginning of the nineteenth century, the second in 1898 (the agony of which was prolonged in Morocco in the early twentieth century). Because of these defeats, Spain lost a huge empire and was reduced to being a third-rate power. Unlike the British Empire in 1947 and 1956, Spain lost almost all contact with the ex-colonies. Latin America and the Philippines vanished from the point of view of Spanish state builders. Of course, the Spanish periphery maintained economic ties with the ex-colonies. Moreover, the crisis of 1898 unleashed an important flow of Spanish migrants to some Latin American countries—especially to the Spanish Caribbean—that lasted until the 1960s. However, the reality of these continued links failed to generate any interest in the Americas. For much of the nineteenth century, Spain had scorned and insulted the Latin American republics and never accepted the legitimacy of their aspirations for independence. This scorn and distancing were reinforced at the end of the nineteenth century after a long and devastating war against Cuban and Filipino patriots. Only in the twentieth century did Spaniards try to develop a rapprochement with the former colonies.

In the early decades of the twentieth century, Spain's liberal establishment forged relationships with Latin American intellectuals that were much more intense than in the nineteenth century. For the precarious Spanish intelligentsia of this period, the great Latin American cities and capitals offered a market (linguistically determined) that created the illusion of foreign influence, something indispensable in a Europe under the iron control of Great Britain, France, and Germany. These developments continued until the dramatic excision of the Spanish Civil War (1936–1939). Although sympathies were divided in Latin America concerning the Spanish conflict, it was Spain's republican exiles who fled to those countries. After the war, the Franco regime disseminated in Latin America a radicalized version of *hispanidad*, a neo-imperialist ideal that remained official ideology until the very end of the regime. For a fascist government that was culturally isolated from the world's major power blocs after World War II, *hispanidad* and *africanismo* were two sides of the same coin regarding its foreign policy and international image.

These considerations are crucial if one is to understand the backwardness of Spain's social sciences (to this very day) regarding its colonial past, not to mention entire areas of its own history. What Spain was missing from its intellectual life was the pressure of national/colonial interests like those that shaped academic work in Great Britain, France, or the Netherlands. The intellectual life of those countries developed in relationship to their colonies and their broader area of influence, leading to constant and diverse readings and rereadings of the past. Spain suffered not only from this colonial vacuum, but also from an aggressive Spanish patriotic offensive in the twentieth century, a reaction to the loss of the last colonies in 1898 and to Spain's subaltern position in the international order. That aggressive patriotism emphasized the most rhetorical elements of the inherited cultural tradition. Spanish historians reinvented medieval Christian Spain and the empire in the Americas as the axes of Spain's historical greatness. This curious defense of Catholicism as the national essence and of Spanish imperialism's noble intentions — ideas that the Franco regime derived to some extent from nineteenth-century liberal historical discourse — had several nefarious effects. Not only did it become impossible to generate critical perspectives on most of the Spanish past, but [also] the historical sense of several generations of Spaniards was corrupted. Moreover, this vision of history increased the gap between Spanish intellectual life and the most important innovations taking place in Europe and worldwide in the social sciences. The overall result was to alienate Latin American intellectual elites even more from Spanish culture because this rancid interpretation of the past was completely at odds with the "creole" foundations of their nation-building projects.

The crisis of these cultural assumptions allowed the slow emergence of a distinct interpretative model, but only very late in the twentieth century. It was the Catalan historian Jaume Vicens i Vives, the principal reformer in medieval and early modern Spanish history, who called for a drastic revision of the historiographical tradition, including the assumptions of the dominant imperial history. The first manifestation of his program of historiographical reform was the collective work *Historia social de España y América*, published in 1957. However, this first effort produced uneven results and did not bring about a real change in the direction of Spanish historiography. What's more, because of the continued dominance of reactionary nationalist and Catholic attitudes, Spain missed out completely on the major revisions of Latin American historiography being carried out in the United States by Woodrow Borah, Shelbourne Cooke, Charles Gibson, and John Leddy Phelan and by numerous historians in Latin America.

These qualifications are fundamental for understanding why in Spain imperial and colonial history were so slow to change and why their focus was so local and oftentimes idiosyncratic. This backwardness was largely, if not solely, due to the weight of the Francoist dictatorship and its fiercely repressive character. In my view, the real change came about only when the discussions of the 1960s concerning the origins and development of capitalism erupted into the Spanish academy. In other words, only when economic historians began to address the role of foreign trade, especially with the colonies, in the economic development of early modern and modern Spain did Spanish historiography significantly change. In this debate, the contributions of Pierre Vilar's seminal study of Catalonia in the eighteenth century and John H. Elliott and John Lynch's elegant works on early modern Spain and the empire were decisive. They opened the road to the international debate and helped end the isolation of Spanish historiography. We can place this moment of change between the mid-1960s and the mid-1970s.

The major renewals came in early modern historiography, especially in the interpretations of the empire between the sixteenth and eighteenth centuries and its role in Spanish history. The "rediscovery" of Latin America and the Spanish colonial world as unavoidable factors quickly led historians to the nineteenth century as well. This new focus produced a reconsideration of great importance: Though nineteenth-century Spain, postimperial Spain, was a minor power after the Spanish American revolutions, it still controlled an important colony until 1898 — Cuba. Indeed, over the course of the nineteenth century, the island acquired even greater economic value for Spain as it developed a massive plantation complex worked by slave labor. Integrating this variable into historical studies led to the "rediscovery" of nineteenth-century Cuba, one of the richest, if not the richest, colonies in the world. Moreover, it meant that Spanish historians had to engage with the great twentieth-century Cuban historians of both the pre- and postrevolutionary period: Fernando Ortiz, Ramiro Guerra, Julio Le Riverend, Raúl Cepero Bonilla, Juan Pérez de la Riva, Jorge Ibarra, and Manuel Moreno Fraginals. Moreno Fraginals's book, *El Ingenio*, on the Cuban sugar plantations, became an inspiration for many Spanish historians of my generation, not only for the breadth of its description and analysis, but also for the beauty of its prose.[7]

These issues in Spanish colonial history dovetailed with important international debates at the time concerning the role of the slave plantation in the development of capitalism and the reasons for the abolition of slavery in the nineteenth century, not to mention debates over the role of colonial systems in the genesis of the modern world. Thus, as the imperial nostalgia that underlay the idea of *hispanidad* became more untenable and unconvincing, it lost ground to the new and quite different concerns with the formation of Spanish capitalism. For this reason, there is a certain logic to the fact that Catalan historiography was the most advanced in addressing these new ideas and topics. For obvious political reasons, twentieth-century Spanish nationalism as a historical paradigm enjoyed little prestige in Catalonia; in some cases Catalans viewed it as the antithesis of the [Catalan] nationalist ethos that impregnated the regional culture. Furthermore, because Catalonia was at the leading edge of industrialization, the precedents of which Vilar had found in the eighteenth century in his great book, and because of the region's intense engagement in the colonial enterprise, the concern with capitalism and colonialism [was] especially strong. The historians who worked under the rigorous intellectual guidance of Vicens i Vives came of age in the 1970s and busied themselves with these new topics, writing works that irrevocably changed the direction of Spanish and Catalan historiography. Miquel Izard's work on Venezuela and Jordi Maluquer de Motes's on the relations between Spain and Cuba represented the coming of age of this new historiography by presenting perspectives completely absent from Spanish historiography only twenty years earlier. The debates of the 1980s over the importance of the Bourbon reforms in the crisis of Spain's empire in the early nineteenth century formed another crucial turning point. This time, historians from throughout Spain were involved, with especially important contributions from Josep Fontana, Josep M. Delgado, and Pedro Pérez Herrero. The contribution of Catalan historians — such as myself, Delgado, Fontana, Carlos Martínez Shaw, and José M. Oliva — to this debate was the reconstruction of almost one hundred years of colonial commerce with the Americas. To a certain extent, the questions relating to classic themes in early modern imperial history and those pertaining to the principal colonies that remained after the Spanish American revolutions — Cuba, Puerto Rico, and the Philippines — reinforced one another.

2. QUESTION: Most contemporary revisions of European imperialism, such as Frederick Cooper and Ann Stoler's *Tensions of Empire*, ignore Spain's nineteenth-century colonial experience and the breakup of empire in the Caribbean and Pacific. Is that marginalization justified? That is to say, do you think that the Spanish empire in that period is abnormal and peculiar, or do you see it sharing in the broad trends — political, economic, cultural — of the "age of empire"?

ANSWER: The absence of the Spanish colonial regime from the international discussion on the meanings and consequences of European expansion and from comparative perspectives on European colonialism has serious implications. Historians and social scientists have a poor understanding of the importance of the Spanish empire — not only the early modern empire, but also the reconstructed one of the nineteenth century. Their misconceptions arise from dominant explanatory "paradigms," the history of which is not unconnected to the history of European colonialism. Let me explain. Regarding the early modern period, it is clear to me that there is considerable confusion about the nature of the Spanish colonial enterprise, a confusion that originates during the Enlightenment, especially the Scottish Enlightenment and the work of Adam Smith. In Smith's interpretation of colonialism, which I want to emphasize was quite sophisticated and subtle, the Spanish were unique among the European conquerors in that while they were driven by the premodern desire for precious metals, they expressed no modern economic motivations. This politicized interpretation of the nature of the early modern empire — an empire much sought after by the French and British, as well as by the Dutch before them — inscribed the emergent ideology of political economy and traditional Protestant anti-Catholicism into an apocalyptic vision of the complex reality of Spanish imperialism. This skewed interpretation of three hundred and fifty years of imperialism — a duration that in itself begs interpretation and explanation — remained dominant until quite recently, affecting, for instance, some of the great twentieth-century North American historians I mentioned previously.

If this Smithian perspective is no longer taken seriously by Latin American historians, it nonetheless continues to shape international discussions of colonialism and decolonization. Assumptions about Spanish and Catholic backwardness obscure two crucial elements in any long-term analysis of European expansion and the development of European capitalism. The first is the fundamental fact that the Spanish monarchy made a titanic effort to weld the empire into a machine for producing precious metals, a machine that functioned effectively from the late sixteenth century until 1810, as Stanley and Barbara Stein have recently demonstrated in their brilliant work. The flow of precious metals was important not just for Spain, but [also] for the rest of the world. For instance, the debate over the price revolution begun by E. J. Hamilton was only the preface to a much broader discussion on a global level in which the contributions of D. O. Flynn and the works of J. F. Richards have shown the changes wrought in the state structures of China and India caused by the flow of silver from the Spanish empire. But the flow of precious metal was only one side of the coin. The other was the dramatic internal restructuring, with enormous long-term consequences, of the American societies to facilitate the production of silver. From the point of view of the state and the Spanish colonizers, this restructuring was an unqualified success, but from the point of view of indigenous society it was destructive and painful, as Spain dispossessed the native Americans of the best lands and brutally imposed a foreign language and religion. (Unfortunately, this is a process too complex to discuss here, as it also requires analysis of the perpetual dialectic between the colonizers and the colonized over an immense territory and time period.)

To the enlightened European world of the eighteenth century, Spain's effort to exert its dominion over such a vast territory and diverse population was absurd. The Enlightenment emphasized the brutality of the Spanish experiment, a brutality it saw as related to Spain's apparent ignorance of cost-benefit analysis in terms of economic exploitation. Paradoxically, however, as this Enlightenment critique of the Spanish empire was achieving interpretative dominance, the North European colonial enterprises were coming to most resemble those of their Iberian predecessors, especially in the case of the British in Bengal and the Dutch in Java in the second half of the eighteenth century. In reading about the efforts of the East India Company to control peasant tribute, or about the debates in Calcutta and Batavia over just government (for example, during the impeachment of Hastings), or about the function of native intermediaries, the Spanish historian cannot help but smile because these are echoes, two centuries later, of similar debates held by Spanish functionaries and by the theologians of Salamanca. The Spanish colonial enterprise is less a historical anomaly than the origin of a historically dense process that must be explained from the start. In my view, Spanish imperialism is the necessary starting point for any understanding of European expansion and the rise of today's global order, beginning already with the internal colonization of the Iberian Peninsula in the thirteenth and fourteenth centuries, a process that involved, not coincidentally, the destruction of a preexisting political order and peasant society.

The other major problem with the traditional visions of Spain concerns Spanish colonialism in the nineteenth century. One of the worst consequences of interpreting Spanish colonialism in terms of the Protestant ethos has been the complete inability to comprehend the changes and reforms (in terms of both colonial policy and metropolitan objectives) that explain Spain's extraordinary longevity as a colonial power. The persistence of Spanish colonial rule in the Philippines, Puerto Rico, and Cuba can only be explained by the changing strategies of the metropolis. Moreover, the factors that contributed to change and continuity in the Caribbean (pacting with the planter class and manipulating a polarized social order to gain consent) were utterly different from the changes made in the Philippines. These innovations in colonial policy represent a major historical problem, one that cannot be isolated from our work on what was still the most highly valued imperial tradition in the late eighteenth century (until India changed Britain's view of colonialism and colonial policy). Moving ahead in time, perhaps we could argue that Spain continued to be a colonial power in the nineteenth century because of the major reforms undertaken in the later eighteenth century, while the nature of its capitalist development did not allow it to overstretch itself. For instance, Spain was an almost insignificant player in the global partition formalized in 1885 at the Congress of Berlin. The persistence of Spanish colonialism is paradoxical, but a paradox that needs to be explained through the double history of colonial transformations and capitalist development, two distinct but inseparable variables. In neither case is Spain anomalous, though like every country, it has its peculiarities. Historians' work will consist of explaining historical particularities and breaking free of the assumptions inscribed in inherited paradigms. For Spaniards, comparisons with the North European countries are the logical comparative counterpoint, but the global description of European expansion can advance only by incorporating the venerable Iberian imperialisms, both the Spanish and the Portuguese.

3. QUESTION: With the triumph of local history in contemporary Spanish historiography, is it still possible to write a narrative of Spanish history? If so, how does the now vast literature on empire transform our vision of nineteenth- and twentieth-century Spain?

ANSWER: Regional studies on immigration to the colonies in the early modern and modern periods (including to Cuba, Venezuela, Argentina, and other countries in the twentieth century), on the economic flows that linked different regions to the colonies, or on the political or military careers of distinguished local and regional figures reflect, without a doubt, the profound nature of the connections among the Peninsula, the Americas, and the Philippines. In many instances, these studies provide important data and are by no means bereft of theoretical reflection. I do not share the academic paternalism that holds that any history strongly informed by local concerns and focus cannot be of general interest and value. Moreover, it is undeniable that after forty years in which the leaden idea of "Spain" produced so much futile rhetoric, studies with a strong local or regional concentration have been the logical response. Many of these works are done with a sureness and sensibility to detail that academic historians generally do not possess. Nonetheless, it is clear that local and regional history should inscribe itself in the more general historical discussion. Here is where academic historians should take a leading role by introducing new questions to reflect on, both methodological and interpretative.

As for the possibility of writing a general Spanish narrative, it seems to me that the question is not so much one of possibility or impossibility but what we want this narrative to reflect or address. This is not a minor question, even apart from the political connotations that it reflects or encompasses. Leaving politics to the side for a moment, it is clear that the hypertrophy of "Spain" in Spanish historiography and culture still has serious consequences, especially in two areas. First, there is a systematic confusion of the imperial monarchy of the early modern period with the Spanish nation-building project of the nine-teenth century, a project that does not take off until the collapse of the empire in the early nineteenth century and that, in fact, begins only because of the imperial debacle. Although many historians refuse to accept it, it is precisely the imperial ideal's continuing validity that explains the lack of a recognizably nationalist or protonationalist movement in Spain before the nineteenth century. Thus, any narrative of Spain until 1824 [the end of the Spanish American revolutions] must be a narrative of the empire.

Second, the peninsular part of the empire was always formed by culturally, politically, and economically diverse entities. If the advent of the Bourbon monarchy in the eighteenth century equalized the political status of the ancient peninsular kingdoms, the differences in other areas continued to grow, especially in the economy, as we discussed in the first question. A single narrative of Spain is impossible until the nineteenth century, whether we view it from below, from the perspective of the peninsular state, or from the complex and diverse overseas empire. Nor is a unified narrative possible for the period immediately following the destruction of the American empire, even though it is in that period that we see the first semblance of a nation-building project, elaborated by small nuclei of liberals tired of the absolutist monarchy's efforts to restore the imperial order.

The development of nineteenth-century Spain was so varied and unequal on a regional level that nation formation had very particular and varied con-notations, something it is critical to recognize. The novelty of the period following the imperial debacle was that a shared nation-building project did indeed exist — even if the visions of the nation were quite diverse — a project in which the restructuring of colonial rule in the Philippines and in the Antilles helped forge a consensus regarding the nature of the liberal state and the "imagined community" of the nineteenth-century nation. It is no coincidence that the foundational moment of the Basque and Catalan nationalist move-ments (here I will not get into the major differences between the two move-ments and their ideas of the nation) was in 1898, with the loss of the remaining colonies.

Basque and Catalan nationalisms show that while the historian can speak of a shared narrative, a Spanish narrative if you like, he/she cannot ignore these problematic aspects of the nation-building process by folding them into the ideal construct of what the nation should be. From this point of view, and without forgetting this question's basic theme, the regional participation in Spanish colonialism in the nineteenth century was fundamental and impossi-ble to dissolve in a single and suprahistorical narrative. These qualifications are valid to the present day. It seems to me that the intellectual goal in writing about Spanish and other nationalisms should be a complex integration that includes these diverse political and ideological developments. Nationalisms need to be integrated into shared spaces in the colonial and metropolitan world, while the importance of the different sorts of "imagined communities" (the idea of "Spain," as well as that of "Catalonia," "Galicia," or "Euzkadi" or colonial identities in Cuba, Puerto Rico, and the Philippines) in the historical process must be acknowledged. We need to focus not only on specific variables, but also on their multiple interconnections — for instance, the prestige of Spanish nationalism after specific colonial adventures, such as the Moroccan war of 1859–1860, or the popular appeal of the war against Cuban and Filipino separatists, or, in contrast, the exhaustion caused by the Franco regime's constant appeals to imperial greatness while the population continued to suffer terrible hardships twenty years after the civil war.

4. QUESTION. Many commentators have noted that since the transition to democracy Spain is no longer a country of emigrants to Northern Europe but now a prosperous nation that receives immigrant laborers, especially from Africa, Latin America, and Asia. While most writers see this as a novel situation in which Spaniards are now confronted with the issue of an increasingly multiracial, multicultural polity, it seems to me that Spain dealt with exactly these questions throughout its long colonial history. Do you think that history informs the present concerns over immigration, or has the memory of Spain's experiments in constructing a multiracial polity been effaced and forgotten?

ANSWER: Spain is clearly no longer a country of emigrants. A cycle of massive immigration that began with the agrarian crises of the later nineteenth century has finally come to a close. For the first time in a long time, Spain is experiencing a sustained flow of immigration that is slowly changing people's perception of these issues. The overall size of immigrants in the total population is still small (1.5 percent according to data from 1998), much smaller than in other European countries but still on the rise. If in the 1960s Spanish cinema and literature, with the limitations imposed by the policies of the Franco regime, reflected the hard life of the men and women who left Spain to work in the great European countries, now they are beginning to reflect the hardships suffered in our country by workers from Africa (24.9 percent of foreign residents in Spain), Latin America (18.1 percent), and Asia (8.4 percent). Nonetheless, it appears that the Spanish experience of colonialism and immigration has been of little help in confronting the issues raised by this situation, although it is difficult to know what rests in the subconscious of Spain's working classes. In some of the major cities and in some agrarian sectors (in agribusiness in particular) with a high density of immigrants, there have been dramatic outbursts of xenophobic aggression, acts of aggression that require careful scrutiny, and demands for more effective intervention by the public authorities.

Undoubtedly, the Spanish case is peculiar when compared to other European countries. Spain did not experience the pattern of decolonization with immigration that Great Britain and France did in the twentieth century. The presence of immigrant workers is novel for Spaniards. [The] Rom are the only minority that Spaniards have know in their own country, a group that, while integrated into the Andalusian image of Spain, has been brutally segregated and oppressed in real life. Even the minuscule Protestant minority was harshly repressed during the Franco regime. Thus, for Spaniards the encounter with African and Asian workers, with Muslims and Buddhists, is unprecedented. The very presence of foreigners, with different patterns of sociability and places of worship, represents a challenge for one of the societies that most effectively practiced "ethnic cleansing" in the fifteenth and sixteenth centuries.

For this reason and because there is no collective memory of the racial discrimination practiced in the early modern empire or the nineteenth-century colonies, it is vital for historians to discuss and to establish in our culture (and not only in academic culture) the profound importance of the imperial and colonial past and the racial subordination and exploitation of the American Indians, Africans, and Filipinos. In this overall context, reconstructing the moments in which some sectors of Spanish society challenged racist policies is crucial, though historians must be careful not to lapse into a historical apologetics that falsifies and distorts their findings. Episodes like the theological debates in sixteenth-century Castille over the personality of the conquered Indians or the abolitionism of the nineteenth century certainly deserve to be recuperated. But this act of recuperation must not whitewash the miseries inflicted by the Spanish empire; rather, it should reveal and make comprehensible the horror — driven by the peninsular colonizers' lust for wealth and the monarchy's fiscal rapacity — that became the norm in colonial society. In short, social scientific research must parallel the state of academic debate. At the same time, we must keep in mind the mistakes of the past. If before we deplored the disastrous interpretations rendered by nationalist and neo-imperialist manipulations under the Franco regime, we must also affirm the responsibility that our work demands. In other words, we must always be aware of our present political circumstances, even if we cannot bend our work to them.

Notes

1 Philip Curtin, *The Atlantic Slave Trade: A Census* (Madison: University of Wisconsin Press, 1969), p. 25.

2   Francisco Scarano, "Liberal Pacts and Hierarchies of Rule: Approaching the Imperial Transition in Cuba and Puerto Rico," *Hispanic American Historical Review* 78 (November 1998): 583–601.

3   Josep M. Fradera, *Indùstria i mercat: Les bases comercials de la indùstria catalana moderna (1814–1845)* (Barcelona: Crítica, 1987).

4   Consuelo Naranjo, Miguel Angel Puig-Samper, and Luis Miguel García Mora, eds., *La nación soñada: Cuba, Puerto Rico y Filipinas ante el 98* (Madrid: Doce Calles, 1996); Juan Pablo Fusi and Antonio Niño, eds. *Vísperas del 98* (Madrid: Biblioteca Nueva, 1997); Juan Pan-Montojo, ed., *Más se perdió en Cuba: España, 1898 y el fin de siglo* (Madrid: Alianza Editorial, 1998).

5   For an introduction to Fradera's work, see the essays collected in *Gobernar colonias* (Barcelona: Península, 1999). Other works appear in the bibliography.

6   I submitted the following questions to Professor Fradera in the spring of 2000. In July, we met in New York to discuss them. He then sent me written responses in Spanish, which I translated in consultation with him. A longer version of this essay appeared in *Bulletin of the Society for Spanish and Portuguese Historical Studies* 25 (winter–spring 2001): 2–14.

7   Manuel Moreno Fraginals, *El Ingenio: Complejo económico-social cubano del azúcar*, 3 vols. (Havana: Editorial de Ciencias Sociales, 1978).

ROBERT GREGG

Making the World Safe for American History

The stage is set, the destiny disclosed.
—Woodrow Wilson, on his return to the United States from Versailles, July 8, 1919

Itemize this, please, as my contribution to the "internationalizing of American history," which is very much in vogue right now. We see it popping up in the pages of our *Journal of American History;* we hear from scholars from different nations telling us how they do "American history" in their countries; next we read essays telling us how American history can and should be internationalized, alongside conference announcements that tell us to which European country we should go to participate in this collective contemplation.[1] Then we begin to see the fruits of this enterprise: articles representing the latest efforts in this new endeavor; even the president of the American Historical Association bearing news of his internationalist leanings; and, fresh in the morning post, the final report from the conference funded by the Organization of American Historians (OAH), convened over the last few summers at New York University's (NYU) Villa La Pietra in Florence.[2]

Behind this movement lies a feeling, perhaps, that historians need to respond to developments we have witnessed in the emergence of the New World Order, unified by the "new" global market. It is as if, following the "victory" of the United States in its cold war with the Soviet Union, there is a collective sense that it is now time to return to a European mansion in the manner of that great internationalizer of American history, Woodrow Wilson, to see whether we can get our colleagues abroad to accept a new League of Americanists. We could even get them to sign a covenant and then withdraw our support, when, after our return, the taste for domestic Bourbon revives.

Woodrow Wilson, arriving in Paris following the armistice to dictate terms to Europeans and sundry, may be said to have stood at a pinnacle of American attempts to internationalize their own history. The logic of American history, certainly as Wilson had pronounced it, seemed to indicate that the Great War would truly become "the war to end all wars" and that decolonization would be carried along in the train of the American Revolution. But Wilson was a Southerner and a racist, and the kind of historical enterprise he was navigating was one of national self-determination for European *volk*, with a "prime directive" that colonialism be mandated and independence postdated for the rest. Was it possible for Wilson to step out of his Bagehotian and Princetonian skin to pronounce an alternative view of the world not generated by the rebirth of his own sense of the nation? Can *we* step beyond our professional and national entanglements to proclaim American history internationalized? Or when we do so, will we merely hear the echo coming back to us, pronouncing faintly but distinctly, "Long Live American History"?

Mario and the Magicians

Like myself he was half American, and here I must resist the temptation to digress on a fascinating topic: England's intellectual debt to America. Nearly all the remarkable Englishmen of the last fifty years have a strong seasoning of Yankee blood. Great is the temptation to dwell on Winston Churchill and develop a theme which has not yet received proper attention. Where would the modern poetaster be without T. S. Eliot? But I shall forbear: perhaps we have suffered too much from racial theorists.
— Sir Harold Mario Mitchell Acton, *Memoirs of an Aesthete*

Never judging a book by its cover is not always to be trusted as a sound rule. For the *La Pietra Report*, judging by the cover seems only fair, and for most people it may be a timesaving device. It is fair since the lavishness of the pamphlet's presentation is intended to make an impression, albeit a positive one. This is the impression it made on me.

The cover presents us with the title of the pamphlet, an interesting photograph of Villa La Pietra (with Greco-Roman statues on the imposing gate), and mention of sponsorship by the OAH. Right from the get-go, this identification between a project on internationalizing the study of American history and an Italian villa seems rather an unfortunate lapse. When we learn, by turning to the preface, that this connection is by design, not misfortune, we certainly have to wonder whether we need to read further. This is from the preface: "The title [of the report] is taken from the Villa La Pietra, where the international body of historians who participated in the project met. It was thought appropriate, given the theme of the project, to meet abroad, and the availability of meeting facilities at Villa La Pietra, New York University's magnificent center in Florence, Italy, made that possible."[3]

On the surface, convening the meeting overseas seems like a sensible plan. But, in fact, internationalizing American history might be more effectively demonstrated by endeavoring to bring out the global buried within the local. Of course, attempting this, perhaps by holding the conference in one of the less attractive locations in the United States that may be thirsting for our inter-national band's dollars, might not be quite so appealing to a group of pro-fessionals used to meeting only in Sheratons and Hiltons, not to mention Adams Marks.

But even if we accept the need for a foreign venue, we need to ask ourselves whether this was indeed either the most convenient or the cheapest one. It was certainly one that most Americanists would find attractive and to which they would wish to travel. It was also readily available through the auspices of NYU, which had been given the building for the purpose of holding international conferences. But even if it were truly the most convenient (which I doubt), is convenience always to override the importance of avoiding a symbolic Euro-American bias that such a venue might signify?

More than convenience, however, the preface continues by letting us know of the villa's own symbolic credentials:

In fact, the recent history of the villa illustrates in its own way the transnational theme of the conferences. The villa was given to NYU by Sir Harold Acton, whose father had purchased it after marrying an American woman from Cleveland who brought to the marriage the resources that made the purchase possible. And it was this American connection that prompted Sir Harold Acton to offer the villa to an American university, which dedicated it in part to be a center for international academic conferences.[4]

So dare we suggest a subconscious desire to revive the great Anglo-American marriage lurking beneath this enterprise? If this is the extent of our interna-tionalization — an Italian villa purchased by what appears to be an Englishman, with American money — then we have not advanced very far from the begin-ning of this century, when such arrangements fed the dreams of many an Anglo-American racial supremacist: a Theodore Roosevelt, a Winston Chur-chill, or a W. T. Stead (all of whom were chart busters in the globalization business).[5]

But if we listen closely, we may hear rumblings of a text lying dormant beneath the weight of this preface. First, we may learn from Sir Harold's memoirs that, in fact, the Mitchell money that bought La Pietra was from Chicago rather than Cleveland, which, as the "capital of the West" back then, may perhaps do more for our globalizing sensibilities than Cleveland.[6] As Sir Harold might have said, it is so much more delicious an idea to conjure with. And when we add to this the strong probability that some of the Hawaiian money flowing into the family was coming (directly or indirectly) from sugar plantations, then our taste buds really just tingle with excitement. And in the wake of this foppery, for which Sir Harold was renowned, we are not surprised to learn that our host was the model for Anthony Blanch, that "prancing faun," Evelyn Waugh's character in *Brideshead Revisited*. When we factor into our consideration Waugh's provision of a South American mother for Blanch, racializing Sir Harold's aesthetic, as well as all the imperial imaginings that wandered through the minds of Sebastian Flight and Charles Rider, then we do have a delightful feast, the smells of which may indeed emanate from within the walls of Villa La Pietra.[7]

But the magic of the transnational embodied in Sir Harold's aesthetics is present neither in the cover of this report, which gives no signal beyond the Euro-American, nor in the material that lies within. For this conference was constructed on a foundation made up of that steely alliance of Academy and Foundation—what we will for convenience dub the Foundation-Academy Complex (FAC). Scholars of un-American history will remember that it was the FAC that brought us (with heavy State Department and CIA backing) area studies. Indeed, the FAC was able to establish conformity over intellectual endeavors in quite formidable ways, as witnessed in the emergence of the Chicago (St. Valentine's Day) School with its distinctive and largely hegemonic approaches to urbanization, immigration, ghettoization, and development, among other things. One can see this beginning to be replicated in the case of internationalizing history. Those organizing the La Pietra conference are donning the mantle of "godfather," so that as new global and international history centers are established in universities around the United States, their positions will be filled either by those scholars who were participants in the La Pietra meetings, or by people recommended from within this family of scholars. New publications in this area will also seek the imprimatur of the family's inner circle, and we can predict that Thomas Bender's *Rethinking American History in a Global Age* will receive significantly heavy marketing to give it iconic status.[8] The foundations, meanwhile, are busily looking for the alternative to their earlier, now failed ventures in area studies and are ready to fund anything coming downstream that appears programmatic.[9]

Let's be honest now. My real beef with the OAH's conference on internationalizing the study of American history at La Pietra was that I was not a participant. Had I been invited, let's face it, I would be endorsing the *La Pietra Report* in a snap, like all the other worthies on the participant list. Maybe—maybe not!

"I am a debtor both to the Greeks and the Barbarians. And, pardon, figuratively speaking, I have had higher education too."
— G. V. Desani, *All about H. Hatterr*

The first thing to note about the La Pietra, Inc. (henceforth LP, Inc.) report is that it is founded on the notion that there is a clear correspondence between historiographical shifts and social change, in this case the shift brought about by the end of the cold war. While it is true that historians are influenced by the society in which they work, so that they are clearly affected by shifts in the *zeitgeist*, undue emphasis on this attaches an air of uniformity to historiography — to works that preceded these new transnational initiatives. Even in those cases where the impact of social change on historical writing seems most obvious — for example, the civil rights movement generating whole new interpretations dealing with slavery and segregation — presenting historiographical change in a uniform fashion downplays ways in which difference and disagreement had been embedded in earlier historiographical trends.[10] In the case of this report, LP, Inc., suggests that we have arrived at the point of such a historiographical shift, and in the process it tends to diminish, even erase, prior conflicts that existed among historians. Thus, there is an underlying irony in the report: it claims that there is nothing new about the global influences we have been witnessing recently while at the same time it fails to see that there is nothing new about the transnational element in American historiography either.

The report, therefore, seems to have created a category of "Americanist" which is formed around the idea of a representative historian who has (until recently) pushed the global to a distance and who lacks much awareness of the world. In this view, the international domain has merely been absent from earlier historical endeavors. And, as such, the remedy lies in educating the "Americanist" about the significance of international terrain, cleansing the student body in the process as well. Such an "Americanist," embodying the plurality of historians of the United States and North America, does not exist, however, and educating him/her in the internationale will thus not produce the results claimed.

It would be another irony if Americanists truly had ignored the international when the people they have had to focus on have had such varied backgrounds. Indeed, many Americans have often been more keenly aware, not less, of the world than people from other nations. It is, instead, a paradox that the people who are often most aware have been cast off as the least conscious —

the old stereotype of the "ignorant American." At the political level alone, as much money has been spent per capita on determining the nature of the external "Other"—whether British, German, Japanese, Russian, Iranian, or Iraqi, to mention a few—as in any other imperial civilization in human history. This is the land of area studies, after all! It is not ignorance that is the problem; it is a willingness and ability to develop mechanisms to forget, hide, distance, and make unique, to make "an area" of the United States.[11] The notion of American exceptionalism itself is not founded in ignorance—as a cursory glance at the work of American historians of the turn of the twentieth century will make abundantly clear; it is founded in a stunning ability to fashion uniqueness, invent tradition, and imagine community, all by silencing aspects of the past.

With this in the back of our minds, let us commence our cross-examination of the *La Pietra Report*. The second sentence of *Rethinking American History in a Global Age* reads:

Since the professionalization of the discipline in the nineteenth century, the nation has been treated as both the principal object and the context for historical inquiry. Study of the United States offers no exception to this generalization. Its historiography may even offer a particularly strong example of this approach.[12]

What are the particular strengths of this historiography? We might want to question the report's assertion here, but if we do believe that it is possible to make this claim about U.S. historiography, then surely we need to examine what these strengths might be and why we think they are indeed strengths— therein lie some of our politics—before moving on to our new initiatives. Otherwise, as I think is detectable in the rest of the document, we will still draw on previous historiography unwittingly, and by failing to interrogate this question, we will reify many of the categories that we claim to now be historicizing.

At present, however, intellectual trends in the general culture are pointing in a different direction. Recent discussions of "globalization," for example, may be uninformed by history, but they have nonetheless promoted important thinking about the historicity of the nation itself.[13]

In what ways are current discussions about globalization "uninformed by history"? How can something actually be uninformed by history? (Are historians the only people who think about history?) These discussions may be uninformed by a history with which LP, Inc., agrees, but surely they are informed by assessments about the past that imply that there is something new to the current process of globalization. And is it perhaps the case that the way globalization is being thought about by LP, Inc., and the kinds of histories that are being sought to provide us with our context and historicity, hide other kinds of global interaction in the past — those things that went into the construction of the peculiar nation-state endorsed by representatives of the earlier historiography and that remain uninterrogated here.

These new understandings of the nation-state invite more complex understandings of the American nation's relation to a world that is at once self-consciously global and highly pluralized.[14]

Is it not curious that so soon after stating a desire to interrogate the nation-state, we have it established here as our unit of analysis? Moreover, I am surely not alone in finding it troubling that in a document that tries to reveal a new sensitivity to the "pluralized" world, we have the United States defined as "the" American nation. Okay, this is a slip. But I've always thought if a Freudian slip fits, one really ought to wear it!

If historians have often treated the nation as self-contained and undifferentiated, it is increasingly clear that this assumption is true neither in the present nor the past.[15]

This sentence may be all well and true. But what has been the impact of these assumptions on the way many historians now think about the nation-state? If the nation's past was never self-contained and undifferentiated, what is the significance of all the energy some historians put into making these things appear so? Maybe they were blind to reality. But would it not be worth considering to what extent this was so? What kinds of maneuverings through concepts of historical objectivity and scientific method enabled them to write off some people as somehow un-American if they remained outside the consensus? Moreover, in the aftermath of all this historical writing, do we end up with a situation where we can comfortably expand on the work of the past, filling in the pasts for the minorities within and the majorities without?[16]

Further, aspects of the historians' assumption may still prevail in the critique of it that has emerged. Let us take an example from the social history of immigration. Earlier descriptions of immigrants as "uprooted" were considered problematic by social historians owing to the manner in which they denied agency and respect to immigrant groups. Social historians made their own assumption that these things (agency, in particular) needed to be attributed to people.[17] But such an assumption is based on further gender and racial assumptions that grew in the same soil out of which ideas of nationhood and American identity emerged (in the aftermath of slavery and emancipation and in a context of republican theories of independence and dependence), so that the urge to locate and attribute agency to the subject may be the act that denies these very same things to others who fall outside the view of the historian or beyond the boundaries of "American history." In short, what baggage may we be carrying with us as we travel into these uncharted lands of international history? It is merely a couple of carry-ons, constantly in our view, or are we making the trip with checked-in bags, neatly stored out of the way in the hold?

A history that recognizes the historicity of different forms of solidarity and the historical character of the project of nation-making promises to better prepare students and the public to understand and to be *effective* in the world we live in and will live in.[18]

"Ask not what you can do for your country; ask what your country can do for you"? While it is nice to be finally moving beyond Kennedyesque hocus pocus, abstract idealism still lies at the heart of this. What we do in history, according to the report, is "prepare students and the public to understand and to be effective in the world." But what do these things mean really? Who are the students? And are we really at the service of "a public," a term that in a way allows the state in by the back door when we had barred it at the front? We want to historicize (and so potentially destabilize) the nation-state and yet find it here shaping our needs and concerns.

Surely if the world is as global as we now imagine it to be, we will bring this into our classrooms to the extent that we (as individual historians) find it politically and/or intellectually appropriate to do so and to the extent that we feel we need to respond to the particular demands of our audiences. Unless we are no more than public functionaries, we ought to attend to global issues when we see them and when we feel that they are significant — not because we have heard that it is in the (singular) public interest to do so.

Additionally, we need to recognize that the more global a situation may be, the more the desire to keep global issues at some distance from our teaching may in fact be evidenced. In other words, "effective" is a politically charged term about which historians will disagree. Some may want a greater public understanding of world poverty, to increase the awareness of the need to maintain strict immigration controls; others may want it to increase the sense of sympathy for the plight of the world's poor.

A more limited history, one insensitive to a multiplicity of contexts and scales of experience, would be a partial and inadequate history, telling far less than the history of the United States.[19]

One has to admire the intent here, but even so the statement is not necessarily true. One would like historians not to be "insensitive to a multiplicity of contexts and scales of experience," but given a failure to examine the ways in which earlier historians remained insensitive even while they thought they were being otherwise, we can easily imagine that the deliberately insensitive historian might write a less partial and inadequate history than the sensitive one, simply because s/he has interrogated her/his own partiality and has acknowledged her/his insensitivity.

Further, one might wonder what *the* (singular) history of the United States might be if it is not a saga of insensitivity. Expanding the parameters of U.S. history, therefore, without interrogating these things may be merely seeking to write narratives that allow for the incorporation of all groups into a message that is unwittingly triumphalist, and thereby insensitive. Moreover, the attempt to provide "preparation" for the public may in fact lead down the opposite road, further immunizing students to the reality that professional history is shaped (not tainted) by politics and that historians do not provide access to truth but rather provide interpretations.

The main point I am making here relates to the top-down aspect of this enterprise. Both the OAH and LP, Inc., representing Americanists, want to pave the way toward new interpretations that maintain a protected and privileged status for the professional historian. This is certainly a curious posture for historians to be taking (since historians have seldom required such open protection, even within the academy), and it seems to me that it is founded in some degree on anxiety about what the role of the historian is to be in the new global order, where access to information is easy and the potential for democratization of knowledge might be considered threatening to members of a professional elite. We have seen new ideas relating to imperialism and literary criticism and so forth coming to the fore. These have been ungrounded in "history," according to LP, Inc. But in effect there is the potential for the equivalent of a sit-down strike coming from the grassroots (whatever form these might take), and historians seem to be anxious about where they fit in this whole process. They have seen what has happened in the academic provinces to British studies with the empire striking black and the traditionalists being forced to fight their Oxford-history-of-the-British-Empire rearguard battle to keep the barbarians from the gate.[20] This must not happen to American history. With the alternative narratives seeping into historical debate, like so many crime families moving in on the historian's turf, the only antidote must be change coming in a controlled fashion from on high, with foundations and professional organizations, like the OAH, footing the bill for this new protection racket.

And that is only the first three paragraphs of this Report!

Growing weary of close analysis, I will cut to the LP, Inc., chaser, which is the outline for an internationalized U.S. history survey course. Note that with all the talk of historicizing the nation, the central topic and actor still remains "the" American nation. It is, LP, Inc., informs us, "properly a focal point for the creation of an internationalized American history." All that is required is a bit of empiricism in the pursuit of "the people, the money, the knowledges, and the things," and one finds "oneself internationalizing the study of American history."[21] It is merely a wonder why American empiricists had not recognized this before.

LP, Inc., then provides some examples of approaches that "might be pursued to connect American history more strongly to historical themes that are not exclusively American."[22] Viewed together, these are interesting. The examples seem to do one of two things: bolster ideas about American history that are already evident without the leap to the international level, or pass over some of the interesting work that has been done around issues that already brought the nation-centered narratives into question.

The first example is one of placing British America "within a context of other world-wide colonial empires and native Americans." This is being done already, I warrant. And the further suggestion that other migrations besides British ones be considered has already emerged out of a focus on ethnic studies that comes from within the traditional nation-centered historiography. By presenting this theme in this way, it seems to me, the earlier endeavors are, in a way, placed under erasure: they are there, and yet they are not so.

The second example talks about the early history of the Americans as part of an Atlantic-wide contest over the control of labor. This is again something that African Americanists have been sensitive to for years, and if their efforts have not brought these concerns into the survey courses yet, then doing so under the guise of the global is another example of placing the political under erasure. Historians endeavoring to develop "minority histories" and perspectives derived therefrom have needed to combat established interpretations of American history in the past, and the politics involved in these efforts and the manner in which the practice of history has been contested terrain get passed over in this top-down effort to install the global dimension.[23]

Next we learn that the American Revolution and its aftermath need not be treated as a singular event. It was still, according to LP, Inc., "the initiating event" of the age of revolutions, thus overlooking the kind of perspective provided by Peter Linebaugh and Marcus Rediker, which places the English Civil War (read through lenses shaped by Atlantic, racial, and gender considerations) in this position.[24] Anyway, one imagines that examining the international crosscurrents would throw up other genealogies as well. We also have the rather easy acceptance of the democratic character of the revolution(s), which would remain a contentious issue for many years, especially given the relationship of slavery to these upheavals. (The English may, after all, claim, especially in the face of "The Patriot," that they Dunmore for emancipation and a wider democracy than a bunch of Virginia slaveowners and their Boston slave-trader friends.) But merely assigning Eric Williams's chapter on the American Revolution from *Capitalism and Slavery* and following it up with C. L. R. James's *Black Jacobins* would probably take care of this.[25]

Having ignored race in revolution, we are now asked to examine the Civil War "as an episode in an international process of consolidating national territories and empires." Now, clearly, the reorganization of systems of labor referred to is meant to bring slavery into consideration, but at a time when so much has been unearthed about the actions of the slaves in rebellion (from New York City to St. Domingue to Charleston to Southampton and to Harper's Ferry) or in flight, thereby contributing to the causes and outcome of the Civil War, it seems a curious way to internationalize this saga (though one may indeed want to understand the issues raised by national consolidation). It is another example of depoliticization and further distances African Americans from "the" story.

This might be shown by looking at how an outsider might have viewed the Civil War. Let's take as our example Pandita Ramabai, an Indian Brahmin woman who spent a brief period in Philadelphia and retained strong connections with the American missionaries who supported her philanthropic work in the Bombay Presidency. Writing about the Civil War, she described it in terms of its meaning for both African Americans and women; she highlighted Lincoln, the emancipator (even before he had much intention of emancipating anything), Sojourner Truth, and the women missionaries supporting the cause of the freedpeople. For her, the story was not about national consolidation at all but was rather an allegory about anti-imperialism, women's rights, and equality; it was an event, as the American Revolution was also (regardless of its failings with regard to the issue of slavery), that could speak to Indians who wished to contest (in myriad ways) British colonialism.[26]

Next, LP, Inc., presents the industrial revolution, and in this case we have the link between the global economy and New World slavery and worldwide colonial systems nicely presented. Here we have an enlargement of industrialism that we were given back in the 1940s by Eric Williams, and so we are heartened to some degree, though the overall sense of anticolonialism that arose from his work and his engagement with capitalism as an economic and political system is missing here — but this is a post-Marxian age, so what do we expect! We learn that "In time industrialism was itself a global phenomenon," which makes this development seem like the spread of a natural organism, spreading outward from Lancashire, rather than something that might have taken on and expanded an Afro-Asian economic (global) system.[27]

Finally, we are given the tribute to Daniel Rodgers's *Atlantic Crossings:* "The Progressive Movement and the New Deal might be contextualized as part of an international age of social politics."[28] While one certainly has to stand in awe of this work's accomplishments, it is still important to recognize that it almost entirely overlooks women and gender, African Americans and race, empire and imperialism, alongside fascism, in its understanding of social politics. As the culmination of LP, Inc.'s examples, this seems fitting.

Considered together, the examples do not deviate much from what one would expect to find in an American/U.S. history survey course currently being taught: British Empire, American Revolution, industrialization, Civil War, progressivism — all the foundational moments that have been well established for a long time now. Of course, there is a desire to nudge people out of the current mode of thinking toward internationalism, but if these examples represent where we are going, why make all the effort?

Who's Next?

Meet the new Boss,
Same as the old Boss.
— Pete Townsend, "Won't Get Fooled Again"

How do we make the great leap forward? How do we make the long march toward the promised land of internationalism? Can it be done in one five-year plan, or will it take several? How do we accomplish this without on the one hand using inflationary rhetoric about our proximity to our goal or, on the other, raising the self-interest rates? Is there a light at the end of the tunnel as we move through a period of questioning "the nation" to some overarching plan sensitive to the global? More seriously, is any plan that we try to establish not in some way going to reify the boundaries of "American" and "international" and in so doing undermine the possibility that we may transcend them?

Rather than being programmatic about the global and the international in ways that reify the past, I would suggest we need to deploy them as questions that may provide the limits to our endeavors as historians. It is merely sufficient, I would argue, that we enlarge our perspective so that we enable ourselves to raise questions about ourselves and about the kinds of histories we write and in which we believe. Here are some examples of questions that animate my interventions (and I stress that they may interest only me; others will have to find their own "way in the world" according to the kind of work in which they are engaged): Why do we place the American Revolution as the determining event in North American history and ignore the arguably more important revolution in St. Domingue? Why would we make the decision to do this when a historian like Henry Adams did not, at least to the same degree? Why do we instinctively conform to the Burnsian paradigm that American history is the story of the Civil War and baseball, with the West thrown in for good measure and to provide a manifest destination, all with a jazz soundtrack? Is it necessary to do more than ask these questions and keep asking them, whether or not we like the answers? If we follow this line of thinking and questioning, we will find, I believe, that the international, like all the ingredients in *ragu* spaghetti, is "in there" already and that in this regard the notion of internationalizing American history will be no more than a tautology.

But if we are to follow the programmatic strictures of LP, Inc., and the FAC, then, in the words of the Immortal Bard II, "don't you know that you can count me out." And I make no apologies for this. For, it seems to me, when the notion of the "American" rests in the erasure, or (as Michel-Rolph Trouillot might describe it) the "silencing," of that which is fundamentally international, then the notion of internationalizing American history constitutes an oxymoron.[29] "American" history, after all, has appropriated the term ("American") for a national history or concern, and as such it has been founded in the contradiction of the international, the establishing of boundaries for an altogether rather Whiggish history. "We" have cheered for the American revolutionaries, excoriated "traitors," established "our" icons (many with localized meanings masking internationalism — e.g., the Statue of Liberty), and created our national sports (baseball!) and music (jazz?). But to create one national history out of the many histories that come together in the southwestern frontier, in the response to the Philippine insurgency or the Boxer Rebellion, in the attempt of women to play professional baseball after World War II, in the experiences of American prostitutes living in Shanghai and Johannesburg, in the flight of capital to the Sunbelt and offshore — to name just a few things that interest me — has required silencing the international at the expense of the national. Such "American" history cannot in fact be internationalized (or reconnected) except in self-serving ways that make it seem that "we" are exporting "our" product to the global market like so many bales of wheat or reels of Hollywood movies, making the world safe for American history.

This has been a feature of much American comparative history, as Daniel T. Rodgers has noted, concentrating on comparison rather than connection.[30] Often boundaries have been cemented and presuppositions confirmed via comparison, when opening up the analytical framework to consider connections would reveal (what I consider) the imperial domain that passes over such boundaries and confounds such presuppositions.[31] Indeed, the notion of American exceptionalism itself, which I have considered at length elsewhere,[32] is dependent on comparison and cannot be founded on ignorance of other societies and their social arrangements, the failure to consider other possibilities, or the ill-informed aspect of American historians. How could it possibly be so? Notions of what constitute "American" derive from deeply comparative sensibilities, whether from the republican ideologies of a revolution that cast off the nation from its "motherland" or from the progressive ideologies emergent at a time when Kipling was eulogizing the "white man's burden," evident in American imperialist ventures into Cuba and the Philippines. But those sensibilities evince a marked political concern to repress commonalities and connections while celebrating the particular and the apparently unconnected.

Enough said. To end, though, let me just say that I hope this latest FAC intervention, which in many ways attempts to step into the gap left by the perceived demise of area studies, prospers as well as its forerunner. As G. V. Desani's Benarrji would say, "And good luck to them!"[33]

Notes

1 Special issues of the *Journal of American History*.
2 Eric Foner, "American Freedom in a Global Age," *American Historical Review* 1 (February 2001): 1–16; *La Pietra Report* (New York: New York University, OAH, Project on Internationalizing the Study of American History, 2000). For an interesting overview of the new emphasis on transnational history, see Robert A. Gross, "The Transnational Turn: Rediscovering American Studies in a Wider World," *Journal of American Studies* 34, 3 (December 2000): 373–393. With regard to Foner's essay, which, like his book, *The Story of American Freedom* (New York: W. W. Norton, 1998), places great emphasis on the exceptionalism of Americans' belief in notions of freedom and liberty, it is worth noting his refusal to consider the possibility of problems interpreting the meaning of freedom that derive from issues of translation and the difficulties of determining equivalence across cultural and political systems. Dipesh Chakrabarty, *Provinicializing Europe: Postcolonial Thought and Historical Difference* (Princeton, N.J.: Princeton University Press, 2000), is crucial here. It is also interesting to note that Foner draws on Daniel T. Rodgers, *Atlantic Crossings: Social Politics in a Progressive Age* (Cambridge, Mass.: Harvard University Press, 1998), in his discussion of internationalizing history, when one of this book's main contributions is to question notions of exceptionalism evidenced in Foner's essay. Finally, a comparison with Edmund S. Morgan, *American Slavery, American Freedom: The Ordeal of Colonial Virginia* (New York: W. W. Norton, 1975), which is less celebratory than Foner's work, would be instructive.
3 *La Pietra Report*, p. 3.
4 Ibid.
5 See, for example, W. T. Stead, *The Americanization of the World* (New York: Garland, 1972 [1902]).

6 Acton writes: "My grandfather, William Mitchell, had taken an active part in Chicago's growth, having founded the Illinois Trust and Savings Bank and a large family, ramifications of which spread to Hawaii, Spain, and, in our case Italy." He was however, "remote from the vulgar conception of a Chicagoan"; Harold Acton, *Memoirs of an Aesthete* (London: Methuen, 1970), p. 18.

7 Evelyn Waugh, *Brideshead Revisited* (New York: Knopf, 1993).

8 University of California Press, 2002.

9 The report's author acknowledges the Ford Foundation's efforts to "rethink area studies"; p. 24.

10 This particular historiographical shift, for example, leaves out the contributions to American historiography of W. E. B. Du Bois, who, along with numerous other African American intellectuals, had never fit within the southern consensus on race and civil rights and was marginalized from the old perspective and the new (sometimes by historians who seemed to be directly appropriating his ideas). See Robert Gregg, "Giant Steps: W. E. B. Du Bois and the Enterprise of History," in *W. E. B. Du Bois, Race and the City*, ed. Michael B. Katz and Thomas J. Sugrue (Philadelphia: University of Pennsylvania Press, 1998), pp. 77–99.

11 Peter Linebaugh and Marcus Rediker, in *The Many-Headed Hydra: Sailors, Slaves, Commoners, and the Hidden History of the Revolutionary Atlantic* (Boston: Beacon Press, 2000), refer to a "hidden history." See also Michel-Rolphe Trouillot, *Silencing the Past: Power and the Production of History* (Boston: Beacon Press, 1995).

12 *La Pietra Report*, p. 3.

13 Ibid.

14 Ibid., p. 5.

15 Ibid.

16 With regard to this point, see Chakrabarty, *Provincializing Europe*, pp. 97–113.

17 See, for example, Oscar Handlin, *The Uprooted* (Boston: Little, Brown, 1990); Herbert Gutman, *Work, Culture and Society in Industrializing America* (New York: Knopf, 1976); John Bodnar, *The Transplanted* (Bloomington: Indiana University Press, 1985).

18 *La Pietra Report,* p. 5. Emphasis added.

19 Ibid.

20 The new *Oxford History of the British Empire* is edited by W. Roger Louis (Oxford: Oxford University Press, 1998). Some of the most interesting insights on these tensions in British studies are to be found in Antoinette Burton's work; see "Who Needs the Nation? Interrogating British History," *Journal of Historical Sociology* 10, 3 (1997): 227–248, and "When Was Britain? Nostalgia for the Nation at the End of the 'American Century,' " *Journal of Modern History*, June 2003.

21 *La Pietra Report,* p. 5.

22 Ibid.

23 Morgan, *American Slavery, American Freedom*, provides just one example of this understanding of global dimensions underlying American history. The extensive literature on comparative slavery (and almost no work in slavery is without a comparative dimension, implicitly or explicitly) provides another.

24 Linebaugh and Rediker, *The Many-Headed Hydra*.

25 Eric Williams, *Capitalism and Slavery* (Chapel Hill: University of North Carolina Press, 1994); C. L. R. James, *The Black Jacobins* (New York: Vintage, 1963).

26 Meera Kosambi, ed., *Pandita Ramabai, through Her Own Words* (Delhi: Oxford University Press, 2000), pp. 222–227; A. B. Shah, ed., *The Letters and Correspondence of Pandita Ramabai* (Bombay: Maharashtra State Board of Literature and Culture, 1977).

27 For a critical response to such a view, see Mike Davis's new book, *Late Victorian Holocausts: El Niño Famines and the Making of the Third World* (London: Verso, 2001). See also Basil Davidson, *Africa in History* (New York: Collier Books, 1991).

28 *La Pietra Report*, p. 13; Rodgers, *Atlantic Crossings*.

29 Trouillot, *Silencing the Past*.

30 Rodgers, *Atlantic Crossings*.

31 This point has been discussed at length in my earlier work, *Inside Out, Outside In: Essays in Comparative History* (New York: St. Martin's Press, 1999), and in Rodgers, *Atlantic Crossings*.

32 Robert Gregg, "Apropos Exceptionalism: Imperial Location and Comparative Histories of South Africa and the United States," in Gregg, *Inside Out, Outside In*, pp. 1–26.

33 G. V. Desani, *All about H. Hatterr* (New Paltz, N.Y.: McPherson, 1986).

AUGUSTO ESPIRITU

Asian American Global Discourses and the Problem of History

What I would like to present is an attempt to expand the boundaries of "Asian American" studies. There is nothing "new" in this, as such a project has been well under way for the last decade, and arguably, ever since the "founding" or "foundings" of Asian American studies. I want to offer my critique of the field as an attempt at both spatial and temporal dislocation, both a synchronic and diachronic intervention. I want to embed these criticisms in a vibrant and deeply contested arena—Asian American cultural studies, or Asian American cultural criticism. In particular, I want to examine the terrain of global culture that has been opened up by investigations variously named "transnational," "diasporic," "postcolonial," and "postnational."

I want to put forward a very direct criticism of this body of work—the unproblematic place of *history* in the discourses of the global—and to demonstrate this in several examples. My critique is in part inspired by Paul Gilroy's conceptualization of the "Black Atlantic," especially as a sphere of cultural continuity and conversation that has been repressed by imperialism and nationalism.[1] Mine is a polemical piece that is designed to elicit discussion about how Asian Americans think of the "global," a "region" of interest toward which much ink has been spilled.[2] The stakes are high, involving no less than the future of the "discipline" or "social movement" called Asian American studies, which is now more than thirty years old and becoming an important force in academic and intellectual life in the United States. The debate that I seek to map here finds parallels in debates or reexamination in various ethnic and area studies.[3]

There have been numerous attempts to map the discursive terrain of the Asia-Pacific.[4] From what I can tell, mine is not the first and certainly will not be the last of these topographical efforts. What drives them are the rapid globalizing transformations that have been occurring in the last twenty years and the anxieties produced by their effects. Asia's newly industrializing countries have emerged during this period as among the most vibrant areas of economic activity in the world. The volume of trade between the United States and these countries has increased exponentially, while the traffic in migrants, legal and illegal, on both sides of the Pacific Ocean, has likewise accelerated.[5] In the last ten years, we have witnessed the impact of these developments on Asian communities across the Pacific. We have seen, for instance, the intensification of a new round of conflict between India and Pakistan, accompanied by the rise of labor organizing among taxi cab drivers in New York. We have seen the dismantling of U.S. military bases in the Philippines, attempts at reunification between North and South Korea, and the opening of Vietnam to international trade. These events were paralleled across the Pacific by struggles against racial stereotypes of Filipinas in the media, Korean American organizing in light of the Los Angeles civil disturbances, and the southern California Vietnamese community's protest against a video store owner who dared to put up a poster of Ho Chi Minh inside his establishment. Finally, the tensions in U.S.-China relations have created their counterparts in the United States in the Democratic Party campaign finance scandal of 1997 and the case of Wen Ho Lee, a Chinese American unduly maligned and incarcerated for flimsy suspicions of espionage.

I have not arranged these events accidentally but in anticipation of what I see as three different, largely separate, discussions of Asian Americans and global cultural processes, perhaps responding to the unique constellation of forces that have shaped particular migrations. Postcoloniality, propelled by the prominence of South Asian intellectuals in American academe, constitutes one realm of global theorizing among Asian Americans. What it has raised are critical questions of orientalism and representation in gender politics, caste, and religion, as well as a sustained questioning of panethnic Asian categories.[6] With U.S. colonialism very much alive in the legacies of their "homelands," Filipino, Korean, and Vietnamese scholars have tended to privilege an approach, inspired by Edward Said, that attempts to rewrite imperialism into American studies.[7] This version of transnationality highlights the U.S. wars that have been fought in the Philippines, Korea, and Vietnam in the twentieth century and the legacies of genocide, partition, dictatorship, and migration that affect cultural representations in the diaspora.[8] Finally, what Aihwa Ong has eloquently, if not prematurely, argued is *the* "cultural logics of transnationality," *flexible citizenship*, has emerged in the study of Chinese transnational elites and middle classes.[9] These, as Ong demonstrates, were displaced, on the one hand, by the political instability of China and Southeast Asia and excluded, on the other hand, by the racialization of Chinese in the United States, which bars them from acceptance into the American mainstream and forces them to acknowledge a certain measure of equality with the historically stigmatized lower class of overseas Chinese and Chinese Americans.[10]

These transnational discourses have been challenged by what I see as a conservative tendency in Asian American studies. Perhaps the most interesting example of this is the *Amerasia Journal* special issue on theory, which appeared several years ago.[11] In it, we can see the contrast among Chinese American scholars, who take contrary positions and attitudes toward the introduction of theory, much of it on the question of diaspora and postnational theories. On the one side, Shirley Hune and Lisa Lowe argue for an expansion of comparative projects across national boundaries and the sponsorship of projects that frame Asian American cultural developments within the analytics of global capital, commodification, and imperialism and an antiteleological view of migrant cultures.[12] On the other side are the *Amerasia Journal* editors (Russell Leong and Glenn Omatsu), Sau-ling Wong, and Ling-Chi Wang, who in different ways question the import of these diasporic theories.[13] Leong, who in 1989 had been a cautious proponent of diaspora studies, now expresses frustration over what appears as postcolonial and transnational theories' diversion of Asian American studies away from the "community."[14] Wong, who puts forth a brilliant summation of cross-national developments and rightly cautions against the aestheticizing and depoliticizing effects of theory, nonetheless fails to critique some of the nativist assumptions of Asian American studies her work opens up.[15] And finally, Wang, who puts forward a useful dual subordination model that traces the effects of homeland politics and U.S. racism on the construction of Chinese American identities, nonetheless proposes a narrow version of Asian American coalitional efforts that attempts to severely limit or dictate transnational political projects.[16]

Yet whether for or against the rise of these new theoretical orientations, these cultural criticisms display a markedly superficial engagement with Asian American history, particularly in the realm of Asian American political and cultural history that informs contemporary cultural projects. With the exception of gestures toward the international origins of Asian American studies, an entire tradition of transnational Asian American historical writing has been elided. Long-standing traditions of protest in almost every Asian community have been ignored or forgotten, creating the truth effect that transnationality is a recent phenomenon instead of one that has a far longer history and complex genealogy. The casualty has been an international dimension to Asian American political culture that has always existed side by side with legal and labor struggles for inclusion, emancipation, and equality within the American nation. Indeed, without the constant work of unburying transnational *relationships*, informed by a deeper historicization, Asian American cultural discourse always threatens to collapse into a nation-bound approach.[17]

A casual glance at one foundational text of Asian American studies illustrates that concern for transnationality has been of long standing and reveals the importance of historical transnational political activity in the self-consciousness of the field's first scholars. *Counterpoint*, which is deceptively subtitled *Perspectives on Asian America*, was published in 1976.[18] The collection is subdivided into several areas that seem to have little to do with transnationalism: "Critical Perspectives," "Contemporary Issues," and "Literature." But a careful examination of the section on Critical Perspectives shows a preponderant concern for the interpenetration between Asia and Asian America and the circulation of Asian migrants across the Pacific and beyond: early Issei socialists and Chinese immigrant leftists; the racialized lives of Filipinos in the U.S. Navy; Korean nationalist activities in the U.S.; evacuees from Vietnam, the Marcos coercion in the United States, and the work of the Korean Central Intelligence Agency (KCIA); the Kuomintang in China and China politics in the United States; and an exploration of the internal colonial model.[19] These articles reflect a real engagement with international developments historically. The picture would become more complex if insurgent newspapers and journals such as *Gidra*, *Kalayaan International*, *Rodan*, *Getting Together*, and other "movement" papers were included. These political tracts considered developments in the Chinese Cultural Revolution, Vietnam, the Philippines, and the Pacific islands as integral parts of what it meant to be "Asian American."[20]

But one might say that *Counterpoint* is only one book, out of print, to which today's students have limited access, especially if they are not in Asian American studies programs. Beyond *Counterpoint* there is a plethora of historical writing, much of it from the 1980s and 1990s, that does not appear on the radar screens of Asian American cultural critics writing on transnationality. Works by Yuji Ichioka and his students on Japanese immigrant nationalism and Nisei study tours in Japan; Sucheng Chan's calls for comparative studies of Asian and European immigration, as well as her essays on international politics, including one in *Asian Americans: An Interpretive History*, a standard textbook; essays by K. Scott Wong, Renqiu Yu, and Robert Lee on Chinese intellectuals, the Chinese Hand Laundry Association, and immigrant radicalism; critical *Amerasia Journal* articles by Kingsley Lyu and Eun Sik Yang on Korean and Korean American women's nationalism; essays by Steffi San Buenaventura, Melinda Kerkvliet, and Jonathan Okamura on the international religious phenomenon of Hilario Moncado, the working-class figure of Pablo Manlapit, and the Filipino diaspora; Joan Jensen's *Passage from India* on Indian nationalists and Vijay Prashad's admirable "historical anthropology," *The Karma of Brown Folk*. Missing also are engagements with the Hawaiian sovereignty movement, including the work of Haunani Kay Trask or the collection of writings of the American Friends Service Committee.[21]

The extent of historical erasure is remarkable and raises several important questions:

What accounts for this selective memory in Asian American cultural criticism? What accounts for the forgetting of this strand of transnational historical thinking and historical writing?

Is this "transnational" history repressed in the desire to claim transnationality and diaspora approaches as something new — or to claim a space, a location of enunciation and power vis-à-vis the overall celebration of poststructuralism, postmodernism, and postcolonialism? Or do the new approaches simply consider colonialism, nationalism, and anticolonialism passé, something already archaic or superseded?

Or does the exclusion of these texts from the field of cultural criticism perhaps reflect a distaste for politics, especially for the left, Marxist, nationalist politics that characterize so many of these movements? In making such a historical marginalization of socialist or nationalist politics, are cultural critics today indifferent to or unaware of these historic and contemporary struggles, or are they making an ideological statement?

Finally, does the lack of engagement with such histories in cultural criticism reflect the failure of historians of Asian America to intervene or to engage in the ongoing academic debates about diaspora and transnationalism? Do their "materialist" outlooks create a barrier to the examination of cultural phenomena and a dialogue with those critics for whom language and representation inform any discourse of objectivity?[22] Does the repression of transnationality reflect a generational failure, a failure of transmission of knowledge and culture and appreciation for "internationalism"?

In raising these questions, it is not my intention to impugn Asian American cultural criticism or cultural critics but to incite discussion, debate, and reflection upon such crucial areas as reading practices, canonicity, and theory, especially as regards global, transnational processes. The sphere of the "global" provides a tremendously powerful analytical perspective that I embrace, for both scholarly and political reasons. But its spread is not inevitable, as this essay shows. There are gaps in historical engagement and politicization in the current global discourse among Asian Americans that raise skepticism among various theorists. Like many critical theorists, I share the view that a transnational perspective that is not informed by considerations of institution and power will end up being an "empty prize."[23] I have sought to "correct" this situation by highlighting one important path of investigation — a consideration of transnational political processes and engagement with Asian and Asian American political histories. Future discussions of transnationality, I hope, will engage the fascinating and highly relevant traditions of protest across the Pacific and thereby shake up the contemporary discourses on "globalization" that tend to be skewed toward neo-imperial or national-imperial purposes.

Notes

This essay is a version of a paper first presented at the Asian American Studies Conference in Toronto, March 29, 2001. I thank Antoinette Burton for her encouragement and interest in this project and for her invaluable suggestions.

1 Paul Gilroy, *The Black Atlantic: Modernity and Double Consciousness* (Cambridge, Mass.: Harvard University Press, 1993).

2 For a current, critical review of the literature on the "global" and "globalization," see "The Great Globalization Debate: An Introduction," in *The Global Transformations Reader,* ed. David Held and Anthony McGrew (Malden, Mass.: Blackwell, 2000).

3 For instance, see Christopher Shea, "A Blacker Shade of Yale: African-American Studies Takes a New Direction," *Lingua Franca*, March 2001: 42–49; *Weighing the Balance: Southeast Asian Studies Ten Years After*, proceedings of meetings held in New York City, November 15 and December 10, 1999 (New York: Southeast Asia Program, Social Science Research Council, n.d.). I thank Antoinette Burton and Michael Salman for bringing these two references to my attention.

4 For two different approaches to the subject, see Philip F. Kelly and Kris Olds, "Questions in a Crisis: The Contested Meanings of Globalization in the Asia-Pacific," in *Globalization and the Asia-Pacific: Contested Territories*, ed. Kris Olds et al. (New York: Routledge, 1999), pp. 1–15, and Shirley Geok-lin Lim et al., eds., *Transnational Asia Pacific: Gender, Culture, and the Public Sphere* (Urbana: University of Illinois Press, 1999).

5 See Paul Ong, Edna Bonacich, and Lucie Cheng, "The Political Economy of Capitalist Restructuring and the New Asian Immigration," in *The New Asian Immigration in Los Angeles and Global Restructuring*, ed. Paul Ong, Edna Bonacich, and Lucie Cheng (Philadelphia: Temple University Press, 1994).

6 Influential texts include Gayatri Spivak, *In Other Worlds: Essays in Cultural Politics* (New York: Routledge, 1988); Sarah Harasym, ed., *The Post-Colonial Critic: Interviews, Strategies, Dialogues* (New York: Routledge, 1990); Chandra Talpade Mohanty, *Third World Women and the Politics of Feminism* (Bloomington: Indiana University Press, 1991). The list of South Asians writing on postcoloniality and Asian Americans is long. Among others, they include R. Radhakrishnan, "Is the Ethnic Authentic in the Diaspora," in *The State of Asian America*, ed. Karin Aguilar-San Juan (Boston: South End Press, 1994), pp. 219–234; Lavina Dhingra Shankar and Rajini Srikanth, eds., *A Part, Yet Apart: South Asians in Asian America* (Philadelphia: Temple University Press, 1998); Deepika Bahri and Mary Vasudeva, *Between the Lines: South Asians and Postcoloniality* (Philadelphia: Temple University Press, 1996); Susan Koshy, "The Fiction of Asian American Literature," *Asian American Studies: A Reader*, ed. Jean Yuwen and Min Song (New Brunswick, N.J.: Rutgers University Press, 2000), pp. 467–496; Gayatri Gopinath, "Nostalgia, Desire, Diaspora: South Asian Sexualities in Motion," *Positions: East Asia Cultures Critique* 5, 2 (fall 1997): 467–490; Vijay Prashad and Biju Mathew, "Satyagraha in America: The Political Culture of South Asians in the U.S.," *Amerasia Journal* 25, 3 (1999/2000): ix–xv.

7 See Edward Said, *Culture and Imperialism* (New York: Knopf, 1993).

8 For instance, see the collection in *Positions: East Asia Cultures Critique* 5, 2 (fall 1997) special issue, "New Formations, New Questions: Asian American Studies," esp. Oscar Campomanes, "New Formations of Asian American Studies and the Question of U.S.

Imperialism," pp. 523–550; Viet Thanh Nguyen, "Representing Reconciliation: Le Ly Hayslip and the Victimized Body," pp. 605–642; and Helen Heran Jun, "Contingent Nationalisms: Renegotiating Borders in Korean and Korean American Women's Oppositional Struggles," pp. 325–356.

9 Aihwa Ong, *Flexible Citizenship: The Cultural Logics of Transnationality* (Durham, N.C.: Duke University Press, 1999). This is not the place to undertake a critique of this bold attempt at synthesis. Nonetheless, I say "prematurely" because it is my belief that "transnationality" involves a much more heterogeneous field than Ong has made allowance for in her argument. For instance, the specter of colonialism and colonial histories, which she has chosen to leave out or bracket from investigation, haunts the work, as much as it today haunts contemporary reality. Transnationality within such colonial or neocolonial relations — say, in the case of the Philippines, Guam, Puerto Rico, and numerous Pacific nations still under colonial rule — will have different inflections than "flexible citizenship" alone.

10 See especially chapters 3 and 4 on cultural capital and the "Pacific Shuttle" of Chinese transnationals in the United States in A. Ong, *Flexible Citizenship*, pp. 87–138.

11 "Thinking Theory in Asian American Studies," *Amerasia Journal* 21, 1 and 2 (1995).

12 Shirley Hune, "Rethinking Race: Paradigms and Policy Formation," pp. 29–40, and Lisa Lowe, "On Contemporary Asian American Projects," pp. 41–54, both in *Amerasia Journal* 21, 1 and 2 (1995).

13 Russell Leong, "Lived Theory (Notes on the Run)," pp. v–x; Sau-ling Wong, "Denationalization Reconsidered: Asian American Cultural Criticism at a Theoretical Crossroads," pp. 1–28; L. Ling-Chi Wang, "The Structure of Dual Domination: Toward a Paradigm for the Study of the Chinese Diaspora in the U.S.," pp. 149–170 — all in *Amerasia Journal* 21, 1 and 2 (1995).

14 See "To Our Readers," "Asians in the Americas," special issue of *Amerasia Journal* 15, 2 (1989): esp. xiv–xv: "While the diaspora perspective is useful for mapping the past dispersion and direction of groups such as Asians to the Americas in a comparative context, it is less useful in probing the present or in predicting the future of our settlement and development here, in my view. Other terms, such as migration or immigration, are more fluid and open in that they do not carry *the burden or boundary of a 'homeland,'* embedded within" (my emphasis). This was followed by Leong's "Lived Theory." Leong is being partly ironic in the following passage but perhaps just as serious in his frustration: "Because academics and other Asian Americanists — including myself — 'pimp off' the community to varying degrees, I feel that it is our responsibility to turn part of the profits [back] to the community" (p. ix). Leong also has a list of useful suggestions for "translation activities," community teaching, and so forth that academics could undertake to reduce the gap between academia and community, which we would all do well to heed. What he does not address, however, are the complex issues involved in the "depoliticization" — or perhaps "repoliticization" might be a better word — of Asian American studies. Asian American studies has become more problematic, in my view, in light of its relatively successful institutionalization. Activists of the last few decades risked their lives and limbs to open up the doors to the institution, ironically in the name of breaking it down. Now I think the problem of Asian American studies has shifted, not only to the concept that has often been bandied about, which is institutionalization, but also in terms of hegemony. Now that Asian American studies is "in the door," I think one realizes that the terrain of resistance is much more complicated. Indeed, the political perspectives reflected by Asian American studies — relevance, community consciousness, etc. — are a distinct minority within the

university. The task of the administrators of Asian American studies and of those Asian Americanists who had been politicized to think of themselves as such has been how to position Asian American studies as a field and as an insurgent intellectual and social movement within the context of the larger debates in academia and in student affairs and to continue to undertake the task of translation and adaptation of these ideals to the challenges of the present. I think some kind of a larger discussion is needed in this direction. Transnational studies becomes in this sense both an important indicator of the anxieties in the field and a real problem or opportunity, depending on one's perspective, that could radically alter Asian American scholarly work, politics, and social organization.

15   An example of this is the oversight in the segment entitled "A Personal Postscript." The opening paragraph reads: "On the door of the Asian American Studies Program is a sign: THIS IS NOT ASIAN STUDIES, SOUTH AND SOUTHEAST ASIAN STUDIES, OR EAST ASIAN LANGUAGES." How does Wong explain this jarring note? She says it was put up for "practical concern" by a "frustrated secretary" who has to deal with numerous "misdirected inquiries and interruptions." For Wong, it "epitomizes the institutional reality within which Asian American studies still operates today. It is a reminder of the precariousness of Asian American studies' discursive space" (Wong, "Denationalization Reconsidered"). I would agree with Wong, but I also see something else at work here. At issue is the performative "NOT," which seems to exceed its intended meaning. I submit that there is a nativist subtext to this sign, a kind of ressentiment. Indeed, it seems like an attempt to police the boundaries institutionally — and by extension intellectually — between Asian and Asian American studies. Notice that Asian American studies is set against other disciplines that could be construed as foreign. In the context of the anti-immigrant Proposition 187 law that Wong says we should be contesting, the sign assumes a different meaning.

16   Wang writes: "The proposed [dual subordination] paradigm reaffirms the validity of the founding principles and approach of ethnic studies and supplements it with transnationality, but only to the extent they affect Asian American experiences, with two additional analytical dimensions: the diplomatic relations between the U.S. and affected East and Southeast Asian countries and the extraterritorial interaction between the Asian American communities and their respective home countries" ("The Structure of Dual Domination," p. 166). Wang sees transnationality in instrumental or utilitarian terms only to the extent that it affects Asian American experiences. How would or could one limit the play of the "transnational"? This would be a difficult, if not unrewarding, task indeed. One senses or sympathizes with what seems like Wang's wariness or anxiety about a play of signification — the global — that could overrun Asian American studies.

17   For two important literary and cultural critiques in this direction, see Oscar Campomanes's important polemic on the nativist bias of Asian American cultural studies, "Filipinos in the United States and Their Literature of Exile," in *Reading the Literatures of Asian America*, ed. Shirley Geok-lin Lim and Amy Ling (Philadelphia: Temple University Press, 1992), pp. 49–78, and King-Kok Cheung's critique of the masculinist assumptions of this Asian American cultural nationalist rhetoric, "The Woman Warrior versus the Chinaman Pacific," in *Conflicts in Feminism*, ed. Marianne Hirsch and Evelyn Fox Keller (New York: Routledge, 1990), pp. 234–251. Even some of Asian American studies' most perceptive social theorists are not immune to the seductions of the nation. While this deserves extended commentary, which must be taken up elsewhere, note for instance this passage from a canonical work of the field: "A sort of 'exceptionalism' turns out to be necessary if one is to address racial dynamics in the U.S. (and probably in respect to any

particular nation's racial dynamics); this is what we seek to provide with our 'racial formation' perspective." Michael Omi and Howard Winant, *Racial Formation in the United States: From the 1960s to the 1980s* (New York: Routledge, 1986), p. 54.

18 Emma Gee, ed., *Counterpoint: Perspectives on Asian America* (Los Angeles: University of California Press, 1976).

19 See the following in Gee, ed., *Counterpoint*: Yuji Ichioka, "Early Issei Socialists and the Japanese Community," pp. 47–62; H. Mark Lai, "A Historical Survey of the Chinese Left in America," pp. 63–80; Don Nakanishi, "Minorities and International Politics," pp. 81–85; Raymond Okamura, "Iva Ikuko Toguri: Victim of an American Fantasy;" Jesse Quinsaat, "An Exercise on How to Join the Navy and Still Not See the World"; Kingsley K. Lyu, "Korean Nationalist Activities in Hawaii and America, 1901–1945"; Le Anh Tu: "The Vietnam Evacuees: What Now?"; "The Story of the Marcos Coercion," pp. 134–139; "KCIA Agents All Out to Get New Korea and the Activities of the South Korean Central Intelligence Agency in the United States," pp. 140–145; Brett de Bary and Victor Nee, "The Kuomintang in Chinatown," pp. 146–151; H. Mark Lai, "China Politics and the U.S. Chinese Communities," pp. 152–159; and John Liu, "Towards an Understanding of the Internal Colonial Model," pp. 160–168. The early transnational conversation might be stretched back even further to Amy Tachiki et al., eds., *Roots: An Asian American Reader*, (Los Angeles: University of California Press, 1971).

20 See a list of movement journals in Tachiki et al., eds., *Roots*, p. 343. The book might qualify to be the foundational text of Asian American studies and has specific references to transnational themes, although I have chosen the more accessible and more scholarly *Counterpoint*.

21 Yuji Ichioka: "Japanese Immigrant Nationalism: The Issei and the Sino-Japanese War, 1937–1941," *California History* 59, 3 (fall 1990): 260–275; "*Kengakudan*: The Origin of Nisei Study Tours of Japan," *California History* 73, 1 (spring 1994): 30–43; Brian Hayashi, "*For the Sake of Our Japanese Brethren*": *Assimilation, Nationalism, and Protestantism among the Japanese of Los Angeles, 1895–1942* (Stanford, Calif.: Stanford University Press, 1995); Eiichiro Azuma, "Racial Struggle, Immigrant Nationalism, and Ethnic Identity: Japanese and Filipinos in the California Delta, 1930–1941," *Pacific Historical Review* 67, 2 (May 1998); Sucheng Chan: "European and Asian Immigration: A Comparative Approach," in *Immigration Reconsidered: History, Sociology, and Politics*, ed. Virginia Yans-McLaughlin (New York: Oxford University Press, 1990), pp. 37–75, and *Asian Americans: An Interpretive History* (Philadelphia: Temple University Press, 1990); K. Scott Wong, "Liang Qichao and the Chinese of America: A Re-evaluation of His Selected Memoir of Travels in the New World," *Journal of American Ethnic History* 11, 4 (summer 1992): 3–24; Renqiu Yu, *To Save China, To Save Ourselves: The Chinese Hand Laundry Alliance of New York* (Philadelphia: Temple University Press, 1992); Robert Lee, "The Hidden World of Asian Immigrant Radicalism," *The Immigrant Left in the United States* eds. Paul Buhle and Dan Georgakas (Albany: State University of New York Press, 1996), pp. 256–288. Kingsley Lyu: "Korean Nationalist Activities in Hawaii and the Continental United States, 1900–1945. Part I: 1900–1919," *Amerasia Journal* 4, 1 (1977): 23–90, and "Korean Nationalist Activities in Hawaii and the Continental United States, 1900–1945. Part II: 1919–1945," *Amerasia Journal* 4, 2 (1977): 53–100; Eun Sik Yang, "Korean Women of America from Subordination to Partnership, 1903–1930," *Amerasia Journal* 11, 2 (1984): 1–28; Steffi San Buenaventura, "The Master and the Federation: A Filipino-American Social Movement in California and Hawaii," *Social Process in Hawaii* 33 (1991): 169–193; Melinda Kerkvliet, "Interpreting Pablo Manlapit," *Social Process in Hawaii* 37 (1996): 1–25; Jonathan Okamura, *Imagining the Filipino American Diaspora: Transnational Relations, Identi-*

ties, and Communities (New York: Garland, 1998); Joan Jensen, *Asian Indian Immigrants to North America* (New Haven, Conn.: Yale University Press, 1988); Vijay Prashad, *The Karma of Brown Folk* (Minneapolis: University of Minnesota Press, 2000); Haunani-Kay Trask, *From a Native Daughter: Colonialism and Sovereignty in Hawai'i* (Monroe, Maine: Common Courage Press, 1993); American Friends Service Committee, *He Alo A He Alo: Face to Face, Hawaiian Voices on Sovereignty* (Honolulu: Hawaii Area Office of the American Friends Service Committee, 1993).

22 For instance, see Gordon H. Chang, "History and Postmodernism," Thinking Theory in Asian American Studies, *Amerasia Journal* 21, 1 and 2 (1995): 89–94, which rejects the relevance of "postmodernism" to history and sees social history as remaining the predominant form of historical writing, even as numerous historians have moved toward cultural history and theory.

23 I am inverting a much cited phrase of the early Asian American movement. Penny Nakatsu, keynote address to *Proceedings of National Asian American Studies Conference II*, ed. George Kagiwada et al., (Davis: University of California, 1974), pp. 5–9. In 1974, Nakatsu wrote: "If Asian American Studies is not *rooted* within the life-experience of each of our *communities* and does not illuminate the forces which bear upon our communities' destiny and foster the development of significant social change, the attainment of institutional credibility would be an *empty prize*" (my emphasis). Cited in Gary Okihiro, "African and Asian American Studies: A Comparative Analysis and Commentary," *Frontiers of Asian American Studies* eds. Gail Nomura, Stephen H. Sumida, Russell C. Leong, and Russell Endo (Pullman: Washington State University Press, 1991), p. 24. Perhaps the key word here is "communities," for indeed what so impresses us about contemporary life is the problematization of communities as a result of the dislocations of capital, war, famine, and so forth and the new paths of migration and movement opened up by the "end" of the cold war.

RADHIKA VIYAS MONGIA

Race, Nationality, Mobility: A History of the Passport

In a sense, every modern nation is a product of colonization.
— Etienne Balibar

The global monopoly of a system of states over the international movement of people seems an unremarkable fact in the present world. This essay is concerned, in part, with how this came to be the case. Here I chart a history of the modern passport in relation to theories of nation, race, and state. Given the current ubiquity of the passport as a necessary document for international mobility, one might expect that a passport system emerged, full-blown, into a world of nation-states. But it has a rather more checkered, piecemeal, and counterintuitive development. In other words, there are no definitive "origins" for the passport system and, indeed, even today it is a system that lacks systematization and standardization.[1] My focus here is the sequence of events and protracted debates between 1906 and 1915 that surrounded the Canadian demand that Indians emigrating to Canada should have passports. This demand was largely made on the grounds of race, though rerouted via arguments of lack of labor demand, cultural incompatibility, and unsuitability of the climate, and eventually accepted on the grounds of national sovereignty. An analysis of these events and debates demonstrates that the passport not only is a technology *reflecting* certain understandings of race, nation/nationality, and state, but was also central to *organizing* and *securing* the modern definitions of these categories.

I shall thus advance two primary arguments: first, that the modern economy of migration, grounded in race and imperialism, is fundamental to the creation of a geopolitical space dominated by the nation-state. Second and relatedly, I shall argue that a blurring of the vocabularies of nationality and race is a founding strategy of the modern (nation) state and, as such, it should be impossible to inquire into the modern state without attending to its creation in a global context of colonialism and racism. The passport, as we shall see, is one concrete technology that harnesses this strategy and produces the "nationalized" migrant. In using the term "nationalize(d)," I wish to draw attention to its peculiar valence as signaling a certain conjuncture between the "nation," which is held to be a primarily sociocultural category describing forms of community, and the "state," which relates to forms of governance. To suggest that the passport is a technology that nationalizes bodies along racial lines is, therefore, to track the itinerary of a process of subject production where both terms, "nation" and "state," are implicated in discourses of race.

Before proceeding any further, some background on Indian emigration and state intervention prior to the twentieth century is in order. In August 1834 Britain abolished slavery in its colonies. Abolition generated a huge scarcity of labor in the labor-intensive economies. This demand for labor was met, in part, via the introduction of indentured Indian labor. As early as 1835, the Court of Directors of the East India Company (in charge, at the time, of British administration in India), installed mechanisms of state control to monitor this massive movement, and under its recommendations the British Parliament ratified the first act for regulating this movement in 1838.[2]

As such regulation lacked legal precedence, this occurred amid challenges to the authority and legality of the state in monitoring the movement of "free" subjects (as opposed to "unfree" subjects of the African slave diaspora). These challenges were answered on two grounds: the first stemmed from the paternalism of the state, which felt it "could not divest [itself] of the interest which [it] felt bound to take in the well-being of those who might be tempted to try their fortune by engaging as laborers in other countries."[3] While recognizing "that this practice [had] no foundation in existing law," the regulations, representatives for the company argued, were warranted to ensure the security and well-being of the laborers, especially given the "necessary ignorance" of the "class of persons so engaging themselves."[4] The primary concern animating these early regulations was not to constrain movement but to establish a series of criteria by which the migration of indentured labor could be construed as "free" and thus distinguished from the slave trade. Second, the challenges to the regulation of "free" subjects were defended on the grounds that "it is a distinction common to every metropolis, that their colonies are governed . . . by special laws, because the elements of society are not the same therein as in Europe."[5] The peculiar situation of the colony, in other words, justified the differential application of the law and made the term "British subject" itself "susceptible of important division and modification."[6]

Our most common understanding of the nonuniversal application of supposedly universal principles is to view it as the blatant violation and hypocrisy of certain historical state formations. Within this understanding, then, the project of the Enlightenment itself is not in question; what is needed is a series of corrections and rectifications that may gradually bring all of humankind under its embracing and universal umbrella. Holding an uncommon view,

Partha Chatterjee has called this tactic — of asserting the truth and universality of post-Enlightenment thought while simultaneously instituting, in practice, the colony as an exception to this universality — the "rule of colonial difference."[7]

Chatterjee has suggested that modes of governance premised on the rule of colonial difference should not be thought of as aberrations from the universal and universally valid principles of the modern state but, rather, as "part of the common strategy for the deployment of the modern forms of disciplinary power."[8] He thus contends that it serves no analytic purpose to differentiate between the colonial state and the modern state — or to see the colonial state as "simply another form in which the modern state has generalized itself across the globe."[9] By suggesting that the colonial state is mistakenly thought of as a particular variety of the modern state, which we can now relegate to the museum of past horrors, Chatterjee draws our attention to how analyses of the colonial state must be immanent to analyses of the modern state; hence, the accepted polarity of the state in Europe and the state in the periphery is brought to crisis, and the presumed analytic validity of an insular "West" and an "East" is revealed as untenable.

State regulation of migration (and the colonial emergence of the passport) is, of course, an obvious site at which to trace this co-implication of the colonial state and the modern state and, thus, the coproduction of the state in the "West" and in the "East." As we shall see, the rule of colonial difference would come to structure the international system of states as it sought to regulate the movement of "free" subjects through the installation of the passport.

Under the indenture system, Indians were transported to a number of colonies, *including* Mauritius, Guyana, Fiji, Jamaica, Trinidad, Tanzania, Kenya, Uganda, *and* South Africa. However, until the early twentieth century, the state monitored only the large-scale movement of indentured Indian labor and did not interfere with the scattered, infrequent migration of those not participating in the state-controlled indenture system. Indeed, within the law, the terms "emigrate," "emigration," and "emigrant" referred *only* to indentured labor. Thus the Indian Emigration Act XXI of 1883, the definitive Indian emigration legislation until 1915, states: "'Emigrate' and 'Emigration' denote the departure by sea out of British India of a native of India under an agreement to labor for hire in some country beyond the limits of India other than the island of Ceylon or the Straits Settlements."[10] The term "to labor," moreover, had been interpreted as "manual labor," thus exempting, in particular, emigrants from the wealthier classes. Further, the act expressly specified the countries to which one could "emigrate." Thus, state control over "emigration" covered *only* the large-scale movement of indentured labor to specific countries.

Given the nature of the legislation, emigrants who did not contract to labor prior to embarking on their journeys or those not engaged in "manual labor" were thus free to travel unhindered, especially between parts of the British empire. In other words, thus far, the state did not exercise a monopoly over the mobility of people. Within the history of Indian emigration regulations, it is only with the migration of small groups of "free" Indians to Australia and Canada, in the first decade of the twentieth century, that we see the initial demands to extend state control to cover all types of migration in recommendations to require passports to restrict such "free" movement.

The anxiety over the migration of Indians to Canada begins in earnest in about 1906, with the arrival of about two thousand Indian men at Vancouver. The anxiety is evident in the correspondence and in what was to become an intense, frantic communication, primarily via telegrams and a series of confidential memos and reports, among the clunky state triangulation of Canada (a self-governing British dominion and thus still part of the empire), Britain (the seat of imperial power), and India (a non-self-governing colony populated, nonetheless, by "British subjects"). The arrival in Vancouver of "some 2,000 people from Northern India" prompted the governor general of Canada to telegram the secretary of state for the colonies in London, stating that the men had "doubtless come under misrepresentation as they are not suited to [the] climate, and there is not sufficient field for their employment. Many in danger of becoming public charge and thus subject to deportation under law of Canada."[11]

The three points raised by the governor general in this brief telegram concerning the climate, the alleged lack of labor demand, and the possibility of destitution would quickly find their way into a five-point memorandum, issued by the Government of Canada on November 2, 1906, as the bona fide reasons for discouraging Indian immigration to Canada.[12] Two of the five points directly cite the climate as the chief reason to restrict the movement since the "transfer of any people from a tropical climate to a northern one . . . must of necessity result in much physical suffering and danger to health."[13] In addition, the memorandum claims that "[the] caste system which is universal among these people is seriously in the way of their employment,"[14] and "the work, for which they are required is necessarily rough and hard, and not of a character . . . for which they are physically fitted."[15] The memorandum therefore concludes that "should the immigration continue, large numbers must become a [public] charge . . . in which case they would be subject to deportation under Canadian immigration laws."[16]

The Canadian state had to resort to arguments regarding the severity of the climate and the constant unsubstantiated panic about impending large-scale destitution in an attempt to curb the migration due to the inapplicability of

Indian Emigration Act XXI of 1883. Since the emigrants were not *already* under a contract "to labor," they did not count as "emigrants" under the act, which could thus not be enforced to prevent the migration. The *emi*gration, in other words, was deemed "free," such that the Government of India could not, within the prevailing legislation, control it.[17] The Government of Canada, on the other hand, was constrained in drafting restrictive *immi*gration legislation specifically targeted toward Indians since this would have exposed, in an indubitable way, that notwithstanding citizenship of empire, different "British subjects" were endowed with differential access to mobility. The involvement of the state in restricting the migration *at either end* would, in other words, have revealed the rule of colonial difference in a particularly salient and unacceptable manner.

It is in this context that the Government of Canada suggests, in 1907, the implementation of a system of passports, issued selectively, to curtail the migration. The prime minister, Wilfrid Laurier, offers two options for the consideration of the Colonial Office in London and the Government of India. The first is a monetary requirement: that each immigrant have on his person $200 to be permitted entry into Canada. This is deemed "necessary to avert real suffering and distress and consequently would appear to us to be called for in the best interests of humanity."[18] The second option is to require passports from all Indians traveling to Canada while simultaneously restricting the number of passports issued and authorizing the Government of Canada to deport all Indians arriving there without passports.[19]

The viceroy of India rejects the passport system, writing in a telegram:

We recognize peculiar difficulties of Canadian Government and appreciate the conciliatory attitude with which it has approached this difficult question, but after very careful consideration, regret we are unable to agree to any proposal for placing in India restrictions such as are suggested on emigration of free Indians or to suggest any further action on our part to check it. Any such measure would be opposed to our accepted policy: and it is not permissible under Indian Emigration Act XXI of 1883. . . . In present state of public feeling in India we consider legislation of this kind to be particularly inadvisable.[20]

In 1908, the "present state of public feeling in India" was becoming deeply anticolonial and nationalist. Indeed, it was in 1908 that the Indian National Congress adopted *swaraj* (self-rule), "like that of the United Kingdom," as its goal, and there was enormous pressure on the state to concede at least partial self-government. And alongside the more moderate, "constitutional" approach of the Congress, there emerged numerous other radical and revolutionary groups opposing colonial rule.

The situation of Indian emigrants in different parts of the empire only added to the ferment and the nationalist demands within India. At the time, the most significant of these were the agitations of Indians in South Africa, which, under the leadership of Gandhi had not merely become a troublesome matter in South Africa (then attempting to partially sever its links with empire and secure responsible government), but had also led to an uproar in India. With the emigration question becoming a central issue in Indian politics and anticolonial demands, the Government of India wanted to avoid situations such as legislative measures expressly containing policies of discrimination against Indians. It suggested instead that Canada pursue suitably disguised methods of discrimination that would achieve the desired ends of curtailing the immigration. For instance, it could "require certain qualifications such as physical fitness . . . and the possession of a certain amount of money."[21]

Simultaneous with the sensitive situation in India, the "public feeling" in Canada was becoming overtly racist toward "Asiatics" and "Orientals." Where the official authorities cite "humanitarian" considerations of climate and labor demand as reasons to restrict the immigration, both N. D. Daru (an Indian official attached with the Geological Survey of Canada) and Falk Warren (a military official committed to an imperial ideology) point to the "anti-Asiatic sentiment" as the problem that needed to be addressed. The immigration they claimed was opposed by "the whole labor element of the country," who had engineered a campaign of "calumny and vituperation" against the Indians;[22] and by the press, which had "not merely taken up a hostile attitude [toward the immigrants], but [had] not scrupled to publish the rankest falsehoods about the Indians,"[23] as well as organized Anti-Asiatic Leagues in Canada and the United States. In fact, on September 6 and 7, 1907, there had been riots in Bellingham, Washington, and in Vancouver against Indians and "Asiatics" orchestrated by the Anti-Asiatic Leagues. The riots in Bellingham had caused some four hundred Indians to leave the United States and move to Canada, "seeking the protection of the British Crown."[24] The Canadian state thus found itself in an odd position: of attempting, on the one hand, to restrict the immigration of Indians and being bound, on the other hand (due to its membership in the empire), to provide refuge for Indians. Racism was clearly operating on numerous registers—ranging from the culturalist racism of the state to the physically violent racism of the rioters. And it was race, articulated to a space increasingly described as "national," that would subtend subsequent immigration regulations, including the emergence of the passport.

The entire machinery of empire, from the Government of Canada to the Government of Hong Kong to the different district authorities of the Government of India, was enlisted to inquire into every aspect of the migration. A report on the character of "the Hindus" was prepared by no less an authority than the minister of the interior of Canada; a secret agent was employed to infiltrate the Anti-Asiatic League of Canada in order to determine its support base and funding source; authorities in Hong Kong were directed to provide information on every ship that sailed, including details of the number of Indians on board and their financial situation; reports on the factors encouraging the migration were elicited from the Government of India; ethnographies of the immigrants themselves were carried out to understand their motivations; the role of shipping companies in assisting the traffic was assessed; Mackenzie King, then deputy minister for labor (later to serve twenty-five years as the much loved prime minister of Canada), was dispatched to have secret consultations with the Colonial Government in London on "the subject of immigration from the Orient and the immigration from India in particular."[25] In short, what the seemingly insignificant migration of Indians to Canada instigated was the eruption and use of a variety of mechanisms for generating, obtaining, and collating knowledge on every aspect of the movement of Indians to Canada.

From the knowledge of information amassed through this elaborate fact-finding mission, it was learned that a proportion of the Indian immigrants to Canada were reimmigrants — that is, they had often completed their term of indenture or service in a country other than India and came to Canada in a spirit of adventure and due to the circulation of stories that "fortunes" could be made there. Otherwise, the bulk of the emigrants came from Punjab and left India via the port of Calcutta for Hong Kong and thence to Canada. With this detailed and minute information in hand, on January 8, 1908, the Government of British Columbia passed an ingenious Order in Council stating that "immigrants shall be prohibited landing, unless they come from [their] country of birth or citizenship by continuous journey, and on through tickets purchased before starting."[26] This order effectively prevented both reimmigrant Indians and immigrants directly from India from going to Canada — the former since they did not come from their "country of birth or citizenship" and the latter since the "continuous journey" condition was literally impossible for Indians to fulfill since there was no steamship company that operated a direct transit from India to Canada and thus companies did not sell "through tickets."

The precise wording of the ordinance did, however, have some rather amusing — and telling — effects. For example, a Russian and a Frenchman were denied admission into Canada since they had not come by "continuous journey" from their "country of birth or citizenship," but rather from Japan.[27] Under the regulation of January 8, both would have been deported back had it not been for U.S. immigration officials at Vancouver who were "glad to pass them on into the United States."[28] The secret agent commenting on the incident to Wilfrid Laurier, the prime minister, says: "I, of course, have no status to advise in such a matter, but I know that the Regulation was never intended to be enforced in this absurd manner." He thus recommends that the regulation should be reworded to state that immigrants *"may* be prohibited [landing] — not *shall* be [prohibited landing]."[29] The aim of the regulation was specifically to prevent the entry of Indians into Canada; its original phraseology, combined with the bureaucratic logic of the state functionaries, led to the unintended consequence of its being implemented in an "absurd manner." Needless to say, the ordinance was immediately reworded so as to enable officers to permit the entry of white immigrants, regardless of where they embarked on their journeys.

Canada was actively pursuing the suggestion of the Government of India, mentioned above, that it follow strategies of selective racial discrimination without naming race as such. In addition to the continuous journey regulation, it imposed the monetary requirement of $200 on Indian immigrants. The rationale offered for these restrictions, let us recall, was twofold: the first was the old appeal to the inability of people from a "tropical climate" to "readily adapt themselves to surroundings so entirely different;"[30] the second was the claim that the migration "would result in a serious disturbance to industrial and economic conditions in portions of the Dominion, and especially in the Province of British Columbia."[31] Hence, an effective restriction on the immigration of Indians was deemed desirable "not less in the interest of the East Indians themselves than in the interest of the Canadian people."[32]

Together, the continuous journey stipulation and the monetary requirement made the entry of Indians into Canada virtually impossible. In fact, between 1909 and 1913, only twenty-seven Indians managed to enter Canada.[33] The migrants had been allowed entry since they were able to establish that they were returning immigrants with Canadian domicile. However, the Canadian government continued to press for the adoption of a passport system along the lines of its 1907 proposal.[34] This was in large part due to the confidential report submitted by Colonel Swayne, governor of British Honduras.[35] Swayne's report not only stated that barring the immigration on grounds of climatic considerations was hogwash, but also that many employers, such as mill owners, preferred to employ the "Sikhs" over white men since they "can be more safely relied upon to give continuous employment."[36] The cause for anxiety now was that Indian immigrants, despite the "hostility of the white trade unions," were making and saving substantial sums of money.[37]

Thus Swayne speculates that the return of the "Sikhs," "enriched with the savings of five years' employment in British Columbia, would have a disquieting effect on the Punjab population."[38]

The "disquieting effect" to which Swayne refers concerned the agitation that would ensue with the realization that the rationale of climatic considerations that was offered to prevent the migration was unfounded and that the returning immigrants were in a position to provide new emigrants with the funds necessary to meet the monetary requirement imposed by Canada. Though not explicitly stated, the concern of the Canadian government was that the continuous journey impediment was insufficient to guard against a fresh attempt at migration. This prompted its claim that "unless some further regulations restricting the influx can be established, there may be a danger of new developments arising with results possibly prejudicial to British interests *in* India."[39] If, moreover, the Government of India did not impose restrictions on emigration, then "the only alternative would appear to be the adoption of further, and from an Imperial point of view undesirable, regulations restricting British Indian emigration to Canada by His Majesty's Canadian Government."[40] Despite the veiled threats of imminent doom, the Government of India refused to acquiesce to adopting the passport system and maintained that the continuous journey impediment was sufficient to guard against the migration: "No new arguments have been adduced which would justify us in abandoning the position we have so far adopted on this subject . . . [and] we cannot propose any measures, such as the suggested introduction of a system of passports, which would *publicly* identify us with the policy of exclusion of Indians from the other portions of the Empire."[41]

A number of fundamental issues were at stake in the passport proposal and the Canadian regulations more generally. Not least of these was the very foundation and legitimacy of the British Empire, which had now come to rest crucially on the definition of the term "British subject." The governor general of Canada was entirely correct in remarking that the imposition of further restrictions was "from an Imperial point of view undesirable." Indians in Canada had sent a petition to the Colonial Office questioning both the monetary requirement and the continuous journey regulation and "demand[ing their] rights as British subjects with all the emphasis [they could] command":

The present Dominion Immigration Laws are quite inconsistent to the Imperial policy because they discriminate against the people of India who are British subjects; as they are forced to produce a sum of $200 before landing, whereas other British subjects are not. . . . The present Dominion Immigration laws are humiliating to the people of India . . . [since we] are not allowed to enjoy the birth-right of traveling from one part of the British Empire to the other. . . . [We also] bring to your notice that no such discriminat[ory] laws . . . [exist] against us in foreign countries . . . to whom we do not owe any allegiance whatsoever . . . [and] which impress upon us that we enjoy better privileges under foreign flags than those under the British flag.[42]

The petition further claimed that "as long as we are British subjects any British territory is the land of our citizenship."[43] Though put forth partially as an appeal to the state, the petition was tacitly questioning the legitimacy of the state and its guarantee to safeguard the well-being of its subjects.[44] If the matter of being "British subjects" and claiming that "any British territory is the land of our citizenship" was exercising the minds of the Indians in Canada, it was at the forefront of the official correspondence I have been detailing. The repeated refusals by the Government of India to accept the passport system hinged on this very fact. The conundrum to be overcome was how to distinguish among members of a state — that is, among "British subjects" — without calling the entire edifice of the empire into question. It is crucial that we note that it is a notion of empire and not the nation that is paramount here. Indeed, I would go so far as to venture that the "nation-state," as it is commonly understood, does not come into being in Europe until the rise of nationalist movements in the various empires. My point here is simple: since the so-called nation-state, whose "origins" are conventionally seen to lie in Europe, comes into existence in an age of empire, it is so deeply imbricated with an imperial formation that we must treat "nation" and "empire" in a unified field of analysis; in other words, the European nation-state is, more accurately, the European empire-state. This position is simple but deceptively so. For what I am suggesting is that we must reexamine the narrow view of nation-states as territorially circumscribed rather than as territorially expansionist. It is the long process of the end of empires that generates the nation-state as a contained entity that, significantly, is the first kind of state formation to have a monopoly over migration.

Let me return to the archival materials that help us see how control over migration has a crucial bearing on the emergence of the nation-state. The Canadian restrictions vis-à-vis Indians had not only prevented the further migration of Indians into Canada, but they had also effectively functioned as a mechanism causing the exodus of Indians already there since their families were unable to join them. Thus, from 6,000 men in 1906, the number of Indians in Canada had dropped to 4,500 (of whom only three were women) by 1915.[45] The regulations that were implemented, as we have seen, attempted to retain the appearance of an unfissured imperial citizenship and keep intact the status of

"British subject," even as the actual motivations and effects of these regulations were quite the opposite. As the intricacies involved in using a racist strategy without naming race were becoming increasingly complex and impossible to disguise, the difficulties with retaining the juridical appearance of an unfissured "British subject" were also being exacerbated. There are, in other words, only so many convolutions one may enact around race without naming it.

Until September 1913, the Government of India had been steadfast in its refusal to participate in a passport system to restrict emigration to Canada, grounding its refusal in the principle of "complete freedom for all British subjects to transfer themselves from one part of His Majesty's dominions to another." Thus, S. H. Slater, the undersecretary to the Government of India, states that "We have consistently declined to be parties to such a policy [i.e., a system of passports], and there seems no reason why we should abandon our attitude."[46] Further, given the limitations of Act XXI of 1883, the Government of India had "infact [sic] no legal power to insist that every emigrant to Canada should obtain a passport before starting."[47] Reiterating its position from 1908 concerning the "state of public feeling in India," the Government of India writes that "the state of public feeling now [i.e., September 1913] renders any such legislation even more undesirable . . . [and] if we attempted it, we should raise a storm of protest all over India; and without legislation we have no power to restrict free emigration."[48] By 1913, the situation of Indian emigrants in Canada and South Africa had become something of a political cause célèbre within India.

But two related events would cause the position of the Government of India on the Canadian passport proposal to be radically altered. The first of these was the October 1913 arrival at Victoria of fifty-six Indians aboard the *Panama Maru*. All claimed prior domicile as the basis for (re)admission into Canada. The translator, John Hopkinson, who doubled as the intelligence agent for the Indian police, let in seventeen, whom he thought he recognized.[49] The remaining thirty-nine immigrants were denied admission on the grounds that they had violated the Orders in Council. One of them, however, escaped from the immigration hall where the immigrants were locked up.[50] The Indian community managed to challenge the decision of the Board of Inquiry of the Immigration Department by demonstrating that the language of the Orders in Council, which had been cited to prohibit the thirty-nine immigrants from entry into Canada, did not conform to the language of the Canadian Immigration Act of 1910. In other words, since it was the Orders in Council that had been used as the basis for denying admission to the Indians and they were not in consonance with the Immigration Act, the decision of the Board of Inquiry was rendered void.[51] Thus, thirty-four of the remaining thirty-eight immigrants were allowed entry. Four were denied admission on medical grounds, but they too succeeded in running away from the Immigration Hall.[52] In sum, all fifty-six Indians who had arrived on the *Panama Maru* managed, in one way or another, to enter Canada.

The news of the Indian victory in the courts in the case of the passengers of the *Panama Maru* soon spread, and it was this, combined with the active encouragement of the revolutionaries in Canada, that provided the impetus for Sardar Gurdit Singh to hire a ship, the *Komagata Maru*, to sail from Hong Kong to Vancouver, with stops at Shanghai in China and Moji and Yokohama in Japan. In all, the ship gathered 376 passengers, mostly Sikhs, and arrived at Vancouver on May 23, 1914.[53] The Canadian government had by now eliminated the dissonance between the Orders in Council and the Immigration Act that had allowed the passengers of the *Panama Maru* entrance into Canada;[54] however, there were still grave risks in having the absurdity of the continuous journey regulation as the definition of a "British subject" being scrutinized in court. Moreover, since Sardar Gurdit Singh had initially attempted to hire a ship to sail directly from India, the arrival of the *Komagata Maru* indicated the precarious status of the continuous journey regulation, causing a furor in the Canadian House of Commons as well as in India. Since outright appeals to biological racism and racial superiority could not be countenanced, the debate in Canada proceeded to substitute cultural racism for biological racism while simultaneously advocating for the principle of the sovereignty of states based on *national* grounds. Thus, for instance, Frank Oliver, who had been minister of the interior at the time of such measures as the continuous journey regulation but now formed part of the opposition, voiced his objection to the immigrants:

The immigration law as it stands is a declaration on the part of this country that Canada is mistress of her own house and takes the authority and responsibility of deciding who shall be admitted to citizenship and the privileges and rights of citizenship within her borders. . . . This is not a labor question; it is not a racial question; it is a question of national dominance and national existence. . . . This [the *Komagata Maru* incident] is an organized movement for the purpose of establishing as a principle the right that the people of India, and not the people of Canada, shall have the say as to who may be accepted as citizens of Canada.[55]

While Frank Oliver attempts to cover over the racist motivations for disallowing Indians into Canada in terms of the threat they posed to the very definition of the sovereignty of the state, Wilfrid Laurier, now also part of the opposition, is more direct in his comments: "The people of Canada want to have a white country, and certain of our fellow subjects who are not of the white race want to come to Canada and be admitted to all the rights of Canadian citizenship. . . . These men have been taught by a certain school of politics [i.e., liberalism] that they are the equals of [white] British subjects; unfortunately, they are brought face to face with the hard facts only when it is too late."[56]

Laurier's comments are remarkable in their candidness since the kernel of the entire struggle over the passport system was precisely about how to effect racial exclusion without naming race. Thus, while the necessity and validity of racial exclusion was widely accepted, as is abundantly clear from the confidential correspondence, the overriding discourse of liberalism made it impossible to actually implement policies that directly cited race. We have seen how the different arms of the liberal empire-state, by incorporating caveats into each policy, utilized the strategy of bureaucratic discretion, time and time again, to circumvent this problem.[57] The fundamental dilemma, let me reiterate, was the fact that Indians were British subjects, and thus, unlike, for instance, the case with China, the discourse of the liberal state made it exceedingly difficult to distinguish among subjects of the British Empire.[58]

As with the 1910 petition from Indians in Canada protesting the continuous journey regulation on the basis of membership in the empire, the meetings and memorandums caused by the *Komagata Maru* incident appealed, once again, to the notion of Indians as British subjects: "The deep loyalty of Indians to the British Raj springs from the consciousness that the British maxim par eminence is that of equal justice and fair play. Under the aegis of the British ideal of justice, Indians only seek for equal changes with their fellow-subjects in other parts of the Empire, so that they may legitimately feel the pride of being citizens, in the full sense, of the Great Empire over which the sun never sets[!]."[59] Based on the notion of justice and fair play, the memorandums also questioned the unrestricted entry of (white) inhabitants from other parts of the British Empire into India.[60] Further, they issued the threat "that Canada must be made to understand that she is dealing not with 600 [*sic*] men only, but with 33 crores [330 million] of Indians."[61]

The *Komagata Maru* incident precipitated a rapid transformation in policy. In fact, the very same S. H. Slater of the Government of India who in September 1913 had vehemently rejected the passport system would seven months later voice a diametrically opposed position: "Circumstances are now compelling a stricter definition of such phrases as . . . 'membership of the British Empire.' It is now conceded that such membership does not carry with it the right of free entry to all parts of the Empire. [Therefore] in this narrower view . . . it will no longer be held that every measure of exclusion of Asiatics from territories forming part of the Empire is necessarily and ipso facto an injustice to Indians."[62]

But regardless of the "circumstances" that were "compelling" this "narrower view," how was it to be justified — especially in the face of the increasingly militant and vociferous protests from Indians around the globe? R. W. Gillian, in his comments in the correspondence, offers the clearest statement of the rationale to justify broader migration regulations. Gillian points out that the Government of India's policy in rejecting the passport proposal and its reluctance to interfere with "free" migration, though resting on the principle that "a British subject [had] a right to go and reside in any part of the Empire," had a "double aspect."[63] For the government, while on the one hand refusing to interfere with "free" emigration from India, had not, on the other hand, balked at suggesting that different parts of the empire impose all manner of restrictions on immigration, so long as their racist motivations were suitably disguised. This, writes Gillian, "is what appears to me an inconsistency. We adhere to our policy, while abandoning the principle on which it has always rested."[64] Moreover, the intransigent position of the Government of India could not, in Gillian's view, "be defended on its merits, since it denies in effect the right of our Colonies and even of other countries to settle their own affairs."[65] Gillian here echoes Frank Oliver's comments in the Canadian House of Commons that control over immigration is somehow fundamental to the very definition of state sovereignty, a line of reasoning that would soon catapult into bringing all migration under state control.

However, as Gillian continues, "If the right of Canada or Australia to manage their own affairs is admitted, what about India? If the right is denied to her, the result is immediately to emphasize her subjection in an extremely unfortunate manner." What was required was a mechanism that would "secure some kind of reciprocity"[66] and "which [would] above all things . . . have the *appearance* of giving equal treatment to British subjects residing in all parts of the Empire."[67] It was imperative to vigorously cling to inscribing the letter of the law as universal while ensuring that in practice this universality would function differentially.

And it would be the "universal" category of nationality, already overlaid with culturalist racism, that could be mobilized in such a way as to tether people to geographical space. It was thus through a recourse to the idea of states as securing sovereignty through an appeal to the "national" that the principle of the "complete freedom for all British subjects to transfer themselves from one part of His Majesty's Dominions to the other" was abandoned, and the category of "British subject" was rendered available for division and differentiation based on the rule of colonial difference. Since, writes Viceroy Hardinge, "thoughtful people will agree that states and countries have an inherent right to decide whom they will or will not admit within their borders,"[68] the solution decided upon is to "undertake to furnish passports to emigrants entitling them to admission into the Colonies and India respectively. The number of these permits or passports would be limited by agreement."[69] It was, further, fortuitous that by now the war was well under way, thus lending credence to the notion of state security. Indeed, the official rules for requiring passports from all Indians proceeding outside India — though, significantly, this did *not* apply to indentured labor — appear as the Defence of India (Passport) Rules, which were a subsection of the Defence of India (Criminal Law Amendment) Act, 1915. This act made embarking on a journey from any port in British India without a passport a criminal offense.[70]

The legitimation for state sovereignty has historically been made on various grounds. One of the features that distinguishes the nation-state from other state formations is that the state secures sovereignty via an appeal to the nation.[71] The acceptance of the passport system is not only underwritten by this barely emergent understanding of the sovereignty of states premised on the national, but is also central to ensuring its effectivity. Ironically, the debate had come full circle and was resolved on exactly the same lines as the initial 1907 proposal put forth by Wilfrid Laurier to which the Government of India had objected for ten years. The crucial distinction, however, was that the appeal to the national enabled a principle of pseudoreciprocity and thus pseudo-universality to be inscribed within the passport system. The passport emerges here as a state document that purports to assign a national identity rather than a racial identity — a mechanism that would conceal race and the racist motivations for controlling mobility in the guise of a reciprocal arrangement among states described as national. Simultaneously and crucially, however, this formation of the passport generates "nationality" as the intersection between the nation and the state. Inscribed on the body of the migrant are the traces of both the state and the nation-race. This produces what I called in my introduction to this essay the "nationalized" migrant, which entails a yoking together of "nation" and "state" on the terrain of race. The development of modern racism and the modern state are thus coproduced in such a way as to nationalize state-territorial boundaries, which are explicitly raced.

Despite Hardinge's remark that states have an "inherent right" to monitor migration, the history I have presented here shows how it took ten years for this inherent right to become evident. It is clear that the rights that accrue to states are historically specific and emerge from certain historical exigencies. The emergence of the nation-state as the first state formation to exercise a monopoly over migration indicates not that control over mobility begins *after* the formation of the nation-state but that the very development of the nation-state occurs, in part, to control mobility along the axis of the nation-race. It is thus that "nationality" comes to signify a privileged relation between people and literal territory, and it is this relation, which sutures nationality to territory, that the passport helps consolidate daily. One might then say that modern migration produces nationality — not in the sense of a craving for a homeland that is identified as a nation, but rather in the subtle, supple, and yet uncircumventable sense of how today the historical burden of a technology such as the passport demands a "nationalized" subject who might engage in legal mobility. An attention to the resilience of such concrete technologies should also give us pause when we make pronouncements regarding the death of the nation-state and the emergence of an era of globalization.[72]

To conclude, then, while presently we tend to think of the passport as not merely a necessary document for international travel but also one that facilitates such movement, its history reveals that it is born out of an attempt to restrict movement along national lines that are explicitly raced. Among the histories calcified in the history of the modern passport is a history of twentieth-century racism and a history of naturalizing the territorial boundedness of a national space as self-evidently the legitimate abode of certain people. The nineteenth-century state interventions regulating the movement of indentured Indian labor were animated by a concern to distinguish the movement from the slave trade and justified by a rule of colonial difference anchored in the "civilizing mission." The twentieth-century state interventions regulating the movement of "free" Indians, embodied in the passport, were justified by a rule of colonial difference anchored in "nationality." The passport is thus a document that has effectively naturalized the "rule of colonial difference" in what one might call the "rule of postcolonial difference," where the marker of difference is not "race," but the "universal" category of "nationality." It is therefore no surprise that today different "nationalities" have differential access to mobility.

Notes

1 On the lack of systemization of the passport system, see John Torpey, "Coming and Going: On the State Monopolization of the Legitimate 'Means of Movement,'" *Sociological Theory* 16 (1998): 239–259.

2 See House of Commons, "An Act for the Protection of Natives of Her Majesty's Territories in the East Indies Contracting for Labour to Be Performed without the Said Territories, and for Regulating Their Passage by Sea," *Parliamentary Papers*, 1837–1838, vol. 3.

3 Edward Lawford (solicitor to the East India Company) to David Hill, June 12, 1838, in *Papers Respecting the East India Labourers' Bill* (London: J. L. Cox and Sons, 1838), pp. 2–3; India Office Library and Records, London. V/27/820/4.

4 Ibid.

5 P. D'Epinay to Hollier Griffiths, January 5, 1836, in *Papers Respecting the East India Labourers' Bill*.

6   Ibid.

7   Partha Chatterjee, *The Nation and Its Fragments: Colonial and Postcolonial Histories* (Princeton, N.J.: Princeton University Press, 1993), pp. 16–22.

8   Ibid., p. 18.

9   Ibid., p. 14.

10 Home Department (Sanitary/Plague), "Question Whether the Term 'Emigrant' Applies to Soldiers Recruited in India under Agreement with the Colonial Secretary for Service in Africa," *Proceedings*, February 1899, no. 114–117. This and all subsequent archival references are to the National Archives of India, New Delhi.

11 Copy of telegram dated November 13, 1905, forwarded from Secretary of State, London, to the Viceroy of India, November 19, 1906. Department of Commerce and Industry, *Emigration Proceedings A*, May 1907, no. 7, ser. no. 1. All further citations of *Proceedings A* and *Proceedings B* are parts A and B respectively of Department of Commerce and Industry, *Emigration Proceedings*.

12 "Memorandum: Re: Immigration of Hindoos [*sic*] to Canada," *Proceedings A*, May 1907, no. 7.

13 Ibid.

14 Ibid. I cannot dwell here on some of the incongruities of asserting that the caste system obtained among the Sikh community. For an analysis of how caste emerges as a key colonial category for ordering India, see David Ludden, "Orientalist Empiricism: Transformations of Colonial Knowledge," in *Orientalism and the Postcolonial Predicament*, ed. Carol Breckenridge and Peter Van der Veer (Philadelphia: University of Pennsylvania Press, 1993).

15 "Memorandum: Re: Immigration."

16 Ibid.

17 Secretary of State for India to Under Secretary of State, Colonial Office, October 19, 1906, *Proceedings A*, May 1907, no. 7, ser. no. 5.

18 Governor General of Canada to the Secretary of State for the Colonies, telegram received November 11, 1907, *Proceedings A*, February 1908, no. 18–33.

19 Ibid.

20 Viceroy of India, Calcutta, to the Secretary of State for India, London, telegram received January 22, 1908, *Proceedings A*, February 1908, no. 28, ser. no. 16 (confidential).

21 Ibid.

22 Colonel Falk Warren to the Under Secretary of State for India, November 22, 1906, *Proceedings A*, May 1907, no. 7, ser. no. 10.

23 N. D. Daru to the Under Secretary of State for India, November 19, 1906, *Proceedings A*, May 1907, no. 7, ser. no. 10.

24 Lord Grey, Governor General of Canada, to Secretary of State for India, September 24, 1907, *Proceedings A*, February 1908, no. 18–33, ser. no. 12.

25 "Report of the Committe of the Privy Council, Approved by His Excellency the Governor General on 2nd March 1908," *Proceedings A*, May 1908, no. 6, ser. no. 22, encl. no. 9.

26 Governor General of Canada to the Secretary of State for the Colonies, London, telegram dated January 15, 1908, *Proceedings A*, May 1908, no. 6, ser. no. 22. encl. no. 3, annex 1.

27 Secret Agent T. R. E. McInnes to Wilfrid Laurier, March 15, 1908, *Proceedings A*, May 1908, no. 6, ser. no. 22, encl. no. 3, annex 2.

28 Ibid.

29 Ibid. Emphasis in original.

30 Governor General of Canada to Earl Crewe, Colonial Office, January 7, 1909.

31 "Report of the Committee of the Privy Council."

32 Ibid.

33 Hugh Tinker, *Separate and Unequal: India and Indians in the British Commonwealth, 1920–1950* (Vancouver: University of British Columbia Press, 1976), p. 29.

34 Dispatch from the Secretary of State for India to the Government of India, April 2, 1909, *Proceedings A*, May 1909, no. 11–12, ser. no. 5.

35 Colonel Swayze had been involved in the matter since the initial scheme was to try and redirect the Indians coming to Canada to Honduras. The scheme came to naught since "the Indians would not go." "Indian Office Memorandum on Indian Immigration into Canada," 26 August 1915, Proceedings A, October 1915, no. 68 (confidential).

36 Governor General of Canada to Earl Crewe, Colonial Office, January 7, 1909.

37 Ibid.

38 Ibid.

39 Ibid.

40 Ibid.

41 Government of India to Viscount Morley, Secretary of State for India, May 20, 1909, *Proceedings A*, May 1909, no. 11, ser. no. 6. Emphasis added.

42 Communication from British Indian subjects in Canada to Colonial Office, London, April 24, 1910, *Proceedings A*, October 1910, no. 47, ser. no. 8, encl. no. 1, annex 1.

43 Ibid.

44 Several Indians in Canada were involved in revolutionary or "seditious" activity and were vehemently opposed to colonial rule. For details, see "Race, Nationality, Mobility: A History of the Passport," *Public Culture* vol. 11 no. 3 (fall 1999): 527–556. Hereafter RNC.

45 President of the United Provinces Congress Committee, Allahabad, to the Secretary to the Government of India, January 25, 1915, *Proceedings A*, June 1915, no. 1–2.

46 Comments of S. H. Slater regarding telegram from the Secretary of State, September 19, 1913, *Proceedings A*, October 1913, no. 29–30 (confidential).

47 Comments of J. F. Gruning regarding telegram from the Secretary of State, September 22, 1913, *Proceedings A*, October 1913, no. 29–30 (confidential).

48 Ibid.

49 For details on the activities of John Hopkinson, see RNC.

50 Hugh Johnston, *The Voyage of the Komagata Maru: The Sikh Challenge to Canada's Colour Bar* (New Delhi: Oxford University Press, 1979), p. 20.

51 Confidential letter from the Governor General of Canada to Colonial Office, December 31, 1913, *Proceedings A*, June 1914, no. 10–11, encl. no. 2.

52 Ibid.

53 Johnston, *The Voyage of the Komagata Maru*, pp. 29–38.

54 Report of the Committee of the Privy Council, approved February 23, 1914, *Proceedings A*, June 1914, no. 10–11, encl. no. 11.

55 "Official Report of a Debate in the Canadian House of Commons on Asiatic Immigration," *Proceedings A*, October 1914, no. 1.

56 Ibid.

57 The state functionaries, moreover, were fully aware of this. Thus a confidential memorandum states: "The efficacy of these Acts, in fact, rests to some extent on a subterfuge." "India Office Memorandum on Indian Immigration into Canada," August 26, 1915, *Proceedings A*, October 1915, no. 68 (confidential).

58 For a more detailed analysis of the discourse of liberalism and the dilemmas posed by empire, see RNC.

59 "Memorial Regarding the Grievances of Indians in Canada," *Proceedings A*, April 1914, no. 13–16.

60 Ibid.

61 "Confidential Weekly Diary for the Week Ending the 13th of June 1914 of the Superintendent of Police, Lahore," *Proceedings A*, July 1914, no. 3.

62 Comments of S. H. Slater to R. E. Enthoven, May 26, 1914, *Proceedings A*, September 1914, no. 18–20 (confidential).

63 Comments of R. W. Gillian, June 23, 1914, *Proceedings A*, September 1914, no. 18–20 (confidential).

64 Ibid.

65 Ibid.

66 Ibid.

67 Comments of R. E. Enthoven, June 13, 1914. Emphasis added.

68 Comments of Lord Hardinge, Viceroy of India, July 8, 1914, *Proceedings A*, September 1914, no. 18–20 (confidential).

69 Comments of R. E. Enthoven, June 13, 1914.

70 "Compulsory Passport Regulations," *Proceedings A*, June 1917, no. 8–22.

71 For an overview of different grounds of state sovereignty, see J. Samuel Barkin, "The Evolution of the Constitution of Sovereignty and the Emergence of Human Rights Norms," *Millennium: Journal of International Studies* 27 (1998): 229–252.

72 Here my position diverges from, for instance, Arjun Appadurai's work on globalization and the emergence of "postnational" identities. See Arjun Appadurai, *Modernity at Large* (Minneapolis: University of Minnesota Press, 1996).

3

Reorienting the Nation:

Logics of Empire, Colony, Globe

CLEMENT HAWES

Periodizing Johnson: Anticolonial Modernity as Crux and Critique

We must consider how very little history there is; I mean real authentick history. That certain Kings reigned, and certain battles were fought, we can depend upon as true; but, all the colouring, all the philosophy of history is conjecture.
— Samuel Johnson in Boswell's *Life of Johnson*

Those in the field of eighteenth-century British literature have long been accustomed to schemas of literary history in which the eighteenth century features as an evolutionary stepping-stone. The eighteenth centuries of our literary anthologies and survey courses have evidently been constructed, as Lawrence Lipking has observed, "by the interests of a later time."[1] Moreover, a great deal of scholarship confirms that the cultural phenomenon we now call "Romanticism" marks the point of consolidation for the evolutionary formulas from which modern historical periodization itself derives. There is a sense, then, in which Romanticism — a self-proclaimed genesis — was, above all, a massively influential narrative.[2] Nineteenth-century Britain claimed to have achieved a triumphant shift from a vertical and class-ridden society to a significantly more democratized one: a politically reformed and culturally "mature" nation. Douglas Lane Patey describes the resulting *nationalization* of the cultural past thus: "The history of any art becomes a history of stages — periods — corresponding to, because informed by, larger movements of the national mind and institutions."[3] The modes of literary-historical periodization we inherit from the nineteenth century thus articulate a developmental metanarrative of a national identity that has been retrospectively forged precisely from that era: the moment when a firmly secured "Britishness" was being consolidated over and against a disorderly past.

Whiggish historicism cast the eighteenth century as representing the unnatural artifice of the *ancien régime*: the bewigged and decadent foil against which all later progress allegedly occurred. Such a narrative obviously trivializes the significant ideological conflicts within the period — conflicts, indeed, that deserve to be rethought in the wake of the "imperial turn." And though

Herbert Butterfield suggested as early as 1944 that "the story of British expansion overseas" constituted "the real alternative to whig history in recent times," few scholars working in the eighteenth-century period have fully grasped the unexpected ways in which a more global unit of analysis might revitalize their field.[4] Indeed, a powerful inertia evidently afflicts the writing of literary history about the British eighteenth century.

To the familiar marginalization of "pre-Romantic" teleologies, moreover, there have now been added others. For contemporary theorists assert that postmodern thought has achieved a clean break with intellectual and political developments that are almost always traced back to the eighteenth-century Enlightenment. The Whiggish glorification of a continuous march of bourgeois progress has thus yielded to the postmodern laceration of a grand narrative of bourgeois hegemony. Once again, a historical break has been defined, and once again, the eighteenth-century moment figures as the devalued past to be broken from. As that which is made to stand for the origin and essence of modernity's undeniable violence, the period itself comes in, yet again, for a considerable drubbing. This postmodernist version of the eighteenth century does little more than invert the Whiggish "grand narrative," largely consolidated in the nineteenth century, which constructed the eighteenth century as the embryonic origin or harbinger — now surpassed and fulfilled — of all progress and reform.

The eighteenth century thus does double duty in the broader sweep of literary and cultural historiography. Only a uniquely transitional century, it seems, could require such a double negation: first as the quintessence of the old regime and then as the hateful epitome of "violent modernity." I contend that the conspicuously elusive nature of the eighteenth century as a distinct period in cultural history derives precisely from its sheer recalcitrance as regards the nature of the critical lenses that have been brought to bear on it. To the false teleology of Whiggish historiography about "the growth of liberty," the reply must be to invoke the wider context of empire — what Partha Chatterjee has termed the "rule of colonial difference."[5] To the one-sided polemics of contemporary postmodern theorists against the "Enlightenment project," the riposte must be to highlight the crucial *liminality* of the eighteenth-century moment as regards modernity. This liminality frequently exceeds the amnesiac categories of historical periodization transmitted to us by the sedimented layers of imperial and nation-based historiography. And indeed, a surprising reassessment of the British eighteenth century emerges from these amended critical instruments. For a conspicuous element of that historical liminality, when viewed in the wake of the "imperial turn," involves immanent critiques of the global fashioning of imperial Britishness.

Perhaps no better epitome of this recalcitrant liminality can be found than the writings of Samuel Johnson: a body of written work continually neglected in favor of the provocative table talk skillfully mediated by Johnson's biographer, James Boswell. The *oeuvre* of Johnson—who consistently challenges and resists the emerging currents of imperial Britishness—stands as a very considerable embarrassment both to a nineteenth-century nation that needed to affirm its natural sense of imperial entitlement and to its inverted mirror image, a contemporary caricature of the Enlightenment that is exceedingly reluctant to concede the force of any critiques arising from within. The challenging crux of Johnson's most misunderstood achievement—his articulation of an anticolonial modernity—awaits a historiography that is prepared to rethink the usual territorial boundaries of "inside" and "outside" as they have often been drawn. In the wake of the "imperial turn," Johnson's invocations of a global framework for political analysis deserve to find new contexts and constituencies.

Samuel Johnson, a proudly professional writer, certainly belongs to the modernizing context of building a vernacular national culture in Britain. He wrote unashamedly for cash; he preferred to address his works to an anonymous public rather than to a leisured coterie; and he often worked, no less than the most exploited hack, under the pressure of commercially imposed deadlines. He wrote many pamphlets on public affairs, and he wrote scores of periodical essays for a reading public engaged in working through an impressive litany of newly problematized social issues: the tyranny of parents, the plight of prostitutes, the ethics of capital punishment, and so on. Above all, perhaps, Johnson made such landmark contributions to a vernacular literary culture as his *Dictionary of the English Language* (1755), his Shakespeare edition (1765), and his *Prefaces, Biographical and Critical to the Works of the English Poets* (1779–1781). When he refers in his biography of Jonathan Swift to England's current status as a "nation of readers," Johnson locates himself squarely within the eighteenth-century making of a print-based public culture. This was a process of imagining community, as Benedict Anderson has shown, that was intimately connected to the cultivation of "modern," relatively egalitarian identities on the print-mediated scale of the nation. By any account, Johnson is a major figure in the vernacular production of Englishness.

Johnson fully registers the crucial political gain—the increased transparency of political institutions and decision making at many levels of society—entailed by the building of a vernacular public sphere. In "The Duty of a Journalist," Johnson emphasizes the anti-elitist implications of his vocation, asserting that it was the duty of a journalist "to consider himself not as writing to students or statesmen alone, but to women, to shopkeepers, to artisans, who have little time to bestow upon mental attainments, but desire, upon easy terms, to know how the world goes." Surveying the Harleian collection of pamphlets generated a century earlier by the English Civil War, Johnson highlights in 1741 the Habermasian significance of the public sphere that England had developed as inhering in "the form of our government, which gives every man that has leisure, or curiosity, or vanity the right of inquiring into the propriety of public measures, and, by consequence, obliges those who are intrusted with the administration of national affairs to give an account of their conduct."[6] And it is precisely to serve the function of public accountability that Johnson reported on parliamentary debates for the *Gentleman's Magazine*, circumventing the laws against such reporting through the tongue-in-cheek fiction that his reports concerned the public affairs of "Magna Lilliputia."

At the same time, however, Johnson represents a distinctly cosmopolitan alternative to the politics of national chauvinism. He is wary of the violent exclusions entailed by an excessive emphasis on the unity or boundedness of national cultures. He warns that "the love of our country, when it rises to enthusiasm, is an ambiguous and uncertain virtue; when a man is enthusiastic he ceases to be reasonable."[7] Indeed, it is precisely by refusing to invest a specifically sacred awe in any secular national icon that Johnson positions himself outside the mainstream of any cultural nationalism. By withholding "superstitious veneration" for Shakespeare, for instance, and thus enumerating his faults in a sobering disquisition some found shocking, Johnson goes against the grain of a growing Bardolatry that Michael Dobson describes as, in the full anthropological sense, a national religion.[8] By the same token, only a scant handful of Johnson's literary biographies affirm the greatness of the poets described therein. His "soft" or civic nationalism precludes so insular an approach to critical judgments.

The most remarkable dimension of Johnson's selective negotiations with modernity, however, lies in his consistent critique of the European imperial project in general and of the British one in particular. His carefully nuanced response to the key ideological theme of "progress" is especially telling in this regard. Johnson is duly skeptical, and often wearily pessimistic, about the likelihood of genuine progress in human affairs. Nevertheless, he tends to embrace "progressive" reforms on the domestic front without nostalgia, even as he resoundingly rejects the central legitimating theme of imperial ideology: that the invading colonizer confers "the gift of progress" abroad. What makes Johnson's views compelling now, however, is precisely that they cannot be dismissed either as premodern or as a mere stalking-horse for Eurocentrism. Consider how Johnson, in the crucial introduction to his serial coverage of British parliamentary debates for the *Gentleman's Magazine*, understands his ethical and political obligations as a journalist. Though intervening in a highly visible *national* discussion, he insists from the start on extending the bound-aries of political concern to humanity as a whole. Thus, in 1738, he frames the affairs of "Magnum Lilliputia," or Great Britain, within the context of a mac-ropolitical conflict that he describes as both immoral and an unlawful violation of sovereignty:

The people of Degulia, or the Lilliputian Europe . . . are, above those of the other parts of the world, famous for arts, arms, and navigation, and, in consequence of their superiority, have made conquests and settled colonies in very distant regions, the inhabitants of which they look upon as barbarous, though in simplicity of manners, probity, and temperance superior to themselves; and seem to think that they have a right to treat them as passion, interest, or caprice shall direct, without much regard to the rules of justice or humanity; they have carried this imaginary sovereignty so far that they have sometimes proceeded to rapine, bloodshed, and desolation. If you endeavour to examine the foundation of this authority, they neither produce any grant from a superior jurisdiction, nor plead the consent of the people whom they govern in this tyrannical manner; but either threaten you with punishment for threatening the Emperor's sovereignty, or pity your stupidity, or tell you in positive terms that *Power is right.*[9]

It is precisely through this framing strategy that Johnson maintains a dual allegiance both to a modernizing national project and to a world polity in-creasingly blighted by the imperial dynamics of European expansion.

Such a globalizing gesture, in the most prominent periodical of the day, belies a common excuse for strictly insular histories of Britain. As David Armi-tage points out, contemporary historians who wish to minimize the domestic significance of the British Empire often invoke as an excuse "the aggressive amnesia of eighteenth and nineteenth-century Britons" as regards the colo-nies.[10] That ideologically sanctioned amnesia, however — what Armitage terms "isolationist imperialism"[11] — is far more characteristic of the nineteenth cen-tury than the eighteenth, which had not yet consolidated the quarantine that would conceive of "British" and "imperial" history as things apart. Indeed, the eighteenth century's much fuller registration of global entanglement was pre-cisely what the nineteenth century had to repress. In that sense, globalization itself has a history that leads inexorably, as Emma Rothschild argues, back to the eighteenth century: the moment when new sciences of wealth and society emerged hand in hand with the international activities of, for example, the Dutch, English, French, and Swedish East India Companies.[12] The fierce an-tagonisms ensuing from this process produced militant expressions of imperial greed of a sort that a later age would sweep under the carpet. However, these antagonisms likewise produced, by way of ideological contestation, significant anticipations of contemporary efforts to think beyond the horizons of the nation. The visibility of tentacular globalization begat globalizing critiques. Johnson repeats his own globalizing strategy in 1759, when he reframes the contents of *The World Displayed* — a twenty-volume collection of European voyage-and-discovery literature — with an introduction instructing readers in the anticolonial analysis of historical sources. He frames this fraught collection of documents, that is to say, by reading its implications against the grain of its surface content. He foregrounds, and repeatedly comments on, issues of violated sovereignty, pitiless greed, capricious violence, and callow bigotry that permeate this collection.

Of one incident among many involving Portuguese violence against Africans — neutrally recounted by Lafitau — Johnson comments as follows:

On what occasion, or for what purpose, cannons and muskets were discharged among a people harmless and secure, by strangers who without any right visited their coast, it is not thought necessary to inform us. The Portuguese could fear nothing from them, and had therefore no adequate provocation; nor is there any reason to believe but that they murdered the negroes in wanton merriment, perhaps only to try how many a volley would destroy, or what would be the consternation of those that should escape.[13]

The subsequent lines, in condemning the brutal attitude expressed in such violence, reverse the usual colonial ascription of barbarity:

We are openly told, that they had the less scruple concerning their treatment of the savage people, because they scarcely considered them as distinct from beasts; and indeed the practice of all the European nations, and among others of the English barbarians that cultivate the southern islands of America, proves, that this opinion, however absurd and foolish, however wicked and injurious, still continues to prevail.[14]

Elsewhere Johnson similarly debunked the much fetishized date of 1492 and noted that no part of the world had "reason to rejoice" that Columbus had eventually received the necessary financial backing for his venture.[15] He told Boswell, in the same vein, "I love the University of Salamancha; for when the Spaniards were in doubt as to the lawfulness of their conquering America, the University of Salamancha gave it as their opinion that it was not lawful."[16]

Johnson never relies on the infamy of Iberian colonial atrocities, moreover — on the "Black Legend" of the uniquely cruel Spanish conquistadors — merely to legitimate by comparison a supposedly more benign British expansionism. In his "Introduction to the Political State of Great Britain" (1756), published just as the Seven Years' War with France was heating up, Johnson uses the English phase of early European expansion to unmask the militaristic political ethos of mid-eighteenth-century Britain. Of the slavery-based colony of Jamaica, Johnson remarks that it continues, even to this day, as "a place of great wealth and dreadful wickedness, a den of tyrants, and a dungeon of slaves."[17] Johnson goes even further in *Idler* 81, an attack on patriotic war fever that was published some three years later. In this essay, Johnson assumes the perspective of an "Indian" chief dispassionately hoping the competing British and French armies will decimate one another: "Let us look unconcerned upon the slaughter, and remember that the death of every European delivers the country from a tyrant and a robber."[18] This passage concludes as follows: "Let us endeavor, in the mean time, to learn their discipline, and to forge their weapons: and when they shall be weakened with mutual slaughter, let us rush down upon them, force the remains to take shelter in their ships, and reign once more in our native country."[19] As James Basker has pointed out, Johnson was indeed not just "an opponent of slavery, but an apologist for violent resistance."[20] Indeed, aside from his famous toast at Oxford "to the next insurrection of the negroes in the West Indies," Johnson endorses acts of anticolonial violence in no fewer than five passages in his "Life of Sir Francis Drake."

Johnson's resistance to colonial aggression rests on universalist principles that he expresses early and late. In his preface to Father Jerome Lobo's *Voyage to Abyssinia* (1735), Johnson argues "that wherever human nature is found, there is a mixture of vice and virtue, a contest of passion and reason; and . . . the Creator doth not appear partial in his distributions."[21] Some forty years later, these ideas recur in "A Brief to Free a Slave" (1777). In this brief, Johnson made a successful legal intervention on behalf of Joseph Knight, a black slave suing a court in Scotland for freedom from the Scottish master from whom he had escaped. Johnson bores in on the lack of proof that Joseph Knight has ever — whether as a criminal or as a military captive pleading for life — forfeited his universal right to liberty:

He [Joseph Knight] is certainly subject to no law, but that of violence, to his present master, who pretends no claim to his obedience, but that he bought him from a merchant of slaves, whose right to sell him was never examined. It is said that, according to the constitutions of Jamaica, he was legally enslaved; these constitutions are merely positive, and apparently injurious to the rights of mankind, because whoever is exposed to sale is condemned to slavery without appeal; by whatever fraud or violence he might have been originally brought into the merchant's power.[22]

He pauses to register the crude injustice of the race-based legal system that Knight would face if Jamaican law were to be invoked: "The laws of Jamaica afford a Negro no redress. His color is considered as a sufficient testimony against him." He then concludes as follows, with a ringing assertion of universal rights: "The sum of the argument is this: No man is by nature the property of another. The defendant is, therefore, by nature free."[23] Johnson is here explicitly extending human rights beyond any sort of "color line" and beyond the boundaries of nationhood.

In the *oeuvre* of Johnson, the scrupulously balanced themes of anticolonial politics and vernacular modernization come together in his responses to the controversy that surrounds the name of "Ossian." These responses mark his refusal to countenance an imperial rewriting of the past. By about 1750, it had become increasingly common in Britain to celebrate local, "home-grown" poetry over and against the universalist claims of the classics. Such "native" poetry was often seen as authentic—as an unmediated expression of *British* genius— precisely because the author was supposedly unlettered and thus had no debts to a continentwide classical tradition centered in Rome. It was indeed on the basis of a valorized ignorance of classical tradition that the authenticity of "native genius" was ideologically founded. Nationalist mythmakers thus began a relentless questing for so-called roots, the eighteenth century being "a great age of origin-seeking."[24] A significant role in this emergent nationalism belongs to speculative philology. The "arch-druid" William Stukeley, for example— whose *Stonehenge* (1740) argued for the prehistoric colonization of Britain by the Phoenicians—attempted to derive the Welsh language from ancient Hebrew. A Scottish philological tradition, emerging from the antiquarian speculations of David Malcolme, Jerome Stone, and William Maitland, likewise argued that Gaelic was the *ur*-language. Such antiquarian projects blurred fiction and fact with varying degrees of self-consciousness, opening the door to poetic reinventions of "national genius." The "Ossian" episode epitomizes the violence that the new "bardic nationalism" would do to the writing of history. Johnson's intervention into literary history's most infamous episode of historiographical fabrication encapsulates his response to such genealogical reinventions of the national pedigree.

The particular appropriation of Celtic antiquities associated with the fabrication of "Ossian" was spawned in the 1760s by the nationalistic desire for a homegrown "British" counterpart to Homer by which the achievements of classical civilization could be trumped. With the support of some leading Scottish literati, James Macpherson laboriously contrived a third-century Highland poet, "Ossian," allegedly surviving fragments of whose Gaelic poetry he purported to translate into cadenced English prose. Though banking primarily on the mystique of a pristine oral tradition, supposedly transmitted with great linguistic purity from bard to bard for some sixty generations, Macpherson unwisely claimed to have certain manuscript sources as well. These he obstinately refused to display for public inspection, with predictably disastrous results for his reputation. Eventually Macpherson was driven to the extreme of fabricating, through a reverse translation, a Gaelic pseudo-original of his Ossianic epic *Fingal*. Macpherson's forgery was framed by an elaborate apparatus of misleading scholarship and ethnographic speculations. These editorial speculations also attempted to launch a preemptive strike against well-attested Irish antiquities, attempting thereby, in Clare O'Halloran's words, "to undermine the potential of Irish literary and historical sources to demonstrate that his Ossian was fraudulent."[25] The anti-Irish angle of Macpherson's project falsified Celtic history in general, recasting Scotland as the Celtic motherland and Ireland as the derivative colony. Macpherson, as Leith Davis points out, supplied "a founding myth for the British empire rooted in native, not continental soil."[26] Macpherson, though often assumed to be a sentimental Jacobite, belongs instead to a specifically Celtic strain of Whiggish historiography. He is an antiquarian "finder" of Whig values in the Scoto-Celtic past, and "Ossian" consummates, by a forgery, the roots-finding philological tradition of Malcolme, Maitland, and Stone. Macpherson's Whiggism, as Colin Kidd writes, "was British in scope, regarding the contributions of both Scoto-Celtic and Anglo-Germanic manners and mixed forms of government to the history of British liberty."[27] Macpherson's version of history is inflected to assert the interests of Lowland Scots, by a convenient appropriation of a Highland culture they had often attempted to extirpate, within the unionist and Hanoverian framework of the British Empire, at the expense of Catholic Ireland.

Johnson's many-faceted response to this famous controversy remains a model for the critical analysis of "invented traditions." He denounced the fraud as such, dryly recommending in *A Journey to the Western Islands of Scotland* (1773) that "If we know little of the ancient Highlands, let us not fill the vacuity with *Ossian.*" He tweaked Macpherson's many distinguished sponsors and defenders in Edinburgh for "loving Scotland more than truth." He likewise tweaked English readers hoping for a vicarious experience of the exotically backward in his account of the Highlands. He insistently exposed the mystification involved in glossing over the historical antagonism between Highland and Lowland Scots culture. While surmising that Macpherson's sources may in the end prove to be Irish, Johnson also gave support to the Irish Catholic antiquarian scholar Charles O'Conor, considered one of the very few eighteenth-century scholars of Gaelic. O'Conor's well-documented studies of Irish antiquities were linked to a public campaign to repeal the odious "penal laws" that dispossessed Catholics on all fronts of daily life.

Above all, Johnson devoted scathingly critical attention to the actual British policies—the "regulations" mentioned above—involved in the continuing economic and cultural demoralization of Highland culture after the military defeat of the Jacobites in 1746. He gives an unflinching contemporary description of the post-Culloden demoralization of Highland culture by British oppression. Of the Highlanders he writes, "Their pride has been crushed by the heavy hand of a vindictive conqueror, whose severities have been followed by laws, which, though they cannot be called cruel, have produced much discontent, because they operate on the surface of life, and make every eye bear witness to subjection."[28] As an antidote to mass emigration from the Highlands, Johnson recommends government concessions on both the arms issue and the question of traditional plaid, also banned by law in 1746. He summarizes his judgment on British treatment of the Highlands as follows: "To hinder insurrection, by driving away the people, and to govern peaceably, by having no subjects, is an expedient that argues no great profundity of politicks. . . . It affords a legislator little self-applause to consider, that where there was formerly an insurrection, there is now a wilderness."[29] Gibes such as these, which seriously annoyed George III, have led some to the dubious conclusion that Johnson was a closet Jacobite. Such labels, in any case, tend to miss the nimbleness of a multipronged response that encompasses, among the various mediations of "Ossian," British oppression of the Highlands, Lowland appropriation of the Highlands, and Scottish annexation of Irish antiquities.

Johnson's antipathy to roots-finding projects such as "Ossian" was in fact based on a principled suspicion of building any national identity around the mystique of reconstructed origins. Given his comments on the credulity of Scots as regards the fantastic antiquity of "Ossian," moreover, it is salutary to register his claim, during his tour of Scotland, that he could produce a ballad-based English equivalent to Macpherson's chorus of true believers. According to Boswell's *Tour of the Hebrides*, Johnson told Lord Elibank he would undertake "to write an epick poem on the story of Robin Hood, and half England, to whom the names and places he should mention in it are familiar, would believe and declare they had heard it from their earlier years."[30] His well-known scorn for the ballad-based "Gothic revival" of the later eighteenth century thus springs from an abiding mistrust of the continuous history "made" through folkloric nationalisms. "There is," as he told Boswell, "no permanent national character; it varies according to circumstances. Alexander the Great swept India: now the Turks sweep Greece."[31]

Johnson's particular target in the "Ossian" controversy, then, is neither old poetry nor popular poetry per se—much less Scotland—but rather "the creation of a mythic vernacular literature."[32] Indeed, precisely this nationalistic recuperation of history into myth arguably marks a fateful ideological appropriation: the redirection of the progressive achievements of the Enlightenment toward empire-building agendas. Johnson's "soft" nationalism remains pointedly civic and anti-essentialist precisely because the mystical and folkloric brands of nationalism are so easily hijacked for racial and expansionist myths — myths, in Laura Doyle's words, "of an ancient soil-rooted folk fit to become modern, global conquerors."[33]

A reading of the eighteenth-century moment in properly dialogical terms would serve to remind us that the oppositional themes of our own moment refract, from a new angle, a great many eighteenth-century debates.[34] However, the crucial ruptures and obtrusive sutures in the cultures of the Enlightenment have been papered over by the dominant strains of contemporary theory, which depend for self-legitimation on a monolithically baleful Enlightenment. This contemporary failure — the reluctance to engage with the Enlightenment's capacity for self-critique — induces a certain intellectual and political stagnation. Indeed, the extent to which the "subversive" discourses of our own moment have now hardened, à la Flaubert, into a lexicon of *idées reçues* is confirmed by the appearance in 1999 of *The Routledge Dictionary of Postmodern Thought*. The immanent critique of the Enlightenment present in Johnson's writings illustrates an alternative to both Whig historiography's triumphalism and postmodern obituaries for (in the words of the above-mentioned dictionary) the "Enlightenment dream of mastery." Johnson responded to the contradictions of his moment with a prescient balancing act that evades the usual labels by which we imagine that we have taken the full measure of the past. Johnson attempted to advance the modernizing project domestically while strenuously dismantling its rearticulations as imperial ideology. As a self-conscious public intellectual, he engaged in deliberate and selective negotiations with a nation-making he simultaneously embraces (in the building of a more democratized vernacular culture) and sharply denounces (in its tendency to fabricate mythical national and racial origins). He repeatedly articulates the relations between the national and the global by focusing on Britain's particular implication in a global narrative of colonial exploitation. His writings exemplify an anticolonial modernity later foreclosed by the Eurocentric and national imperatives of Britain's increasingly imperial trajectory. This historically *liminal* quality of eighteenth-century "Britishness" has a special resonance now precisely because it suggests that imperial ideology was no less vulnerable in its eighteenth-century emergence than in its twentieth-century decline. An emerging metaphysics of "Britishness" was being visibly made up in the eighteenth century, visibly cobbled together — and, perhaps above all, visibly *contested* — before one's very eyes. A genuine remaking of history "after the imperial turn" ought to undertake a dialogue with the alternative modernity to be found in the eighteenth-century moment: a self-critical modernity based neither on what came before nor on what now claims to have superseded it.

Notes

1 Lawrence Lipking, "Inventing the Eighteenth Centuries: A Long View," in *The Profession of Eighteenth-Century Literature: Reflections on an Institution*, ed. Leo Damrosch (Madison: University of Wisconsin Press, 1992), p. 9.

2 See Robert Griffin, *Wordsworth's Pope: A Study in Literary Historiography* (Cambridge: Cambridge University Press, 1996).

3 Douglas Lane Patey, "Ancients and Moderns," in *The Cambridge History of Literary Criticism*, vol 4: *The Eighteenth Century*, ed. H. B. Nisbet and Claude Rawson (Cambridge: Cambridge University Press, 1997), p. 45.

4 Herbert Butterfield, *The Englishman and His History* (Cambridge: Cambridge University Press, 1944), p. 81.

5 Partha Chatterjee, *The Nation and Its Fragments: Colonial and Postcolonial Histories* (Princeton, N.J.: Princeton University Press, 1993), p. 10.

6 Samuel Johnson, "Introduction to the Harleian Miscellany: An Essay on the Importance of Small Tracts and Fugitive Pieces," in *The Oxford Authors: Samuel Johnson*, ed. Donald Greene (Oxford: Oxford University Press, 1984), p. 123.

7 Samuel Johnson, "Reply to a Paper in the Gazetteer of May 26, 1757," in Green, ed., *The Oxford Authors*, p. 520.

8 Michael Dobson, *The Making of a National Poet: Shakespeare, Adaptation, and Authorship, 1660–1769* (Oxford: Clarendon Press, 1992), p. 6.

9 Samuel Johnson, "The State of Affairs in Lilliput," *Gentleman's Magazine* 8 (June 1738): 285.

10 David Armitage, "Greater Britain: A Useful Category of Historical Analysis?" *American Historical Review*, April 1999: 439.

11 Ibid.

12 See Emma Rothschild, "Globalization and the Return to History," *Foreign Policy* 115 (summer 1999): 106–116.

13 Samuel Johnson, "Introduction to *The World Displayed*," in *The Works of Samuel Johnson*, 15 vols., ed. Arthur Murphy (Edinburgh, 1806), vol. 2, pp. 217–218.

14 Ibid., p. 218.

15 Samuel Johnson, "Taxation No Tyranny," in *Political Writings*, ed. Donald J. Greene (New Haven, Conn.: Yale University Press, 1977), p. 421.

16 See James Boswell in *The Life of Samuel Johnson*, 3 vols., ed. Arnold Glover (London: J. M. Dent, 1925), vol. 1, p. 301.

17 Samuel Johnson, "An Introduction to the Political State of Great Britain," in *Political Writings*, Greene, ed., p. 137.

18 Samuel Johnson, *Idler 81*, in *The Idler and the Adventurer: Yale Edition of the Works of Samuel Johnson, Vol II* (New Haven: Yale University Press, 1963) ed. W. J. Bate, John M. Bullitt, and L. F. Powell (1963), p. 254.

19 Ibid.

20 James Basker, "The Next Insurrection: Johnson, Race, and Rebellion," in *The Age of Johnson* (New York: AMS Press, 2000), vol. 10, 37–51.

21 Samuel Johnson, "Preface to Lobo's *A Voyage to Abyssinia*," in *The Oxford Authors*, Greene, ed., p. 41.

22 Samuel Johnson, "A Brief to Free a Slave," in Boswell, *The Life of Samuel Johnson*, vol. 2, p. 368.

23 Ibid.

24 Ian Haywood, *The Making of History: A Study of the Literary Forgeries of James Macpherson and Thomas Chatterton in Relation to Eighteenth-Century Ideas of History and Fiction* (London: Associated University Presses, 1986), p. 35.

25 Clare O'Halloran, "Irish Re-Creation of the Gaelic Past: The Challenge of Macpherson's Ossian," *Past and Present* 124 (1989): 74.

26 Leith Davis, "Origins of the Specious: James Macpherson's Ossian and the Forging of the British Empire," *The Eighteenth Century* 34, 2 (1993): 132.

27 Colin Kidd, *Subverting Scotland's Past: Scottish Whig Historians and the Creation of an Anglo-British Identity, 1689–c. 1830* (Cambridge: Cambridge University Press, 1993), p. 233.

28 Samuel Johnson in *A Journey to the Western Islands of Scotland*, ed. R. W. Chapman (London: Oxford University Press, 1978 [1924]), p. 89.

29 Ibid., p. 97.

30 See James Boswell, *Journal of a Tour of the Hebrides with Samuel Johnson, LL.D.*, ed. Frederick A. Pottle and Charles H. Bennett (London: Heinemann, 1963), p. 380.

31 Ibid., p. 25.

32 J. C. D. Clark, *Samuel Johnson: Literature, Religion and English Cultural Politics from the Restoration to Romanticism* (Cambridge: Cambridge University Press, 1994), p. 82.

33 Laura Doyle, "The Racial Sublime," in *Romanticism, Race, and Imperial Culture, 1780–1834*, ed. Alan Richardson and Sonia Hofkosh (Bloomington: Indiana University Press, 1996), p. 22.

34 See Robert Markley, "The Rise of Nothing: Revisionist Historiography and the Narrative Structure of Eighteenth-Century Studies," *Genre* 23 (summer/fall 1990): 79.

LARA KRIEGEL

The Pudding and the Palace: Labor, Print
Culture, and Imperial Britain in 1851

After putting his children to bed on Christmas Eve, Mr. Oldknow, a fictive
patriarch, sat in his kitchen and puffed on his cigar. Oldknow was the protagonist of a fantastical tale about a Pudding that appeared in the 1850 Christmas
number of *Household Words*, an inexpensive weekly magazine published by
Charles Dickens for a middle-class, domesticated, urban reading public. His
wife and children in bed, Oldknow mused over the family recipe book, which
catalogued the ingredients required for baking his yearly luxury, the Christmas
Pudding. The recipe contained a number of foreign commodities — raisins,
currants, nutmeg, raw sugar, and ginger. It also included such domestically
produced staples as milk and eggs. An enthusiastic reader of travel books and a
connoisseur of London's panoramas depicting faraway lands, Oldknow reflected on the "mercantile history" of these commodities as he filled the room
with smoke. To his delight, a series of exotic topographies materialized in the
kitchen. Within each vista appeared a genie who embodied one of the ingredients in the Christmas Pudding. The Genius of the Raisin surfaced in the
shape of an Andalusian donning a Cashmere shawl, while the Genius of the
Bread appeared as a "stalwart" Kentish ploughman from provincial England.
The Genius of Sugar followed in the form of a freed slave, and the Egg Collec-
tor of Cork as an "Irish Market-woman."

As they appeared before him, the animated commodities discussed with
Oldknow the labor and trade practices of the nations they represented. The
patriarch assessed his spectral guests against the English ideals of hard work,
diligent labor, and free trade. He applauded the Genius of the Currant, a
"little free trader" who pronounced the virtues of intercourse among nations.
Oldknow chided the ploughman, who uttered a plea for "protection." In
Sugar, he found a vindication of abolitionism, proof that with freedom from
chattel slavery came diligence and toil. When the parade concluded, Oldknow
celebrated the hybrid concoction as Albion's "national dish." "Behold that
Pudding," the patriarch remarked, as he proclaimed it the Christmas reward
for England's laborers, the "artisans of Birmingham and Manchester" and

the "seamen of London and Liverpool" alike. In the Pudding, the product of free trade and diligent labor, Oldknow found yuletide proof of England's "commercial eminence" and the promise of future glory for the imperial nation.[1]

The pudding tale appeared just six months before the Great Exhibition of 1851, the first world's fair, opened in London's Hyde Park. The Exhibition celebrated "progress" as it was embodied in its display of raw materials, machinery, and manufacturers. Its founders — the Prince Consort Albert and the civil servant Henry Cole — imagined that the matchless collection would attest to the march of free trade, democratic consumption, and empire. Like the scene in Oldknow's kitchen, the Great Exhibition "annihilated" the distance among nations by containing worldly commodities within its "great glass case," Joseph Paxton's exalted and mythologized Crystal Palace. By walking through the Palace, visitors to the Exhibition could find a bounteous world "alive and stirring" without too much "trouble or fatigue," just as Oldknow had done in his reverie.[2] Two seeming encapsulations of the globe, the Pudding and the Palace, are both artifacts of the "Society of the Spectacle" that was built by the entwined enterprises of industrial capitalism and empire.[3] They reveal a pervasive cultural logic at work in England at midcentury, when commodities represented their places of origin and so brought the world "home" to metropolitan consumers.[4]

The real and imagined presence of foreign commodities in the metropole, epitomized by the Pudding and the Palace alike, has provided practitioners of Britain's new imperial history with an effective avenue for pressing two points that have become nearly commonplace and indisputable within this body of scholarship: first, that "home" was saturated, shaped, and constituted by empire; and second, that imperial processes permeated domestic life on the level of the everyday and the seemingly mundane.[5] By tracing the history and biography of commodities, numerous scholars have illuminated the persistent workings of imperial power in a circuit that spans metropole and colony. Historian Timothy Burke has demonstrated this dynamic to great effect in his study of cleanliness and commodification in Zimbabwe. His *Lifebuoy Men, Lux Women* chronicles the complex processes through which goods attain meaning and significance, including marketing, advertising, and local custom.[6] "The Pudding and the Palace" follows the work of Burke and others by examining one particular mechanism through which goods acquired meaning in 1851: the mechanism of print culture.

The Pudding tale offers just one instance of goods' assuming significance in print at midcentury. Through its parade of genies, the fantastical tale of the Pudding provided a sort of prophetic, if imperfect, fulfillment of Karl Marx's wish, expressed seventeen years later in *Capital*'s famous exposition of commodity fetishism, that goods could "speak" and thereby express the labor spent in their production.[7] Given voice by the genies, the ingredients that comprised the pudding made imaginary versions of the imperial and foreign labor that rendered them visible to metropolitan consumers. It was a prominent conceit in 1851 that the displays in the Crystal Palace could themselves speak, just like those in Oldknow's tale. One of the event's many catalogues, John Cassell's *Illustrated Exhibitor*, provides a compelling instance of this practice. As it led his readers around the Exhibition's famed Indian Courts, this guide for England's artisans waxed lyrically of the displays: "What stories they tell."[8] Historians and literary critics have cast the Great Exhibition as the triumph of the spectacle, a regime of production and representation where, as literary critic Thomas Richards has argued, the commodity assumed "center stage."[9] This narrative of the vanquishing mid-nineteenth-century commodity bears reconsideration in light of print culture. At the Great Exhibition, the commodity could not speak for itself or by itself. Instead, the displays inspired — or even compelled — the publication of numerous texts, including catalogues, travelogues, ephemera, newspapers, and periodicals. These artifacts of popular print culture served a number of purposes. They promoted the Exhibition and interpreted its showcases, often well before visitors set foot in the Crystal Palace. As they meditated on the Exhibition, the texts endowed the commodities with narratives, saturating them with meaning. Like the Pudding tale and like the Exhibition itself, this literature made empire, and England's dominion over it, imaginable. To use the formulation of sociologist Simonetta Falasca-Zamponi, the Exhibition's narratives produced imperial power even while representing it.[10]

The notion that Exhibitions and world's fairs were sites for kindling imperial sentiment is now a pervasive one. With the 1988 publication of *Ephemeral Vistas*, Paul Greenhalgh cast exhibitions as a compelling topic for students of empire.[11] Historians, art historians, literary critics, and geographers have subsequently illustrated the myriad ways that exhibitions displayed and ordered Britain's empire while simultaneously refashioning the colonial nation.[12] Their rich body of scholarship implicitly refines the work of Guy Debord by demonstrating that it was not simply industrial capitalism, but imperialism too, that played a constituent role in the production of the spectacle in its nineteenth-century form. Often more explicitly, scholarship on imperial spectacle renders specificity to the ideas of Benedict Anderson by outlining the ways that nation and empire are "imagined" on the most material of levels, whether through architecture, collecting, or display.[13] It is now luminously clear that race and gender played a constituent role in these imperial imaginings — whether as categories that underwrote the spectacle or ones that gained redefinition through it.[14] Missing, however, from many analyses of the topi—and often from the new imperial history itself—is an emphasis on labor, save perhaps in discussions of the "human showcases" or living villages of Irish and African workers who entertained visitors to world's fairs from the later nineteenth century onward.[15] Jeffrey Auerbach and Peter Henry Hoffenberg have sought to redress this problem in their recent studies of metropolitan and colonial exhibitions. They maintain that the commodity spectacle at the Great Exhibition and at subsequent world's fairs mystified—or worse, eviscerated—the figure of the imperial laborer.[16]

By focusing on print culture, I posit an alternate view. In 1851, labor was not hidden or invisible. In fact, it served as a pivotal category for conceiving nation and empire alike—not simply in the Pudding tale, but at the Great Exhibition as well. As they meditated on the goods inside the Crystal Palace, the Exhibition's texts animated the displays by evoking figures of English and imperial labor. These inescapably national figures organized the productive relationships between England and its imperial possessions. Labor was thus an integral component of what Felix Driver has called the "imaginative geography" of empire at midcentury.[17] The remainder of this essay carries out this interpretive line by analyzing the narratives produced around the displays from India, Ceylon, Ireland, Scotland, and China. I draw upon a range of texts, but especially *Household Worlds*, the *Illustrated London News*, and the *Illustrated Exhibitor.* Products of the expanding press of the 1840s, these publications were part of a broad, if internally contradictory, liberal tradition that transcended class, party, and region to laud diligent labor, imperial expansion, international trade, and democratic consumption.[18] Like the Great Exhibition itself, these texts sought to impart to their readerships, which were comprised of the middle and working classes, a sense of wonder toward the real and the everyday.[19] Producing fictional narratives of labor around the commodities on display offered one way to manufacture this sort of enchantment. The protagonists of these narratives ranged from the dextrous Indian weaver to the slothful Cingalese craftsman to the introspective Chinese carver. Like the genies who emerged from the Pudding, these figures exemplified popularly held notions of the nations they purported to represent. And just as the genies had, these imaginary personas functioned as foils to the English ideals of vigorous trade and labor. These print artifacts demonstrate that if commodities and their display made empire visible in the metropolis, labor functioned as a category through which metropolitan subjects conceived of empire and its component parts at midcentury—albeit in fictional and aestheticized incarnations.

* * *

Let us turn now to the Exhibition's vast Indian Courts. The displays from England's prized imperial possession provide one of the richest opportunities for examining the relationship among print culture, empire, nation, and spectacle. Compiled, arranged, and painstakingly indexed by the East India Company, the collection aimed to delight visitors with its lavish array of art manufactures. It also sought to impress them with its staggering aggregation of raw materials. By "dazzling and astounding" Exhibition goers, the East India Company aspired to convince them of the worthiness of imperial engagement on the subcontinent at a transitional moment in its history, as the dictates of rule were shifting from trade to militarism. The Exhibition seemed to offer the company an opportunity to refashion itself as a steward of empire for a new era and to rebut the liberal elements of the British press that had lambasted its protectionist policies for decades.[20] Artifacts of what Louise Purbrick has called the Exhibition's "dense significance," the myriad publications that described the Indian Courts appeared on the whole to support the East India Company's vision.[21] They cast the subcontinent alternately as a rich and fertile land or an oriental treasure trove. As it narrated the collection for visitors, readers, and posterity, Exhibition literature evoked a range of laboring figures. Portrayed in national guises, they epitomized the rudeness of uncultivated territory, the refinement and romance of a long-standing artisanal tradition, and the promises of an empire of free labor and free trade.[22]

Raw materials and agricultural implements occupied a prominent place within the Indian Courts. As they inventoried these displays, the Exhibition's texts conjured a land of "natural fertility," a territory so rich that it could single-handedly produce "the useful products of every other quarter of the globe."[23] As Jeffrey Auerbach has shown, the subcontinent seemed to offer fruitful ground for growing such English staples as cotton, tea, and sugar. However, large-scale cultivation did not appear immediately feasible in the minds of most commentators, who declared that the agricultural arts of the subcontinent had remained stationary for "centuries." Writers took the displays of rough hand-mills and bows — used from "time immemorial" to remove seeds and dirt from raw cotton — as material testimony to this fact. Statements such as these might be read as indictments of the East India Company, which had failed to kindle a booming economy on the subcontinent during its years of rule.[24] Rather than assigning blame, however, the Exhibition's texts deployed the material culture of India in the service of its civilizing mission.[25] They preached the many benefits that would come with the endeavor of cultivating the subcontinent. Harnessing its fertility would elevate the lowly Indian peasant, the epitome of debased, if skillful, rural labor, who appeared repeatedly in the pages of the *Illustrated London News* and *Household Words*. It would release the poor peasants from the poverty and stasis that their "singularly rude" ploughs suggested. Improving agriculture on the subcontinent would prove beneficial for England as well, not simply because it would promise a steady supply of raw cotton, but also because it could free the nation from its dependence on American slave labor — a specter of the U.S. Courts, a subject of parody, and an institution decried in Exhibition literature as "the worst of modern times."[26] When they examined India's raw materials, the Exhibition's interlocutors thus conjured images of backward, yet tractable and nimble, workers who provided a mandate for sustained engagement on the subcontinent. When liberated from the shackles of stagnancy by the succoring arm of empire, Indian peasants would become reflections of freeborn Englishmen, making England all the more a beacon of liberty itself.

Indian art manufactures — whether Cashmere shawls, ornate howdahs, or intricate arms — proved to be an even more provocative inspiration for narratives that performed the work of empire than the store of raw materials. When they pondered the spoils of the East, Exhibition commentators exalted India's artisans as bearers of an enduring tradition and an "unerring taste." In a maneuver that would echo the observations of the early modern explorers discussed by Michael Adas, Exhibition writers expressed a sort of disbelief at the disparity between such rude tools as fish jaws or iron rollers and the ornate products that they yielded.[27] As they discussed the art manufactures, Exhibition commentators employed the same tropes of simplicity and timelessness that had guided their examinations of the raw materials. In the process, they produced numerous images of Indian labor, some of them seemingly contradictory. One figure to emerge out of these discussions was the female Hindu spinner. The living repository of the artisanal, the natural, and the preindustrial, the spinner epitomized the notion of "anachronistic space" — an expressly imperial dynamic described by Anne McClintock, wherein geographical distance is expressed as difference over time.[28] Nature, rather than the clock, regulated the spinner's workday. She rose before the sun had "dissipate[ed] the dew on the grass" to spin her "finest thread" before dawn. The spinner relied on rough tools, as well as her "sensibility of touch" and "delicate organization." She was only one figure who appeared to repudiate a version of the English work ethic preached by Oldknow. As they invoked figures like the spinner to meditate on the spoils of the subcontinent, several commentators expressed a longing for a mythic, artisanal past. Other Exhibition writers responded differently. Several equated the lavish displays of arms, jewels, and cloths in the Indian Courts with oriental despotism. Cambridge scientist William Whewell was only one who found in the finery of the Indian Courts a materialization of the differences between liberty and oppression. In the East, he noted, so many laborers toiled for so few—a far cry from the vision of democratic consumption in Britain that he endorsed and that Oldknow had celebrated in the Pudding tale.[29] One a source of inspiration and the other a symbol of despotism, the glorified spinner and the oppressed artisan might reflect the contested philosophies of governance—orientalism versus Anglicanism—that informed debates over imperial rule during the early nineteenth century.[30] By illuminating these prior discussions, the art manufactures of the subcontinent demonstrate the role of material culture as a purveyor of the "embedded conflicts" that shape imperial rule.[31]

More than any other display in the Indian Courts, a series of "Ethnographic Models" suggests the importance of labor to the imperial imagination at mid-century. This display, which presaged the living villages that would thrill visitors to future world fairs, showcased 150 miniatures representing various Indian trades. It employed the category of "trade" capaciously to include not only cotton spinners and blacksmiths, but cooks, nursemaids, and snake charmers as well. Commentators responded to this museological gesture of colonization with a rhetoric of dismay or even "repulsion," as they sought simultaneously to capitalize on and contain "the shock of the visual" presented by the Ethnographic Models.[32] The Exhibition chronicler Edward Concannen found himself sickened by the "distorted," thin, and effeminate bodies of the models, which he described as "poor, half-clad, [and] rice-fed." As it reminded its readership of British workers of their good fortune, the *Illustrated Exhibitor* emphasized the despicable poverty of their Indian counterparts, "a lean, starved-out regiment of squalid beggars" with "scanty folds of coarsest cotton flung around their wasted limbs."[33] By highlighting the strangeness, poverty, and effeminacy of Indian workers, such descriptions facilitated the celebration of disciplined labor performed by healthy Englishmen that Oldknow had extolled as well.[34] They employed the gendered body politics of colonialism to great effect. They elevated the English worker as a vigorous masculine figure, one who provided a foil to the unmanly laborers of the subcontinent. As it invoked these images, Exhibition literature suggested that material culture played a pivotal role in the production of a gendered body politics that scholars of imperialism have demonstrated to be central to the dynamics of colonial rule.[35]

In the Exhibition's texts, Indian laborers surfaced in many forms—as debased peasants, dextrous spinners, and sickly artisans toiling under a regime of backward despotism. By invoking these figures, Exhibition commentators made engagement on the subcontinent compelling, whether in terms of economic necessity, humanitarian impulse, or orientalist fascination. The inspiration for so many narratives, India stood "preeminent" among Britain's imperial possessions at the Great Exhibition. It was, however, just one of many colonies on display in the Crystal Palace.[36] Oldknow's reverie attests to the presence of multiple foreign and colonial influences in the metropole in 1851. It also offers a model for a multisited imperial history.[37] The Crystal Palace showcased the material culture of several imperial possessions, among them Ceylon, Scotland, and Ireland. Although they were dwarfed by the Indian Courts, the displays from these colonized locations also provided an inspiration for narratives of labor and nation in 1851. Like the texts that gave voice to the Indian Courts, the print productions around these displays relied on the trope of rudeness versus refinement. Haphazardly collected and displayed, these smaller collections did not motivate the proliferation of narratives that the subcontinent's courts had. But as they invoked fictive — and inescapably nationalized — laborers, they worked all the same to undergird England's status as the heart of the empire and India's as the "jewel" in the imperial crown.

The Ceylon Court, a modest assembly of raw materials and handicrafts, provides a case in point. A site of insurrections earlier in the Exhibition year and throughout the nineteenth century, this "farthest Indian Isle" seemed to offer only limited hope for England's empire in 1851.[38] Commentators noted Ceylon's rich supply of raw materials — especially its coffee and cinnamon — but cast its inhabitants, who had not harnessed the wealth of the island, as the exemplars of "Oriental laziness."[39] While the poor farmers of India appeared as tractable imperial subjects worthy of cultivation, the inhabitants of Ceylon emerged as unruly, uncivilized savages marked by "extraordinary slothfulness" and "extreme turpitude."[40] Their labor habits seemed to mirror those of recently emancipated Jamaicans depicted by Thomas Carlyle in his infamous "Occasional Discourse on the Negro Question," published just two years before the Exhibition.[41] Critics brought the notion of indolent labor rendered by Carlyle to bear on their discussion of the material culture from this eastern imperial isle. They inflected their discussion of the Cingalese handicrafts with disregard, deeming the miscellaneous assortment of tortoiseshell ornaments, umbrellas, and decorated coconuts "more curious than valuable." It was a testimony to the intractability and savagery of the island's laborers that its celebrated ivory carvings were absent from the Exhibition. As the *Illustrated London News* explained, it was "impossible to persuade a Cingalese carver to work faster than is his custom."[42] The habit that was written as patience for the artisans of India thus emerged as obstinacy in the case of the Cingalese. Hardly as plentiful or contradictory as the Indian figures, these images of labor cast the island as a site for disapprobation rather than awe. By portraying Ceylon in this way, the Exhibition's commentators reinforced notions of English superiority and Indian potential.[43]

Exhibition writers furthered the project of imagining the empire as they narrated the displays from the Scottish Highlands and Ireland—possessions whose dual status as parts of the United Kingdom and members of the empire was on display at the Crystal Palace. By subsuming the contributions from the Celtic nations into the United Kingdom's massive collection, the commissioners had participated in the endeavor of binding the "Four Nations" together as a political, commercial, and material unity. The narratives around them served, however, to reinforce the status of the Celtic nations as imperial possessions. When they discussed the scant contributions from the Scottish Highlands, the Exhibition's texts consolidated an image of a "rude" people sprinkled over "wild hills and pathless moors." Though they did not approach the turpitude of the Cingalese, the Highland farmers were "destitute" of the "pushing energy and hard and keen spirit of industry" that characterized England. If the Highlanders approximated the Cingalese at the moment of the Exhibition, Ireland occupied a structural and rhetorical space that was similar to India's. Like India, Ireland received acclaim for its handicraft traditions, especially those of lace making and flax spinning, which were performed by women. Ireland also resembled the subcontinent because it was rich in raw materials that had not been harnessed to their fullest extent. As they depicted scenes of rural hardship, Exhibition commentators invoked the Irish peasant, who suffered under a regime of scarcity and ruin. Like the Indian farmer, the Irish peasant served as a symbol of ultimate poverty and dejection for the English reading public in the years just after the Famine—a reminder of the liminal, colonized status of the Celtic nations in 1851.[44]

Members of the empire—India, Ireland, Scotland, and even Ceylon— emerged as presences that metropolitan government and culture could incorporate into the notion of an emerging Greater Britain—ruly and unruly to varying degrees. Another oriental presence at the Exhibition, China, figured as the ultimate outsider, foreign and impenetrable. A decade before the Crystal Palace stood in Hyde Park, Britain had opened China's ports, though not its interior, through the Opium Wars.[45] At midcentury, China was the material and ideological apotheosis of impenetrability, the ultimate barrier to be broken or distance to be crossed.[46] A piece of the "informal" empire, it was a contrast to knowable, colonizable India. The Great Exhibition reinforced this counterpoint in its very mode of collection. While the East India Company had exhaustively collected and systematized the subcontinent, forty independent contributors provided the sundry assortment of materials that comprised the

Chinese collection at the Crystal Palace. There, a miscellaneous array of curiosities — snuff boxes, opium pipes, chopsticks, and nested ivory balls — represented the "Celestial Empire."[47]

The birthplace of the silk and porcelain industries, China alone shared India's designation as an ancient and enduring civilization in 1851.[48] Even so, its manufactures and the laborers who produced them did not inspire the same degree of admiration. At the moment of the Exhibition, the "whimsical and fantastical taste" exhibited by the Chinese provoked disgust, criticism, and amusement. Infamous for such monstrosities as drinking cups that deliberately squirted water, the Chinese were branded with an affection for the deformed and debased. Their artisans featured in a range of periodical productions, including *Blackwood's Edinburgh Magazine*, an elite organ of Whig ideology, and the *Builder*, a professional journal for a growing class of architects. *Blackwood's* assayed that the Chinese were the "one people who cultivate[d] the ugly, the monstrous, the deformed," the one nation that favored the "grotesque" over the "graceful."[49] While commentators admired Indian artisans for their access to timeless artistic traditions, China's laborers emerged as a "plodding, persevering, unchanging people." The *Builder* deemed them "servile copyists" lacking in innovation and creativity. A Chinese tailor who allegedly made so exact a replica of a vest that he "copied all the holes and tatters of the original" exemplified this propensity for slavish imitation.[50] Even worse, Chinese laborers appeared unethical at heart throughout the print literature on the Exhibition. They were petty tricksters, forgers, frauds, and pirates.[51]

China was more than a foil to India in 1851. "Partly real, partly imagined," the ideals of trade and labor that the popular press attributed to the Chinese were directly antithetical to the liberal goals of the Great Exhibition and to England itself.[52] This relationship emerges most clearly in an article printed in *Household Words* entitled "The Great Exhibition and the Little One" and written by Charles Dickens and R. H. Horne. Dickens and Horne drew on a long-standing opposition as they invoked England as the exemplar of progress, openness, and usefulness and China as the epitome of decline, insularity, and futility.[53] While England had cultivated "commercial intercourse with the whole world," China had stymied because the nation had "shut itself up, as far as possible, within itself." The displays of machinery and manufactures in the Great Exhibition provided material evidence of these differences — that is, to the "greatness of the English results, and the extraordinary littleness of the Chinese." Dickens and Horne juxtaposed the English cotton-spinning industry, which enriched Britain and the world, to the Chinese practice of carving ivory balls. A labor-intensive, time-consuming, and intricate craft that had remained unchanged for centuries, ivory ball carving employed and benefited few. "Ball within ball and circle within circle," the trinkets—and the fictive laborers who produced them—represented China's insularity. The practice of carving nested ivory balls also exemplified the Chinese tendency toward painstakingly detailed, if wasteful, toil, so evident in such objects as "paper made of rice."[54]

Dickens and Horne were just two of many writers to meditate on *chinoiserie* in 1851. Other writers detached the designation "Chinese" from a specific geography; they extended its use to indicate tendencies toward backwardness and insularity in Britain. French political economist Adolphe Blanqui referred to economic protection, for example, as the "old Chinese brick wall of the insulation of nations."[55] The ardent free trader "Helix," who wrote in the liberal *Westminster Review*, invoked the "Chinese" to describe a number of practices that he deemed antithetical to ingenuity and progress. He showered accolades on the modern Renaissance man Joseph Paxton, who had designed the Crystal Palace, by referring to him as a "thorough Englishman" and "an Anti-Chinese."[56] For Dickens and Horne, scrutinizing the vast nation of China enabled them to indict the small-mindedness of those who opposed free trade at home. These rhetorical moves suggest that the "Chinese" threat did not emanate from Asia but surfaced much closer to home. For Dickens and Horne, the real threat was the "true Tory spirit," which would have "made a China of England if it could." In a formulation that John Stuart Mill would echo with his publication of *On Liberty* in 1859, Dickens and Horne declared that the "China" they actually abhorred was a version of England itself, one devoted to "stoppage" rather than "progress."[57] Even if China appeared unassimilable in 1851, the ultimate foreign presence or antidomestic, it was always encroaching on England and Englishness, subverting trade, industry, and improvement—ideals that Oldknow had extolled and values that the Great Exhibition sought to enshrine as well.

*   *   *

I began this essay by drawing a comparison between the Christmas Pudding and the Crystal Palace, two artifacts that suggest a pervasive cultural logic at work in mid-nineteenth-century England. By evoking figures of imperial and foreign labor, the Pudding and the Palace both made empire imaginable for England's reading public. In so doing, they bear out two assertions made by historian Madhavi Kale—first, that labor is an imaginative and analytical "category" and not simply an activity or an identity; and second, that this category is defined within the "crucible" of empire.[58] The imaginary laborers who emerged out of the Exhibition's print culture made the empire visible to domestic readers; at the same time, they seemed to challenge received notions of Englishness. The Indian displays prompted some writers to question the unequivocal benefits of mechanization, industry, and the division of labor — pillars of England's "commercial eminence." China's miscellaneous collection led Dickens and Horne to indict Tory England as backward and insular. The Exhibition's texts suggest the potential of print culture not only to challenge dominant cultural or commercial narratives, but also to undermine the commodity fetishism that is part and parcel of modern capitalist societies and the spectacle alike.[59] By invoking imaginary labor, it seems that the Exhibition's texts could redress the separation of production and image, which is one of the defining aspects of imperial spectacle.[60] They might also critique Britain's imperial project and produce a sort of "counterexhibition" in print.[61] However, as they fashioned and circulated these laborers, the works I have analyzed aestheticized imperial labor rather than critiquing its exploitation. These narratives made imperial engagement seem desirable, necessary, and compelling, just as the Pudding tale had. Rather than its refutation, the Exhibition's narratives — enabling documents for the intensification of empire — proved to be the handmaiden of the imperial spectacle in 1851.

Let me conclude with a final parallel that lurks behind that between the Pudding and the Palace. This is a parallel between the Great Exhibition and Christmas itself. At the moment of the Exhibition, which celebrated England's labor, trade, and empire, Christmas was on its way to becoming the country's "national" holiday. If the Great Exhibition was the spectacle writ large, then Christmas amounted to the spectacle writ small — commodity capitalism available for consumption throughout the nation, conceived, pace Benedict Anderson, as a series of identical middle-class households. Like the Exhibition, Christmas relied on and celebrated a hybrid and cosmopolitan notion of the nation, yet one that presented itself as a homogeneous entity.[62] This is evident not simply in the Pudding, that emblem of Englishness forged alchemically through the union of foreign and imperial commodities, but in the Christmas tree as well. It is noteworthy that Queen Victoria's husband, Albert the Prince Consort, holds a place in popular histories not only as a progenitor of the Great Exhibition, but also as the figure responsible for popularizing the Christmas tree across the channel from his native Germany. Albert is just one actor who links these two moments. Bureaucrat Henry Cole is celebrated as the progenitor of the Christmas card. And to the delight of the reading public, the author of the Pudding tale, Charles Dickens, published *A Christmas Carol* in 1843. More than any other text or event, it is Dickens's tale that is credited with kindling the sentimentalism of the modern Christmas. Like the pudding tale published seven years before, *A Christmas Carol* relied on spectral forces evoked through the engine of print culture — the ghosts who showed Ebeneezer Scrooge what had been, what was, and what might be — to effect the domestication of capitalism that has become part and parcel of Christmas as we know it. Had Tiny Tim, object of the reformed Scrooge's devotion, made it inside the Crystal Palace, we can only imagine his response to the world domesticated and commodified under glass. In a spirit that echoed Oldknow's in awe at the apparent bounty, he likely would have exclaimed, "God bless Us, Every One!"[63]

Notes

Many friends and colleagues have enriched this essay, but special thanks go to Sally Alexander, Antoinette Burton, Karen Fang, K. Dian Kriz, and Judith R. Walkowitz.

1 "A Christmas Pudding," *Household Words* 2 (December 21, 1850): 300–304.

2 William Whewell: "The General Bearing of the Great Exhibition on the Progress of Art and Science," *Lectures on the Results of the Great Exhibition of 1851* (London: Bogue, 1852), p. 13; see also [Anon.], "Iron and Glass Buildings," *The Builder*, December 7, 1850, p. 585; *Tallis' History and Description of the Crystal Palace, and the Exhibition of the World's Industry in 1851*, vol. 1 (London: John Tallis, 1851), pp. 238–240.

3 For a theoretical exposition of spectacle and its relationship to industry, see Guy Debord, *Society of the Spectacle*, trans. Donald Nicholson-Smith (New York: Zone, 1995), chs. 1 and 2, esp. pp. 12–14, 19–21, 28–30.

4 For a discussion of this phenomenon at the end of the nineteenth century, see Annie E. Coombes, *Reinventing Africa: Museums, Material Culture, and Popular Imagination in Late Victorian and Edwardian England* (New Haven, Conn.: Yale University Press, 1994), pp. 4, 63, 85.

5 This literature is vast. Some of its most influential expositions include the following: Tim Barringer and Tom Flynn, eds., *Colonialism and the Object: Empire, Material Culture, and the Museum* (New York: Routledge, 1998); Antoinette Burton, *At the Heart of the Empire: Indians and the Colonial Encounter in Late-Victorian Britain* (Berkeley: University of California Press, 1998); Coombes, *Reinventing Africa*; Anne McClintock, *Imperial Leather: Race, Gender, and Sexuality in the Colonial Contest* (London: Routledge, 1995).

6 Timothy Burke, *Lifebuoy Men, Lux Women: Commodification and Cleanliness in Colonial Zimbabwe*, (Durham, N.C.: Duke University Press, 1996). See also Arjun Appadurai, "Introduction: Commodities and the Politics of Value," and Igor Kopytoff, "The Cultural Biography of Things: Commoditization as Process," both in *The Social Life of Things: Commodities in Cultural Perspective*, ed. Arjun Appadurai (New York: Cambridge University Press, 1986).

7 Karl Marx, "The Fetishism of Commodities and the Secret Thereof," in *The Marx-Engels Reader*, ed. Robert C. Tucker (New York: W. W. Norton, 1978), pp. 319–329, esp. p. 328.

8 John Cassell, *Illustrated Exhibitor*, October 4, 1851, pp. 317–318.

9 This phrase is from Thomas Richards, *The Commodity Culture of Victorian England: Advertising and Spectacle, 1851–1914* (Stanford, Calif.: Stanford University Press, 1990), ch. 1. See also Debord, *Society of the Spectacle*, pp. 29 and 34. Louise Purbrick's analysis of the "originary" freight of the exhibition calls Richards's periodization into question. See Louise Purbrick, "Introduction," in *The Great Exhibition of 1851: New Interdisciplinary Essays*, ed. Louise Purbrick (Manchester: Manchester University Press), pp. 1, 15–16.

10 Simonetta Falasca-Zamponi, *Fascist Spectacle: The Aesthetics of Power in Mussolini's Italy* (Berkeley: University of California Press, 1997), p. 3.

11 Paul Greenhalgh, *Ephemeral Vistas* (Manchester: Manchester University Press, 1998), chs. 3 and 4.

12 See note 5. See also Jeffrey Auerbach, *The Great Exhibition of 1851: A Nation on Display* (New Haven, Conn.: Yale University Press, 1999); Antoinette Burton, "Making a Spectacle of Empire: Indian Travelers in Fin-de-Siècle London," *History Workshop Journal* 42 (1996): 127–146; Patricia Morton, *Hybrid Modernities: Architecture and Representation at the 1931 Colonial Expo, Paris* (Cambridge: MIT Press, 2000).

13 Benedict Anderson, *Imagined Communities: Reflections on the Origin and Spread of Nationalism*, 2d ed. (London: Verso, 1991).

14 On this latter point, see Coombes, *Reinventing Africa*, pp. 3, 5.

15 Annie Coombes's work on later nineteenth- and early twentieth-century exhibitions provides a model here. See *Reinventing Africa*, chs. 4, 5, 9, and Paul Greenhalgh, *Ephemeral Vistas*, chs. 3 and 4.

16 Jeffrey Auerbach, *The Great Exhibition*, ch. 6, and Peter Henry Hoffenberg, *An Empire on Display: English, Indian, and Australian Exhibitions from the Crystal Palace to the Great War* (Berkeley: University of California Press, 2001), esp. ch. 6.

17 Felix Driver, *Geography Militant: Cultures of Exploration and Empire* (Oxford: Blackwell, 2000), p. 148.

18 Paul Greenhalgh writes that "Exhibitions up to 1914 were saturated with Liberal ideology." See *Ephemeral Vistas*, p. 27.

19 On imperial culture as an everyday dynamic and negotiation, see Antoinette Burton, *At the Heart of the Empire*, introduction, p. 180. Louise Purbrick provides a contrasting argument with regard to the Great Exhibition. She emphasizes that exhibitions are "not of the everyday." See Purbrick, "Introduction," p. 5.

20 For a rich discussion of the criticisms faced by the East India Company, see Timothy L. Alborn, *Conceiving Companies: Joint-Stock Politics in Victorian England* (London: Routledge, 1998), ch. 2.

21 Purbrick, "Introduction," p. 7.

22 "Modern India," *Bentley's Miscellany* 31 (1851): 465–473, esp. p. 470; see also Philip Lawson, *The East India Company: A History* (New York: Longman, 1993); Thomas Metcalf, *Ideologies of the Raj* (New York: Cambridge University Press, 1994), ch. 2; C. Lestock Reid, *Commerce and Conquest: The Story of the Honorable East India Company* (Port Washington, N.Y.: Kennikat Press, 1947; reissue 1971), p. 195; "Shall We Retain Our Colonies?" *Edinburgh Review* 93 (1851): 475–498.

23 *Official Descriptive and Illustrated Catalogue of the Great Exhibition of 1851*, (London: William Clowes and Sons, 1851), vol. 2, pp. 860, 874. On empire as a cornucopia of raw materials, see Purbrick, ed., *The Great Exhibition of 1851*, ch. 6; Hoffenberg, *An Empire on Display*.

24 Lawson, *The East India Company*, p. 160.

25 On the use of material culture, and especially technology, as a gauge of civilization, see Michael Adas, *Machines as the Measure of Men* (Ithaca, N.Y.: Cornell University Press, 1989), introduction, esp. p. 3. See also chs. 3 and 4.

26 *Illustrated London News*, May 31, 1851, pp. 487–489; June 14, 1851, p. 563; August 2, 1851, p. 163; *Official Descriptive and Illustrated Catalogue*, vol. 2, 881–883, 932–976; "British Cotton," *Household Words* 5 (1852): 51–54; "The Field of the Cloth of Flax," *Household Words* 5 (1853): 466–469.

27 Adas, *Machines as the Measure of Men*, pp. 38–138.

28 McClintock, *Imperial Leather*, pp. 39–40.

29 *Official Descriptive and Illustrated Catalogue*, vol. 2, pp. 933–936; Whewell, "General Bear-

ing," pp. 18–19, J. F. Royle, "Art and Manufactures of India," *Lectures on the Results of the Great Exhibition*, p. 352; *Illustrated London News*, April 26, 1851; May 3, 1851; May 10, 1851, p. 392; May 31, 1851, p. 491; June 14, 1851, p. 563. See also *Cassell's Illustrated Exhibitor*, October 4, 1851, pp. 317–318; "Helix," *Westminster Review* 55 (1851): 200; Matthew Digby Wyatt, *Industrial Arts of the Nineteenth Century;* "Wanderings in the Crystal Palace," *Art Journal*, 1851: 196; *Tallis' History and Description of the Crystal Palace* pp. 33–34, 238.

30   On this debate, see Adas, *Machines as the Measure of Men*, pp. 275–284.

31   This phrase is Tim Burke's. See *Lifebuoy Men, Lux Women*, introduction, p. 116.

32   See Antoinette Burton's reading of Rey Chow in "Introduction: The Unfinished Business of Colonial Modernities," in *Gender, Sexuality and Colonial Modernities*, ed. Antoinette Burton (London: Routledge, 1999), p. 7.

33   Edward Concannen, *Remembrances of the Great Exhibition* (London: Ackerman, 1852[?]), n.p.; *Cassell's Illustrated Exhibitor*, October 4, 1851, pp. 317–318.

34   The foundational discussion of the production of the categories of the "manly Englishman" and the "effeminate Bengali" as a strategy of rule is Mrinalini Sinha's. See *Colonial Masculinity: The "Manly Englishman" and the "Effeminate Bengali" in the Late Nineteenth Century* (Manchester: Manchester University Press, 1995), introduction.

35   See Burke, *Lifebuoy Men, Lux Women*, introduction, ch. 1; Saloni Mathur, "Wanted Native Views: Collecting Colonial Postcards of India," in Burton, ed., *Gender, Sexuality and Colonial Modernities;* Sinha, *Colonial Masculinity.*

36   *Tallis' History and Description of the Crystal Palace*, p. 31.

37   Catherine Hall, "The Nation within and Without," in Catherine Hall, Keith McClelland, and Jane Rendall, *Defining the Victorian Nation: Class, Race, Gender and the Reform Act of 1867* (New York: Cambridge University Press, 2000), has been provocative in this regard.

38   *Speech of the Rt Hon Viscount Torrington on the Affairs of Ceylon in the House of Lords, April 1, 1851, with an Appendix Containing Extracts from the Minutes of Evidence Taken before the Select Committee on Ceylon.*

39   "Ceylon and the Singhalese," *Bentley's Miscellany* 29 (London: Richard Bentley, 1851), 224–232. See also Isaac Tompkins, *Cheap Coffee and Cheap Government, or the Case of Ceylon* (1850?).

40   Ibid.

41   Catherine Hall's discussion of Carlyle's text has been influential for me. See "Competing Masculinities: Thomas Carlyle, John Stuart Mill, and the Case of Governor Eyre" in Catherine Hall, *White, Male, and Middle Class: Explorations in Feminism and History* (New York: Routledge, 1992), p. 270.

42   *Illustrated London News*, May 3, 1851, p. 371; June 14, 1851, p. 462.

43   *Official Descriptive and Illustrated Catalogue*, vol. 2, pp. 937–938; *Tallis' History and Description of the Crystal Palace*, p. 49.

44   *Illustrated London News*, September 20, 1851, p. 353; October 4, 1851, pp. 417–418; *Tallis' History and Description of the Crystal Palace*, pp. 175–182. See also John Sproule, ed., *The Resources and Manufacturing Industry of Ireland* (Dublin: Sproule, 1854); Wyatt, *Industrial Arts of the Nineteenth Century;* "Calcutta," *Bentley's Miscellany* 30 (1851): 361–368; on the representation of the Irish and Irish villages at turn-of-the-century exhibitions, see Coombes, *Reinventing Africa*, ch. 9, pp. 208–210.

45   "China with a Flaw in It," *Household Words* 5 (1852): 368–374; see also Samuel Warren, *The Lily and the Bee: An Apologue of the Crystal Palace of 1851* (London: Blackwood, 1854).

46   The length of time it took for letters to get to China was the ultimate test of the progress in speed nagivation; *Illustrated London News*, May 31, 1851, p. 496.

47 *Official Descriptive and Illustrated Catalogue*, vol. 3, pp. 1412–1430.

48 Ibid., vol. 2, pp. 508, 929. See also Royle, *Lectures on the Results of the Great Exhibition*, vol. 2, pp. 336–338, 370.

49 "Voltaire in the Crystal Palace," *Blackwood's Edinburgh Magazine* 70 (1851): 142–153.

50 *Builder*, May 25, 1850, p. 255; November 1, 1851, p. 688.

51 *Tallis' History and Description of the Crystal Palace*, pp. 235–237, 240; *Illustrated London News*, July 5, 1851, p. 19; "Pottery and Porcelain," *Household Words* 4 (1851): 36.

52 Michael Adas used this terminology to discuss eighteenth-century assessments of chinoiserie. *Machines as the Measure of Men*, p. 79.

53 Jeffrey Auerbach's reading of the Chinese collections at the exhibition is helpful on this score. See *The Great Exhibition*, pp. 174–179, and Adas, *Machines as the Measure of Men*, pp. 9, 84, 88, 91, 123.

54 Charles Dickens and R. H. Horne, "The Great Exhibition and the Little One," *Household Words* 3 (1851): 356–360. See also Tim Dolin's reading of this article: "Cranford and the Victorian Collection," *Victorian Studies* 36 (1993): 179–206, and Mrs. Corner, *China: Pictorial, Descriptive, and Historical* (London: H. G. Bohn, 1853); *Tallis' History and Description of the Crystal Palace*, p. 14; *Illustrated London News*, August 30, 1851; December 20, 1851.

55 *Tallis' History and Description of the Crystal Palace*, p. 202.

56 "Helix," *Westminster Review* 55 (1851): 178–204.

57 Dickens and Horne, "The Great Exhibition and the Little One"; John Stuart Mill, *On Liberty*, 2d ed. (London: John W. Parker and Son, 1859), p. 129.

58 Madhavi Kale, *Fragments of Empire: Capital, Slavery, and Indian Indentured Labor Migration in the British Caribbean* (Philadelphia: University of Pennsylvania Press, 1998), esp. pp. 2–3.

59 Michael Taussig, *The Devil and Commodity Fetishism* (Chapel Hill: University of North Carolina Press, 1980), pp. 5, 8, 17, 21, 26, 28, 30, 31.

60 On the spectacle and separation, see Debord, *Society of the Spectacle*, pp. 12–24. For an interesting reading of the *Illustrated Exhibitor*'s attempts to redress this separation and one whose interpretation of this periodical contrasts with my own, see Brian Maidment, "Entrepreneurship and the Artisans: John Cassell, the Great Exhibition, and the Periodical Idea," in Purbrick, ed., *The Great Exhibition of 1851*, pp. 79–113, esp. p. 97.

61 On the counterexhibition, see Patricia Morton's *Hybrid Modernities*, ch. 3.

62 Essays by Daniel Miller and Adam Kuper in *Unwrapping Christmas*, ed. Daniel Miller (Oxford: Clarendon Press, 1993) have informed my interpretation here. Also helpful has been Elizabeth Pleck, *Celebrating the Family: Ethnicity, Consumer Culture, and Family Rituals* (Cambridge: Harvard University Press, 2000), especially pp. 2, 44–49, 234–237.

63 Charles Dickens, *A Christmas Carol* (London: Peal Press, n.d.), p. 119.

IAN CHRISTOPHER FLETCHER

Double Meanings: Nation and Empire in the Edwardian Era

The Edwardian era — the turbulent years from the South African war of 1899–1902 to the outbreak of World War I in 1914 — is rich with historiographical possibilities after the imperial turn. One mode of rewriting Edwardian history is global and synchronic in nature, emphasizing the interactions — from below as well as from above, centripetal as well as centrifugal — that constituted the imperial state and its subjects across the metropole and colonies. Such interactions might be tracked along axes that link two "nations," as Mrinalini Sinha and Peter van der Veer have recently done for Britain and India, or along more weblike lines.[1] Given the isolation of many North American academic historians from current struggles for global peace and justice and the smart but disengaged histories we produce as a consequence, this chapter seeks especially to bring political contention back into the "new imperial history." I begin by juxtaposing Lord Milner's *The Nation and the Empire*, Mohandas K. Gandhi's *Hind Swaraj*, and J. E. Casely Hayford's *Ethiopia Unbound* to suggest some of the ways imperialists and nationalists deployed, contested, and appropriated notions of nation and empire. I show how these "floating signifiers" were entangled with each other and how their meanings were always already divided and doubled. I then turn to Erskine Childers's *The Framework of Home Rule* and the controversy it generated to highlight the imperial context of metropolitan politics and the "whiteness" of Irish nationalism. Placing metropolitan and colonial politics within a single analytic frame underlines not just the scope of the imperial state, but also the emergence of an imperial public sphere in which various forms of anticolonial criticism could find expression. Not unlike our own predicament in the "age of globalization," imagining alternatives in a world system of imperial states and subject peoples was a challenging task. An interrogation of categories and politics we share with the Edwardians might point to the possibility of a usable as well as a radical history after the imperial turn.

* * *

In 1913 the statesman Lord Milner published *The Nation and the Empire*, a collection of his speeches delivered over the previous fifteen years on the prospects of the imperial state. Milner had served as Britain's "man on the spot" in South Africa between 1898 and 1905, where he schooled a "kindergarten" of young protégés who later launched the Round Table movement for closer imperial union. Although he certainly held distinctive views, a glance at the proceedings of the contemporaneous colonial and imperial conferences shows that his book condenses many of the assumptions, swerves, and silences that shaped mainstream imperial thinking in the Edwardian era.[2]

For Milner, the British nation and empire were overlapping domains. He believed that the peoples of the United Kingdom and the self-governing dominions were "one body-politic," sharing a single nationality and entitled to a common citizenship.[3] This primal identity stemmed from the "racial bond" between Britons in the metropole and the colonies, which coexisted with the emergence of the dominions as nations in their own right.[4] Milner distinguished among the various white races, as well as the white and colored or black races. At the same time, he believed that the empire had the capacity to incorporate the French Canadians and other colonial settler communities of European descent. In South Africa, he recognized that "deep divisions" persisted but still held out the prospect of "the two great European races" fusing "into one nation."[5] Milner avoided equating Britishness with Englishness and was full of praise for the imperial contributions of "the Scottish people" and "the Scottish race."[6] He vouched for the "truly Imperial spirit" and "strongest sentiments of patriotism" of British workers he had encountered but worried about the "toiling millions" who seemed unaware of or indifferent to the empire.[7] A committed Unionist, he had little to say about Irish nationalism except to make invidious distinctions between loyal Irish subjects in the dominions and disaffected Irish Americans and between the Irish people and the home rule "faction" and its "foreign paymasters."[8] Not surprisingly, the enemy within the United Kingdom was comprised of "Little Englanders, Cosmopolitans and Separatists."[9]

Milner's deployment of the categories of nation and empire was complicated by his notion of the "two nations" and "two empires." Representing himself as a radical — by which he meant acceptance of democratic government and support for social reform — he did not hide the fact of "social cleavage" and "class antagonism" in Britain.[10] Linking the Disraelian specter of a class-divided society to his own anxiety about a declining core state at the center of a worldwide empire, he made an imperial case for the reunion of the "two nations." Speaking of women's "influence" through social work, he suggested that women were more likely than men to uphold "public, national, Imperial interests" over party politics. He acknowledged the existence of "the women's movement" around the empire and encouraged greater communication and cooperation in the interest ultimately of "a higher type of civilisation."[11] The "two nations" were inextricably bound up with the "two empires," for Milner divided the empire along "racial" and "climatic" lines into the United Kingdom and the dominions, which needed "consolidation," and the dependencies, which required defense and "development."[12] However, the United Kingdom's mounting social and economic problems made it increasingly difficult to govern the crown colonies alone. What was needed was a "partnership" with the dominions as these nations assumed more and more regional responsibility for the empire.[13] And yet, the eventual shape of this collaboration remained to be seen. For example, Milner doubted the feasibility of northward expansion of the South African state. Somewhere in the Rhodesias a "border-line" existed, beyond which the mixing of white and black became "unnatural and undesirable."[14] Thus the supplements of sexual and racial difference were never far behind invocations of national and imperial unity.[15]

Milner's sharp racial divide, supposedly crystallized in the different political forms of dominion and dependency, was impossible to sustain except by such strategies as remaining silent on the presence of indigenous peoples in settler colonies like Australia, Canada, and New Zealand. In South Africa, where whites enjoyed "political supremacy" over a native majority, Milner feared the "social" effects of "contact with a less civilised race."[16] Yet he also understood that his was "a migratory age," in which diasporas of people of color were changing the nature of colonial encounters.[17] In Australia and Canada as well as South Africa, Milner noted the problem of the immigration of "alien coloured races" from India and the crown colonies.[18] Assuming the paternalistic role of the "imperial man" with long experience of people of color, Milner advocated a policy of protecting the native and regretted the "crude ignorance" of colonial whites who could not distinguish between the "high-class and cultured Asiatic gentleman or noble" and the "humblest coolie."[19] At the same time, in his role as go-between for the United Kingdom and the dominions, he was unwilling simply to blame the latter and instead attributed the "misunderstanding" over immigration to an inadequate appreciation of the "interdependence" of the empire.[20]

The Edwardian era was a period of rapid political as well as physical movement. In 1908, on the morrow of the great swadeshi struggle in Bengal, Milner had described Indian self-government as "a hopeless absurdity," but only a few years later other members of the Round Table movement were conceding its plausibility.[21] Even Milner's own rhetoric registered the struggles of colonial subjects and people of color for legal equality and political representation. In a speech delivered in 1912, Milner imagined a day when the "two patriotisms" of nation and empire would be seamless identities and "any civilised man," regardless of color, might claim allegiance to the imperial state.[22] And despite the current spirit of discontent among "the educated classes," he held out hope for "the future of Imperial patriotism in India" if opportunities for participation in government were increased and "disabilities and indignities" suffered by Indians in the dominions were eliminated.[23]

Of course, Milner and the *Round Table* were far from the only participants in discursive and political projects to articulate nation and empire in the Edwardian era. Some were colonial subjects and people of color asserting themselves in widely dispersed locations in the metropole and colonies against the abuses and inequities of colonial rule and the color line. Emerging from the flow of people and ideas across the spaces of empire, their early but complex forms of anticolonial criticism cannot be reduced to a premature anti-imperial nationalism. In fashioning new (trans)national, diasporic, and cosmopolitan identities, these writers and activists conveyed a sense of "imagined community" quite unlike the imperial nationalisms of the United Kingdom and the dominions.[24]

Thus the imperial public sphere, through which circulated critical as well as official discussion of the problems of the imperial state, included Ramananda Chatterjee's *Modern Review*, published in Calcutta; Dusé Mohammed Ali's *African Times and Orient Review*, published in London; and other forums that engaged both metropolitan and colonial audiences and constituencies. A glance at the pages of the *Modern Review* opens new perspectives on nation and empire. It published essays and comments on Indian history and ethnography; literature and philosophy; science and industry; and, of course, politics, world affairs, and social questions. Far from promoting a narrow form of nationalism, the journal projected a capacious sense of Indianness even as it dealt with supposed racial differences between "Aryans" and "Dravidians"; political antagonism between Hindus and Muslims; and social conditions of women, Adivasis, Dalits, peasants, and workers.[25] One of the most intriguing aspects of the journal was its attention to overseas Indians — in the United Kingdom, Canada, South Africa, Japan, the United States, and elsewhere. It chronicled Gandhi's imprisonments in the Transvaal, exposed the sufferings of Indian plantation laborers in various British colonies, and hailed the accomplishments of Indian students in many countries. Alongside criticism of colonial law and administration and analysis of metropolitan opinion and politics, readers could find discussions of oriental civilization that insisted on its modernity and conceded little or nothing by way of inferiority to the West. Much the same can be said about the *African Times and Orient Review*, which brought together the worlds of Africa and the African diaspora, Islam, and the Orient.[26]

This dense yet far-flung culture of print and politics was the context for Mohandas K. Gandhi's *Hind Swaraj* and J. E. Casely Hayford's *Ethiopia Unbound*, two outstanding works of Edwardian political thought. Gandhi was at this time a leader of the Indian community's struggle for civil rights in South Africa. His text presented a dialogue between an editor representing Gandhi's views and a reader whose questions and comments gave voice to opinions usually associated with the "extremist" and "terrorist" tendencies in Indian nationalism. Hayford was, like Gandhi, a lawyer and journalist and a rising British West African nationalist. Ranging in time from the late nineteenth century to an imagined 1925, his text was also hybrid in nature — part novel, part essay, part prophecy. These innovative strategies of opening the text to different perspectives and temporalities called into question authoritative renditions of identity and community.

Both Gandhi and Hayford employed the trope of doubleness and dividedness in their critiques of metropolitan as well as colonial society. Yet their divergent approaches to imagining alternatives to the imperial state confounded homogenizing representations of "the Asiatic" and "the native." In *Hind Swaraj*, the struggle between modern Western and moral Indian civilization was not depicted as if it were waged between two separate entities or two different epochs but rather as a struggle from within as well as without. Although he focused on the dislocating effects of doctors, lawyers, railways, and machinery on India, Gandhi pointed as well to the destructive consequences of capitalist modernity in Britain, symbolized by the plight of women workers and the protests of militant suffragists. The imperial encounter brought together Anglo-Indians and "almost half-Anglicized Indians," neither of whom were identical with the British and Indian nations as a whole.[27] Rejecting the British argument that India was not a nation, Gandhi insisted that Indian nationality was inclusive of Hindus, Muslims, and other religious communities and that even Britons could become "Indianised."[28] Paradoxically, British rule depended entirely on the collaboration of Indians: "We alone keep them."[29] Self-rule, both individual and national, required a radical emancipation from the ideological as well as material hegemony of colonialism.

In *Ethiopia Unbound*'s opening metropolitan scenes, Hayford's depiction of the strivings of West African students offered a sharp contrast to the inner discontent of two Englishmen, a colonial official and a faithless missionary. His subsequent scenes of colonial life included the inefficient railways and other public services, the alcohol trade, the misguided Christian converts (as opposed to indigenous Muslim believers), and the indignities large and small imposed by white supremacy on educated and professional men of color. Hayford used the stories of several men and their wives and families to propound his views not only of love, marriage, and culturally correct conduct, but also of the complementary roles of public men and essentially domestic women in national and racial development. The two main characters, the lawyer Kwamankra and his equally highly educated and well-travelled wife Mansa, exemplify the cultural and intellectual syncretism of a new generation of Africans. Transformed after her death into a goddess, Mansa entrusts Kwamankra with the spiritual duty of restoring the older Fanti polity and regenerating a far wider African nationality. Emphasizing human universalism rather than racial particularisms, Hayford appropriated the legacy of ancient Greece from the Victorians and Edwardians of the metropole. He portrayed Kwamankra telling his son Ekra Kwow about "similitudes of thought and action . . . between the Greek and the Fanti," such as the way these peoples mingled with their gods.[30] In the end, Hayford projected a vision of world peace, "for what was to have become a great race war had become a mighty truce. . . . The white needed the black and the black needed the white."[31]

If, counterposed to Milner's idealized imperial nationalism, Gandhi and Hayford expressed the visionary limits of Edwardian anticolonial criticism, the concomitant controversy over Irish home rule offered a practical political reminder of the centrality of racial hierarchy in constructions of nation and empire.[32] The 1910 founding of the dominion of South Africa made the government of Ireland appear all the more anachronistic and intolerable to nationalists.[33] In *The Framework of Home Rule*, the English writer Erskine Childers recognized the nexus of nation and empire in his notion of a "colonial analogy" between Ireland and the dominions. Describing Ireland as "the oldest and the nearest of the Colonies," he argued that imperial history offered a series of lessons in the destructive consequences of metropolitan misrule and the restorative effects of colonial self-rule.[34]

Passionately committed to an imperial republican vision of self-government and citizenship, Childers examined the colonization of America and Ireland, the revolutions that brought about American and (briefly) Irish independence, and the union of Ireland and Britain before tracing the evolution of dominion self-government in Canada, Australia, and South Africa. For example, in a suggestive "Canadian parallel" to Ireland, Childers noted that the union of Upper and Lower Canada in 1840 failed to merge the culturally distinct Francophone and Anglophone communities, and the confederation of Canada in 1867 saw the reemergence of a separate province of Quebec.[35] But imperial history showed that neither federation nor union was necessary or inevitable. New

Zealand remained a viable polity without federating to Australia; the same was true of Newfoundland despite its proximity to Canada. On the eve of home rule, Irish public life showed encouraging signs of "national revival," from non-sectarian movements among farmers, women, and Gaelic enthusiasts to political movements like Sinn Fein.[36] Childers favored what he called "Colonial Home Rule," in essence the establishment of a self-governing Irish dominion.[37] This sweeping change was a political prerequisite for any forward movement toward home rule all around the British isles and closer imperial union of the United Kingdom and the dominions. Reversing the common sense of politics, Childers derided Unionists for their "anti-Imperialist" policy and predicted that the Irish home rule leader, John Redmond, would be recognized as "among . . . those who have saved the Empire from the consequences of its own errors."[38]

Childers's imperial case for Irish self-rule, which even received a respectful review in *Sinn Fein*, helped set the terms of a wide-ranging debate.[39] In *The New Irish Constitution*, a collection of essays by Liberal supporters of home rule, Sir Alfred Mond described the colonial analogy as "most misleading," for dominion self-government was a "geographical accident" of overseas location that did not apply to the British isles.[40] Nevertheless, he discussed the federal forms of government in Australia and Canada, which offered useful precedents for the proper balance of power between provincial or state governments and the central dominion government. In a rival collection of essays, *Against Home Rule*, Unionists seized upon Childers's argument to discredit the whole project of self-government. Calling Childers's book "the ablest, as well as the most courageous, piece of Home Rule advocacy" but claiming that it was founded on "a series of confusions," Leo Amery deployed his own examples from imperial history to draw opposite conclusions.[41] The provinces of Canada, the islands of New Zealand, and the former Boer republics of South Africa were all pressed into service to show that the tendency of the imperial state was toward union and that Ireland, with its scores of nationalist and unionist MPs at Westminster, already enjoyed self-government as part of the United Kingdom.

In *The Two Irish Nations*, W. F. Monypenny decried as "unthinkable" Childers's "whole scheme" of reproducing the empire's decentralized polity, with "its five centres of national life vaguely related," inside the British isles.[42] Countering those "fanatics of colonialism" who welcomed Childers's analogy, Monypenny put forward the "argument from proximity" that strategic and other considerations prevented Britain from accepting the existence on its doorstep of a dominion seeking independence.[43] Like Mond and Amery, he elaborated his own colonial analogy for Ireland. It was not South Africa, where Britons and Afrikaners were agreed on dominion self-government, but Canada, where a federation of Ontario, Quebec, and several other provinces had defused tensions between Anglophone and Francophone communities. According to Monypenny, the parallel arrangement in the United Kingdom would be home rule all around, not limited to England, Ireland, Scotland, and Wales, but also extended to Ulster. This was, however, "a system which no one desires or imagines to be possible."[44]

A nearly simultaneous discussion of nation and empire was unfolding in the *Irish Review*, an independent forum of Irish letters and opinion. Writing as "Ulster Imperialist," one contributor suggested that "local patriotism" manifested itself on the four levels of parochial, provincial, national, and imperial "public spirit." The Irish nation, no less than the Scottish or English nation, was a fusion of "smaller identities," and the task of the British Empire was to "develop its multiple Nationalities, present or future, to the limit of which each is capable." The difficulty lay in the "double meaning" of these terms. Understood in their "true" or "real" rather than "political" sense, nationalism and imperialism were not incompatible. Noting "that certain Nationalists in Ireland are beginning to acknowledge their citizenship in the Empire," "Ulster Imperialist" concluded with the idea that Ireland was embarked on "a double evolution" toward "a true Nationality" and a "larger Imperial patriotism."[45] This iconoclastic essay provoked the ire of the Sinn Fein leader Arthur Griffith. The advocate of a dual monarchy for Britain and Ireland modeled on Austria-Hungary, he was not quite a little Irelander. Indeed, even as he equated the empire with "English ascendancy," he left the door open to the possibility that a "Hiberno-British" empire might find support in Ireland.[46] "Ulster Imperialist's" reply pointed to the growing consensus in the United Kingdom and the dominions that the empire was a joint enterprise among them and went on to envision Ireland taking its place among these nations on a footing of equality.[47] A further essay called attention to Childers's book and predicted that "the Imperial argument" would be decisive in winning support in the United Kingdom for the granting of home rule to Ireland.[48]

Symbolized by their appropriation of his analogy, Childers's interlocutors shared with him an increasingly influential view of the interdependency of nation and empire. Gone were the days when the relationship between Ireland and England/Britain could be discussed in insular terms, and gone too were the days when, as Ernest Boyd showed in a biting comparison of Unionist and Gaelic attitudes, the chauvinism of the "Celtic Imperialist" could pass unremarked.[49] Moreover, Childers and other commentators were committed to a set of racialized assumptions about nation and empire that went far beyond the tendency to use "nation" and "race" interchangeably as signifiers of what might be considered cultural and ethnic difference. This political common sense was the equation of whiteness and fitness for self-government, which was closely connected to the formation or fusion of white nations and the rule of whites over other races.[50] Even *Sinn Fein*, with its sympathetic coverage of Chinese, Egyptian, and Indian nationalists, could publish an article on "Some Constitutions of the White Man."[51]

Likening Ireland to Jamaica and Malta, Childers insisted on its anomalous position among "white communities" and went on to argue that "No white community of pride and spirit would willingly tolerate the grotesque form of Crown Colony administration, founded on force, and now tempered by a kind of paternal State Socialism, under which Ireland lives to-day."[52] White men apparently had a natural capacity for self-government, which, however, deteriorated in its absence. Childers blamed Britain's malgovernment of Ireland for preventing the fusion of its inhabitants and the development of white self-government: "If left to themselves, white races, of diverse nationalities, thrown together in one country, eventually coalesce, or at least learn to live together peaceably."[53] Irish and British settlers had fused into one people in colonial America, whereas they remained apart in a relation of native and settler in Ireland. Biracial America was constituted by whites and blacks; biracial Ireland, by two different kinds of whites, of whom the indigenous people formed a servile class. The high degree of "physiological" and "ethnological" difference had preserved the "dominant race" in America, but the relative similarity of the Irish and the British had led to considerable degeneration of the ruling class in Ireland.[54] The consequences were global, for "the Irish race all over the world, fine race as it is, would be finer still if Ireland had been free."[55] Ireland had helped build the empire, and "the result is hers as much as Britain's." The establishment of an Irish dominion would help bring together not only the empire, but also "the English-speaking races," according to Childers, as "a fifth of the present white population of the United States is of Irish blood."[56]

Whiteness as a component of imperial governmentality was predicated on a formal distinction between the government of whites and blacks and on the constitutive role of the government of whites over blacks. Thus Childers distinguished between Ireland and the dominions, where white self-government prevailed, and "India and other coloured dependencies where despotic, or semi-despotic, systems are in vogue."[57] A critic of home rule, "Ulster Imperialist" also raced Ireland, taking it as a given among both unionists and nationalists that "we Irish are white men of the same set of racial stocks as the other inhabitants of Western Europe; hence we react to what we consider injustice or fair play much in the same way as do the other white races. The relationship of the coloured races to the whites is a problem in many ways distinct from that of the relationship of us whites among ourselves."[58] Childers, however, explicitly recognized the interrelationship of self-rule and ruling others. In tracing South Africa's evolution, for example, he was critical of the early colonial state's precipitous emancipation of the slaves and its policy of "impracticable equality between white and coloured men."[59]

Other participants in the debate acknowledged their adherence to the notion of racial hierarchy and its political effects. In his contribution to *The New Irish Constitution*, L. T. Hobhouse distinguished between race, the expression of "physical kinship," and nationality, "the possession of a common country, common interests, common traditions, a common mode of life and sentiment."[60] Acknowledging that nations were often "blends of many races," he enumerated three scenarios of government in which "two or more races are intermixed": in the first, one race rules the other, "as generally happens when white and black live together"; in the second, an outside power sets one race over the other, in the form of "an 'Ascendency' caste"; and in the third, the two races "govern themselves with mutual toleration," and "In proportion as it succeeds the two races blend, and a new nationality is formed."[61] Needless to say, Hobhouse had Ireland in mind for his second scenario and Canada and South Africa for his third. Significantly, he did not linger over his first scenario of white supremacy and its implications for fostering a sense of nationality. Monypenny was rather more forthcoming in his formulations. To add weight to his case for recognition of the "smaller" of the two Irish nations, characterized by "separate religions, separate ideals, separate traditions, and separate affinities," he pointed out that there were more Protestants in Ireland than all the whites in South Africa.[62] In fact, the continuing divisions in Ireland invited comparison with the success of reconciliation of Britons and Afrikaners. One factor, which Monypenny identified as missing in Ireland, nevertheless resonates with the whole discussion of the colonial analogy: "the presence of a native population greatly outnumbering the two white races supplies an overwhelming reason for co-operation between them."[63] It would seem that whites could not be one without the other.

If Milner's and Childers's outlooks were largely circumscribed by the "Anglo-Saxon" world, Gandhi's and Hayford's horizons were wider. Indeed, Gandhi employed the colonial analogy not to praise dominion self-government in Canada and South Africa, but to query whether it was "good enough" in relation to the true meaning of *swaraj* (self-rule).[64] Going beyond Childers's gestures to Irish America, Hayford engaged in an extended dialogue of sorts with W. E. B. Du Bois and other African Americans.[65] Once again, the differences between Gandhi and Hayford are equally intriguing. Both saw parallels to other national movements, with, ironically, Hayford praising the example of Gaelic cultural nationalism in Ireland. Gandhi's reader took heart from the example of Japan, but his editor countered that "it is the British flag which is waving in Japan, not the Japanese," for Japan was a "westernised" country in thrall to the same power represented by Britain in India.[66] By contrast, Hayford saw much to admire in the Japanese way of life and made connections between the panics over the "yellow peril" and "black peril" and the global struggle against white supremacy.[67] Even as Gandhi and Hayford claimed their entitlement to participate in a public sphere configured by an imperial state that privileged certain "nations" and "races," they enacted their sense of belonging to wider, alternative, and overlapping diasporic and civilizational worlds.

*   *   *

The Edwardian era is a rich moment for interrogating the double meanings of nation and empire and, furthermore, the ways in which these contingent categories are underpinned by notions of race. In the political and discursive struggles around Irish home rule — not to mention South African union, Indian *swaraj*, the White Australia Policy, Egyptian administration, and women's suffrage in both metropole and colonies — they were employed to exclude as well as include, to designate citizens and subalterns among the subjects of the imperial state. In this dialogical play of forces, however, dominant meanings were contested and appropriated even as they bore heavily on colonial subjects and people of color. Anticolonial criticism had its limits, of course, with many critics speaking for others, subscribing to notions of racial difference and hierarchy, and believing in the essential compatibility of nationalism and imperialism. Some of this was on display in forums like the 1910 Nationalities and Subject Races Conference and the 1911 Universal Races Congress in London. In bringing together figures as diverse as Milner and Gandhi and emphasizing political contention across the imperial state, this chapter looks outward as well as in, forward as well as back. It is possible to rewrite Edwardian history along lines that problematize rather than ratify the nation. Moreover, a "globalized" Edwardian history, tracking the crisscrossing struggles over rule and representation, rights and resources, belongs to a critical history of the present. Such historical knowledge, particularly about the formation of new political subjects and alliances across borders, may yet help us understand and rise to the challenge of our times.

Notes

My grateful thanks to Mansour Bonakdarian, Antoinette Burton, Jean Tucker Fletcher, Willard Allen Fletcher, Yaël Simpson Fletcher, Rachel Neiwert, Kavita Philip, and the staff of the Logue Library, Chestnut Hill College, Chestnut Hill, Pennsylvania.

1 Mrinalini Sinha, *Colonial Masculinity: The "Manly Englishman" and the "Effeminate Bengali" in the Late Nineteenth Century* (Manchester: Manchester University Press, 1995); Peter van der Veer, *Imperial Encounters: Religion and Modernity in India and Britain* (Princeton, N.J.: Princeton University Press, 2001).

2 Compare Maurice Ollivier, ed., *The Colonial and Imperial Conferences from 1887 to 1937*, vol. 1: *Colonial Conferences*, and vol. 2: *Imperial Conferences*, Part 1: "The Imperial Conferences of 1909, 1911, 1917, 1918 and 1921" (Ottawa: Edmond Cloutier, 1954). For more on Milner's book and his milieu, see Bernard Semmel, *Imperialism and Social Reform: English Social-Imperialist Thought, 1895–1914* (Garden City, N.Y.: Anchor, 1968), ch. 9; John Kendle, *The Round Table Movement and Imperial Union* (Toronto: University of Toronto Press, 1975); and Andrew S. Thompson, "The Language of Imperialism and the Meanings of Empire: Imperial Discourse in British Politics, 1895–1914," *Journal of British Studies* 36, 2 (1997): 147–177.

3 Lord Milner, *The Nation and the Empire* (London: Constable, 1913), pp. xxxiv, 278.

4 Ibid., pp. xxxv, 142.

5 Ibid., p. 339.

6 Ibid., pp. 238, 412–413.

7 Ibid., pp. 252, 353, 452.

8 Ibid., p. 458.

9 Ibid., p. 350.

10 Ibid., p. 496.

11 Ibid., pp. 354–355, 358.

12 Ibid., pp. 290, 292.

13 Ibid., p. 299.

14 Ibid., p. 232.

15 See Annie E. Coombes, *Reinventing Africa: Museums, Material Culture and Popular Imagination in Late Victorian and Edwardian England* (New Haven, Conn.: Yale University Press, 1994), esp. ch. 9; Jonathan Hyslop, "The Imperial Working Class Makes Itself 'White': White Labourism in Britain, Australia, and South Africa before the First World War," *Journal of Historical Sociology* 12, 4 (1999): 398–421; Paul B. Rich, *Race and Empire in British Politics*, 2d ed. (Cambridge: Cambridge University Press, 1990), esp. chs. 1–3; more generally, Anna Marie Smith, *New Right Discourse on Race and Sexuality: Britain, 1968–1990* (Cambridge: Cambridge University Press, 1994), esp. ch. 2.

16 Milner, *The Nation and the Empire*, p. 340.

17 Ibid., p. 313.

18 Ibid., p. 296.

19 Ibid., p. 297. The phrase "imperial man" is Catherine Hall's.

20 Ibid., p. 296.

21 Ibid., p. 294; Kendle, *The Round Table Movement*, pp. 224–229. For a dawning sense of the rapidly changing Indian political situation, see "India and the Empire," *Round Table* 8 (1912): 587–626; "India: Old Ways and New," *Round Table* 9 (1912): 52–80.

22 Milner, *The Nation and the Empire*, p. 489.

23 Ibid., p. 493.

24 See Shompa Lahiri, *Indians in Britain: Anglo-Indian Encounters, Race and Identity, 1880–1930* (London: Frank Cass, 2000); Jonathan Schneer, *London 1900: The Imperial Metropolis* (New Haven, Conn.: Yale University Press, 1999), chs. 8–9; Philip S. Zachernuk, *Colonial Subjects: An African Intelligentsia and Atlantic Ideas* (Charlottesville: University Press of Virginia, 2000), ch. 3.

25 For a broad treatment of the vicissitudes of Indian national identity formation, see Partha Chatterjee, *The Nation and Its Fragments: Colonial and Postcolonial Histories* (Princeton, N.J.: Princeton University Press, 1993).

26 See Ian Duffield, "Dusé Mohammed Ali, Afro-Asian Solidarity and Pan-Africanism in Early Twentieth-Century London," in *Essays on the History of Blacks in Britain: From Roman Times to the Mid-Twentieth Century*, ed. Jagdish S. Gundara and Ian Duffield (Aldershot: Avebury, 1992), pp. 124–149.

27 M. K. Gandhi, *Hind Swaraj and Other Writings*, ed. Anthony J. Parel (Cambridge: Cambridge University Press, 1997 [1910]), p. 115.

28 Ibid., pp. 52–53, 73.

29 Ibid., p. 41.

30 J. E. Casely Hayford, *Ethiopia Unbound: Studies in Race Emancipation* (London: Frank Cass, 1969 [1911]), pp. 204–205. For a bracing discussion of the possibility of a history that can include gods and spirits as well as human beings, see Dipesh Chakrabarty, *Provincializing Europe: Postcolonial Thought and Historical Difference* (Princeton, N.J.: Princeton University Press, 2000).

31 Hayford, *Ethiopia Unbound*, p. 208.

32 For a wide-ranging discussion, see Stephen Howe, *Ireland and Empire: Colonial Legacies in Irish History and Culture* (Oxford: Oxford University Press, 2000), esp. chs. 4–5.

33 Symptomatic of such an attitude is the South African coverage in the radical nationalist weekly *Sinn Fein*, October 30 and November 13, 1909; January 8, 15, February 5, and March 5, 26, 1910.

34 Erskine Childers, *The Framework of Home Rule* (London: Edward Arnold, 1911), p. 1.

35 Ibid., p. x.

36 Ibid., p. 155.

37 Ibid., pp. 198–203.

38 Ibid., pp. 144, 341.

39 *Sinn Fein*, December 9, 1911. For an important account that, however, is not concerned with Childers or questions of race, see John Kendle, *Ireland and the Federal Solution: The Debate over the United Kingdom Constitution, 1870–1921* (Montreal: McGill-Queen's University Press, 1989), chs. 5–7.

40 Sir Alfred Mond, "Colonial Forms of Home Rule," in *The New Irish Constitution: An Exposition and Some Arguments*, ed. J. H. Morgan (Port Washington, N.Y.: Kennikat Press, 1971 [1912]), pp. 412–413.

41 Leo Amery, "Home Rule and the Colonial Analogy," in *Against Home Rule: The Case for the Union*, ed. S. Rosenbaum (Port Washington, N.Y.: Kennikat Press, 1970 [1912]), pp. 128–129.

42 W. F. Monypenny, *The Two Irish Nations: An Essay on Home Rule* (London: John Murray, 1913), pp. 75–76.

43 Ibid., p. 76.

44 Ibid., p. 87.

45 Ulster Imperialist, "Nationalism and Imperialism," *Irish Review* 1 (1911): 63–71.

46 Arthur Griffith, "True and False Imperialism," *Irish Review* 1 (1911): 269–272.

47 Ulster Imperialist, "True and False Imperialism," *Irish Review* 1 (1911): 383–389.

48 Ulster Imperialist, "An Appreciation of the Situation," *Irish Review* 2 (1912): 4.

49 Ernest A. Boyd, "The Jingoism of the Gael," *Irish Review* 3 (1913): 59.

50 For an earlier manifestation of this racialized political logic around Canada, Ireland, and Jamaica, see Catherine Hall, Keith McClelland, and Jane Rendall, *Defining the Victorian*

Nation: Class, Race, Gender and the Reform Act of 1867 (Cambridge: Cambridge University Press, 2000), ch. 4. See also David Scott, *Refashioning Futures: Criticism after Postcoloniality* (Princeton, N.J.: Princeton University Press, 1999), ch. 3.

51 *Sinn Fein*, December 2, 1911.

52 Childers, *The Framework of Home Rule*, pp. 1, 144.

53 Ibid., p. 7.

54 Ibid., p. 14.

55 Ibid., p. 145.

56 Ibid., p. 148.

57 Ibid., p. 190.

58 Ulster Imperialist, "True and False Imperialism," p. 384.

59 Childers, *The Framework of Home Rule*, p. 122.

60 L. T. Hobhouse, "Irish Nationalism and Liberal Principle," in Morgan, ed., *The New Irish Constitution*, pp. 367–368.

61 Ibid., p. 368.

62 Monypenny, *The Two Irish Nations*, p. 12.

63 Ibid., p. 84.

64 Gandhi, *Hind Swaraj*, p. 27.

65 Hayford, *Ethiopia Unbound*, esp. chs. 16–18. This is yet another instance of the wider diasporic formation brilliantly interrogated by Paul Gilroy in *The Black Atlantic: Modernity and Double Consciousness* (Cambridge, Mass.: Harvard University Press, 1993).

66 Gandhi, *Hind Swaraj*, pp. 41, 66.

67 Hayford, *Ethiopia Unbound*, pp. 108–110, 115–118, 169–172.

KRISTIN HOGANSON

The Fashionable World:
Imagined Communities of Dress

In October 1914, the drama *My Lady's Dress* made its U.S. debut in the New York City Playhouse. Written by Edward Knoblauch, an expatriate American playwright who had spent the majority of his adult life on the continent and in Britain, it told the story of a dress in a series of vignettes. It started with the British woman who had purchased it and fully intended to wear it despite her husband's protestations of its risqué cut and extravagant cost; the ensuing scenes took the audience on a continental tour of the origins of the component parts. After depicting Italian peasants who raised silkworms, the play moved on to weavers in France, a lace tatter in Holland, a flower maker in the East End of London, a fur trapper's stockade in Siberia, and back to London, to a pretentious dressmaker's establishment. Even as it suggested the universality of themes such as vanity, jealousy, and self-sacrifice, the play drew attention to a specific historical development: the increasing internationalism of Western fashion. Said the astounded Sir Charles upon visiting the dressmaker's: "Strikes me you have to rummage all over the world to put a dress together nowadays."[1] Although Knoblauch began and ended the play in his adopted city of London, never venturing across the Atlantic, he dramatized trends that fashionable American women could hardly miss: stylish dresses and other articles of clothing documented unprecedented international linkages.

During the course of the play, the owner of the gown in question comes to appreciate its cosmopolitan history in a dream sequence. Upon awakening, she regards her purchase in a new light, as an emblem of international labor. Moved by the struggles of the people who helped produce her dress, she professes a desire to try to make the world better. The play underscores her sense of identification with far-flung workers by having the same actress who plays the modish Anne also play characters in each of the other scenes. Critics regarded the play's efforts to uncover the history of the dress favorably. The *New York Times* praised the drama for demonstrating the "interdependence of our modern, co-operative civilization."[2] It presented Anne's newfound sense of belonging to a community of people attached to her dress as a novelty, and it was indeed novel because the overwhelming majority of fashion writing at the time promoted a very different imagined community: one based on consumption.

Whereas it took a dream sequence to bring the international community of *producers* behind Anne's dress to the fore, the international community of *consumers* had far greater visibility to American women in the late nineteenth and early twentieth centuries. The popular press took the lead in delineating the imagined communities of consumption implied by clothes. In writings on fashion, clothes never just stood for themselves; they signified the adornment necessary for belonging in particular groups. Although some of the imagined communities sketched out by fashion reportage were local or national, a significant proportion were further reaching. Above all, these linked women in the United States to wealthy, well-dressed women in Europe.

The specter of American women looking to European cities such as London, Berlin, Vienna, and above all Paris for the modes flew in the face of the conviction, widespread among white, native-born, middle-class Americans, that women should model nationality. Just as white women's bodies marked racial boundaries by being sexually off limits to all but white men, bourgeois women's bodies marked national boundaries by serving as metaphors for the nation.[3] Depictions of "the American girl" presented her as physically distinctive — a symbol of national youth, vigor, and beauty. In nationalistic drawings and cartoons, she towered over foreign men and women, puny aristocrats among them.[4] According to the nationalist line of thought — and it had a significant following in the late nineteenth century — women's bodies and bodices alike should delineate national difference. As the *New York Times* put the matter in 1909, "Our national character is more reflected in the clothes of our women than in anything else."[5]

This gendered nationalism has been echoed by recent historians, who have tended to adhere to the idea that the nation-state has played a definitive role in distinguishing among middle-class women, even when they have occupied marginal positions in their national polities. This practice is consistent with Benedict Anderson's emphasis on the national boundaries to imagined communities, and insofar as the history of U.S. women is concerned, it reflects a larger tendency to exceptionalize American history.[6] But this nationally bounded approach to history recently has come into question by historians who, influenced by the imperial turn, have advocated a more transnational approach.[7] Although women's historians have participated in this historiographical trend — most notably in studies of women's transnational organizational activity — histories of the international political economy still tend to focus on corporations and exports.[8] Not only has his led to an emphasis on men, but it also has cast the United States as an exclusively colonizing nation, bent on Americanizing the world.

Turning to consumption, however, shows the inadequacy of a national framework for encapsulating bourgeois women's experiences; at the same time it shows that bourgeois women have played a pivotal role in globalizing developments. As growing trade connections have linked producers and consumers in distant parts of the world, they have also given rise to imagined communities of consumption larger than the nation. Along with fostering a wider sense of affiliation, global linkages have fostered a wider sense of disaffiliation. Through their purchases, bourgeois women have differentiated themselves from the masses of women not only in their own nations, but also worldwide. Consumption has helped turn bourgeois women into markers of civilizational boundaries (heavily inflected by class and race), as well as national ones. Beyond helping to reframe bourgeois women's experiences in a transnational context, paying attention to consumption complicates narratives of national self-assertion. Focusing on consumption demonstrates how the United States has been simultaneously colonial (in a culturally dependent sense) and colonizing, continuing to look to Europe for cultural capital even as it came to play an increasingly dominant role in the international marketplace.

As *My Lady's Dress* suggests, bourgeois women's participation in transnational trade networks and the imagined transnational affinities and disaffinities that consumption advanced can be seen in the phenomenon of fashion. Late nineteenth-century protestations of fashion nationalism obscure the degree to which style-conscious women followed international trends. In 1888, Jenny June (Jane C. Croly), until recently the chief staff writer of *Madame Demorest's Mirror of Fashions*, assessed the state of American fashion as follows: "It is true that in America we are as yet only an echo. We do not originate our clothes, not in fashionable circles. Today, we echo La Belle France."[9] Things had not changed substantially by 1912, when the *New York Tribune* declared that the fashion openings in Paris "are always awaited with keen interest all over the world. Buyers from far and near have been camping for weeks as near as possible to the ateliers of the great French designers, who, despite all protestations and arguments, govern the world of fashions to-day."[10] Headlines such as "Fashion's Dictates from Paris" and "Seen in the Shops of Paris" revealed, even as they promoted, the reach and allure of Parisian fashion.[11] Along with fashion writers, retailers, milliners and dressmakers (the last made most high-end dresses in an age when ready-made wear for women was just catching on) emphasized their French connections if they were lucky enough to have them or brazen enough to fabricate them.[12]

Photographs and descriptions of the clothes worn by middle-class American women between the Civil War and World War I bear witness to the widespread following that French fashion attracted. After analyzing a wide range of nineteenth-century photographs, Joan L. Severa has concluded that by the 1840s, all but desperately poor women knew about and adopted aspects of French fashions within a year of their introduction in Paris. It became difficult to procure dress goods during the Civil War, especially in the Confederacy, but American women nonetheless continued to follow French designs. Paris maintained its hegemonic grip on middle-class and wealthy women's fashion until the 1890s, when the tailored look popularized by Charles Dana Gibson attracted a large following. But even then, French fashion tenaciously maintained its appeal, above all in elegant dresses better suited for leisure than work.[13]

Strangely, all the attention to French fashion played out against a backdrop of U.S. fashion productivity. By 1855, the clothing industry had become New York City's largest; by 1900, over 134,000 New York men and women made their living as dressmakers, tailors, and garment workers.[14] The United States imported more clothing than it exported through 1910, but imports nonetheless represented a small proportion of the total market for clothes in the United States.[15] Domestic manufacture met most of the booming domestic demand.

Besides manufacturing clothing, the United States had a strong pattern-making industry. One leading company, Mme. Demorest's, churned out an average of twenty-three thousand patterns a day in 1871; more popular designs soon sold as many as fifty thousand copies.[16] In contrast to Demorest, who marketed patterns primarily to professional dressmakers and their middle-class clients, her rival, Ebenezer Butterick, marketed patterns to the masses. In 1871, Butterick sold over 6 million patterns.[17] Both companies had international ambitions. Demorest's highlighted its international connections and appeal; Butterick's ran ads in Spanish and German and gave prices for Mexican customers in its fashion magazine, the *Delineator*.[18]

As the international markets obtained by U.S. pattern makers indicate, the U.S. fashion industry started to reach beyond the nation's borders in this period. Government trade data for 1870 reveal over $680,000 in clothing exports, mostly to Asia, the Pacific (especially Hawaii), and the Americas.[19] By 1910, the numbers had risen to over $10.4 million, and by 1920 the United States was exporting over $113 million in clothes.[20] Clothing exporters trumpeted their international successes to their domestic audiences. B. Altman & Co., for example, proudly announced in its 1880 catalog that it mailed goods to "all parts of the United States and Territories, Canada, Central and South America and West Indies, etc."[21] Fashion experts likewise gloried in their international following. In 1896, *Vogue* claimed sales in Canada, Mexico, Japan, Great Britain, continental Europe, India, South America, and Australia.[22] "When a fashion changes in New York, its influence is felt from the Atlantic to the Pacific, and from Canada and British America to the Gulf of Mexico," boasted fashion writer Frances Faulkner in the pages of the *Ladies' World*. Yet even Faulkner had to admit that the original source of these fashions was exogenous. "The chief cities of the United States, more especially New York and Boston, are in constant touch with the great fashion centers of Europe," she noted.[23]

Faulkner's invocation of the "great fashion centers of Europe" serves as a reminder that despite the productivity of the U.S. garment industry and the regional influence of U.S. fashion, much of the design inspiration for the U.S. fashion industry came from Paris, frequently passing through New York before being disseminated more broadly.[24] Even Demorest and Butterick based their patterns on European designs. Rather than shrinking the reach of French fashion, the success of U.S. pattern manufacturing helped spread it by enabling home sewers to craft garments that echoed couture clothing.[25] The New York merchant who admitted to sewing copies of Paris labels into his domestic dresses because "American women have been brainwashed into thinking French clothes are superior" illustrates the tenacious allure of French fashion even in an age of New York fashion ascendance.[26] Rising exports notwithstanding, in the late nineteenth century, the colonial character of U.S. design continued to counterbalance its colonizing aspects.

Given the urgent appeals for nationalism in dress and the availability of U.S. materials and designs, what explains the cult of French fashion in the United States? Does it reveal a deep-seated Francophilia among American women, a sense of exceptional affinity with the French people? Not quite. The women who sought French fashions may have regarded the French favorably, but in all probability this was as much a *result* of their fashion preferences as a cause of them. The imagined community implied by French fashion was not France per se. French peasant women had no place in this community, and French working-class women existed only on its periphery. Nor did French fashion necessarily evoke images of wealthy French women: fashion writings were just as likely to associate it with the *haut monde* from other nations. To participate in the world of fashion was to imagine connections not only to the wealthy within the United States, but also to the original source, to the conspicuous consumers from across Europe. Like other women committed to the Western fashion system, American women looked to Europe, and particularly Paris, for fashion because they thought that meant getting the best in the world. Guided by fashion writers and purveyors who spoke of "the newest and best the world has to offer" and couturiers "of world wide fame," they embraced the idea of fashion as an international (albeit overwhelmingly European) system that happened to be centered in Paris.[27]

Writings on France as a fashion mecca made it clear that American women were not the only ones who looked to Paris for their clothes; they often mentioned Russian, British, German, and other European women who shopped in Paris.[28] The key to the appeal of French fashion lies in the imagined community it implied, and this community stretched across national boundaries, uniting upper-crust consumers. The world of fashion, in its quintessential form, was an aristocratic world of independently wealthy pleasure seekers who lived in close proximity to and yet, in terms of their lifestyles and status, far apart from ordinary people in places like Paris, Monte Carlo, Newport, and stately English country houses. Rather than being defined by distinctive boundaries that could be drawn onto a map, the fashionable world divided near neighbors and spilled over national lines. As *Vanity Fair* said of the fashionable women at Monte Carlo, "They belong to Paris, to Vienna, to St. Petersburg. They are the citizens of the world."[29] The U.S. press, which covered the doings of this world in great detail, acknowledged the domestic component of the fashionable world but made it clear that its center lay in Europe. Those at the top of the U.S. social hierarchy might enjoy enviable riches and aloof status, but as their embrace of European dress indicated, they were at best peripheral representatives of the fashionable set, for the central position belonged to European aristocrats.

Aristocrats made the imagined world of fashion seem more tangible by providing distinctive personas to emblematize it. This can be seen in the gossipy tone of fashion writing. Indeed, gossip writing could be viewed as the most effective fashion writing, for if one point of fashion was to prove belonging in high society, what better way to learn of what it took to belong than in the society pages? Fashion experts claimed authority by profiling dresses worn by duchesses, countesses, vicomtesses, princesses, and other titled *grandes dames*.[30] Just as fashion writing often strayed into the realm of gossip, the reverse was also true: gossip reporting often conveyed fashion news. Numerous articles in *Vogue* illustrate this trend: they mixed descriptions of social functions attended by the "exclusive set" with pictures of the latest toilettes.[31] The blurry line between fashion and gossip writing enabled the women who followed the fashionable world to buy the connotations along with the clothes, and foremost among the connotations were aristocracy and wealth. Historians have found the nineteenth century to be a democratizing age in women's fashion — largely because of the spread of paper patterns — but the wider dissemination of the latest fashions should not blind us to fashion's undemocratic associations.[32] The imagined world of fashion was a world of consumption, not production, even though producers could claim fleeting affiliation through emblematic purchases. These might not root them firmly in the fashionable world, but they could at least express a commitment to belonging. Through couture clothing and lower-cost copies alike, American women claimed membership in a class-stratified world that placed aristocrats at the pinnacle.

If the interest in European fashion manifested by the American press seems inconsistent with the tendency to see bourgeois women as embodiments of the nation, it seems equally inconsistent with republican traditions of antipathy to inherited privileges. Nineteenth-century critics dismissed aristocrats as degenerate and exploitative, as throwbacks to a feudal past rather than as harbingers of a modern future.[33] To underscore their points about aristocrats' immorality, patriotic critics did not hesitate to censure aristocratic women's dress. One denounced gowns seen at court functions for giving the women the appearance of courtesans.[34] If not immodest, their dress struck critics as ridiculously extravagant.[35] Dress reformer Abba Goold Woolson denounced fashion itself as an absurdity of "duchesses and queens, whose daily lives are of little value to the world or to themselves, and who can afford to give their time to the display of costly follies."[36] In light of such republican sentiments, what explains the popularity of a fashion system understood to be fundamentally aristocratic?

The most obvious answer to this question is that women who imagined aristocratic connections imagined affiliations with power and privilege. The paramountcy of class helps explain why fashion subordinated nationality. Would-be denizens of the world of fashion scorned national boundaries in their efforts to identify themselves with an entitled transnational elite. Rather than opting out of the fashion system on nationalistic grounds, the American women who followed French styles cast their lot with upper-class internationalism. Aristocrats might not have had as much money as plutocrats — hence their need for transatlantic marriages — but they had considerably greater cultural capital. However small their economic reserves, their cultural prestige made them symbols of what Europe as a whole seemed to offer the United States. To Americans who felt their country lacked tradition, history, and culture, European aristocrats offered standards of taste. Beyond this, they offered examples of power that inhered not just in pocketbooks and political might, but also in social positioning.

What made aristocracy particularly attractive to *women* was the conviction that the perquisites of rank were not limited to aristocratic men, that women could wield cultural power even when other forms of power eluded their grasp. Men might lead in politics and business, but social life revolved around women. In contrast to American high society — in which men's accomplishments in the marketplace seemed relatively more important in determining status — aristocrats seemed relatively less devoted to the masculine world of commerce than to the feminine world of ritual and display. By expressing allegiance to the world of fashion, American women could thus express a commitment to a social system that seemed to offer women — at least those lucky enough to belong to its inner circles — seemingly unrivaled opportunities to exercise power.[37]

If part of the appeal of the fashionable world inhered in its difference, in its ability to offer imaginative entitlement and escape, another part of its attraction lay in its familiarity. The plentiful coverage of aristocracy in U.S. publications domesticated aristocrats by bringing them into U.S. households and making them an accustomed part of everyday life. Newspapers and magazines devoted great attention not only to the royal families of the great powers, but also to minor courts and royals, from Denmark to Bulgaria.[38] The most intimate affairs of European aristocracy made headlines in the United States. Such tell-all coverage may have bred contempt, but it also bred fascination and an avid following for aristocrats, who came across as foreign enough to merit interest and familiar enough to retain it. Those who placed aristocrats at the heart of the imagined community of fashion placed not only a class, but also discrete individuals, known for particular habits, tastes, and histories, into the center of the circle. Their individuality helped make the world of fashion seem like a real community and not just a collection of disembodied dresses.

But aristocrats represented more than class privilege. With their inherited treasures and leisured refinement, they symbolized something of the utmost importance to their fin-de-siècle American admirers: civilization. Just as fashion promised incorporation into an exclusive community with aristocratic pretensions, it promised inclusion in the civilized world. Fashionable dress showed that the nation had cultural standing worthy of its economic standing. Dressing like European aristocrats proved that the United States was not a provincial backwater. It demonstrated Americans' social worthiness, their ability to fit into the most exclusive social circles. And these circles, though centered in the haunts of the European aristocracy, were understood as extending their reach across the globe.

American women who followed the styles emanating from Paris kept company not only with wealthy European women, but also with wealthy women from the entire Western and Westernizing world. Elite Latin American women favored European clothes just as much as wealthy women in the United States.[39] U.S. publications made it clear that Latin American women who could afford to do so purchased their clothes in Paris.[40] But one need not travel all the way to Europe to find well-dressed Latin American women. Paris designer Mme. Paquin had a branch in Buenos Aires. In the 1910s, Havana won a reputation for being a "transplanted Paris," slightly behind the times in women's dress but still brilliant. Those hoping to spot some local color looked in vain for mantillas at elite Cuban gatherings, for French fashion reigned supreme.[41]

Just as the commitment to French fashion proved the modernity of Latin American women—or at least those who discarded mantillas and other items of traditional dress—U.S. fashion writing presented the spread of European fashion as an index of civilization in Asia and the Middle East. Coverage of Japan's efforts to claim a place "among modern civilizations" emphasized that "a chief phase of the movement is the decision of the Japanese women to adopt the European dress."[42] The empress herself ordered designer gowns from Paris.[43] Similarly, accounts of the modernizing Young Turk movement highlighted Turkish women's Parisian tastes in clothes.[44] If women from around the world were looking to France for fashion, not to do so would mean being stuck in a provincial backwater, outside the major currents of the time. It would mean settling for second rate in an era of international standard setting. In its broadest terms, the fashion system emanating from Paris stood for civilization and modernity. As such, it served to affiliate American women, or at least fashionable American women, with the entitled and the trendy and, at the same time, to differentiate them from most of the women of the world.

Along with promoting geographically expansive feelings of affiliation, fashion demarcated borders that separated "us" from "them." These lines tended to divide the Western world from the rest of humanity, but they also divided the haves from the have-nots within Western societies. The irony of the narrow scope to the imagined community of fashion was that Western fashion was becoming more and more appropriative in this period, as goods from around the world flowed into Western markets. U.S. fashion writing and advertising made it clear that well-dressed women drew heavily on a wide variety of foreign markets for their raw materials.[45] In addition to procuring goods from distant markets, Western designers transgressed national and class boundaries in their search for design inspiration. Yet the further the Paris-based fashion system reached, the greater its power to demarcate supposed civilizational differences. The imagined community of consumption, though transnational in scope, failed to keep pace with the expanding world of production. The ever-broadening commercial networks that linked bourgeois American consumers to fashion producers from around the world failed to produce a corresponding sense of identification in American women's imaginations (hence the novelty of *My Lady's Dress*). For most American women, the community of production captured little imaginative space. It existed only in the fashions themselves — in clothing made from materials from far-flung lands, based on design ideas equally far-reaching.

If, from a political economy perspective, the internationalization of fashion emerged from an imperial world system, with lower wages paid in areas dominated by the Western powers, from a cultural perspective, the internationalization of Western fashion owed much to Paris designers. In their search for novelty, French designers looked far beyond the bounds of the wealthy Western communities to which they catered, thus popularizing a wide range of materials and styles. Closest to home, they revived and reinterpreted regional folk designs from around Europe.[46] Occasionally French designers looked to the United States. After the Buffalo Bill show stopped in Paris, for example, milliners made hats with wide, rolling brims that they dubbed "Buffalo" and "Annie Oakley."[47] In their search for inspiration, French designers more commonly looked to the East, crafting brightly colored oriental fantasies, a tendency that led the New Orleans *Times-Picayune* to characterize French design in 1920 as "One Step from Savage, but Fashionable."[48]

U.S. fashion writings covered such borrowings, making it clear that French fashion was eclectic in its origins. An 1892 fashion report in the *New York Tribune* expressed awe at the *bricolage* of fashion: "Never assuredly have there been so many different styles inaugurated by that autocrat known by the name of 'La Mode.' In one and the same drawing-room or salon one sees to-day costumes in the style of Louis XIV, of Russia, of the French Empire, of Walachia, of Greece, and of Japan."[49] American women who kept up with fashion writing knew that "La Mode," though ostensibly French, was based on appropriation. This can be seen in the names attached to the modes. U.S. fashion reports of the period mentioned Breton bonnets, Spanish mantillas, Bulgarian embroidery, Italian ruffles, and the like.[50] Following the French lead, fashionable American women also welcomed styles that struck them as essentially oriental. Starting around 1910, corset-determined curves gave way to straighter lines. Observers often acknowledged that the new silhouette owed a debt to Eastern dress. The *Ladies' Home Journal*, for example, noted in 1914 that "we are borrowing from almost every Oriental country and the effect is most picturesque. We have adapted the Persian lampshade tunic and headdresses, the Chinese colors and embroideries, kimono effects and collars from Japan, and burnoose draperies from Arabia. Evidently all is grist that comes to the fashion mills."[51]

The links to Eastern fashion won fullest acknowledgment in writings on "boudoir attire."[52] Whereas other garments tended to be acknowledged as adaptations, boudoir attire tended to be cast as more authentic. Most popular of all were Japanese-inspired kimonos, which one fashion writer admonished women not to wear outside their bedrooms.[53] In choosing to wear kimonos at home, Western women identified themselves with what they imagined to be Eastern — and above all Japanese — elegance, grace, sensuousness, and eroticism. But in choosing not to wear them on the streets, they maintained some distance from the Japanese women who did. Even as they drew on Eastern dress, fashionable Euro-American women still wanted to maintain some distance from non-Western women. What ultimately enticed many into a limited orientalism — an orientalism of small decorative touches, a less constricted figure, and exotic-looking fabrics — was that the Paris-based fashion system validated it. The acceptability of Asian motifs in U.S. fashion depended, in large part, on the imprimatur of French acceptance. American women could dress "Asian" and still be fundamentally European. Indeed, since French designers looked to the East for inspiration, American women had to do the same to maintain a chic, European demeanor.

However much designs and materials from around the world influenced Western fashion, the people who originated the designs and manufactured the materials still stood on the fringes of the imagined community of dress. As the realm of production became ever more global, the imagined community implied by fashion stayed tightly bounded. Fashion writers did acknowledge the wide-ranging origins of goods and styles — they would have been blind to have missed this — but they did not present the ever more integrated world of production as a true community and certainly not as a community with which American consumers would want to imaginatively affiliate themselves. In contrast to Anne's imagined affinity with European workers, most fashion writings did little to associate the latest modes with any workers other than the leading couturiers.

The class presuppositions that kept most European (along with U.S.) workers outside the boundaries of an imagined community of fashion combined with racial presuppositions to keep non-Western producers even further from its enclosure, for fashion writings were much more likely to present women outside the West as producers than as consumers. This can be seen in an ad for silk hosiery that showed a Japanese woman and girl spinning silk from cocoons so that the ankles of "fair ladies" would "shimmer and gleam." The advertisement did not include an image of the fair ladies with shimmering ankles, but their implied life of pleasure stood in contrast to the toil of the Japanese workers, both with solid ankles and bare feet.[54] Whereas fashionable women's doings and personalities merited detailed coverage, the daily lives of producers received relatively little, and their personal qualities virtually none. In *My Lady's Dress*, Anne acknowledges China's role in silk production but then dreams about Italian silkworm breeders. Anne was exceptional insofar as she imagined a sense of community with workers, but even she did not extend this sense of community to workers outside of Europe.[55]

That the world of fashion stood in stark contrast to the expropriated world of the local — and particularly to toilers outside of Europe — can be seen especially clearly in ethnographic writings, including ones adjacent to fashion columns on women's pages. Rather than presenting all dress as ethnic, ethnographic accounts drew a line between Western fashion — which they associated with modernity, civilization, and power — and the clothes worn by most of the world's women. Folk costumes might be picturesque, but in contrast to fashionable dress (by which they meant upper-class Euro-American fashion), they were parochial, backward, and lower class. If the fashionable world was the world of the appropriators, the rest of the world was appropriated. To buy into the fashion system centered in Paris thus meant to distinguish oneself from lower-class, colored, and colonized people.

Perhaps the best-known commentator on fashion in the late nineteenth century was Thorstein Veblen, known for his observation that fancy dress demonstrated membership in the leisure class. But Veblen did not limit his remarks to the class implications of fashion; he also suggested that fashion indicated civilizational standing and modernity, to the discredit of both. "It is well known that certain relatively stable styles and types of costume have been worked out in various parts of the world; as, for instance, among the Japanese, Chinese, and other Oriental nations; likewise among the Greeks, Romans, and other Eastern peoples of antiquity; so also, in later times, among the peasants of nearly every country of Europe," he wrote. "These national or popular costumes are in most cases adjudged by competent critics to be more becoming, more artistic, than the fluctuating styles of modern civilised apparel."[56] According to Veblen, Orientals, ancient peoples, and European peasants all existed outside of the world of fashion. This did not mean that their clothes were unattractive — to the contrary — but it did mean that they did not change from year to year. They also had limited appeal, as seen in their having only a national or local following.

Veblen's appreciation of Eastern dress echoed the sentiments of nineteenth-century dress reformers who had regarded it as healthier for women. Dress reformers blamed confining corsets for female invalidism and, because of their implications for reproduction, even racial degeneracy. Looking for alternatives to the Western silhouette, they frequently invoked oriental women as models. Responding to those who found Eastern dress unattractive, one reformer shifted perspectives, claiming that oriental women regarded the corseted "civilized" woman as "ugly and stiff and unnatural."[57] Another asserted that "Paganism and the Chinese women only bandage their feet, while Christian women bandage, with equally unrelenting self-sacrifice, the vital organs."[58] The Western woman might deplore the bound feet of the Chinese woman, but she should envy her unfettered waist. And she ended up copying this waist. Aesthetic women in the Gilded Age adopted a corsetless dress, influenced by Eastern costumes, that served as a precursor to the fashions of the 1910s.[59]

Despite dress reformers' intention to commend alternative practices to American women, they nonetheless ended up highlighting what seemed so clear to less radical contemporaries — the huge gulf that separated the world of fashion from other systems of dress. Although many contemporaries agreed on the existence of this gulf, they did not share the favorable interpretation of the world outside the reach of Western fashion. Frances Faulkner revealed a more typically negative attitude toward women outside the purview of the Paris fashion system: "The higher the civilization, the more important is the part played by costume, and the more subject to marked changes and fluctuations in its fashioning. This is due to the mental activity, the spirit of invention which is abroad, as well as to the culture and refinement of a highly civilized people. . . . In Oriental countries there is no change in costume; law, custom, tradition and necessity forbid it." According to Faulkner, fluctuations in dress signified the superiority of Western civilization rather than its wastefulness and frivolousness. Indeed, they indicated civilized status, for they reflected mental activity and an inventive spirit.[60]

To be sure, U.S. observers often described European folk costume as picturesque. They appreciated its historical roots and, no less significant, its current ephemerality. By the late nineteenth century, U.S. fashion writing made it clear that European folk costume was passing, that it should be seen as a carryover from a bygone age.[61] The sentimentalizing of European folk clothes did not mean untrammeled enthusiasm for them, however. Travelers who noted the persistence of folk clothes might regard them as attractive, but they almost invariably described them as peasant garb. Ethnographic accounts published in the United States did provide images of picturesque peasant women happily frolicking in local fetes and carnivals, but these were shadowed by images of desperately poor, miserably uncomfortable, prematurely aged, and frightfully ugly peasant women.[62] Folk costumes, however attractive at their finest, were suspect, for they connoted poverty, hard labor, ignorance, and backwardness to the observers who eyed them from the perspective of the fashionable world. And in contrast to fashion, which implied a transnational community of consumption, folk costume implied provincial sensibilities and tightly constricted communities.

Perhaps worst of all, European folk costumes signified affinities with non-

Western women, who also wore clothes that seemed strange to middle-class American women. The association between European and non-European folk costume can be seen in a *Chicago Tribune* article that featured hats from "those places where women still wear their native costumes." These places included Switzerland, Alsace, the Netherlands, Naples, Turkey, Algiers, and Tunis.[63] From the white Dutch headdress to the close-fitting Tunisian "fez" (a misnomer because only men wore fezzes in Tunisia), all the hats came across as ethnic curiosities. However disparate the women, they nonetheless had something in common: they were all outsiders to the world of fashion. Though participants in globalizing processes to the extent that their trappings fell within the purview of the Chicago paper, their headdresses marked them as local anomalies in an age of growing international connections.

Though European peasant women struck many ethnographic writers as throwbacks to a more localized age, women in Africa, Asia, Latin America, and the Pacific generally struck them as most backward of all. To be sure, some won recognition for adopting Paris fashions, but these women came across as elite pathbreakers. As an article on Mexican women noted, "The people who can afford it wear the Frenchiest of French creations in the way of hats," but the majority of women just wore light scarves. Indeed, the "great middle class," clad only in sandals, still went without stockings.[64] These Latin American women were a far cry from their compatriots who shopped in Paris.

A more sinister tone characterized much writing on Eastern women's dress. The horrors of foot binding proved particularly compelling to those who reported on China.[65] Though not as physically constricting, veils also came to symbolize bondage. Travelers to the Middle East reported disparagingly on concealing headresses.[66] On the opposite end of the spectrum from excessively constricting and obscuring clothing lay scanty dress. This too struck Western observers as being beyond the pale.[67] In turn-of-the-century accounts, the exposed skin of tropic peoples clearly called for Western sartorial intervention. The Christianizing and civilizing project embraced by Western missionaries, governments, and corporations included reclothing non-European women in the garb of Western modernity, or at least a simplified version thereof.

If non-Western dress could be seen as unduly restraining or as inappropriately revealing, Western dress supposedly conveyed power. This extended beyond the financial power demonstrated by consuming goods produced by others to include the social power of standard setting and display. This can be seen in the example of May French-Sheldon, a New Yorker by birth, a Briton by marriage, and an adventuress by inclination. Leaving her husband behind, she traveled extensively in Africa in the early 1890s, accompanied only by African servants, described in one account as "her savage escort." A prolific writer and an entertaining speaker, she attracted a following among middle-class women in the United States who thrilled to her stories of exotic adventures and her claims of having visited places never before seen by a white man, much less a white woman.[68] In relating her successes, she credited not only her race and her demeanor, but also her wardrobe, and the press picked up on this theme.

In an account of an expedition from Zanzibar, *Housekeeper's Weekly* cut right to this point. "What did she wear?" it asked. The answer? "Mrs. Sheldon's mind was firmly made up that she would show the African tribes, who had never seen a white man save in a travel-stained and bedraggled condition, that a white *woman* could look fresh, neat, and even dainty under all disadvantages. Accordingly she took with her thirty-six wash-dresses of silk, outing cloth, and flannel . . . and a court dress!" On the march she wore a "jaunty white flannel suit," but when she approached a village she stopped to change. She then "received" the chief dressed in a "magnificent trained court dress of white silk covered with silver gauze, collar and girdle of jewels, and a blonde wig whose curls fell to her waist. The simple natives thought her a goddess, and loaded her with gifts on her departure."[69] Those who followed Sheldon's adventures had grounds for regarding women's dress—and above all, garments such as her court dress that signaled aristocratic privilege—as an instrument of imperial power. According to Sheldon, gauze could be more effective than guns in winning the homage of scantily clad natives. Western fashion, she believed, articulated power in a language intelligible to "savages" and the readers of *Housekeeper's Weekly* alike.

The lower-class, backward inflections of dress originating outside of the Paris fashion system make fashionable women's enthusiastic adoption of folk motifs seem somewhat odd. If working-class and non-European women existed outside the scope of the imagined community of fashion, why did fashionable Western women not shun their styles as antithetical to everything with which they hoped to affiliate themselves? One reason is that pastiche displayed the power of appropriation—that is, the power to incorporate what others had produced. If this could be read as a sign of appreciation, it also could be read as pride in the ability to exploit. Sometimes this exploitation was nakedly obvious, perhaps nowhere more so than in a European diplomatic reception described by the widow of an American diplomat. Shortly after the Chinese ambassador arrived, an American woman entered. "The ambassador caught sight of her instantly, and his agitation was painful to see. For she wore the coronation robes of the Empress of China!" These robes had recently been, as the ambassador and many of the assembled guests well knew, looted from the imperial palace by foreign troops in the aftermath of the Boxer Rebellion. As the ambassador sank trembling into a chair, onlookers led the woman away. "We all thought it was the most disgraceful thing we had ever witnessed. But in speaking about it in America, I was astonished to find many people take the woman's part." Their reasoning: "If a woman wanted to wear them to a party instead of a Paquin gown — they wouldn't especially admire her taste — but why wouldn't she?"[70] The logic of "why wouldn't she" helps explain the arrogation of folk motifs. Rather than signify exclusion from the fashionable world, they signified the fashionable woman's audacity and appropriative power. The ability to borrow from other design traditions could signal distance from the originator just as readily as it could signal proximity. Fashionable women could feel confident that their energetic search for novelty — a fundamental premise of the modes — differentiated them from ignorant peasants and non-Europeans with little understanding of and power over the wider world.

If, on the one hand, adherence to the Paris-based fashion system signaled empowerment, on the other, it reflected profound anxiety over maintaining cultural hierarchies in the face of globalizing connections. Just as the affiliative urge extended beyond the nation, so did the need to draw distinctions. As media connections and commerce drew far-flung consumers and producers ever closer, bourgeois U.S. women clung to the Paris-based fashion system in part to prove their civilizational distance from the world's dispossessed. U.S. women's adherence to a transnational system of fashion testifies to a historical moment in which, thanks to the popular geography conveyed by writings on dress, they could locate virtually the entire world in reference to a particular fashion system. And as fashionable U.S. women positioned themselves in a global context prior to World War I, their colonial attitudes toward European cultural production balanced their colonizing ambitions of cultural assertion. Recognizing the U.S. following of the Paris-based fashion meant acknowledging the transnational identities cultivated through consumption in a globalizing age and, in the process, giving middle-class American women a central role in the increasingly decentered historical narratives of our time.

Notes

I would like to thank Jim Barrett, Antoinette Burton, Vernon Burton, Clare Crowston, Ken Cuno, Charles Gammie, Fred Jaher, Deanne Karr, Jackson Lears, Mark Leff, Kathy Oberdeck, Elizabeth Pleck, Cynthia Radding, Mary Renda, Daniel Rodgers, Eleanor Thompson, and Juliet Walker for their comments and assistance.

1   Edward Knoblauch, *My Lady's Dress* (New York: Doubleday, Page, 1916), p. 134.
2   "*My Lady's Dress* Most Interesting," *New York Times*, October 12, 1914.
3   Katrina Irving, *Immigrant Mothers: Narratives of Race and Maternity, 1890–1920* (Urbana: University of Illinois Press, 2000), p. 10.

4 Martha Banta, *Imaging American Women: Idea and Ideals in Cultural History* (New York: Columbia University Press, 1987), pp. 2, 206, 211, 500, 557.

5 Thomas L. Masson, "The White Woman's Burden," *New York Times*, May 16, 1909.

6 Benedict Anderson, *Imagined Communities: Reflections on the Origin and Spread of Nationalism* (London: Verso, 1983).

7 Amy Kaplan and Donald E. Pease eds., *Cultures of United States Imperialism* (Durham, N.C.: Duke University Press, 1993); Jane C. Desmond and Virginia R. Domínguez, "Resituating American Studies in a Critical Internationalism," *American Quarterly* 48 (1996): 475–490; Gesa Mackenthun, "Adding Empire to the Study of American Culture," *Journal of American Studies* 30 (1996): 263–269; Ian R. Tyrrell, "American Exceptionalism in an Age of International History," *American Historical Review* 96 (1991): 1031–1072.

8 Leila J. Rupp, *Worlds of Women: The Making of an International Women's Movement* (Princeton, N.J.: Princeton University Press, 1997); Ian R. Tyrrell, *Woman's World, Woman's Empire: The Woman's Christian Temperance Union in International Perspective* (Chapel Hill: University of North Carolina Press, 1991); Emily S. Rosenberg, *Spreading the American Dream: American Economic and Cultural Expansion, 1890–1945* (New York: Hill and Wang, 1982).

9 Jenny June, "Renaissance of Fashion," *Times-Picayune*, November 4, 1888. On June, see Margaret Walsh, "The Democratization of Fashion: The Emergence of the Women's Dress Pattern Industry, *Journal of American History* 66 (1979): 299–313.

10 "French Fashion Openings," *New York Tribune*, August 25, 1912.

11 Grace Corneau, "Fashion's Dictates from Paris," *Chicago Tribune*, January 3, 1904; "Seen in the Shops of Paris," *Atlanta Constitution*, May 2, 1912.

12 On ready-made wear, see Ava Baron and Susan E. Klepp, "If I Didn't Have My Sewing Machine . . .': Women and Sewing-Machine Technology," in *A Needle, A Bobbin, a Strike: Women Needleworkers in America*, ed. Joan M. Jensen and Sue Davidson (Philadelphia: Temple University Press, 1984), pp. 20–59.

13 Joan L. Severa, *Dressed for the Photographer: Ordinary Americans and Fashion, 1840–1900* (Kent, Ohio: Kent State University Press, 1995), pp. 4, 185, 474.

14 Nancy L. Green, *Ready-to-Wear and Ready-to-Work: A Century of Industry and Immigrants in Paris and New York* (Durham, N.C.: Duke University Press, 1997), p. 2.

15 Department of Commerce, *The Foreign Commerce and Navigation of the United States* (Washington, D.C.: Government Printing Office, 1911), pp. 214–217, 262, 290, 331–334, 373–375.

16 On 1860, see Ishbel Ross, *Crusades and Crinolines: The Life and Times of Ellen Curtis Demorest and William Jennings Demorest* (New York: Harper and Row, 1963), p. 21; on 1871, see Walsh, "The Democratization of Fashion," p. 304; Russell Lynes, *The Tastemakers* (New York: Grosset and Dunlap, 1949), pp. 77–78.

17 Walsh, "The Democratization of Fashion," pp. 303, 307.

18 Mrs. C. C. Barker, *Catalogue of Mme. Demorest's Reliable Patterns of the Fashions* (Saratoga Springs, N.Y.: W. Demorest, 1874), n.p.; *Delineator* 60 (April 1898): 382.

19 Department of Commerce, *The Commerce and Navigation of the United States* (Washington, D.C.: Government Printing Office, 1870), p. 1523. On Mexico and U.S. fashion, see Steven B. Bunker, "'Consumers of Good Taste:' Marketing Modernity in Northern Mexico, 1890–1910," *Mexican Studies/Estudios Mexicanos* 13 (1997): 227–269.

20 Department of Commerce: *The Foreign Commerce and Navigation of the United States* (1911), pp. 214–217, 262, 290, 331–334, 373–375; *The Commerce and Navigation of the United States* (Washington, D.C.: Government Printing Office, 1920), pp. 215–218, 258–

259, 383–384, 419. This figure does not include laces, furs, leather products, or goods listed under "all other."

21 *B. Altman and Co., Catalogue of Fall and Winter Fashions* (New York: B. Altman, 1880), p. 2.

22 *Vogue* 7 (May 21, 1896): 348.

23 Frances Faulkner, "Our Skirts and Sleeves," *Ladies' World*, October 1895: 13.

24 Wendy Gamber, *The Female Economy: The Millinery and Dressmaking Trades, 1860–1930* (Urbana: University of Illinois Press, 1997), p. 111.

25 Barker, *Catalogue of Mme. Demorest's Reliable Patterns of the Fashions*, n.p.; *Catalogue for Fall* (New York: E. Butterick, 1874); Walsh, "The Democratization of Fashion," pp. 300, 312.

26 Cited in Caroline Rennolds Milbank, *New York Fashion: The Evolution of American Style* (New York: Harry N. Abrams, 1989), p. 59.

27 On the newest fashions, see "High's," *Atlanta Constitution*, September 6, 1896; on couturier fame, see "J. M. Gidding & Co.," *New York Tribune*, March 21, 1916.

28 Wolf von Schierbrand, "The Women of Russia," *Delineator* 63 (September 1904): 358; "Home and Society," *New York Tribune*, October 23, 1892; "Influence of Paris Fashion," *Atlanta Constitution*, June 2, 1912.

29 Anne Rittenhouse, "Fashion Stages a Fantasy," *Vanity Fair* 2 (April 1914): 61.

30 "Paris," *Vogue* 8 (July 16, 1896): 46.

31 E. M. R., "From the Faubourg St. Germain," *Vogue* 30 (November 7, 1907): 636.

32 Joan M. Jensen, "Needlework as Art, Craft, and Livelihood before 1900," in Jensen and Davidson, eds., *A Needle, a Bobbin, a Strike*, p. 8; Walsh, "The Democratization of Fashion," p. 313; Claudia B. Kidwell and Margaret C. Christman, *Suiting Everyone: The Democratization of Clothing in America* (Washington, D.C.: Smithsonian Institution Press, 1974), p. 17.

33 Maude Andrews, "I Have Seen a King," *Atlanta Constitution*, September 6, 1896.

34 Widow of an American Diplomat, *Intimacies of Court and Society: An Unconventional Narrative of Unofficial Days* (New York: Dodd, Mead, 1912), p. 149.

35 "Women Should Wear More Modest Clothes," *Atlanta Constitution*, February 4, 1912.

36 Abba Goold Woolson, ed., *Dress-Reform: A Series of Lectures Delivered in Boston* (Boston: Roberts Brothers, 1871), p. xii.

37 Leonore Davidoff, *The Best Circles: Women and Society in Victorian England* (Totowa, N.J.: Rowman and Littlefield, 1973), pp. 54, 102.

38 "A Devoted King," *New York Tribune*, January 5, 1896; "The Princess of Bulgaria," *New York Tribune*, January 26, 1896.

39 Jeffrey D. Needell, *A Tropical Belle Epoque: Elite Culture and Society in Turn-of-the-Century Rio de Janeiro* (New York: Cambridge University Press, 1987), p. 158; Benjamin Orlove, ed., *The Allure of the Foreign: Imported Goods in Postcolonial Latin America* (Ann Arbor: University of Michigan Press, 1997), pp. 5, 40–42, 75, 103.

40 "Here Is a 'Bit,'" *New York Tribune*, September 18, 1892.

41 On Paquin, see Diana de Marly, *The History of Haute Couture, 1850–1950* (New York: Holmes and Meier, 1980), p. 50; "Havana a Second, Almost a Gayer, Riviera," *New York Tribune*, January 23, 1916.

42 Gail Hamilton, "New Year Suggestion," *Los Angeles Times*, January 3, 1888.

43 Marly, *The History of Haute Couture*, p. 132.

44 "The Naked Truth about the Turk and His Harem," *Chicago Tribune*, October 6, 1912.

45 "The Coulter Dry Goods House," *Los Angeles Times*, December 1, 1888; "Keely Company,"

Atlanta Constitution, January 19, 1896; *John Wanamaker Catalogue No. 25, Fall and Winter 1888–9* (Philadelphia: John Wanamaker, 1888), p. 22; *B. Altman and Co., Catalogue of Fall and Winter Fashions*, p. 5; *Montgomery Ward and Co.* (Chicago: Montgomery Ward, 1884), p. 3.

46 "Notes from Our Foreign Correspondent," *Godey's* 109 (September 1884): 306–307; "Dress in Paris," *New York Tribune*, April 8, 1888; Mrs. John W. Bishop, "Latest Fashions," *Ladies' Home Journal* 7 (March 1890): 13; "Fashions Recruited from Five Nations," *Vanity Fair* 2 (May 1914): 67.

47 "The Frilled Hat," *Los Angeles Times*, October 4, 1896. Such cowboy wear owed an unacknowledged debt to Mexican clothing.

48 "One Step from Savage," *Times-Picayune*, May 3, 1920; Steele, *Paris Fashion: A Cultural History* (New York: Oxford University Press, 1988), pp. 74, 221.

49 "Never Before," *New York Tribune*, December 4, 1892.

50 On bonnets, see "Hats This Year," *New York Tribune*, July 28, 1912; on mantillas, see "Society Gossip," *Chicago Tribune*, July 18, 1880; on embroidery, see "Latest Styles," *Times-Picayune*, September 2, 1900; on ruffles, see *B. Altman and Co., Catalogue of Fall and Winter Fashions*, p. 14.

51 Alice Long, "What I See on Fifth Avenue," *Ladies Home Journal* 31 (January 1914): 24.

52 On boudoir attire, see "Mandel Brothers, Nikko Shop," *Chicago Tribune*, December 4, 1918.

53 "Women Can Look," *New York Tribune*, July 7, 1912.

54 "McCallum Silk Hosiery," *Vanity Fair* 10 (October 1918): 105.

55 Knoblauch, *My Lady's Dress*, p. 14.

56 Thorstein Veblen, *The Theory of the Leisure Class: An Economic Study of Institutions* (New York: Modern Library, 1899).

57 "Autumn Days," *Atlanta Constitution*, September 4, 1892.

58 Hamilton, "New Year Suggestion."

59 Mary Warner Blanchard, *Oscar Wilde's America: Counterculture in the Gilded Age* (New Haven, Conn.: Yale University Press, 1998), p. 142.

60 Faulkner, "Our Skirts and Sleeves," p. 13.

61 "Dutch Meccas of Modern Artists," *Vogue* 39 (May 15, 1912): 23.

62 "Pictures from Roumania," *Demorest's Monthly Magazine* 19 (June 1883): 492–503.

63 "Easter Millinery in Other Lands," *Chicago Tribune*, April 7, 1912.

64 Jean Urquhardt, "A Girl's Life in Old Mexico," *Ladies' World*, October 1897: 13. On foreigners' disdain for Mexican peasant dress, see William H. Beezley, *Judas at the Jockey Club and Other Episodes of Porfirian Mexico* (Lincoln: University of Nebraska Press, 1987), pp. 70–71.

65 See "The Feet of Chinese Women," *Chicago Tribune*, October 16, 1880.

66 "Costume of Persian Ladies," *Cottage Hearth* 1 (October 1874): 276.

67 "The Fashionable Kaffir," from *The Queen*, in *New York Tribune*, January 11, 1880; "Women of the Transvaal," *New York Tribune*, February 18, 1900. On proving Westernization through bourgeois clothing, see Philippe Perrot, *Fashioning the Bourgeoisie*, (Princeton: Princeton University Press, 1996), p. 79.

68 Louise Michele Newman, *White Women's Rights: The Racial Origins of Feminism in the United States* (New York: Oxford University Press, 1999), pp. 102–107.

69 "A Woman in Darkest Africa," *Housekeeper's Weekly* 2 (May 28, 1892): 2.

70 Widow of an American Diplomat, *Intimacies of Court and Society*, pp. 327–328.

HSU-MING TEO

The Romance of White Nations: Imperialism, Popular Culture, and National Histories

Over the last few years scholars from diverse backgrounds have challenged the nation-state as the natural or inevitable framework of political, economic, social, or cultural investigation. Jon Stratton and Ien Ang, for example, have called for the problematization of the nation in studies of "national" culture,[1] while the imperial historian A. G. Hopkins has observed that "most history continues to be written within a national framework that derives its inspiration from nineteenth-century state-building and state-reforming movements in Europe" because "preoccupation with the national epic has also endorsed a degree of insularity that has tended to marginalize international influences."[2] This chapter argues that the study of popular culture in the postimperial Anglophone world needs to look beyond the boundaries of the nation-state in order to situate and analyze cultural artifacts and practices. Literary works have often been used as exemplars of national culture, resulting in the creation and perpetuation of the national "canon" or "classic," which is somehow supposed to give expression to national identity. Popular literature often has the additional task not only of portraying national culture and expressing national identity, but also of giving voice to jingoistic patriotism as well. Using twentieth-century romance novels as a case study, however, I want to examine the ways in which romances are produced through transnational racializing discourses. While the romance novel has been analyzed by British and American scholars since the 1970s, almost all of this work has focused on class, gender, and sexuality debates. In certain studies authors have been at pains to point out the national differences between the "American" and the "British" romance novel. For example, the American critics Mariam Darce Frenier and Carole Thurston have argued that American romances had a more feminist agenda than their British counterparts, especially where representations of sexuality and gender equality in the home and workplace were concerned—an assertion questioned by British scholar Jay Dixon.[3] Such claims heighten national differences and reinforce national chauvinism without taking into account colonialism and race or ethnicity as categories of analysis. In a recent reappraisal of the extant feminist scholarship on romance, Lynne Pearce and Jackie Stacey acknowledged that "As in other areas of feminist work, white agendas have dominated discussions of love and romance."[4] This article examines how ideas of colonialism and race have been played out in the production of twentieth-century romance novels and how the global reach of the romance industry has disseminated these texts in ways that not only inhibited what they could say about race and racism, but also created a transnational community of white readers.[5] In discussions of the first half of the twentieth century, I focus on British and Commonwealth romances since the American romance industry did not really take off until the 1970s.

The sheer size of the romance market throughout the twentieth century makes it imperative for us to understand what kinds of racialized fantasies were being produced and disseminated among women in the name of "love." Sales of romances increased astronomically throughout the century. In 1999, Harlequin Enterprises — the largest international publisher of romance novels — sold over 175 million books worldwide, reflecting a sale of 5.5 books per second to over 50 million women in more than one hundred countries.[6] Mills and Boon (now the British subsidiary of Canadian-owned Harlequin Enterprises) claimed 32 percent of the paperback market in the United Kingdom, totaling 11 million readers, or 4 out of every 10 women.[7] Sales figures were also high in non-Western countries such as India, which constituted "the largest market for Mills and Boon outside the U.S., the U.K., and Canada."[8] According to the Romance Writers of America, 53 percent of all mass-market fiction published in the United States in 2000 was romance, while the readership consisted of 41.5 million people, 9 percent of whom were men.[9] The culture of the romance novel pervaded women's lives internationally, but despite the huge numbers of nonwhite readers in non-Western countries and the fact that 22 percent of American romance readers were nonwhite, the culture of romance was overwhelmingly white, its authors drawn historically from the United States, Britain, and the imperial dominions of Australia, New Zealand, Canada, and South Africa.

The meaning of whiteness in these countries was, of course, unstable and subject to historical change, as a growing body of work demonstrates. Even within the British Empire, the relation of "whiteness" to "Britishness" was by no means clear-cut. At the most fundamental, irrefutable level, ruling-class Anglo-Saxonism was always white. Apart from that, whiteness was a political, economic, and social process of categorization, varying according to how acceptable non-Anglo-Saxon labor and immigration were at different historical periods in the United States, Britain, and the colonies. Even at the end of the nineteenth century, whiteness was not necessarily linked with Europeans or even with race. Within Europe itself, attempts were made to assert the negritude of the Irish, especially when the Fenian movement was gathering strength,[10] and in the United States historians have examined how Irish, Italian, and other European groups were disadvantaged politically, socially, and economically through their initial exclusion from the category of "white" people, only to be incorporated at a later date.[11] In Australia, whiteness was by no means coterminous with Britishness, for although the Maltese were British subjects, they were excluded under the 1901 Immigration Restriction Act (the "White Australia Policy"). Germans and Scandinavians were considered white and were more desirable as immigrants than Southern Europeans, who were considered ethnically white only after World War II. And in late nineteenth-century Australia, Lebanese people were confusingly considered "Asian" but with "white" characteristics. Furthermore, whiteness entailed class distinctions in the colonies, for how else, as Ann Laura Stoler asked, "do we explain the sustained presence of a subterranean colonial discourse that anxiously debated who was truly European and whether those who were both poor and white should be included among them?"[12] Whiteness was thus an unstable fantasy existing along a spectrum, anchored in Anglo-Saxonism but otherwise shading into an indeterminate "brownness," which, in turn, shaded into "blackness" at the other end of the spectrum. All of these ideas were played out in romance novels, and it is the task of this chapter to examine why romances have perpetuated whiteness throughout the twentieth century and how colonial discourses of race actually produced romance.

In his classic study, *Love in the Western World*, Denis de Rougemont made a significant statement about the nature of romantic desire. In discussing the medieval Tristan and Iseult myth, de Rougemont declared that "What they need is not one another's presence, but one another's absence."[13] Many of the obstacles that keep Tristan and Iseult apart were not insurmountable, even by the rules of feudal fealty and courtly love. De Rougemont showed that in fact Tristan and Iseult went out of their way to create obstacles that would keep them apart. This, he argued, was in order to heighten the intensity of passion they felt. It was, moreover, a structural device to keep the plot going. Without the twists and turns of the numerous obstructions to love, there was simply no story, for the phrase "and they lived happily ever after" was a death knell to narrative. Although the development of the female romantic novel at the end of the eighteenth century transformed the understanding of love and the point of the romance plot in significant ways — centering women as romantic protagonists and concluding in marital domesticity rather than death — nevertheless the domestic romance inherited from the earlier masculine quest romances three fundamental characteristics: first, the protagonists of romance always struggled between desire and self-mastery; second, the deferral of desire or the postponement of sexual fulfillment was the engine that drove the romantic plot; third, the fulfillment of love signified an absolute end to the narrative, for there was nowhere else for the plot to go.

Modern romance writers recognized these three basic principles and structured their books accordingly. In her manual on romance writing, Valerie Parv states baldly that conflict between the hero and heroine drives the romance. "Each time the heroine reaches a barrier she must overcome it, only to find a more daunting one in her way."[14] The obstacles to romantic love have not changed that much through the centuries. Family feuds have been an eternal favorite since *Romeo and Juliet* and are still used in historical romances, although they fell out of favor as plot devices in contemporary romances. Class and/or wealth differences were another classic obstacle to be overcome. The heroine's preservation of her virginity, or her perception of her sexual frigidity, were popular obstacles to sexual fulfillment before the 1980s. And until the 1990s, the sexually potent "other woman" was a productive source of all kinds of misunderstandings that would keep hero and heroine apart until the final chapter. Extreme gender differences — the traditional hypermasculine hero and the quasi-feminist heroine — also provided a fruitful source of conflict, as did different lifestyles, different goals, and different personalities. If difference, conflict, and seemingly insurmountable obstacles were integral to the romance, then interracial relations should have been the romantic dynamic par excellence that propelled the plot. Yet for the last two hundred years, interracial romances have been rare and white-black romances practically nonexistent.

Admittedly, the fact that Britain was a favored setting for "town and country" domestic romances meant that these stories did not lend themselves to considerations of racial or ethnic differences. However, the British colonies provided numerous romantic settings for racial anxieties to be played out. The empire played a significant role where the fortunes of British romance novels were concerned, in terms of both its market and its manufactured fantasies. Publishing houses such as Mills and Boon and Hurst and Blackett looked overseas for sales growth and profit, participating in the general trade practice sometimes referred to as the "imperial publishing [of] colonial editions." Sales of romance fiction were profitable throughout the empire, and authors were encouraged to write love stories set in various exotic destinations. Hurst and Blackett cultivated the Rhodesian author Gertrude Page, Mills and Boon actively recruited colonial writers, while the 1920s and 1930s saw the phenomenon of the Kenyan love story.[15] The empire provided an exotic space of romantic love and female adventure, a locus sometimes idyllic and pastoral, at other times fraught with danger from "the natives." In the first half of the twentieth century, pioneering doctors, engineers, and farmers were fashionable heroes. Colonial Africa was a favorite setting for imperial romances in the novels of Gertrude Page, Florence Riddell, Nora K. Strange, Louise Gerard, Anne Vinton, Ann Hampson, Yvonne Whittal, and many others. Ethel M. Dell, Maud Diver, Joan Sutherland, and Juliet Armstrong set their tales of love in India during the Raj. Rosa Praed and Marie Bjelke-Petersen wrote colonial Australian romances in the early twentieth century, and by midcentury Mills and Boon were seeking Australian and New Zealand authors because these countries were popular destinations for emigration.[16]

Empire romances were written predominantly by Anglo-Saxon women for other white readers—European, American, or colonial—and from very early on their romantic fantasies were inflected, even produced, by race. The service and sacrifice of black people under the regime of colonialism made white romance possible. If, as Jan Cohn argued, the "popular romance tells the story of how the heroine gains access to money—to power—in patriarchal society,"[17] then hypergamy—the upwardly mobile marriage—was possible for the heroine because the hero had been made wealthy by the legacy of imperial enterprise.[18] In colonial romances the white hero and heroine were free to concentrate on the development of the romantic relationship, go on safari, attend parties, spend time sightseeing with each other, and so on because they were surrounded by "natives" serving them. Africans appeared in these romances as grinning porters, cooks, waiters, house servants, guides, and other subordinates. In Gwen Westwood's *Bright Wilderness*, for instance, the heroine, who is nursing her aunt on a farm in South Africa, thinks that household shopping is easy compared to shopping in England. In South Africa, "When you made your purchases, black hands were waiting to carry your parcels out to the car."[19]

"Natives" existed in the romance so that the hero or heroine could demonstrate compassion and lack of racial discrimination, thus justifying their status as the happy protagonists of the love story. For example, in Anne Vinton's *The Hospital in Buwambo*, the hero, a brilliant ophthalmic surgeon, gives up his practice in England to dedicate his medical skill to "Africa and her scourges." Thus he founds a leper colony, treats schoolchildren, and sets up workshops for leprous men. The African Dr. Kalengo acknowledges that even "I—an African—am physically afraid where a white man prepares to tread boldly."[20] "Natives" were there as an appreciative audience to true love. At the end of Vinton's *Nurse Wayne in the Tropics*, "The natives were strangely quiet" as hero and heroine gazed lovingly at each other, and "They seemed to realize these two people were quite alone in their own world, that they should not be peeping in on them at all. Gradually they dispersed and went back to their houses," leaving the African landscape inhabited only by the two white lovers.[21] In Yvonne Whittal's South African romances, Africans were simply erased from the landscape.

"Race" also inflected the romance novel because desire was racialized. In general, white women — primarily of British heritage — were naturalized as the heroines of romance. This was not only due to the mass-market romance novel's origins within the British Empire, but also because historically "white women function as emblematic objects of heterosexual desire."[22] Over and over again, descriptions of white women in the romances created a synonymy between white women and physical beauty. Lola Young has argued that "when it comes to the cinematic aestheticization of the feminine, white women's faces and bodies are privileged signifiers of female beauty and desire."[23] The beauty of the heroine's whiteness subsisted not only in her physical appearance, but also in her moral qualities and, for the most part of the century, her chastity and mastery of her sexual desire. Until the romance revolution of the 1970s that Carole Thurston has identified, whereby the historical, then mass-market, romance novel became highly sexualized, the plot of the romance novel retained its sexual tension by endlessly deferring the moment of sexual intercourse.[24] This plot device was possible with the perpetuation of stereotypes of white women who adhered to middle-class morality. Their abstinence from casual sex, their control over their own bodies, was rewarded by romance and marriage. Even after the romance sexual revolution, white heroines were kept free from the taint of promiscuity because they were portrayed as helpless against an overpowering force of passion.[25] This passion, however, was ultimately related to the corporeal recognition of their one true love. They might not have been virgins when the story started, but neither were they sexually active until the encounter with the romantic hero. Far from betraying them into promiscuity, white women's bodies instinctively recognized true love long before they were consciously aware of "being in love." This story of white femininity, Lola Young argued, was "intimately connected to slavery and colonialism" because the "middle class European woman is idealized and symbolic of the planters' control — control of self, of sex, of Others — and her femininity was made distinctive from that of the African woman and the white women of the 'lower' social orders."[26] In contrast to the portrayal of white women, racial discourse perpetuated stereotypes of black women's debased femininity and hypersexuality, which was pathologized.[27] Dark-skinned women were desired by white men because of their perceived hypersexuality, yet this made them unfit heroines for the romance novel since there could be no struggle between sexual desire and self-mastery to propel the romance plot and heighten the intensity of emotion. Nevertheless, because of the juxtaposition of white women and black people in colonial romances, the meaning of women's whiteness — their moral "purity," class status, fitness as reproducers of the "race," and white patriotism — was always ambiguous and under threat.

White women's pathological desire for dark men — a horrific desire from which they must be saved — is displayed in one of the more remarkable colonial romances of the early twentieth century, Mary Gaunt and John Ridgwell Essex's *The Arm of the Leopard* (1904), in which two English people, David Lindsay and Margaret Rivers, meet and fall in love on the way to Africa but have to contend with the heroine's African fiancé, Dr. James Craven, an Ashanti man educated in England. The language in which her change of heart occurs is the vocabulary of patriotism: she "transfers her allegiance to one of her own race and colour." Craven's attempt to appeal to Lindsay's sense of fair play in the rules of white romance fails. To Craven's question, "Even if it had been done before my face, it would not have been fair; behind my back it was an outrage. Suppose she had been the promised wife of one of your own colour?," Lindsay replies, "You are a man of colour, and as such you are no fitting husband for a girl of my class and race."[28] Eventually, after much diabolical plotting, Craven saves Margaret from a cannibal attack until the British arrive to take charge. He tells her that he is giving up his claim to her because "the white has conquered the black once more. The African is ever a slave."[29] His only reward at the very end of the novel is to have Lindsay grasp and shake his hand, telling him as he dies, "I've wronged you. You're a white man after all."[30] An African's "whiteness" can be achieved only by his sacrifice and death. In this novel the idea of romance is racialized so that it applies only to the love between the two white people, whereas Craven's doomed love for Margaret is pathological, sending him into a spiral of self-destruction. The beautiful but passive body of the white woman becomes the contested site of romantic desire, where colonial politics are played out and the educated "native" subordinated and destroyed. Craven could never be a romantic hero because the very structure of the romance within the context of colonialism prevented the positive closure of interracial romance. The female romance novel must end in domesticity and the creation of stable white families. In this way, women's romances played a vital role in the fantasy of community, nation, and empire building. But the pathologization of interracial relationships meant that there could be no closure in happy domesticity for such relationships; hence they could not be the main focus of a romance.

The dilemma between the sexual desirability of dark men and the structural impossibility of interracial romance was partially solved by the extremely popular "sheik" or "desert" romance set in the Middle East during the 1920s. *The Sheik*, E. M. Hull's best-selling 1919 novel, told the story of a white flapper,

Diana, abducted by an Arab sheik, raped into "feminine" submission until racial disgust was revealed as desire. The pathologized, hypersexual characteristics attributed to black men could also be transferred to nonwhite Others,[31] so it was unsurprising that Hull drew attention to the equivalence between "Arabs" and "blacks" in *The Sheik* when the heroine realized, to her simultaneous horror and delight, that she loved her captor even though "he was an Arab! A man of different race and colour, a native; Aubrey [her brother] would indiscriminately class him as a 'damned nigger.'"[32] The fact that the sheik is revealed to be an aristocratic Englishman at the end of the novel enabled Hull to titillate her readers with the fantasy of interracial romance while ensuring that her romance could have the requisite domestic ending—an ending, moreover, in which the English offspring of the sheik and Diana would be the future dynastic leaders of the Arab tribes. This desert romance was indeed a colonial enterprise.

The interwar sheik romances nevertheless represented an attempt—albeit a clumsy one—to diminish racist sentiments in the romance novel. Credit must be given to the romance industry—particularly Mills and Boon—for exhibiting comparatively "greater tolerance for foreigners" and toning down "prejudice and jingoism" at a time when right-wing fascist movements in Europe—particularly the National Socialists in Germany—were trumpeting calls for racial purity and fanning the flames of racial hatred.[33] The condemnation of overt racism in many interwar Mills and Boon romances contrasts with violent sex and casual racism that pervaded the male paperback market during the same period.[34] However, the increasing dependence of publishing firms like Mills and Boon on international markets placed constraints on both writers and editors. Because of the importance of the conservative Irish market to the firm's sales, taboos had always existed on certain subjects, including drinking, sex, and "foreigners." When Mills and Boon novels began to be printed and distributed in paperback by Harlequin Enterprises in 1957, British, Australian, and New Zealand writers who wished to be distributed in North America found themselves reined in to more conservative romantic plots. Canadian editors, John Boon wrote in 1966, "do not like heroines to be in love with married men, or married heroines in love with other men, or unhappy married situations, and no touching on difference of colour."[35]

Throughout the 1960s certain British, Australian, and New Zealand romance writers tried to advance the cause of civil rights and racial equality in their works, but the outcome was not always satisfactory because of editorial restrictions. In 1964 Alex Stuart submitted a manuscript to Mills and Boon entitled *The Scottish Soldier.* Alan Boon requested that changes be made to the plot because South Africa's apartheid laws were pointedly targeted. Boon liked stories set in Africa, but he preferred characters to be white or "uncoloured," as he put it, thus (apparently) avoiding the whole problem of race.[36] The farthest that Harlequin Mills and Boon was prepared to go where race relations were concerned was to urge tolerance of difference. In New Zealand author Essie Summers's romances, racism was something that happened elsewhere because her upright, decent, church-going New Zealanders would have no truck with the color bar and happily worked side by side with Maoris. In the end, Harlequin Mills and Boon was too restricted by its colonial/Commonwealth market to tackle the subject of race relations and discrimination. This would be left to American romance publishers.

From the 1980s onward, American historical romances proved particularly fertile ground for dealing with contemporary questions of race relations, emphasizing the necessity of accepting cultural or ethnic differences. The settings of historical romances were sufficiently remote from readers' lives, while plots set around the American Civil War were especially popular because, in simplistic schoolbook history terms, the abolitionist North won against the slave-owning South. In the 1990s romance market there were a surprising number of American novelists who attempted to rewrite the history of race relations in the United States by portraying mostly white heroes and heroines who treated blacks and Native Americans as equals, who protested against the practice of slavery or the dispossession of Indians from their ancestral lands, and who decried the discriminatory treatment meted out to racial "Others." Nevertheless, like British and Commonwealth romances, the agents of these stories were nearly always white. White lives were the lives worth living, worth loving. Nonwhites were almost invariably represented as the helpless victims of racism who needed to be saved by tolerant, compassionate white heroes and heroines, who would extend to them white acceptance of their difference. This was part of what Ghassan Hage called the "White nation" fantasy: "this White belief in one's mastery over the nation, whether in form of a White multiculturalism or in the form of a White racism . . . is a fantasy of a nation governed by White people, a fantasy of White supremacy."[37] Whiteness, as discussed above, is fundamentally unstable, not tied in any logical or visible way to race, ethnicity, or even skin color.[38] The fantasy of whiteness was hegemonic precisely because, to a certain extent, whiteness was a quality that could be accumulated, depending on social attributes and cultural capital. The slippery borders of whiteness — who counted or did not count as white during particular eras — are evident in a survey of twentieth-century romance novels. Spanish, Greek, Italian, Mexican, South American, and Mediterranean men have at various times been categorized as intriguing heroes or dangerous "dagos"; sometimes they counted as white men, while at other times they were intolerable hybrids, racial Others who threatened the purity of the white heroine and her offspring. Perhaps these men constituted a category of brown heroes—neither completely white nor black—whose borders also overlapped with Middle Eastern and Native American men.

Gilman has argued that psychological projections of desire onto the Other are double-edged: "They may appear as negative images, but they may also appear as positive idealizations. The 'pathological' may appear as the pure, the unsullied; . . . the racially different as highly attractive."[39] This was certainly the case where the treatment of Native Americans in romance was concerned. Indian captivity narratives had been in circulation since the seventeenth century. In the early nineteenth century it was still possible to consider the uneasy implications of white-Indian romance. Lydia Maria Child's 1824 novel, *Hobomok*, told the tale of a Native American who marries a white woman only to surrender her to a white man at the end while he takes himself off "among some of the red men in the west" who will "dig him a grave."[40] Thereafter Native Americans rapidly fell out of favor as possible heroes, and from the time of Twain's half-breed "Injun Joe" until the late 1970s, Native Americans served only as villains. The 1980s saw the appearance in contemporary romance of the "half-breed" Native American hero who was alienated from reservation life and socialized into white culture. By the 1990s, full Native Americans had become very popular as heroes, especially in historical romances. These heroes were invested not only with the traditionally desirable heroic qualities of sexual potency, strength, intelligence, and self-control, but in the tradition of the "noble savage," they were also portrayed as dignified, inherently spiritual, and in harmony with their environment. The desirability of these heroes had nothing to do with an expanding Native American readership clamoring for greater representation of its own race or ethnicity, for this occurred despite the fact that only 2 percent of the American romance market comprised both Asians and Native Americans. Black American readers, on the other hand, constituted 11 percent of the romance market, and although New York publishing houses Ballantine and Kensington developed "multicultural" or "ethnic" romance lines featuring African American and Hispanic characters in the 1990s, I have not yet come across a popular contemporary romance in which either the hero or heroine was Asian or black.[41] Colonial taboos on interracial romance remained strong to the century's end despite the fact that in the latter half of the twentieth century, the racialization of desire produced romantic fantasies of dark, hypersexual men who were white on the inside.

Twentieth-century romance novels were produced by discourses of race, and they perpetuated fantasies of whiteness and white nations. These fantasies of whiteness were legacies of British, then American, imperialism and the global reach of the romance market. The desirability of beautiful white women remained central to the romance, though the boundaries of ambiguous whiteness expanded slightly to include heroines who were partly continental European and sometimes partly Hispanic. However, nonwhite and Jewish women remained barred from the role of mainstream romantic heroine. And if white women's "dark" desire has historically been projected onto "dark" men, then throughout the twentieth century the mass-market romance novel has exploited the desire for darkness through a sleight of hand that substituted dark-hued white men and brown heroes for darkness, while the historical legacies of colonialism and slavery have worked to keep black people at the margins of romance or to exclude them completely. Because race is a process and not an entity, the meanings of whiteness, brownness, and blackness have changed over the century, as have the categories themselves. Whiteness at the end of the century included a lot more "ethnic" groups than it did at the century's start, while whiteness-as-cultural-aspiration made possible the inclusion of brown heroes. Slavoj Žižek has argued that fantasy is not merely a projection of preexisting desire; rather "fantasy constitutes our desire, provides its co-ordinates; that is, it literally 'teaches us how to desire.'"[42] In romance novels, desire for dark Otherness was often tamed and trained into desire for sun-tanned sameness. What was being sold was not merely an escapist daydream of passionate love and ideal gender relations, but also a racialized imperialist fantasy in which white people were still the principal actors in romantic narrative and geographical space.

It is the problematic meanings invested in the boundaries of this geographical space that have been in question here — the cultural values, events, and products associated with or enacted within the "nations" inscribed over vast tracts of land. There is no question that "nationness" needs to be taken into account in analyses of popular culture and literature, for the specificities of national histories and mythologies provided a reservoir of images, stories, and clichés that writers drew upon, while contemporary politics and cultural preoccupations were also played out in the text. However, in Britain, North America, and the white settler Commonwealth nations, discourses of romance, race, and imperialism also cut across national boundaries and national cultures. Authors from various backgrounds read each other's texts and raided images, motifs, stock characters, rhetorical flourishes, and romantic fantasies in a way that attenuated the boundaries of the nation-state while reinforcing racial discourses and fantasies about whiteness.

In treatises on nationalism, Benedict Anderson's assertion that the nation is "an imagined political community" has been a much quoted phrase. What is less often attended to is his supporting argument that it was "the convergence of capitalism and print technology on the fatal diversity of human language" that made possible "a new form of imagined community, which in its basic morphology set the stage for the modern nation."[43] But the form and content of popular literature often extended beyond the boundaries of the nation-state in its production, dissemination, and consumption. Anderson acknowledged this when he wrote that "the concrete formation of contemporary nation-ness is by no means isomorphic with the determinate reach of particular print-languages."[44] Print culture could create more than the community of the nation; it could create a community of readers who absorbed messages of the supremacy of white (ultimately Anglo-American) lives. Because of the continuing hegemony of British imperial and American neo-imperial culture and the nature of globalized mass-market publishing, investigations of literary cultures — particularly the popular fiction consumed by the vast majority of English-language readers worldwide — need to move beyond the nation-state as their sole frame of reference. There is no natural, automatic alignment between cultural products and national identity. Future studies of imperialism and women's popular literature would therefore need to move beyond national cultural histories in order to examine both the transnational material process of publishing and the international discursive practices that drew from, generated, or maintained fantasies of gender, class, race, imperialism, and even the white nation itself.

Notes

1 Jon Stratton and Ien Ang, "On the Impossibility of a Global Cultural Studies: 'British' Cultural Studies in an 'International' Frame," in *Stuart Hall: Critical Dialogues in Cultural Studies*, ed. David Morley and Kuan-Hsing Chen (London: Routledge, 1996), pp. 361–391.

2 A. G. Hopkins, "Back to the Future: From National History to Imperial History," *Past and Present* 164 (1999): 202–203.

3 Mariam Darce Frenier, *Good-Bye Heathcliff: Changing Heroes, Heroines, Roles, and Values in Women's Category Romances* (New York: Greenwood Press, 1988); Carole Thurston, *The Romance Revolution: Erotic Novels for Women and the Quest for a New Sexual Identity* (Urbana: University of Illinois Press, 1987); Jay Dixon, *The Romance Fiction of Mills and Boon, 1909–1990s* (London: UCL Press, 1999).

4 Lynne Pearce and Jackie Stacey, eds., *Romance Revisited* (New York: New York University Press, 1995), p. 22.

5 As Robert Miles and many others have argued, "race" is not a biological fact of nature but a classificatory system through which a racialized social order is produced. Miles is troubled by the continued usage of "race" and "race relations" (see Miles, *Racism after "Race Relations"* [London: Routledge, 1993]), but I use them here because romance authors and publishers did not distinguish between the idea of "race" and the process of racialization. Their concerns were about the representation of "race."

6 "The History of Harlequin Enterprises Limited," http://www.eharlequin.com/harl/globals/about/00bkrd11.htm#HISTORY .

7 Joseph McAleer, *Passion's Fortune: The Story of Mills and Boon* (Oxford: Oxford University Press, 1999), p. 3.

8 Radhika Parameswaran, "Western Romance Fiction as English-Language Media in Post-colonial India," *Journal of Communication* 49, 3 (summer 1999): 84.

9 Romance Writers of America, http://rwanational.com/statistics.stm, 2000.

10 Richard Dyer, *White* (London: Routledge, 1997), p. 52; Robert Young, *Colonial Desire: Hybridity in Theory, Culture and Race* (London: Routledge, 1995), p. 72; Liz Curtis, *Nothing but the Same Old Story: The Roots of Anti-Irish Racism* (London: Information on Ireland, 1984), p. 55; L. Perry Curtis Jr., *Apes and Angels: The Irishman in Victorian Caricature* (Newton Abbott: David and Charles, 1971).

11 David Roediger, *The Wages of Whiteness: Race and the Making of the American Working Class* (London: Verso, 1991); Matthew Frye Jacobson, *Whiteness of a Different Color: European Immigrants and the Alchemy of Race* (Cambridge, Mass.: Harvard University Press, 1998).

12 Ann Laura Stoler, *Race and the Education of Desire: Foucault's History of Sexuality and the Colonial Order of Things* (Durham, N.C.: Duke University Press, 1995), p. 103.

13 Denis de Rougemont, *Love in the Western World*, trans. Montgomery Belgion (Princeton, N.J.: Princeton University Press, 1983 [1940]), pp. 41–42.

14 Valerie Parv, *The Art of Romance Writing: How to Create, Write, and Sell Your Contemporary Romance Novel* (Sydney: Allen and Unwin, 1993), p. 90.

15 McAleer, *Passion's Fortune*, pp. 45–46; C. J. D. Duder, "Love and the Lions: The Image of White Settlement in Kenya in Popular Fiction, 1919–1939," *African Affairs: The Journal of the Royal African Society* 90, 360 (1991): 427–438.

16 McAleer, *Passion's Fortune*, p. 103.

17 Jan Cohn, *Romance and the Erotics of Property: Mass-Market Fiction for Women* (Durham, N.C.: Duke University Press, 1988), p. 3.

18 See, for example, the colonial farms inherited by the protagonists in Gwen Westwood: *Zulu Moon* (London: Mills and Boon, 1980), and *Blossoming Gold* (London: Mills and Boon, 1976).

19 Gwen Westwood, *Bright Wilderness* (London: Mills and Boon, 1969), p. 25.

20 Anne Vinton, *The Hospital in Buwambo* (London: Mills and Boon, 1957) p. 161.

21 Anne Vinton, *Nurse Wayne in the Tropics* (London: Mills and Boon, 1961; first published as *The Time of Enchantment*, 1956), p. 180.

22 Lola Young, *Fear of the Dark: "Race," Gender and Sexuality in the Cinema* (London: Routledge, 1996), p. 17.

23 Ibid.

24 Thurston, *The Romance Revolution*.

25 Catherine Belsey, *Desire: Love Stories in Western Culture* (Oxford: Blackwell, 1994), p. 27.

26 L. Young, *Fear of the Dark*, pp. 15, 47.

27 Sander L. Gilman, *Difference and Pathology: Stereotypes of Sexuality, Race and Madness* (Ithaca, N.Y.: Cornell University Press, 1985), p. 76.

28 Mary Gaunt and John Ridgwell Essex, *The Arm of the Leopard: A West African Story* (London: Grant Richards, 1904), pp. 40–41.

29 Ibid., p. 289.

30 Ibid., p. 306.

31 Gilman, *Difference and Pathology*, p. 35.

32 E. M. Hull, *The Sheik* (New York: Buccaneer Books, n.d. [1919]), p. 133.

33 McAleer, *Passion's Fortune*, p. 167.

34 Steve Holland, *The Mushroom Jungle: A History of Postwar Paperback Publishing* (Dilton Marsh: Zeon Books, 1993), pp. 99–100.

35 McAleer, *Passion's Fortune*, p. 122.

36 Ibid., p. 270.

37 Ghassan Hage, *White Nation* (Sydney: Pluto Press, 1998), p. 18.

38 "Race" and "ethnicity" are of course problematic concepts, deriving from nineteenth-century biological discourse. See R. Young, *Colonial Desire*.

39 Gilman, *Difference and Pathology*, p. 25.

40 Lydia Maria Child, *Hobomok and Other Writings on Indians*, ed. Carolyn L. Karcher (New Brunswick, N.J.: Rutgers University Press, 1986 [1824]), p. 139.

41 Statistics compiled by Romance Writers of America, http://rwanational.com/statistics .stm, 2000.

42 Slavoj Žižek, *The Plague of Fantasies* (London: Verso, 1997), p. 7.

43 Benedict Anderson, *Imagined Communities: Reflections on the Origin and Spread of Nationalism*, 2d ed. (London: Verso, 1991 [1983]), pp. 6, 46.

44 Ibid., p. 46.

KAREN FANG

Britain's Finest: The Royal Hong Kong Police

The 1997 ceremonies commemorating the handover of Hong Kong from Britain to China graphically depicted the prominent place of the Hong Kong police in the territory's postcolonial identity. At midnight on June 30, 1997, the last day of British rule in Hong Kong, as the naval vessel HMY *Britannia* sailed away from Hong Kong harbor with its retinue of civil servants, the police quietly exchanged the royal crest on their uniforms for the newly minted insignia of the Special Administrative Region, the territory's new designation under Chinese sovereignty. This nonevent, in which only the badge of the police was exchanged, dramatized the erasure of colonial connotations that had occurred in the force over the past few decades. More important, by emphasizing their continuity through the handover, the gesture also called attention to the police as an icon of Hong Kong culture. The act intended to commemorate their withdrawal from one of Britain's last and most valuable colonies in fact cast the former Royal Hong Kong Police as an object lesson in the strange persistence of imperial structures in the period after colonial sovereignty.[1]

In today's era of globalization and devolution, the Hong Kong police survive as guardians of the territory's political stability and cultural identity. The archetypal representations of British colonial administration thus invite us to interrogate perceptions of the nineteenth-century imperial nation-state as monolithic and anachronistic. For example, by excelling at a centralized system of social governance once considered emblematic of Britain, the Hong Kong Police invert the traditional power axis between a sovereign state and its dependency. They suggest the migration of nineteenth-century British imperial supremacy to postcolonial Asia. Such uncontested status enjoyed by the Hong Kong police is remarkable because it exists at a time when police forces across the globe are increasingly subject to public resistance. Moreover, their influence was achieved by a canny conversion of colonial authority into postcolonial importance that ironically was enabled by conditions the colonial administration itself had set in place.

The keys to this late twentieth-century transformation of Hong Kong's formerly colonial police were the remaking of the police to match the local population and their assertion of legitimacy by constant reference to their location in a larger geopolitics, including not just various British imperial spaces, but also China, America, and Japan.[2] This account adds to the existing historiography by emphasizing the hybridity of Hong Kong's various policing structures, ranging from the land and marine jurisdictions to military or non-military powers to state versus municipal authority, all of which were instrumental in gaining public consent. The British Royal Navy and its role in founding the Water (later Marine) Police is an important component of this history because of its policies of localization and professionalization, such as the systemic recruitment of native hires and their promotion to elite levels of administration, practices that would become models for the police force as a whole.[3] This essay departs from much imperial scholarship by showing how, in the history of the Hong Kong police, the flow and exchange that exist between metropole and periphery and from one point in the periphery to another were never dyadic and constant. This essay also challenges multiple conventions of policing studies and postcolonial theory—as well as their amalgam, colonial police history—by calling into question the extent to which a democratizing former colony must move beyond its colonial heritage.[4]

When British Royal Navy gunboats arrived in Hong Kong harbor in 1841, their role in enacting colonial annexation extended to the immediate deployment on land of policing duties such as law enforcement and territorial patrol. Their instrumentality in subordinating the territory was also evident in the swiftness with which a permanent land police force was established in Hong Kong. Hong Kong's first jail opened within a year of colonial possession, and in 1844 the Royal Navy was relieved of its policing duties when London approved funds for a dedicated land police. From its inception, however, the Hong Kong Police were distinguished among other colonial forces for the variety of policing systems that they simultaneously employed. A navy and a land police were both required in early "Hongkong" because the territory encompassed islands and a harbor. (Hence, 1844 also oversaw the commissioning of "China Squadron," a permanent Hong Kong–based branch of the Royal Navy.) Moreover, the early land police were a blend of metropolitan and constabulary policing practices that combined the older, militarized mode of policing first deployed in Ireland (and upon which most other colonial forces had been modeled) with the newer urban system based on Peel's New Police, recently founded by the London Metropolitan Police Act of 1829. Hong Kong's hybrid policing form thus was both innovative and traditional, acknowledging the urban density of the island colony by emulating recent developments in the metropole while also retaining the magistrate capacities of older policing forms. The constabulary element for the Hong Kong police remained useful as late as 1898, for example, when Britain's lease of the New Territories, an extensive rural tract on the Chinese mainland, required the police to clear the newly annexed frontier.

The diversity of ethnicities and nationalities composing their forces also distinguished the early Hong Kong Police. Although British colonial policy usually required the appointment of some native personnel to midranking commissions in an effort to build public consent, stereotypes about Chinese propensities to corruption and vice were intense among British colonial officials and resulted in strict policies of racial exclusion for the Hong Kong force. Thus, the early Hong Kong land police employed native Chinese only for the lowest brigades and supplemented the white officers with trained colonial servants such as Sikh and Gurkha former soldiers. Not surprisingly, cynicism about the police among the colonized Hong Kong Chinese was as harsh as the stereotypes leveled against them. The native Chinese largely viewed the land police as an invasive, oppressive, politically interested, and unreliable organization whose maintenance of law and order was especially suspect because the police were accountable only to the colonial governor. By thus empowering servants from London and elsewhere in Britain and the colonies but forbidding autonomy to the native subjects, the early Hong Kong land police epitomized colonial hegemony.

The Royal Navy, however, differed from the land police because of its early incorporation of native hires. This move to localize marine policing as a representative practice resulted in the Water Police, a specialized branch of the territorial police founded by the navy in 1845. The progressive new division inherited the navy's previously ad hoc marine policing responsibilities but differed from both the navy and the land police by being a locally assembled crew. From its inception the Water Police included Chinese among its ranks. Interestingly, for many years the Water Police also included a number of White Russians, whose lack of affiliation with Britain underscores the Water Police's apparent indifference to imperial hierarchy. Moreover, because they provided formal training and followed the same rules of promotion employed by the Royal Navy, the Water Police also encouraged internal promotion. Such early incorporation of native hires perhaps occurred within the Water Police because their chief function was the prevention of piracy—an externally directed mission that was not thought to be vulnerable to corruption among the native Chinese on Hong Kong land. There is also some evidence that a precedent Chinese marine force, funded by the Chinese government seeking to protect its junks, existed in Hong Kong before the Water Police's founding. At any rate, this early adoption of local hires suggests the Water Police was Hong Kong's first example of a truly local police force, in contrast to the self-consciously imperial structures of the land police. In fact, their structural differentiation from imperial authority existed in spite of the subdivision's continuing practical and perceptual ties to its naval founder. The Water Police continued to train with the Royal Navy until 1930.

Hong Kong's various police factions thus asserted vastly different modes of legitimacy throughout the first century of its existence. From the 1844–1845 founding of the two branches until World War II, the land police focused on achievements in science and technology in order to build a reputation within the imperial system. For example, the Hong Kong land police were leaders in the development of fingerprinting, the new scientific form of criminology pioneered at Scotland Yard and perfected by civil servants in India. The land police made their contribution to empire when they began to use fingerprinting in 1904, only three years after the London Met adopted the practice. In fact, the Hong Kong Police would instruct the metropole when an English-language work by a Chinese clerk in the Hong Kong force became the leading text on fingerprinting for the first half of the twentieth century.[5] The Royal Navy, by contrast, showed an early propensity toward demilitarization and the separation of state from social concerns. The Royal Navy helped Hong Kong establish hospitals, schools, power generators, and postal and fire prevention systems and provided much needed medical aid during the bubonic plague that incapacitated the island in 1894, as Royal Navy surgeons worked side by side with traditional Chinese doctors. The navy's reputation as a local protector was also consolidated during the late nineteenth century, when the threat of various imperial powers seeking to fracture China prompted Britain to increase naval presence. The navy's freedom to cultivate local favor existed because the apparatus, unlike the land police, had no need to augment its global reputation and could focus on mitigating its military presence.

As the navy's protégé, the Water Police also supplemented police presence with a significant development and social service component. The Water Police are credited with introducing land reclamation to Hong Kong by mastering the Royal Navy's technique of massing hulks, and they have always assisted the territory in medical aid, rescue services, and refugee management. In 1904 the Water Police's status within the territory grew significantly when the branch received sole jurisdiction over Hong Kong harbor. By gaining authority over such a valuable district in the territory, the Water Police increased their visibility at a time when the land police remained indifferent or antagonistic. Their success was in large part due to the example of the navy, whose counterintuitive model of increased authority by way of intense colonial involvement set a precedent for the Water Police to shape themselves as a local entity.

The Water Police emerged as an exemplary branch of the force during the period of rapid change in the territory that World War II ushered in. The 1941–1945 Japanese occupation of Hong Kong irrevocably sundered British police control of the colony by first supplanting the colonial forces and then casting attention, after the Japanese defeat and subsequent pullout, on the inadequacies of the current police to restore social stability. (Indeed, because it was the Royal Navy who maintained law and order during this period, the immediate postwar era seemed to reprise the militarized era of colonial annexation.) In 1947 a former commissioner of the prewar Hong Kong Police responded to the crisis in local policing by composing the Pennefather-Evans Report, an analysis and set of recommendations for problems in the existing force. The chief weakness the report identified was the failure of the Hong Kong Police to inspire identification among the public it governed. Among the strategies for police reform, the report advised an increase in local hires, an expansion in operational duties, and an enhancement of professional training. The Pennefather-Evans Report drew upon various sites and stages in imperial policing, such as the commissioner's training in Singapore and his internship by the Japanese in Hong Kong's Stanley Prison, to make recommendations. Notably, the report singled out the Water Police in praise of their long-standing inclusion of native Chinese. The report thus laid the framework in which the marine subdivision was held up as a model for the police force as a whole. Although it would be some time before the recommendations of the Pennefather-Evans Report would be instituted throughout the Hong Kong Police, this early commendation encouraged the postwar expansion of the Water Police (which, in keeping with conditions of imperial exchange, were overseen by a former officer of the Palestine Police). In 1948 the Water Police renamed themselves the Marine Police, acknowledging the central role the Royal Marines played in the liberation of Hong Kong, and announcing itself as a multitalented, elite version of the local police force, occupying in Hong Kong the same pride of place as do the marines in the British Royal Navy.

The path to reform for the land police came more slowly, with social and institutional crises that occurred over two periods: social unrest in the territory in the 1960s and early 1970s, and the reunification process of the 1980s and 1990s. The mid-1960s and early 1970s were the first time that Hong Kong's historically immigrant society harbored a majority native-born population. The first era of reform of the land police was sparked when emerging pressure for autonomy clashed with colonial police authority, and British influence was further eroded by China's Cultural Revolution, the rise of communism in surrounding Asian nations, and the increasing prominence of the United States, as it contained these developments in the Pacific Rim. During this period police legitimacy reached its nadir with the 1966–1967 Star Ferry Riots, a series of street protests whose violent police crackdown was rewarded by the British government with the "royal" honorific, and the 1972 Godber Affair, a corruption scandal that affirmed suspicions of colonial bias when a white police officer escaped embezzlement charges by fleeing to Britain. Clearly, reform was imperative. The police determined that the only way to restore authority was to conform to the consolidation of Hong Kong identity and prevent further failures of justice and accountability. Thus, the land police mandated an increase in local hires, their promotion to higher-ranking positions, and the augmentation of police salaries. These measures were intended to prevent corruption and elevate the force's social standing by promoting internal morale, as well as evoking local pride in the police bureau. Significantly, the plans followed the same principles of localization and professionalization that the Water Police had pioneered. The land police also worked with the territorial administration to create a watchdog agency that would finally subject the force to external review.

Reunification induced the second era of police reform. In the period from the 1984 Sino-British Joint Declaration, negotiating the handover of Hong Kong to Chinese communist sovereignty, to the 1997 handover, anxieties about police power centered on the possible abuse by China of the paramilitary police powers in Hong Kong and the potential replacement of the Hong Kong Police by communist China's secret police. The Tiananmen Square massacre in 1989 only justified these anxieties about the need to curtail police power. Thus in order to quell widespread uncertainty in the colony, the Basic Law negotiated during these years to govern the territory after reunification included codices separating the police and military responsibilities previously conflated in the colonial police. Moreover, the reforms provided specific reductions in future police powers, such as the surrender in 1997 of the Hong Kong Police's previously paramilitary authority. (The exception to this demilitarization was border control, a national defense task that the Hong Kong Police retained as a specific sign of the territory's continuing autonomy.) As the force's showcase branch, the Marine Police were the subject of special reunification changes. In order to foster autonomous operation, the costs of Marine Police expansion since the reunification agreement increasingly had been assumed by the Hong Kong rather than the British government. Changes initiated in this second era of reform also bolstered community relations by annulling the handicapping apparatus of the police, such as its racial elitism and imperial trappings. Plans for the post-handover police included the removal of the controversial "royal" title and were overseen by the first ethnic Chinese police commissioner in the history of the force.

A sharp rise in violent crime during the 1980s and early 1990s, however, also shaped this second era of police reform. Although the issues of municipal law and safety might appear apolitical, the political cast of the crime waves was evident in the fact that they were attributed primarily to illegal mainland Chinese immigrants. The contemporary concerns about police power further complicated the police response. Although the mission of the Hong Kong Police was to protect citizens, the context of reunification and post-Tiananmen anxiety required that police actions not appear as anything that could be construed as authoritarian violence. The solution of the Hong Kong Police was to pit these apparently conflicting anxieties against each other. Their strategy worked because British law and order were the obvious defense, given the territory's colonial history and communist future, against the Tiananmen-substantiated nightmare of Chinese violence in Hong Kong streets. Such a complex response to reunification resulted in a postcolonial police agency with a surprising twist. The formerly colonial Hong Kong Police not only survived colonial withdrawal, but in fact found their presence in increasing demand, and their ascendancy as a postcolonial icon was in large part due to their colonial history. In 1992 Hong Kong's unique relationship to police power was further illustrated by the territory's relatively uncontested consideration of the Police Authority and Criminal Evidence Act (PACE), legislation originally designed to increase police powers in Britain. Because the legislation offered Hong Kong a means of both affirming ties to its colonial sovereign and persecuting the criminals believed to be mainland Chinese trespassers, in handover-era Hong Kong the bill encountered notably less resistance than it had in Britain.

The reforms undergone by the Hong Kong Police in the past half century were a choice between the two modes of British policing that were built into Hong Kong's uniquely hybrid version of imperial policing. But although the Hong Kong Police elected a nonmilitary and locally assembled force for the era after decolonization, embracing a structure more evocative of a metropolitan capital than a colonial frontier and aligning the force with the affluent and increasingly native-born population they represented, at the same time they renewed their imperial heritage by merging this newly domesticated apparatus with its previous commitment to professional expansion and by making certain colonial legacies more visible than before. Curiously, while these changes reversed the police's historical role in subordinating the territory, they also reinstated them as a microcosm of Hong Kong culture as a whole. For example, the bailiwicks originally drawn by the land police to patrol the territory now enable the police to aid commercial growth. Under the aegis of municipal efficiency, the land police impose traffic restrictions that maximize pedestrian movement through commercial thoroughfares. Similarly, whereas a naval captain had been Hong Kong's first de facto governor, in the late twentieth century the navy's once omnipotent influence is present in Watson's Chemist, the chain of commercial pharmacies throughout Hong Kong and Singapore that mushroomed from the first Western dispensary established by a Royal Navy surgeon to prevent disease in Hong Kong. In the mid-1980s the end of British colonial occupation of the territory was symbolized by a lucrative auction in which valuable harbor properties previously occupied by the navy's hulks were sold to the Chinese government. The historical role of the Water Police in controlling the harbor remains visible in the decorative traditions of the postcolonial administration. The ceremonial chair of the harbor master, formerly a responsibility of the chief of the Water Police, is located in the assembly room of the Legislative Council and now is occupied by the chief executive appointed by the Chinese government.

Indeed, public safety and commercial stability have arguably always been of equal importance in Hong Kong, and in the postcolonial era the police continue to fulfill their duties with remarkable proficiency. On land their deployment of Britain's traditional beat-policing modes has ensured that since the early 1980s Hong Kong repeatedly has ranked as one of the world's safest cities. On the seas the Marine Police continue to protect the territory's powerful economy, as the bureau's original responsibility of preventing piracy has grown more important with the eruption of extremely violent, high-stakes piracy that during the past decade has severely impacted the shipping lines in the South China Seas. During reunification both components of the force were crucial to calming investor anxiety in the territory, and in the postcolonial era the police's pre-unification heritage of due process and accountability is instrumental in protecting citizen rights under the Special Administrative Region's "one country, two systems" policy.

Such postcolonial prominence of the former British institution in Hong Kong posits multiple similarities between the sovereign region and former colony. Because Hong Kong, like England, is an island nation whose wealth derives from mercantile growth, the British Royal Navy served the same purpose in Hong Kong as in Britain—that is, to protect the harbor and trade routes that are among the territory's most valuable resources. This function also accounts for the continuing importance of the Marine Police, a naval scion. Other likenesses between Hong Kong and Britain are evident in the parallels between the colony and the British provinces and in the role of empire in realizing aspirations at home. That the Hong Kong land police originated in Ireland's constabulary policing also suggests, reflexively, Ireland's quasi-oriental status and the limited assimilation into Britain it is consequently permitted. For England, the similarity between the two forms of policing exercised in the respective colonies implies that white and neighboring Ireland is as foreign as a distant Chinese island. In fact, Irish subjects often found more professional achievement in Hong Kong than at home. Many of the highest-ranking officers in the history of the Hong Kong police, including a number of police commissioners, were Irish nationals. Indeed, Britain now appears to lag behind Hong Kong in the authority and favor accorded the police. The fact that the PACE legislation, which encountered minimal resistance in Hong Kong, was hopelessly stalled in Britain, the country for which the legislation was originally designed, suggests that metropolitan policing has much to learn from the colonies. Or, conversely, the fact that policing in Britain intensified during the era of decolonization suggests that a declining former colonial authority will find that its outlet for power is at home. (Not coincidentally, George Orwell served in the Burma police before writing *1984*, his famously dystopic vision of a heavily policed London.)

Because the history of the Hong Kong Police is a product of diverse relays among London, the British provinces, and other spaces of empire, as well as vice versa, it is only appropriate that today the success of the Hong Kong Police is measured not just by their internal authority, but also by international reputation. At the start of the millennium the Hong Kong land and sea police together comprised one of the world's biggest forces, in both real and per capita numbers. Their ubiquitous officers, vehicles, technological devices, and architectural sites not only represent their postcolonial authority, but also are recognizable throughout the world as emblems of Hong Kong's development and excellence. The Marine Police alone are the largest constabulary water police on the globe, bigger than most of the world's navies, and competitive in resources and training with the national navy that founded them. They position their global as well as territorial status by providing Interpol with a vital source of Pacific coverage, and their eclipse of comparable agencies — such as the Thames Division of the London Metropolitan Police — shows them surpassing their metropolitan origins. Even the local admiration enjoyed by the Hong Kong Police is used to trumpet their name abroad. With statistics showing unusually high rates of assent for characterizations of the current police as honorable, hard working, and dedicated to the public, the Hong Kong Police are known worldwide as a historical and theoretical impossibility that effected massive growth with the full support of the public.[6] Moreover, such peculiar and unique success of the Hong Kong Police confirms their long-standing history of hybridity and exceptionality by illustrating how the police's ascendancy was predicated on a shift from a colonial to a local to a colonial-as-local identity.

* * *

The history of the Hong Kong Police complicates both British and Asian studies on several levels. Their emergence as a national icon not only constitutes a remarkable erasure of colonial memory, but also contrasts with contemporary global trends toward decentralization by paradoxically presenting an increase of police powers as a sign of popular desire for autonomy and democracy. They cultivate a fluid identity that is neither solely English or Chinese, nor entirely devoid of these facets, and exemplify, along with the parallel histories of hygiene, education, and public housing in Hong Kong, colonial success at social improvement efforts that the colonial power itself had invented and in which it had failed.[7] Their ascendancy after World War II is emblematic of the territory's general vitality in the late twentieth century — an era when Hong Kong citizens generated more tax revenue, experienced a lower rate of unemployment, and enjoyed a higher standard of living than citizens in the sovereign country — and thus invites interpretations of themselves as a phenomenon of the "American" century. Indeed, these two economically powerful former colonies seem to have been galvanized at the same time and under the same circumstances: the Japanese invasion of Hong Kong in 1941 occurred only hours after their attack on Pearl Harbor. The local police also affirm third world colonial cities as precursors of today's world cities by illustrating how their indispensible role in enhancing territorial development helped bring Hong Kong to its current prominence on the world stage.

Hong Kong, I acknowledge, is sui generis. The original island captured by the British had very little indigenous population, and throughout its history the territory's culture predominately has been formed by its absorption of diasporic and transient people. Its adaptation to police practices may be conditioned by both the long history of police in China and the strong traditions of natural surveillance in ethnic Chinese culture. Such adaptation to social structures certainly is a long-standing characteristic of Hong Kong society, as are the crime syndicates whose existence gave the colonial administration a goal that propped up its own legitimacy (and that remains a major focus of current police activity).[8] Friction between the public and the police is also minimized in Hong Kong because the brunt of a hostile police encounter is borne not by Hong Kong citizens but by disenfranchised individuals such as Philippine service workers, Vietnamese refugees, and legal and illegal Chinese immigrants. As a colony, Hong Kong was often overshadowed by other British colonial holdings such as India. Such metropolitan neglect enabled the relatively unchecked development of its colonial structures into autonomous agencies. The police's rehabilitation was dependent on the creation of a powerful external oversight agency and public relations office, both of whose considerable authority is beyond the scope of this survey.[9] As a city-state Hong Kong requires considerable police authority because such authority also doubles as national defense, and the Tiananmen tragedy that had such meaning for Hong Kong ensured that any other police force was preferable to the Chinese People's Liberation Army (PLA). Indeed, the territory's transition from one colonial power to another outside sovereign epitomizes the territory's exceptionality.

The Hong Kong police invite comparisons to other former colonial police forces. The Hong Kong Police survive while other imperial remnants such as the Royal Ulster Constabulary are heavily contested or already disbanded; they differ from the Royal Canadian Mounted Police, the Jamaican Constabulary Force, and the current Zimbabwe Police (formerly the British South Africa Police in Southern Rhodesia), all of whom continue into independence with little structural or titular change because the Hong Kong Police survival required reform. Yet unlike Australia's New South Wales Police, a reformed force that continues to clash with indigenous peoples, the Hong Kong Police enjoy public support. Perhaps not surprisingly, the Hong Kong police appear to have most in common with police forces in other island cities and formerly British colonial regions in East and Southeast Asia, such as the Singapore Police, whose implementation of neighborhood policing was closely studied by the Hong Kong Police; the former Federation Police of Malaya, whose commission during the post–World War II period was to quell communist insurrection; and the Indian Police, whose loyalty to the Indian National Congress was instrumental to that country's independence. The aforementioned parallels between Hong Kong and Ireland are also recalled in the fate of the Dublin Metropolitan Police, which, like the Hong Kong Police, elicited sufficient popular favor that it was absorbed into the wholly civil Garda Siochana. Indeed, the last governor of Hong Kong, Christopher Patten, is now a prominent policymaker in the negotiations over the Royal Ulster Constabulary (soon to be renamed the Police Service of Northern Ireland), and the fact of the Irish Republican Army complicates Irish policing much like the Chinese PLA shaped Hong Kong. In a last instance of the career imperial official applying experience from one colonial front to another, Patten's intervention in the debate over the Irish police illustrates Hong Kong's legacy for the devolutionary processes currently at work in other former imperial forces.

The historiography of the Hong Kong Police is itself an elusive entity. Many of the government's official records of police activity were destroyed during World War II, under orders from the colonial administration to prevent the records from being assessed by the occupying Japanese. This absence of an extensive archive on the police prevents corrections to the triumphal accounts the institution and colonial historians might offer and also may encourage false impressions of the bureau's postwar emergence as a fully formed institution. Much of the current empirical data on the Hong Kong police is the result of public opinion surveys (significantly, a statistical form of evaluation that is itself a remnant of the administration's originally imperial scientific practices) that are constantly levied by the local government or is the work of M.A. theses in sociology authored by Hong Kong Police officers who hope to achieve promotion by attaining an advanced degree. Although neither of these bodies of research are objective data themselves, they call attention to the police as a self-interested institution. Hong Kong's bilingual environment also complicates historical research. Scholars not proficient in written Chinese or the Cantonese dialect (of which I am one) may unknowingly reproduce bias due to their inability to use oral history and their exclusive use of official documents that historically were maintained only in English. Perhaps it is appropriate that a primary source of information on the Hong Kong Police is the considerable number of commercial publications that were designed for popular interest (see the notes to this essay). These popular histories testify to the public relations savvy of the local police bureau, as well as to the enthusiasm with which Hong Kong culture views them, and are intriguing examples of late twentieth-century imperial propaganda.

I want to close by positing the history of the Hong Kong police as a foil to the influential "End of History" argument Francis Fukuyama published in 1989. Fukuyama's essay claimed the global triumph of Western liberal and democratic ideologies at the end of the twentieth century. The essay was written when the protests that would result in the massacre at Tiananmen Square were gathering and cited this evident unrest in China as proof of the penetration of decentralized inclinations that ethnically comparable countries such as Taiwan had already embraced. "Maoism," Fukuyama asserted, had become "an anachronism." Fukuyama stated that "the People's Republic of China can no longer act as a beacon for illiberal forces around the world."[10] But Hong Kong defies Fukuyama's claims on several levels. At the time Fukuyama was writing, the quintessentially capitalist territory already was awaiting reunification with the archetypal ideological state and hence was precisely the exception to Fukuyama's rule. More important, in contradistinction to Fukuyama's claims of decentralization and capitalism as indices of postauthoritarianism, Hong Kong's manifold social, political, economic, and cultural investment in the police instantiates the embrace by such a liberal and capitalist society of a centralized structure directly associated with colonial authoritarianism. Most important, such a counterintuitive turn by Hong Kong toward centralization was explicitly conceived to counteract Maoist centralization, and hence paradoxically an increase in police powers is precisely its sign of identification with Western democracy. Clearly, Fukuyama's blanket statement about the breakdown in authoritarianism throughout Chinese society was premature. Only a few months after the publication of Fukuyama's essay, the massacre at Tiananmen Square occurred.

Hong Kong's exception to Fukuyama's generalizations is rich with irony. Hong Kong is not Taiwan, an ethnic Chinese nation with several centuries of local history preceding its short-lived colonial occupation by a non-Western power. Hong Kong arguably never anticipated an autonomous future, nor could it cultivate an identification with the West as a purely liberating expression. Thatcherism and Maoism look surprisingly similar when they both result in increased power — an oddity that certainly belies Fukuyama's projection about the fall of communism — but the fact that Hong Kong citizens showed a greater tolerance than Britons for increased police powers was in fact the colony's attempt to defend itself against Maoism. My purpose in addressing Fukuyama is to show how in the case of Hong Kong the territory's perfect inversion of his overly dialectical claims might have obscured the colony's real historical insight: that a nationalism considered oppressive in the first world may be a liberating and positive force in the third world or among stateless or otherwise disenfranchised populations; that institutional inertia in structures such as the police can precipitate unanticipated outcomes, as was the case in the actions of Deng Xiao-peng; and that such claims about "the end of history" might be better applied to traditional modes of historiographical scholarship. I offer the history of the Hong Kong Police — an anachronistic reproduction of the British bobby, albeit now with a Chinese face — as testament to the paradoxical persistence of colonial forms in a new world order distinguished for devolution.

Notes

I am grateful to Antoinette Burton, Lisa Kim Davis, Vicki Hsueh, Lara Kriegel, and Donal Lowry for their comments.

1   During the handover era popular interest in the police was evident in 1983 by the runaway success of Kevin Sinclair and Stephanie Holmes, *Asia's Finest: An Illustrated Account of the Royal Hong Kong Police* (Hong Kong: Unicorn, 1983), an unsolicited book that became a best-seller. It was followed in 1997 by the commissioned volume, Kevin Sinclair with Kwok-Cheung Nelson Ng, *Asia's Finest Marches On: Policing Hong Kong from 1841 – Into the 21st Century* (Hong Kong: Kevin Sinclair Associates, 1997), which also was a best-seller. The handover era also saw Kevin Sinclair, *Royal Hong Kong Police, 1844 – 1944: 100th Anniversary Commemorative Publication* (Hong Kong: Police Public Relations Bureau, 1994), a volume commissioned by the police. Both of these commissioned works figured the police as a sign of continuity during reunification.

2   The standard and popular histories of the Hong Kong Police from which this essay draws include the following: Jon Vagg, "Policing Hong Kong," *Policing and Society* 1, 3 (1991): 235–249; Colin Criswell and Mike Watson, *The Royal Hong Kong Police (1841–1945)* (Hong Kong: Macmillan, 1982); Kathleen Harland, *The Royal Navy in Hong Kong since 1841* (Liskeard, Cornwall, U.K.: Maritime Books, 1991); P. J. Melson, ed., *White Ensign, Red Dragon: The History of the Royal Navy in Hong Kong 1841–1941* (Hong Kong: Edinburgh Financial Publishing, 1997); Iain Ward, *Sui Geng: The Hong Kong Marine Police, 1841–1950* (Hong Kong: University of Hong Kong Press, 1991); Harold Traver and Jon Vagg, eds., *Crime and Justice in Hong Kong* (Hong Kong: Oxford University Press, 1991); Raymond Wacks, ed., *Police Powers in Hong Kong: Problems and Prospects* (Hong Kong: Faculty of Law, University of Hong Kong, 1993).

3   Norman Miners, "The Localization of the Hong Kong Police Force," *Journal of Imperial and Commonwealth History* 18, 3 (1990): 296–315.

4   The history of colonial policing is an emerging field. See David M. Anderson and David Killingray, eds.: *Policing the Empire: Government, Authority, and Control, 1830–1940* (Manchester: Manchester University Press, 1991), and *Policing and Decolonisation: Politics, Nationalism, and the Police, 1917–1965* (Manchester: Manchester University Press, 1992); Mike Brogden, "The Emergence of the Police: The Colonial Dimension," *British Journal of Criminology* 27, 1 (1987): 4–14, which notes the ironies of British criticism of its own domestic police system as reminiscent of Hong Kong's.

5   Ng Bing-wu, *The Art of Fingerprints* (1919).

6   *Market Survey on Police Recruitment and Advertisements: An Executive Summary* (MDR Technology, 1991).

7   On public health in Hong Kong, see Philippa Levine, "Modernity, Medicine, and Colonialism: The Contagious Diseases Ordinances in Hong Kong and the Straits Settlements," in *Gender, Sexuality and Colonial Modernities*, ed. Antoinette Burton (London: Routledge, 1999), pp. 35–49. On education, see the work of Anthony Sweeting: *Education in Hong Kong, pre-1841 to 1941* (Hong Kong: University of Hong Kong Press, 1990), and *A Phoenix Transformed: The Reconstruction of Education in Post-War Hong Kong* (Hong Kong: Oxford University Press, 1993); Gerard A. Postiglione, ed., *Education and Society in Hong Kong: Toward One Country and Two Systems* (Hong Kong: University of Hong Kong Press, 1992). On public housing, see Manuel Castells, L. Goh, and R. Yin-Wang Kwok, *The Shek Kip Mei Syndrome: Economic Development and Public Housing in Hong Kong and Singapore* (London: Pion, 1990); Robin Hutcheon, *High-Rise Society: The First 50 Years of the Hong Kong Housing Society* (Hong Kong: Chinese University Press, 1999).

8   On the history of police in China, see Alison Dray-Novey, "Spatial Order and Police in Imperial Beijing," *Journal of Asian Studies* 52, 4 (1993): 885–922; Hwei-shung Gao, "Police Administration in Canton," *Chinese Social and Political Science Review* 10 (1926): 332–354, 669–698, 872–890; Frederick Wakeman Jr., "Policing Modern Shanghai," *China Quarterly* 115 (1988): 408–440. On alternative forms of social organization and organic support for police, see Aline Wong, *The Kaifong Associations and the Society of Hong Kong* (Taipei: Orient Cultural Service, 1972); Yiu Kong Chu, *The Triads as Business* (New York: Routledge, 1999).

9   On the Independent Commission against Corruption (ICAC), see Rance P. L. Lee, ed., *Corruption and Its Control in Hong Kong: Situations up to the Late Seventies* (Hong Kong: Chinese University Press, 1981); Max J. Skidmore, "Promise and Peril in Combating Corruption: Hong Kong's ICAC," in Max J. Skidmore, *The Future of Hong Kong* (Thousand Oaks, Calif.: Sage Periodicals Press, 1996), pp. 118–130. On the Police Public Rela-

tions Bureau, see Karen Fang, "Arresting Cinema: Surveillance and the City-State in the Representation of Hong Kong," *New Formations* 44, 2 (2001): 128–150.

10 Francis Fukuyama, "The End of History?" *The National Interest*, summer 1989: 3–18. Reprinted in Francis Fukuyama, *The End of History and the Last Man* (New York: Free Press, 1992).

JOHN PLOTZ

One-Way Traffic: George Lamming
and the Portable Empire

All the books they read, their whole introduction to something called culture, all of it, in
the form of words, came from outside: Dickens, Jane Austen, Kipling and that sacred
gang. The West Indian's education was imported in much the same way that flour and
butter are imported from Canada.
— George Lamming, *The Pleasures of Exile*

George Lamming's 1960 *The Pleasures of Exile*[1] situates the Barbadian-born
novelist squarely in a familiar postcolonial tradition.[2] In that book, the hegemonic force of British imports, both physical and metaphysical (from butter to
Austen), is imagined as making the colonial subject mimetically into a version
of the colonizing country. Shakespeare's *The Tempest* is that book's most striking example of the West Indian colonial condition. This is in part because the
text represents the colonial situation, but also because the play itself was exported to the West Indies, thus becoming part of the very colonial legacy on
which it reflects.[3]

But Lamming's *In the Castle of My Skin* (1953) depicts British objects operating in quite a different way. That novel, Lamming's first, intervenes tellingly
in debates that raged then, and rage now with even more force, on the nature
of the cultural legacy inflicted on a colony by its conquerors and long-term
owners. Thirty years after his last substantial work and at a scholarly moment
when new ways of parsing both the imperial turn and postcoloniality itself
have returned us to aesthetic texts as avenues into ideological formations,
Lamming's novels reward reevaluation. They have always appeared to be a
direct response to the logic of trade and imperial expansion that made even the
postcolonial West Indies seem an overseas extension of British culture. But our
new attention to the relationship between postcoloniality and globalization
and a renewed scholarly interest in material culture make Lamming's novels
seem something more as well.[4] In his six novels — but most notably in *In the
Castle of my Skin* and *Natives of My Person* — Lamming reveals the ways in which
"the whole sacred gang" of British high culture singularly fails to take hold in

the postcolonial context — even at the moments when such portable imperial culture seems most triumphant.

To acquiesce to the force of the colonial mind-set, Lamming suggests, is "in silence or with rhetoric . . . [to] sign a contract whose epitaph reads: To be in exile is to be alive."[5] But Lamming thinks there is a way out of such an acceptance of exile: it comes by discovering that one's imaginary motherland, the England that made and shaped one, bears no relation to the England of the English. In other words, by refusing its imaginary hold, one can discover that the seeming portability of the imperial motherland is an illusion. In that sense, Lamming's work seems a striking prognosticator of the nature of debates about a distinctively postcolonial literary form (debates that have shaped the field in important contributions by Jameson, Ahmad, During, Hulme, Beverly, and others).[6]

The key question that Lamming approaches is arguably the most important question for framing postcolonial studies today: what is to be made of the export objects that colonizers offered as fetish representatives of the metropole? How, in other words, did British object lessons function in a colonial context to enforce a sense that the metropole is not a distant actor *upon* but a proximal actor *within* a colonial space? That question has been approached in a wide variety of ways by a recent wave of vigorous postcolonial scholarship: in recent years books like Gauri Viswanathan's *Masks of Conquest* and work by such subaltern studies scholars as Gyan Prakash have proposed that the story of British "hegemony" in India be rethought in terms of the complicated struggles among various models for how culture was to be transmitted from the mother country to the colony. And works such as Peter Hulme's have alerted scholars of the Caribbean to the complicated questions of hybridity and dissemination that C. L. R. James's *Black Jacobins* had broached in the 1960s.[7]

However, Lamming's particular contribution to the West Indian debate on the colonial legacy offers a rather different way to evaluate the postcolonial condition. If the best work by Viswanathan, for example, has focused on the export of "culture" read as a dematerialized set of practices and customers, there has also recently been a vigorous scholarly attention toward what is labeled "global circulations" in Lydia Liu's recent collection, *Tokens of Exchange*. Such work, building as it does on both world systems theory and Marxist accounts of commodity exchange and responding to the material turn evidenced in Arjun Appadurai's magisterial collection, *The Social Life of Things*, has opened the way to make postcolonial studies into a detritus field — that is, a field that studies the objects that make up the global trade by which colonies were both initially justified and sustained.[8] Justified because the export of the objects of religion played a key role in legitimating colonization in the first place; sustained because it was the successful export of Britishness itself (tea-cups, domestic interiors, flags, and all manner of civilian materiel) that made the colonies seem livable extensions of Britain itself. Lamming brilliantly ana-tomizes the ways in which British objects, passed down or pressed onto colo-nial subjects, are imagined, from a British perspective, as capable of shaping lives coercively — and anatomizes as well the ways that such objects work in-stead to produce an odd kind of imaginative freedom.

* * *

A telling debate at the heart of *In the Castle of My Skin* spotlights Lamming's interest in classifying the British objects that help both to define and to control the West Indies. The novel at this point is collectively narrated by a group of boys to whom every object is an occasion for the same sort of inconclusive debate that rages about the doubloon nailed to the mast of the *Pequod* midway through *Moby Dick*.[9] In this case, the object is the British penny that each boy has received at a school prize day. As soon as the gift is received, the debates begin among the boys:

Some said it was a drawing of the king made with a pin while the copper was soft. . . . It was a long and patient undertaking. But it had to be done if there was going to be any money at all, an everyone knew how important money was. [Others said] it was very silly to argue that such a job would be done by sensible people. And the English who were the only people in the world to deal with pennies were very sensible.[10]

This debate frames the production of money for Barbados as a gift of the English. Because the children believe that only the English make pennies, they also believe necessarily that there must be both a reason for their production and a reasonable way to produce them. The challenge is to read the mind of the imperium. And the debate is configured around a competition as to who can successfully ventriloquize the penny. Those pennies thus become something like the commodities that Marx believed were capable of bringing their owners to market, or even of making their owners into agents of their (objective) will.

Theories proliferate among the boys; one is that "it was the same penny all the time." The portraits of the king on the penny will not vary because "The king could never find time to press all the pennies in the world."

One penny, that is the first penny ever made, was the real penny, and all the others were made by a kind of stamp. You simply had to get the first penny, and the necessary materials and thousands followed. That meant, someone asked, that you couldn't spend the first penny. Someone wanted to know how the first penny was made. . . . [The penny was made and heated and] finally sent to the king who pressed it on one side of his face.[11]

If this account begins to seem allegorical of the relationship between these boys and their distant ruler — that is, if the later pennies made from that first penny begin to sound like copper-colored allegorical figures for the "Brown Briton" boys themselves — so much the better.

Why does Lamming decide to go on at such length staging this debate on the meaning of the pennies? The absurdity that prevails as each unlikely theory about the penny's origin is introduced is not merely contingent, but also central to the meaning of these debates. The incredible quality of these explanations is exactly the point.

Ngùgì wa Thiong'o's influential account, "George Lamming's *In the Castle of My Skin*," sees the explanations as moving toward a real understanding of the colonial condition. He argues that in this novel, "the yardstick is England. Everything that affects the tender minds of the children is geared towards veneration of England and the British throne."[12] But the yardstick is precisely not the real England. Instead it is the imaginary England that has been summoned up in the children's minds. The final thesis advanced by one of the children is that the king is not responsible for that image because "the king was never seen" and all images flow only from a kind of "shadow king."[13]

That notion of the invisible but omnipotent shadow king points to Lamming's real intent here. The wholesale importation of "Dickens, Jane Austen, Kipling and that sacred gang" has produced not a comprehensive but rather a kind of "shadow" Britishness, and that shadow's relationship to its original is fundamentally unmappable. Just as the children that a "shadow king" sires will have no genetic relationship to the "real king," the daydreams sparked by these shadow imports will have, Lamming supposes, no true relationship to the site from whence the objects came. The children's accounts of the object they see before them is grounded not in evidence but in imagination and is arrived at neither by extrapolation nor interpolation, but pure and simple speculation.

To understand the postcolonial rebellion against British portable objects, as articulated in Lamming, means in part to understand why such exportable objects as those copper pennies came with such significant cultural adhesions, such "aura" as Walter Benjamin put it, attached. The carefully satirical set piece on pennies is oriented against an ideology that had imagined the perfect *portability* of the British nation (and of an imperial culture) by way of objects. Lamming conjures up a world in which the creation of a plausible past for the imported artifact is fatally compromised by the very act of imagination that is required to constitute the object as a lesson of the empire. That is, all the meaning that seems to inhere in the object is actually conjured up by its interpreter. That claim is both necessary and striking because Lamming is writing against an inherited set of object lessons that posit the perfect transmissibility of British culture abroad.

Consider, for example, a British tea service laid out by Britons in India. What is it that makes the object's meaning in India seem to depend upon the object's original meaning in England? Flora Annie Steel, in her 1899 *On the Face of the Waters*, has her heroine call her English garden of "heartease and sweet peas" in India "the shadow of a rock in a dusty land" and go on to describe such parlor appurtenances as a piano in the same terms.[14] Home notes sound loudest. Even playing Beethoven, even struck by Indian hands, the "old country" piano must operate as a marker of Britishness in the Raj.

Like the beloved "old willow-ware" that reminds the sea captain in Emily Eden's *The Semi-Detached House* of life back home, English objects in a range of nineteenth-century British accounts are what make the old island palpably present. To make one's country or family or even oneself feel "at home" overseas required the successful transplantation of not only culture in the most abstract sense, but also of "material culture," rooted in tangible objects.[15] Tea-kettles, Bibles, lockets, and portable copies of Shakespeare instantiate the homeland overseas. The British in India, in Kenya, in the West Indies strung out a sense of their distant metropole in every public space, recreated it in every private interior.[16] Flora Annie Steel's *Complete Indian Housekeeper* at century's end listed all the English items available at good Delhi markets (salad oil, tinned fish) that made an Indian house a para-English one.[17] And Emily Eden's *Up the Country*, letters written from the Indian hinterland in the 1840s, details her ability to create upon an alien landscape an illusion of British domesticity — though it might take a retinue of several hundred servants to implement that feeling of home.[18]

It should not be surprising that it is often literary works, those most culturally loaded of objects, that are imagined as best at constructing parochial Englishness abroad. Consider, for example, Rudyard Kipling's fascinating 1926 short story, "The Janeites," a convincing testament to the felt power of a Jane Austen novel to create an entire English world once Austen has become an object exportable in people's minds, not just their valises. In Kipling's account, it is a shared knowledge of Jane Austen's world (acquired through conversation and the passage of battered texts from hand to hand) that enables true Britons to recognize one another overseas.[19]

Does it make any difference to a Briton's ability to arrive in India unchanged if his collection of Jane Austen novels has arrived there with him? Kipling's account supposes that it does, because in that motion overseas the Austen novels have become metonymical for those "middling counties of England." It is just this that West Indian writers like Lamming understand as the strongest claim that literature can make—and as the most threatening form of imperial extension into the West Indies. For if the book, suitably laden with cultural freight, can be accepted as a piece of Britain, then the imaginative force of literary conquest will have seemed not to triumph, but actually to disappear: there is no literature here anymore, simply a piece of England transported whole to these islands. Literature's triumph would therefore be its disappearance too if imperial mimesis is to become the ultimate ending of any text sent overseas "as England."

This sort of substitutive logic may seem familiar from our understanding of "regional" literature. Consider, for example, the claim of local particularity that is registered by Thomas Hardy's Wessex novels, in which the world of Wessex is definitively bounded by the province (these people belong only here) yet also made exportable as a kind of curio piece contained within the novel itself (a "taste of Wessex").[20] But there is a crucial difference. Hardy offers a representation of Wessex that will not lend itself to that world being recreated as a living whole. Kipling's "Janeites," though, implies that Austen's local truth will function abroad to make up England. The middling counties are suddenly transportable anywhere Austen is legible, so that one can imagine reconstituting England's culture, just as dried soups can be reconstituted to allow British cuisine (terrifying thought) to travel overseas.

It comes to seem, then, that the existence of England overseas depends, in an imperial age, upon the triumph of a readily portable culture, concretized in certain key culture-laden artifacts. This conception of a Britain made portable by way of objects continues, in some forms unaltered, through the middle of the twentieth century.[21] Evelyn Waugh's 1934 "The Man Who Loved Dickens" marks one important break, after which the successful dissemination of British culture (here by way of Dickens) begins to seem not a triumph but a curse on Britain, as its colonial children use that culture to turn the tables on the colonizer.[22] Waugh's account of the terrors that occur when Dickens is made available to racial aliens like the illiterate Mr. Todd (who had to kidnap the Englishman Tony Last to serve as his reader) suggests that it is time to close the floodgates, to truncate the flow of portable objects so as to save little England from the Greater Britain it has—Waugh gloomily believes—successfully created. However, a larger shift is in store. By 1950, in the work of the first post–World War II (and post–Indian independence) generation of West Indian writers, the very idea of portable British culture at times seems not simply outmoded, but fatally flawed from the outset. Small wonder, perhaps, that Australian David Malouf's *Remembering Babylon* begins with a colonial subject crying, "Don't shoot! I am a B-b-b-british Object!"[23]

The problematic of imperial dissemination by way of imperial objects does not inevitably produce a Lamming-like response. Indeed, the responses of writers from the margins of empire to imperial notions of object portability do not always differ widely from the metropolitan accounts that the well-educated colonial imbibes.[24] And even when they do, the results may serve circuitously to affirm the effect that British imperial objects were imagined to have.

There are many writers of the ex-colonized world who accept the legacy of the successfully portaged object and turn to the question of assessing the damage that such objects have done. What have these objects done to us, some writers worry, by manufacturing illusory accounts of that "other life" back in the motherland, the "imaginary homeland"? Salman Rushdie's *Midnight's Children* (1980) brilliantly anatomizes this worry in its account of the allegorical Methwold Estates. Sold to Indians at the moment of independence, the "Estates" are handed over on condition that all its artifacts are left untouched — whisky bottles and glasses, toilet paper, pictures of sweating old Englishmen. The (purely intentional) effect is that within a month the residents are gathering on the veranda for cocktail hour, telling stories of past glories in pseudo-Oxford accents.[25]

After such portability, Rushdie asks, what revenge? What is to be made now of these no longer new things, these "star commodities" that arrive on our shores with their Englishness and imperial might seemingly intact?[26] Rushdie jokes in *Midnight's Children* about the mother country's abiding hold: a radio arrives labeled not "made in England" but "made as England." Whatever comes from the mother country, home of all objects and of all objectivity, serves in the still colonial space as more than a symbol, as a metonymic portion of that mother. Seeing the English object, one thinks more of its country of origin than of the object itself. Go looking for Britain, and it recedes before you; invent it from what has been sent you, and a complete life, seemingly imported from abroad, is on offer. But Anglophone West Indian writers have addressed that legacy somewhat differently.[27] Derek Walcott, for instance, makes colonial deprivation meaningful only by contrasting it to the imagined wealth of the "essential" culture brought from overseas: "Colonials, we began with this malarial enervation: that nothing could ever be built among these rotting shacks, barefooted back yards, and moulting shingle. . . . We knew the literature of empires, Greek, Roman, British, through their essential classics."[28] And V. S. Naipaul, in both *The Mimic Men* (1967) and *A Bend in the River* (1979), takes a look at British objects that seem no longer to hold the sway they should over colonial subjects, and the effect of his examination is to produce an account of colonial imagination that is surprisingly similar to Lamming's. Certainly Naipaul, born in 1932, who sailed (like Lamming) from Trinidad to England in 1950, is of a generation to know something of such colonial nostalgia. To some critics, his work is nothing but variations on that nostalgia — slow discoveries of various ways in which former meaning has waned and left the world the dimmer for it. Trains, stamps, steamboats are all part of the vanished European legacy in *A Bend in the River*, and at times it is hard not to feel that Naipaul fervently believes all can be restored to their colonial magnitude.[29]

That nostalgia, however, is only a way that characters persuade themselves that they once had, and so could have again, a closer relationship to the imperial center than they have now. In Naipaul's account, only two sorts of Western objects endure: denuded trade goods and irrationally aura-laden memorabilia. *A Bend in the River* seems to set up the waning presence of Europeans in Zaire as emblematic of a postcolonial fall away from civilization more generally. In the place of the bygone era of memorable European products — faded posters for Italian wines, postage stamps whereby even illiterate Arab slave traders could learn their own history, a calendar that brought order into the timeless chaos of pre-European lives[30] — Naipaul sees a grubby trade in fungibles, marking the failure of any admirable postcolonial life to replace the vanished empire. The perfect emblem for the diminished flow of culture after the captains and the kings depart is imported zinc basins: "It was antiquated junk, specially made for shops like mine, and I doubt whether the workmen who made the stuff — in Europe and the United States and perhaps nowadays Japan — had any idea what their products were used for." The actual use to which they are put, these deliberately denuded objects, could not possibly have been envisioned back in the first world: "The smaller basins for instance, were in demand because they were good for keeping grubs alive in, packed in damp fibre and marsh earth."[31]

Salim, the protagonist, pointedly distinguishes these basins from the objects that seem still filled with all the allure of neocolonial power. He has a palpable addiction to first world popular science magazines, filled with pictures of what "they" are doing in Europe — "they" being not so much Europeans as scientists of any race, inventors in sterile labs, "people far away from us in every sense."[32] The entire appeal of the magazines is theoretical, or rather, they are appealing because they bespeak a practical meaning for objects that Salim cannot imagine ever entering Zaire. Guy Debord describes the "star commodity," an object that marks the advent of technologically superior North to the retarded South.[33] But in Naipaul's account, the commodity remains a star precisely by not arriving, by not contaminating itself with actual exposure to the zone of retardation.

These inventions are appealing precisely on account of their unavailability. Should a Western object actually successfully arrive in Zaire, it could not help but be corrupted. When a "Big Burger" franchise arrives and thrives, Salim sees it only as a lowest common denominator where corrupt Zairean culture meets the worst of the West. When Salim begins an affair with a Western woman, Yvette, he wants only to possess her while she remains untouched by someone like him. He desperately wants objects to preserve their distant purity of Western promise ("made as England"), and yet he wants those objects right here simultaneously, wants them to enter his life while holding on to their chilly Northern distance from him.

Rather than constructing a suitable way for the portable European object to continue flourishing in this fallen present, however, Naipaul anatomizes the illusions that go along with imagining that European culture is a way out of one's provincial life. Like Lamming with the copper penny, Naipaul plunges into the realm of European objects to pick out one that exemplifies the work that goes into inventing the meaning that seems embedded in a Western object. He does so most tellingly in an earlier novel, *The Mimic Men*. There, he tells the story of a portable British property that never existed and yet overshadowed in the colonized mind objects that actually did: "My first memory of school is of taking an apple to the teacher. This puzzles me. We had no apples on Isabella. It must have been an orange; yet my memory insists on the apple. The editing is clearly at fault, but the edited version is all I have."[34] This apple actually erases the local object and replaces it with what has never been imported. Naipaul can conceive the European portable object's surviving, but only within this edited imaginary world. If the Lamming penny made the boys create in their minds an elaborate England that never existed, the apple creates the poignant illusion of a Western boyhood for someone who lived in a realm where the objects necessary for such a boyhood were not provided, even though the narratives of such boyhoods were.

Naipaul once claimed that "Nothing was created in the West Indies," but the conjuring up of this apple strikes me as a very telling kind of creation, most telling perhaps because the act of creation seems to do no more than mimic the colonizer.[35] Naipaul is experimenting here with something like Du Bois's notion of the "double consciousness" belonging to African Americans living in "the world within . . . the Veil."[36] In Naipaul, the narrator's conviction that the apple memory is simultaneously true and false makes him a single subject who exists both inside the bounds of empire and outside of them. Inside the Veil, the apple is real only in thoughts of the distant motherland, imaginary when associated with one's own provincial home. This form of double consciousness, though, is defined by distance; one's veiled relationship is to the proximal seeming yet distant motherland via the exported objects that arrive to constitute it — via those objects that promise to arrive and never do so. To live beneath the Veil as a "Black Briton" is to construe oneself as British until the moment that one actually arrives in Britain.

Lamming's parable of the pennies turns a seeming deficit into a hidden strength because it credits West Indian distance from the metropolis with endowing its residents with a powerful imaginative life. The West Indian imagination, by this account, is only putatively engaged in interpreting England's objects. In reality, it uses those objects as occasions for the most fabulous invention. Like Homi Bhabha's account of colonial "mimicry" as mimesis that fails even by succeeding, Lamming's account of imaginative interpretation suggests that the very moment at which colonial subjects may seem most invested in their imperial antecedents is the moment at which they have already broken with that empire.[37]

In the penny parable Lamming is, like Sarah Orne Jewett in "The Queen's Twin," praising the imagination that arises around a few scrap mementos as a far more powerful force in the world than mere mundane experience of one's surroundings.[38] In Jewett's 1899 story, the protagonist, Abby Martin, born the same day as Queen Victoria and linked to her by various other seemingly significant coincidences, builds up a collection of pictures of the queen, as well as a fantasy life of secret communication, a life that Jewett finds more admirable than living resignedly in one's own provincial locale.[39] Abby enters into feeling communion with the queen, who is made tangible to her not by pennies but by magazine illustrations and articles. Such imagination is a purely provincial power; her urbane friend, a frequent traveler to England, is incapable of experiencing the kind of thrill these illustrations bring to Abby. As a friend tells her at the climax of "The Queen's Twin," "Don't it show that for folks that have any fancy in 'em, such beautiful dreams is the real part o' life? But to most folks the common things that happen outside 'em is all in all."[40]

Like Jewett, Lamming supposes that the necessary illusions out of which provincial life is made can endow the writer or reader or colonial subject with an imaginative power far exceeding any metropolitan assets. It is not that the colonial objects really bring England with them, nor is it the case that they lie in seeming to do so. Rather, they offer a set of inimitable dreams. Provincial life is shaped not by imported objects, but by the illusion that life is shaped by these imported objects.

Lamming's claim about the force of such necessary illusions is perhaps best articulated in his most recent novel, *Natives of My Person* (1972), an allegorical retelling of such New World exploration narratives as Richard Hakluyt's *Voyages*.[41] The book evidently owes much to *Moby Dick* as well, although here Ahab's quest for the white whale comes across as another version of the quest for the New World.[42] One can begin to understand how Lamming anatomizes the appeal of the imperial object for the provincial subject by noting that *"Inside the Castle of My Skin"* and *"Natives of My Person"* are almost identical titles. Both assert a kind of corporate unity that underlies the apparent disaggregation of persons: all these voices that you hear, scattered all over the social map, are in reality joined together within "my" experience.

The "insideness" of the first novel's skin castle echoes Teresa of Avila's castle, that spiritual retreat from the world. At the same time "skin," in the racialized consciousness of a West Indian subject, necessarily connects that retreat to the persistent master-slave relations that depend on color coding. *"Natives of My Person"* seems to offer the same formulation because it too offers a way for a collection of voices, thoughts, selves, to be gathered under a single roof, within a single life. The novel tells of the voyage of a quixotically driven Commandant and of various of his crew (Steward, Surgeon, Boat-Swain) through diaries, voices, dialogue, the manic recollections of the Commandant himself, and finally "The Women" at sea in another ship altogether.[43]

Yet the context within which the title phrase appears in the latter novel suggests ways in which the corporatism of the earlier novel has been replaced by something a bit more difficult to parse. At the book's end, when the three central characters — Surgeon, Steward, and Commandant — are already dead, their wives and lovers, stranded somewhere in the New World and still expecting their arrival, speak of the way that their own lives are shaped, as women, by submission to another's will. This is a submission that has the effect of forming their subjectivity, in that their decision to make another's life a resident part of their own means that their own actions are effectively taken as agents for that other:

Surgeon's Wife: It was what I had to do. He was a piece of my person.
Steward's Wife: It is the same. My husband had become that too: a native of my
    person. Whenever there is a crisis, we must choose against our interests.[44]

What makes the moment poignant is that death has already dissevered them from those imagined natives of their person, so that their assertion that they are not acting but simply continuing the action of others is undermined by the fact that those dominant others are not left to act. Their own subjective status is revised by the fact that they have become the agents, in effect the objects, of others who no longer exist.

In order to live, Lamming holds, people require the impression that they are working for those persons and objects that surround and define their lives. Thus even at the moment in which their connection to those others has been severed, they continue to imagine those others inhabiting them. Be it the other the king's penny or the dead husband, the form of imaginary connection is equally strong. But finally all these seeming inhabitations of one's own thoughts by the mind of another, or by the imported objects that make up a world, are a form of fetish, a productive illusion. The pluralization in the title — so that one "native of my person" turns into "natives of my person" — seems to suggest that Lamming contains all of his characters as beloved natives. But it also suggests that his own relationship to those others whom his prose ought to contain and indeed to speak for is profoundly unsettled, as illusory (and as productive) as that imagined affinity to a distant Britain mediated through its coinage.

In a recent appraisal of C. L. R. James's *Mariners, Renegades and Castaways*, Donald Pease specifies James's investment in responding to and rewriting *Moby-Dick*. Pease argues that James writes to register "the horror of Melville's failure to provide the crew with the power to revolt against their monomaniacal captain."[45] James's indictment of Melville is echoed in *Natives of My Person*, which rewrites *Moby-Dick* in such a way as finally to liberate the crew from the Commandant's dead hand.

But Lamming goes farther. The revision to *Moby-Dick* proposed in *Natives of My Person* functions not only against Melville, but also against James's acceptance of the ultimate dependence of a West Indian intellectual on the canonical texts of the Anglo-American world. In Lamming's account, James's choice to "number oneself among the mariners, renegades and castaways" (as Pease believes James did) may seem to offer liberatory alternatives but actually traps one within a false conception of the colonial world.[46] *Natives of My Person* fantasizes the discovery that all our imagined connections to those who hold sway over us (our husbands, our captains, our nations) are a delusion from the beginning. And having recognized that delusion, one realizes that one was never subservient to that authority, that the force contained in those guiding British precepts and objects was all along a product of one's own mind, not inherent in the things themselves.

In *Natives of My Person*, the seeming triumph of asserting that one contains another as a "native of one's person" is the psychological corollary to the state of colonization. Both hinge on the delusion that objects and messages can traverse the ocean unimpeded, bearing with them a perfect replica of original intent. Rushdie's Methwold Estates are intended as a satire that bemoans the effectiveness of imperial colonization. By contrast, Lamming tells the story of portable treasures that do not portage any meaning with them; he tells the story of "incorporation" founded on lies or on mistakes. In so doing, he returns to the foundational conceit of overseas colonies and crafts a response devastating not because it topples an old order, but because it suggests that that old order itself had never existed.

Peter Hulme rightly identifies elements of Fredric Jameson's notion of the postcolonial novel as "national allegory" that fit Lamming's work.[47] For Hulme, Lamming's interest in "the shaping of national consciousness" depends on what Hulme calls "an imaginative reassessment of the relationship between metropolis and ex-colony."[48] In fact, *Natives of My Person* makes an even stronger claim: that the shaping of national consciousness comes not by rejecting the colonial culture, but by recognizing that one's seeming ingestion of that culture had all along been an illusion. It turns out that your whole life you had been speaking postcolonial prose and dreaming postcolonial dreams without knowing it.

Notes

1 George Lamming, *The Pleasures of Exile* (Ann Arbor: University of Michigan Press, 1992 [1960]), p. 27.

2 Sandra Pouchet Poquet sums up the critical consensus in the first line of her *Dictionary of Literary Biography* entry: "George Lamming is one of the great Caribbean writers on the subject of decolonization and national reconstruction." "George Lamming," in *Twentieth Century Caribbean and Black African Writers*, 2d series, *Dictionary of Literary Biography*, ed. Bernth Lindfors and Reinhard Sander (Detroit: Gale, 1993), p. 54. Born in Barbados in 1927, emigrated to England in 1950, Lamming is the author of one influential book of essays, *The Pleasures of Exile*, as well as six novels: *In the Castle of My Skin* (1953), *The Emigrants* (1954), *Of Age and Innocence* (1958), *Season of Adventure* (1960), *Water with Berries* (1972), and *Natives of My Person* (1972). He currently divides his time between the United States and Barbados.

3 Frantz Fanon's roughly contemporary *Wretched of the Earth* is one striking example of a similar exploration of the creation of colonial subjects as dark mirrors for their colonizers. The rise of subaltern studies (marked by, for example, Ranajit Guha, "On Some Aspects of the Historiography of Colonial India," *Subaltern Studies* 1: 1–9, is another; but see also the most recent anthologies: Ranajit Guha, ed., *A Subaltern Studies Reader* [Minneapolis: University of Minnesota Press, 1997], and Vinayak Chaturvedi, ed., *Mapping Subaltern Studies and the Postcolonial* [London: Verso, 2000]) is largely constituted as an extension of the legacy of Gramsci in "Marxist heterodoxy" (Chaturvedi's formulation), but it has evolved recently through the work of Chakrabarty, Spivak, and others) into a response to Fanon as well. Another influential response comes in Homi Bhabha, "Of Mimicry and Man: The Ambivalence of Colonial Discourse," *October* 28 (1984): 125–133.

4 Simon During, "Postcolonialism and Globalization: Towards a Historicization of Their Inter-Relation," *Cultural Studies* 14 (2000): 385–404.

5 Lamming, *The Pleasures of Exile*, p. 24.

6 John Beverly, *Against Literature* (Minneapolis: University of Minnesota Press, 1993). Other works cited below.

7 Gauri Viswanathan, *Masks of Conquest: Literary Study and British Rule in India* (New York: Columbia University Press, 1989); Gyan Prakash, *Another Reason: Science and the Imagination of Modern India* (Princeton, N.J.: Princeton University Press, 1999); Partha Chatterjee, *The Nation and Its Fragments: Colonial and Postcolonial Histories* (Princeton, N.J.: Princeton University Press, 1993); Peter Hulme, *Remnants of Conquest: The Island Caribs and Their Visitors* (Oxford: Oxford University Press, 2000).

8 Arjun Appadurai, ed., *The Social Life of Things: Commodities in Cultural Perspective* (Cambridge: Cambridge University Press, 1986), and Lydia Liu, ed., *Tokens of Exchange: The Problem of Translation in Global Circulations* (Durham, N.C.: Duke University Press, 1999). See also Frederick Cooper and Ann Laura Stoler, eds., *Tensions of Empire: Colonial Cultures in a Bourgeois World* (Berkeley: University of California Press, 1997).

9 It is a telling characteristic of Lamming's work that he often features such dialogues of the dupes, lengthy debates among disempowered characters who have no chance of getting the facts right, facts that even the reader knows far better than the participants. One effect of this is to produce, among those who are ignorant and know themselves so, a renewed investment in the success of pure verbal constructs.

10 George Lamming, *In the Castle of My Skin* (Ann Arbor: University of Michigan, 1991 [1953]), p. 53.

11 Ibid., pp. 53–54.

12 Ngũgĩ wa Thiong'o, *Homecoming: Essays on African and Caribbean Literature, Culture and Politics* (New York: Lawrence Hill, 1972), p. 115.

13 Lamming, *In the Castle of My Skin*, p. 54.

14 My sense of the Victorian meanings of (exportable) culture has been shaped by Christopher Herbert's account in *Culture and Anomie* (Chicago: University of Chicago Press, 1991) of Mayhew's idea of a working-class, object-mediated identity. Following Herbert, I speak here of "culture" in the Arnoldian sense of "the best that has been known and said in the world," to which Tylor's 1871 definition of culture as a "complex whole which includes knowledge, belif, art, morals law, custom" (cited in Herbert, p. 4) is a complicated counterpart starting in the late Victorian period.

15 Flora Annie Steel, *On the Face of the Waters: A Tale of the Mutiny* (New York: Macmillan, 1897), p. 23.

16 Ian Baucom's *Out of Place* (Princeton, N.J.: Princeton University Press, 1999), is one important recent account of this process.

17 Flora Annie Steel, *The Complete Indian Housekeeper and Cook: Giving the Duties of Mistress and Servants, the General Management of the House, and Practical Recipes for Cooking in All Its Branches*, 2d ed. (Edinburgh: Murray, 1890).

18 Emily Eden, *Up the Country* (London: Virago, 1983 [1866; actually written 1842–1848]).

19 Rudyard Kipling, "The Janeites," from *Debits and Credits* [1926]; in *Collected Works of Rudyard Kipling* (New York: AMS Press, 1970), pp. 99–128. A new collection, *The Janeites*, ed. Deidre Lynch (Princeton, N.J.: Princeton University Press, 2001), takes the title of this Kipling story as the basis of its exploration of enduring Austen mania worldwide. See also You-me Park and Rajeswari Sunder Rajan, eds., *The Postcolonial Jane Austen* (London: Routledge, 2000).

20 The best recent account of Hardy and regionalism is John Barrell's "Geographies of Hardy's Wessex," in *The Regional Novel in Britain and Ireland, 1800–1990*, ed. K. D. M. Snell (Cambridge: Cambridge University Press, 1998), pp. 99–119.

21 It is worth thinking about how such paradigms of portability altered in the waning days of empire in the works of modernists from Conrad to Ford to Nigel Dennis (*Cards of*

Identity), in whose works the possibility of assembling a persuasive account of a culture through any individual's possessions comes to seem more and more problematic.

22 First published as a short story, this piece was reprinted that same year as the final chapter of *A Handful of Dust.*

23 David Malouf, *Remembering Babylon* (New York: Vintage, 1993), p. 3.

24 Nirad Chaudhuri's *Autobiography of an Unkown Indian* (Berkeley: University of California Press, 1968 [1951]) is one fascinating account of an education in which the reality of the British-export education works so well that even Raphael and Napoleon strike the narrator as preeminently British heroes. And David Malouf's early novels — especially his retelling of Ovid's Black Sea exile, *An Imaginary Life* (New York: Vintage, 1996) — bespeak a connection to British education that focuses all narratives around the question of the provincial relationship to the metropole.

25 Salman Rushdie, *Midnight's Children* (New York: Vintage, 1980), pp. 109–111.

26 The term is Guy Debord's; see his discussion in *The Society of the Spectacle*, trans. Donald Nicholson-Smith (New York: Zone, 1995 [1967]), p. 42, inter alia.

27 The French and Spanish Caribbean legacy is beyond the scope of this essay.

28 Derek Walcott, "What the Twilight Says," in *What the Twilight Says* (New York: FSG, 1998 [1970]), p. 4.

29 Naipaul is often attacked for rejecting his natal island and embracing the distant island that ruled, subdued, and shaped the West Indies. In "The Garden Path: V. S. Naipaul," Derek Walcott describes Naipaul as an "elegiac pastoralist" of England who displays "virulent contempt toward the island of his origin" — a contempt strengthened, he writes, by Naipaul's fascination with "rook, shaw and hedgerow," those little bits of barely portable Englishness: in *What the Twilight Says*, p. 122.

30 All these are images from the first section of V. S. Napaul, *A Bend in the River* (New York: Vintage, 1979), pp. 3–63.

31 Ibid., p. 40.

32 Ibid., p. 44.

33 Debord, *The Society of the Spectacle*, pp. 42 passim.

34 V. S. Naipaul, *The Mimic Men* (New York: Macmillan, 1967), p. 90.

35 Quoted by Reed Dasenbrock in *Interviews with Writers of the Post-Colonial World*, ed. Feroz Jusawalla and Reed Dasenbrock (Jackson: University Press of Mississippi, 1992), p. 109.

36 W. E. B. Du Bois, *The Souls of Black Folk* (New York: Library of America, 1990 [1903]), p. 3.

37 Bhabha, "Of Mimicry and Man."

38 Sarah Orne Jewett, "The Queen's Twin," in Sarah Orne Jewett, *Novels and Stories* (New York: Library of America, 1994), pp. 493–511. Originally published in *The Atlantic*, 1899.

39 Bramwell Bronte, elder brother of Charlotte and Emily, was one of thousands of provincial Britons who had the same relationship, in the nineteenth century, to London. Surrounded by maps and guidebooks to the city he had never visited, he would spend evenings at his local pub waylaying London travelers and demonstrating to them his knowledge of London geography.

40 Jewett, "The Queen's Twin," p. 510.

41 Lamming, *Natives of My Person* (New York: Holt, Rinehart and Winston, 1972). Supriya Nair, *Caliban's Curse: George Lamming and the Revisioning of History* (Ann Arbor: University of Michigan Press, 1996), is the best recent account. Other interesting work on the novel includes Sandra Pouchet Paquet, *The Novels of George Lamming* (London: Heinemann, 1982); Avis G. McDonald, "Within the Orbit of Power: Reading Allegory in George Lamming's *Natives of My Person,*" *Journal of Commonwealth Literature* 22 (1987):

73–86; Peter Hulme, "George Lamming and the Postcolonial Novel," in Jonathan White, ed., *Recasting the World: Writing after Colonialism* (Baltimore: Johns Hopkins University Press, 1993), pp. 120–136.

42 The most revealing recent discussion of allegory in *Natives of My Person* and its relationship to postcolonial concerns more generally is Stephen Slemon's important and controversial "Post-Colonial Allegory and the Transformation of History," *Journal of Commonwealth Literature* 23, 1 (1988): 156–167. The strongest component of Slemon's argument is his claim that "the act of 'revisioning' allegory becomes also an act of 'revisioning' those codes of recognition which we inherit from the imperial encounter" (p. 164). That is, new forms of representation will reverse the causal flows that putatively make the postcolonial dependent on the colonial; in this inverted allegory, the history of the old world will "tell" only when it allegorizes the current events of the new.

43 Nair rightly points out that C. L. R. James's book about Melville, *Mariners, Renegades and Castaways* (Detroit: Bewick, 1978 [1953]), must also have been a crucial influence on Lamming.

44 Lamming, *Natives of My Person*, p. 328.

45 Donald Pease, "Doing Justice to C. L. R. James's *Mariners, Renegades and Castaways*," *Boundary 2* 27, 2 (2000): 6.

46 Ibid., p. 9.

47 Though Ahmad argues convincingly that Jameson's claims about "national allegory" fail to apply to all of postcolonial literature. This well-known debate occurs in Frederic Jameson, "Third-World Literature in the Era of Multinational Capitalism," *Social Text* 15 (1986), and Aijaz Ahmad, "Jameson's Rhetoric of Otherness and the 'National Allegory,'" *Social Text* 17 (1987): 3–25.

48 Hulme, "George Lamming and the Postcolonial Novel," p. 131.

DOUGLAS M. HAYNES

The Whiteness of *Civilization:* The Transatlantic Crisis of White Supremacy and British Television Programming in the United States in the 1970s

The period from the mid-1960s through the 1970s marked a crisis of white supremacy in the Anglo-America world. Rebellions rocked urban America, from Watts and Compton on the West Coast to Detroit and Cleveland in the Midwest to Newark on the East Coast. These rebellions disrupted the false sense of security that consensual legislation—that is, the Civil Rights Act (1964) and the Voting Rights Act (1965)—had addressed the so-called "race problem" in American society.[1] To be sure, they reflected in part the stubborn persistence of inequality, especially in urban centers, in an age of seemingly unlimited prosperity. But in the wake of the 1968 assassination of Martin Luther King Jr., they also testified to a broad-based "black power movement" that challenged the "self- and group-hatred" imposed on African Americans and its corollary—the privileged place of European or "white" culture.[2] Although protean, the hallmarks of this movement included a rejection of the consensual politics of liberalism, the development of self-sufficient institutions, the recovery of Africanness or African identity, and the unmasking of white racial privilege in the past and present.[3]

For many European Americans, the institutions that once reproduced and sanctioned the entitlement of whiteness appeared to be in full retreat. As more African Americans and other people of color attended universities and colleges, they contested the Eurocentrism of the curriculum and demanded more attention to the black presence in the United States and the wider African diaspora in the world.[4] The 1968 student strike at California State University, San Francisco, led to the establishment of the first department of black studies and spurred others. The growth of programs and departments in ethnic and women's studies accelerated an ongoing revision of the curriculum at the leading institutions of higher education.[5] Further, criticism rained down on commercial and noncommercial broadcast networks alike for either the absence of or demeaning portrayals of people of color or the lack of relevant programming. Direct political action, such as public challenges to license renewals and sponsor boycotts, led to "black theme" or socially conscious programming.[6]

This crisis of white supremacy fostered a receptive context for a distinctive type of British cultural programming on public television in the United States. Building on the inroads made by its film and radio industries during World War II, Britain's television industry exported a steady stream of content that raced European culture as unproblematically "white." Absent in the selection of the now familiar costume dramas and documentaries that branded British cultural programming as discriminating television was Britain's historical relationship to its empire, much less the presence of its multiracial population. This erasure should not come as a surprise for an imperial society. The representation of the world under British rule as "different" and thereby inferior enabled the construction of the racial myth of the whiteness of the nation, one that unified a society riven by the fault lines of class, ethnicity, gender, race, and sexual orientation. The empire facilitated the production of wholly new and/or raced existing narratives about the whiteness of freedom and the special mission of Anglo-Saxon people to disseminate its truths — that is, commerce, Christianity, and civilization — to the "dark corners" of the world.[7] As Carl Freedman has noted, this myth and its attendant elisions steadied Britain during its own identity crisis of the 1960s and 1970s.[8] Independence movements, which spread across Africa and elsewhere in the empire, challenged the idea and reality of the entitlement of white rule. Black Britons, who appropriated the strategies of the black power movement in the United States, bore witness against the history of officially sanctioned discrimination in education, housing, and public life in Britain and demanded long-denied racial justice.[9] The politics of decolonization, like desegregation and integration in the United States, may have ended the formal hierarchies of white supremacy, but they also generated a desire for its cultural trappings.

As a growing number of scholars have pointed out, the authority of whiteness derives from its seeming invisibility, its absence of particularity.[10] This characteristic invests whiteness with a universal register of value and meaning. By contrast, people of color have had to justify their humanity in racial terms — that is to say, their blackness — because of a long history of racist oppression and mendacious stereotyping. George Lipsitz observes that "whiteness never has to speak its name, never has to acknowledge its role as an organizing principle in social and cultural relations."[11] This authority is by no means timeless, however. It is instead a product of the racialized history of the United States, not to mention that of the United Kingdom. The historical iterations of white supremacy range from the systems of slavery and segregation, colonialism and apartheid, justified in terms of the racialized differences between whites and blacks grounded in biology, to right-wing political interventions since the 1970s that frame racially compensatory gestures such as affirmative action as a form of white victimization.[12] As Howard Winant perceptively notes, "This imaginary white disadvantage—for which there is almost no evidence at the empirical level—has achieved widespread popular credence, and provides the cultural 'glue' that holds together a wide variety of reactionary racial politics."[13]

Integral to universalizing the entitlement of the white citizen-subject is a cultural framework that explains racial privilege as not only normal and moral, but also as the culmination of human civilization.[14] Whiteness is embedded in the Western teleology of the making of the modern world. The movement of people from Europe to North America produced new political institutions and practices — most notably representative democracy — that unleashed the entrepreneurial spirit that developed the natural resources of the continent while inspiring the creative imagination. Customarily, in the literary and historical imagination white men (and less so white women) have been represented as the natural agents of modernity: they write and paint; speak and act; in a word, create the modern world. This teleology is possible through discursive silences — that is, the indifference to the brutality of the regimes of racial terror, the constitutive role of raced people in producing cultural forms and generating national wealth — or through a resolution of the contradictions of American institutions through the redemptive humanitarian acts of white men on behalf of raced people — that is, freeing black slaves, educating African and Native Americans, and extending basic civil rights to people of color.[15]

Civilization, the BBC-produced series that chronicled the development of human civilization from the Christian era through the nineteenth century, resonated with the transatlantic crisis of white supremacy. As I will show, it affirmed the privileged status and durability of Europe and its values by aestheticizing the whiteness of civilization. It aired first in Britain in 1968. Two years later, with corporate sponsorship by Xerox, National Educational Television (NET) (under the auspices of the newly created Public Broadcasting Service [PBS]) broadcast the thirteen-part program to a national audience in the United States. This program, which pioneered corporate sponsorship of programming on noncommercial television, commenced a transatlantic exchange between the underfunded British television industry and the nascent national public television system in the United States. This relationship provided inexpensive programming with high production values, as well as mollified the guardians of public television who objected to local and national programming that increasingly subjected U.S. foreign policy in Southeast Asia and Latin America and racism and race relations at home to searching examination. Moreover, the success of the racial economy of culture as deployed in Clark's *Civilization* was paralleled by the broadcast of the *Forsyte Saga* on educational stations. This program, based on the pre–World War II novels by John Galsworthy about the disintegration of a prominent London family, would lay the foundation for what would be the signature program on public television in the 1970s that celebrated the whiteness of civilization: *Masterpiece Theater.*

*   *   *

At the suggestion of BBC 2 director David Attenborough, Kenneth Clark, art historian and pioneer of cultural programming on television in Britain, agreed to write and host a program about civilization. When recalling the genesis of the project, Clark breezily volunteered that "I had no clear idea what it meant, but I thought it was preferable to barbarism, and fancied that this was the moment to say so."[16] Still, he had little doubt about the relative importance of the cultural production of Western Europe in its development. He overlooked the ancient and non-European world, citing time limitations and his own narrow linguistic abilities. "Obviously I could not include the ancient civilizations of Egypt, Syria, Greece, and Rome because to have done so would have meant another ten programmes, at least; and the same was true of China, Persia, India, and the world of Islam."[17] These sites of culture are not wholly absent. Clark's deployment of non-European people and culture, especially from Africa, enables him to aestheticize the inherent whiteness of West European civilization. At the heart of his aesthetic is a racial binary that simultaneously defines worthy art or culture as white while defining exoticism as the black presence in Europe.

Critical to Clark's aesthetic is the reduction of black people to mute tropes of savagery, whether as objects of the picturesque or of humanitarian rescue. Clark opens by comparing the Apollo of Belvedere with an African mask. He makes no effort to specify the tribal or cultural function of the mask. But the relative value of the art as an index of human development is clear enough: "[Apollo] embodies a higher state of civilization." Where the mask reflected a "Negro imagination" consumed by "fear and darkness," the Apollo radiates a Hellenistic "world of light and confidence."[18] Later, he presents the ceiling painting of the continents of the world in Balthasar Neumann's palace by Giovanni Tiepolo to illustrate the extravagance of the seventeenth-century Baroque style. In the Africa panel, the black women function as referents to an exotic land. "Africa with it ostriches, camels, and disdainful negresses."[19] Even when black figures share the canvas with European figures, they remain invisible to Clark's gaze. Rather than viewing their presence on the margins of

Hogarth's *Chairing a Member* (from the *Election* series) and *The Orgy Scene* (from the *Rake's Progress* series) or the servant in *Portrait Group* by Arthur Devis as the inextricable connection between Europe's development and black oppression, he simply overlooks them.[20] Indeed, to acknowledge their presence risks complicating the national myth of Britain as a homogeneously white society. At a moment when Afro-Caribbean and South Asian Britons increasingly protested against discrimination, their historical presence not only authenticated their long-term connection to the British Isles, but also challenged official explanations of Britain's racial problem as simply one of the uneven assimilation of "immigrants" into an otherwise tolerant and peace-loving society.

To the extent that black people occupy a presence at all, it is in relation to the transatlantic slave trade as mediated by the white imaginary. It was the so-called "esoteric" nature of the horrors of the trade that provoked abolition sentiment in Britain, Clark insists. "But slaves and the trade in slaves, that was something different: for one thing it was contrary to Christian teaching; for another it was esoteric — it wasn't something that surrounded one like air, as home-made poverty did. And the horrors it involved were far more horrible: even the unsqueamish stomachs of the eighteenth century were turned by accounts of the middle passage."[21] Clark ironically exhibits a repertoire of images and objects to convey the "horrors" of an exotic trade but describes the effects of industrialization on white Britons only as "dehumanizing effect."[22] These range from a display of a body brand (which Clark presses against his pale hand), to a water color painting that depicts cramped black bodies in the interior hulk of a slave vessel, to an eighteenth-century miniature of the infamous *Brookes* ship, to a print of a female being whipped while hanging upside down. These images/objects simultaneously reinforce the binary of civilization and savage chiefly by linking both Africa and black bodies with "exotic" suffering and violence and Europe as a site of humanitarian intervention.[23]

The significance that Clark assigns to the visual narrative of the slave trade ultimately depends on the agency of white men and women to speak and to act on behalf of passive Africans. Clark grounds the credibility of his discussion on the "exotic" trade from none other than the home in Hull of Bishop Wilberforce, whom he credits with leading the political fight for the abolition of the trade in 1807. As if to underscore the whiteness of humanitarianism, Clark lets the camera pause on a painting, above a lifelike figure of Wilberforce at his desk, that depicts (as usual) a nameless black subject with broken chains, looking upward with an expression of submissive gratitude.[24] Clark, too, assigns canonical status to the historical depiction of the *Zong* affair by J. W. M. Turner (*Slavers Throwing Overbroad the Dead and the Dying — Typhoon Coming*) because it mediates the horror of the trade and in turn mobilized British people to end the trade and the condition of slavery in the empire. "For the last fifty years we have not been in the least interested in the horrible story, but only in the delicate aubergine of the negro's leg and the pink fish surrounding it. But Turner meant us to take it seriously."[25] When referring to the abolition of the trade and slavery, Clark adds in the same breath, "One must regard this a giant step forward for the human race, and be proud, I think, that it happened in England."[26]

Where the liberation of blacks outside of Britain advances the "human race," the proximity of whites and blacks complicates the relationship of American society to European civilization. For Clark, Thomas Jefferson and his many achievements — ranging from the inspired neoclassicism of Monticello, to the foundation of the University of Virginia, to authorship of the Declaration of Independence — firmly root America's cultural heritage in the eighteenth-century European Enlightenment. Yet the very physical existence of slavery diminishes this connection. In oblique language, Clark locates the insecurity of contemporary America in the unresolved place of African Americans:

"Self-evident truths" . . . that's the voice of the eighteenth century enlightenment. But on the opposite wall are less familiar words by Jefferson that still give us pause today: "I tremble for my country when I reflect that God is just, that his justice cannot sleep forever. Commerce between master and slave is despotism. Nothing is more certainly written in the book of fate than that these people are to be free." A peaceful-looking scene, a great ideal made visible. But beyond it what problems — almost insoluble, or at least not soluble by the smile of reason.[27]

In spite of Clark's doubts for the future, he remained convinced of the durability of Western civilization. Rather than viewers being silent spectators of its decline, Clark continually enjoins them to shore it up through "confidence." It was the absence of "confidence in the society in which one lives, belief in its philosophy, belief in its laws, and confidence in one's own mental powers" that undermined the civilizations of Greece and Rome. At the close of the series, he enjoins viewers to choose confidence: "I said at the beginning that it is a lack of confidence, more than anything else, that kills a civilization. We can destroy ourselves by cynicism and disillusion, just as effectively as by bombs."[28] Refracted through the troubled decade of the 1960s, this was indeed a reassuring message.

Clark's "personal perspective" reached a wide audience in the United States. A month before the October 1970 broadcast, Xerox Corporation sponsored a one-hour synopsis as a tie-in to the series. Jack Gould, the television critic for the *New York Times*, enthused: "The Public Broadcasting Service and Channel

13 have a hit next month; of that there cannot be the slightest doubt."[29] NET reported strong viewership for the duration of the series. The decision to air the program in competition with commercial network programming was not an accident. Against the usual flotsam of variety shows, situation comedies, and crime shows, *Civilization* distinguished NET as television for the discriminating viewer. Gould declared: "Let today's American television drag dismally on with trivia, a prisoner of format initiated by radio and imbued with Hollywood. For those who want an alternative there is the Public Broadcasting Service's presentation of 'Civilization.'"[30] Clark, too, received other forms of official and commercial validation, ranging from a special exhibition and medal from the National Gallery for distinguished service to education and art to a best-selling companion hardback volume to the program.[31]

Clark's personal view of civilization received its share of critical reviews, especially the companion book. It is worth noting that the bulk of the negative criticism focused on Clark's emphasis on "high art"—that is, the selection of his choices of representative art and/or the disdain for modern art.[32] Still, book reviewers and other commentators accepted the underlying whiteness of civilization. This racial economy of culture privileged whiteness by ignoring the cultural production of black people and/or the discursive connection between white supremacy and black oppression. These elisions made it possible for Clark to present civilization as an Arnoldian narrative—that is, as the self-evident progress of the best that has been written and thought.

This racial economy would become a standard feature of the programming format of public television. Preceding Clark's series was the *Forsyte Saga*, a twenty-nine-part costume drama based on the trilogy by the Edwardian novelist John Galsworthy. The success of the program not only revealed the existence of an audience for costume dramas based on the canonical literature of Europe. It also laid the foundation for *Masterpiece Theater*, which WGBH of Boston launched in 1971. Yet the value of the *Forsyte Saga* as a type of high culture available in a mass medium was neither self-evident nor independent of racial politics. It was in fact framed by the contentious politics of race relations in an early experiment in national public television programming: the Public Broadcasting Laboratory (PBL).

The PBL was designed to demonstrate the promise of public television as a national noncommercial network. Besides a chronic shortage of funding, public television lacked interconnection—that is, over 125 educational stations of the NET were not connected on a national grid. By subsidizing interconnection for a national public affairs programming that included politics, health, science, and social problems and live performances of music, art, and theater, Ford Foundation president McGeorge Bundy and former president of the CBS news division Fred Friendly hoped to persuade Congress, the Federal Communications Commission, and the networks to invest in a domestic satellite system for noncommercial television.[33] With generous Ford Foundation support, the PBL promised to tackle current affairs, especially race relations, without the reporting censorship that commercial sponsors imposed on network broadcasters.

The social mission of the PBL reflected a broader aim of the Ford Foundation to address the state of race relations in the mass media in the wake of the urban rebellions in 1967. A report by the National Advisory Commission on Civil Disorders had confirmed the long-standing criticism of advocates of racial justice that network television "failed to report adequately on the causes and consequences of civil disorders and the underlying problems of race relations."[34] In hopes of enhancing the relevance of public television, the foundation provided grants to public television stations across the country to enhance the minority content of locally produced "newsroom" programs.[35] It also funded programs that promoted racial dialogue in response to black nationalism, such as *Neighborhood*, *Coffee House*, *My New Orleans*, and Jacksonville, Florida's, *Feedback*.[36]

As a matter of fact, Av Westin and the editorial board of the PBL planned an extended examination of the contentious state of race relations in northern cities in the inaugural episode.[37] Using the medium of television as a tool of protest, civil rights activists exposed the inherent violence of white supremacy in the South. This regional orientation ironically fostered the myth of the North as racially tolerant and diverted attention away from racism in northern communities and cities. African Americans confronted this contradiction in their daily lives — in employment and housing discrimination, de facto segregation in public education institutions, routine police brutality and the biased administration of justice, and the systematic violation of their voting rights. It was these very contradictions that ignited the urban rebellions that rocked the final years of the Johnson administration.[38] The intensity of black protest spurred the federal government to push for greater integration in public life and institutions.

Yet the fragile national consensus over racial justice had undergone a sea change by 1967–1968. The unprecedented post–World War II economic boom began to stall. Whites in northern cities grew more economically insecure. In the wake of a more vigorous commitment to integration by the federal government, whites now had to face blacks as equals who competed for jobs and moved into formerly all-white neighborhoods and attended public schools. Politicians such as Richard Nixon and George Wallace (among others) transformed the economic and social insecurities of whites into a more general national "white backlash" by linking urban disorder and crime to racial justice and denouncing integration as unfair to deserving whites. It is no surprise that by 1968 some 52 percent (versus 31 percent in 1963) of ethnic whites believed that the government was pushing too hard and too fast in the areas of housing, education, and jobs.[39]

The PBL program foregrounded tense "black-white" relations in two segments. The first closely examined mayoral elections in northern cities: Cleveland, Ohio, and Boston, Massachusetts. PBL crews followed the campaigns of Cleveland Democrat Carl B. Stokes, an African American seeking the office for a second time, and Boston Republican Louisa Hicks, a European American. Stokes, who would become the first elected African American mayor of a major U.S. city in 1967, ran on a consensus platform of investment in disadvantaged areas and a more robust effort to desegregate public schools. Seth Taft, his Republican opponent, deployed the coded racial language of the New Right when appealing to voters: he promised lower taxes and called for law and order.[40] More so than Taft, in Boston's nonpartisan election Hicks explicitly foregrounded race loyalty. She not only excoriated Republicans, who nominated Edward Brooke, who would become the first African American U.S. senator since reconstruction, and Democrats, who embraced desegregation in public education, Hicks also portrayed herself as the "champion" of the "white working man."[41] A second segment consisted of a film by Russ Meek, a black nationalist, of the neighborhood in which he grew up and which provided the point of departure for a contentious studio audience discussion about racial equality and the "communication gap" between whites and blacks.

Even before the program aired, the PBL Editorial Policy Board expressed some reservations about the "excessive concentration on the urban-racial issue."[42] After reviewing a "dry run" of the studio segment in Chicago, board members voiced concern that "the Black Nationalist spokesman was highly articulate and the others inarticulate." Others on the editorial board added that "the program should somehow have provided alternatives to the extremists' 'solutions.' "[43] After the broadcast, the board sought to introduce more balance — that is, a moderate or integrationist perspective. The board was equally troubled by the attention given to black nationalism in a later segment that featured the experience of Vietnam veteran Lewis Jenkins, who returned to a racially polarized Chicago. Board members commented: "Is it conceivable that Jenkins talked with Negro moderates or plain integrationists?" "This obviously had to be staged, and it seems wrong that, say, the Whitney Young [executive director of the National Urban League] type of middle course was again ignored. As a minimum, it should have been set in perspective by introductory and/or concluding remarks."[44] In the future, the board mandated a more integrationist perspective. "The board requested program planning to correct the balance, suggested drawing upon Young and others, and asked that it be briefed in detail about future racial segments involving clear policy questions."[45]

The anxiety of the board anticipated the sentiment of local stations in northern and southern states. Several either balked at transmitting the premiere episode of PBL or simply broadcast the comparatively mild exposé on truth in advertising for aspirin and cigarette products. Betty Cope, station general manager for WVIZ TV in Cleveland, feared that the program would exacerbate an already charged climate. "We felt that it wasn't wise to present a program with the emotional thrust of this one — with approximately 150 minutes devoted to the race issue — in Cleveland 36 hours before the election."[46] Local stations south of the Mason-Dixon Line omitted the PBL from their programming schedules. Some, like the state-owned educational television network in South Carolina and Texas, cited financial concerns. William H. Hale, the general manager of the station for the University of Georgia, was more candid. He questioned leaving the discussion of the race problem "wholly in the hands of a predominately New York organization unfamiliar with the Southern perspective."[47] After the initial showing, 29 out of 119 stations that agreed to air the program dropped out.[48]

Jack Gould warned in an editorial that the PBL experiment jeopardized the funding, if not the future, of public television. "If the premiere should be regarded as representative of what lies ahead, Congressmen could scarcely be blamed for wondering if a huge permanent investment in noncommercial video is warranted." Gould regarded the electoral coverage as "completely pedestrian and devoid of mature reporting." But he reserved his venom for the confrontation between the white and black studio audience in Chicago. "The confrontation in Chicago on the fascinating nuances and pains of the black-white relationship turned out to be nothing but a showcase for a rude Black Nationalist who merely shouted everyone down. The studio meeting idea not only was old hat . . . but also pandered to mob curiosity in a public floor fight."[49]

Over the next eighteen months PBL heeded the advice of the guardians of public television. The program, to be sure, continued to address the "racial problem" in a variety of contexts. Segments ranged from police–minority relations in urban cities, to the "Poor People's Campaign" organized by Martin Luther King Jr. before his untimely assassination in 1968, to the 1967 report of the National Advisory Commission on Civil Disorders.[50] These segments provided pointed analysis. The police–minority relations segment grounded the harassment of minority communities and members to the institutional culture of racially segregated departments in New York, Atlanta, Philadelphia, Pittsburgh, and Detroit, as well as the racist perception of the criminal nature of black people. "Burn, Baby, Burn," the anthem of urban rebellion, opened the segment on the Kerner Commission. It included a reprise of the confrontation between Russ Meek and white residents in Chicago and closed with the satirical "Honkie Test," which tested how well white Americans understood the culture of the ghetto. The segment on the "Poor People's Campaign" featured King and other activists who criticized the structural inequalities of American society.[51]

Even though aspects of these segments were sharp in their criticism of racism in American society, the structure of the studio evaluation of the problem blunted their impact. Each segment included a discussion of the problem from "experts," which included representatives of the African American professional classes from the academy, clergy, and/or law enforcement.[52] For example, in the police–minority relations segment Alvin Poussaint of Tufts University joined white panelists in a discussion of the sociology of crime and law enforcement. As experts whose blackness authenticated their authority, these individuals mediated the concerns of blacks, particularly the urban poor, in a staged discourse that shifted responsibility for addressing the manifestations of white supremacy in society from individual acts to institutional gestures. In the wake of the urban rebellions, the Reverend Leon Sullivan and Whitney Young respectively discussed the Opportunities Industrialization Center and the efforts by the National Urban League to promote jobs and economic development and coexistence among black and white communities.[53] In the "Poor People's Campaign" segment the Reverend Fontroy of Washington, D.C., stressed the importance of taking steps to discourage black and white extremism.[54]

In 1969 the Ford Foundation decided not to renew funding for PBL. This decision, to be sure, reflected the provisional nature of the original grant and the unresolved autonomy of PBL in relationship to NET, which technically oversaw the program. The decision referred no less to the need to promote the viability of the Corporation for Public Broadcasting (CPB). The CPB became operational only in 1969, after the U.S. Congress had created it in 1967 as an independent, nonprofit corporation. Its stated mission mirrored other Great Society domestic programs of the waning years of the Johnson administration: using federal resources to both expand access to public television and develop excellence in telecommunications and diversity in programming. With limited content at its disposal and few independent production facilities beyond the NET, the CPB took steps to shore up the political credibility of public television.

This imperative created an enabling context for institutionalizing British cultural television programming on a permanent basis. In the year that the PBL ended, the Ford Foundation joined PBS to subsidize a new national program format to the tune of $3.6 million. The format consisted of two complimentary programs, one dedicated to theatrical entertainment and the other to public affairs. The BBC-produced *Forsyte Saga* and *The Advocates* comprised the first installment of this national format. The pairing of *The Advocates* and the *Forsyte Saga* was not simply an example of the segmentation of programming for different audiences. If anything, the contrast between the two programs de-politicized British programming while privileging the whiteness of culture.

In announcing the inaugural broadcast of the *Forsyte Saga*, Jack Gould invoked the appeal of the program in the English-speaking world. "Tomorrow evening the 'colonies' will have the opportunity to view the first episode of 'The Forsyte Saga,' a television series that was called a national 'obsession' by a British Broadcasting Corporation commentator during its two year run in England."[55] The fact that the first broadcast competed well against the usual network draws such as ABC's *Sunday Night Movie*, CBS's *Leslie Uggams Show* and *Mission Impossible*, and NBC's *Bonanza* and *The Bold Ones* not only suggested an audience for British programming, but also framed the hour as television for the more discriminating viewers — that is, for those with a special connection to Britain's heritage.[56] Jack Gould, in a glowing review, noted that "a routine check of many American libraries would have revealed that interest in Galsworthy has been on the rise here for at least a couple of years. Tourists visiting London who saw a segment or two of the BBC production in part were perhaps responsible but more likely the development is one of these inexplicable cyclical surges that lend constant fascination to the literary world. Galsworthy, it seems, is 'in.'"[57]

The political nature of *The Advocates* was transparent. Each week representatives for issues including racial problems, water and air pollution, and the draft and campus disorders debated before a live studio and television audience. To be sure, class politics were present in the *Forsyte Saga* — it was about the disintegration of an upper-class family. But the politics of race, much less whiteness, remained wholly unexplored. The fact that spokespersons discussed the status of African Americans in *The Advocates* underscored the political nature of the status of African Americans in society and, by extension, the problematic nature of blackness. Not only did spokespersons debate race relations, but the studio and viewing audiences could also register their opinions by applause or by telephoning the local station or through an electronic polling system. The framing of the *Forsyte Saga* as the recovery of an authentic past against more contemporary programming and/or concerns such as race relations underscored the racial economy of culture whereby whites produced and possessed culture and blacks did not. One new subscriber to public television from

Millburn, New Jersey, wrote that "'The Forsyte Saga' presentation makes [the enclosed check] imperative. What a wonderful thing to do for this country, particularly at this unsettled time."[58]

*   *   *

The success of the *Forsyte Saga* set the stage for the creation of *Masterpiece Theater*. Even though part of a mass medium, the format of the program framed high culture in terms of a racial aesthetic of whiteness. Like Clark in the *Civilization* program, Alistair Cooke served as docent for American viewers. His authority as a mediator of the cultural heritage of Anglo-Saxons was marked by his white skin as much as by the ease of delivery of the program notes, interspersed with knowing asides about the author, novel, characters, and/or historical period. The worn leather armchair and carefully laid bric-a-brac of a gentleman's study or club all exuded a powerful sense of knowing one's heritage and presumption of its superiority.

The programs that Cooke introduced marked high culture as white and affluent partly owing to the competition with the commercial networks. The networks provided viewers with a predictable programming on Sunday evening after the family hour at 9 P.M. These included network Sunday night movies or variety shows that featured durable, middle-aged actors, such as *The Jimmy Stewart Show* and *Dick Van Dyke*, or those featuring rising recording artists, such as *Sonny and Cher* and *Cher*. Situation comedies, usually dominating the 9–10 P.M. hour, foregrounded the insecurities of Americans. These included *All in the Family* and *Archie Bunker's Place*, which featured a working-class family headed by a lovable bigot. *Alice* and *One Day at a Time* explored the lives of single or divorced women as they struggled on the fringes of the middle class to balance career, romance, and parenting responsibilities. *The Jeffersons* chronicled the lives of a successful African American businessman and his wife as they moved up the social ladder and experienced and projected their own class and race biases in Chicago. Dramatic programming that followed the situation comedies either explored the lives of urban professionals (such as doctors and lawyers) or more likely unmasked crime in American society. These programs included *The Bold Ones* (lawyers and doctors), *Trapper John, M.D.*, *Mannix*, *Barnaby Jones*, *Kojak*, *Bronk*, *Delvecchio*, and *Kaz*.[59]

The seasonal offerings of *Masterpiece Theater* consisted of a combination of literature, historical subjects, and modern mysteries. Not all of the novels were necessarily canonical, but when competing against the fare of network programming, they assumed a privileged status. The dramatized novels during the first decade included Jane Austen's *Pride and Prejudice;* Honoré de Balzac's *Père Goriot* and *Cousine Bette;* James Fenimore Cooper's *The Last of the Mohicans;*

Charles Dickens's *Our Mutual Friend*; Fyodor Dostoyevsky's *Crime and Punishment*, *The Gambler*, and *The Possessed*; Gustave Flaubert's *Madame Bovary*; Thomas Hardy's *The Mayor of Casterbridge* and *Jude the Obscure*; Henry James's *The Spoils of Poynton* and *The Golden Bowl*; Thomas Hughes's *Tom Brown's School Days*; Jean-Paul Sartre's *Kean*; William Thackery's *Vanity Fair*; and Leo Tolstoy's *Resurrection* and *Anna Karenina*.[60]

The historical subjects, like the dramatized novels, privileged the whiteness of Britain's past or that of Western Europe chiefly by concentrating on the pre–World War I era. Unlike the novels of the long nineteenth century, these programs concerned themselves with the lives of royalty, such as *The Wives of Henry VIII* and *Elizabeth R*, or social elites, such as *The First Churchills*, the conservative prime minister Benjamin Disraeli in *Disraeli*, and the affluent Bellamy family in *Upstairs, Downstairs*. Other programming provided a more political message about the women's movement, such as *Shoulder to Shoulder* and *Testament of Youth*. But the emphasis on white middle-class women foregrounded their experience over all others, including women of color and white working-class women. Similarly, the original programming revolved around the lives of upper-class men and women in the twentieth century, based on the novels of such authors as mystery writer Dorothy Sayers (*Clouds of Witness, The Unpleasantness at the Bellona Club, Murder Must Advertise, The Nine Tailors, Five Red Herrings*). This was equally the case with the novels by Somerset Maugham (*Cakes and Ales*) and Lewis Grassic Gordon (*Sunset Song*).[61]

The establishment of *Masterpiece Theater* institutionalized the racial economy of culture on public television. To be sure, the very name was designed to distinguish public television from commercial television. The content of the program, like Clark's *Civilization* series, defined the cultural production of Europe as the best that has been written and thought. Not only did the selection of texts that served as the bases for the dramas on *Masterpiece Theater* define the essential whiteness of culture, it was also confirmed by the absence of a national programming equivalent that similarly privileged the cultural production of Africa or its descendants in the world. In the end, the cultural politics of public television in the wake of the transatlantic crisis of white supremacy in the 1960s and 1970s breathed new life into the racial myth of the whiteness of culture.

Notes

I would like to acknowledge funding support for the research for this essay from the Cultural Diversity Faculty Research Program, Committee on Research, Academic Senate, University of California, Irvine.

1 Gerald Horne, *The Fire This Time: The Watts Uprising and the 1960's* (Charlottesville: University Press of Virginia, 1995); Sidney Fine, *Violence in the Model City: The Cavanagh Administration, Race Relations and the Detroit Race Riots of 1967* (Ann Arbor: University of Michigan Press, 1989); Stephen Grant Meyer, *As Long As They Don't Move Next Door: Segregation and Racial Conflict in American Neighborhoods* (Lanham, Md.: Rowman and Littlefield, 2000).

2 Kenneth Clark, as cited in Manning Marable, *Race, Reform, Rebellion: The Second Reconstruction in Black America, 1945–1990* (Jackson: University Press of Mississippi, 1991), p. 93.

3 The literature is large, but representative publications include Stokely Carmichael and Charles V. Hamilton, *Black Power: The Politics of Liberation in America* (New York: Vintage, 1967); Theodore Cross, *The Black Power Imperative: Racial Inequality and the Politics of Nonviolence* (New York: Faulkner Books, 1984); Robert C. Smith, *We Have No Leaders: African Americans in the Post Civil-Rights Era* (New York: State University of New York Press, 1996); Brian Ward, *Just My Soul: Rhythm and Blues, Black Consciousness* (Berkeley: University of California Press, 1998).

4 Anderson Talmadge, ed. *Black Studies: Theory, Method, and Cultural Perspectives* (Pullman: Washington State University Press, 1990); William H. Exam, *Paradoxes of Protest: Black Student Activism in a White University* (Philadelphia: Temple University Press, 1990); Richard McCormick, *The Black Student Protest Movement at Rutgers* (New Brunswick, N.J.: Rutgers University Press, 1990).

5 Laurence W. Levine, *The Opening of the American Mind: Cannons, Cultures, and History* (Boston: Beacon Press, 1996).

6 *Minorities and the Media: A Ford Foundation Report*, (New York, 1974). See also Leonard Archer, *Black Images in the American Theater: NACCP Protest Campaigns — Stage, Radio and Television* (Brooklyn, N.Y.: Pageant Poseidon, 1973); Jannette L. Dates, "Public Television," in *Split Image: African Americans in the Mass Media*, ed. Jannette L. Dates and William Barlow (Washington, D.C.: Howard University Press, 1993), pp. 329–364; J. Fred MacDonald, *Blacks and White TV* (Chicago: Nelson Hall, 1983), p. 139.

7 See Robert Colls and Philip Dodd, eds., *Englishness: Politics and Culture 1880–1920* (London: Croom Helm, 1986); John M. MacKenzie, *Propaganda and Empire: The Manipulation of British Public Opinion, 1880–1960* (Manchester: Manchester University Press, 1984); John M. MacKenzie, ed., *Imperialism and Popular Culture* (Manchester: Manchester University Press, 1986); J. A. Mangan, ed., *Making Imperial Mentalities: Socialisation and British Imperialism* (Manchester: Manchester University Press, 1990); Michael Hays, "Representing Empire: Class, Culture, and the Popular Theatre in the Nineteenth Century," in *Imperialism and Theatre: Essays on World Theatre, Drama and Performance*, ed. J. Ellen Gainor (London: Routledge,1995); Robert H. MacDonald, *The Language of Empire: Myths and Metaphors of Popular Imperialism, 1880–1918* (Manchester: Manchester University Press, 1994); Laura Tabili, *We Ask for British Justice: Workers and Racial Difference in Late Imperial Britain* (Ithaca, N.Y.: Cornell University Press, 1994); Paul Rich, *Race and Empire in British Politics* (Cambridge: Cambridge University Press, 1986).

8 Carl Freedman, "England as Ideology: From 'Upstairs, Downstairs' to *A Room with a View*," *Cultural Critique*, winter 1990–1991: 79–106; Timothy Brennan, "Masterpiece Theater and the Uses of Tradition," *Social Text* 12 (fall 1985): 102–111.

9 Paul Gilroy, *"There Ain't No Black in the Union Jack": The Cultural Politics of Race and Nation* (London: Hutchinson, 1987); Paul Gilroy and Hazel Carby, *The Empire Strikes Back: Race and Racism in 70s Britain* (London: Hutchinson, in association with the Centre for Contemporary Cultural Studies, University of Birmingham, 1982); Jim Pines, ed.,

Black and White in Colour: Black People in British Television since 1936 (London: BFI Publications, 1992); James Walvin, "From the Fringes: The Emergence of British Black Historical Studies," in *Essays on the History of Blacks in Britain: From Roman Times to the Mid-Twentieth Century*, ed. Jagdish S. Gundara and Ian Duffield (Aldershot: Avebury, 1992), pp. 225–240.

10 For representative accounts that historicize the making of white privilege since the nineteenth century in the United States, see Alexander Saxton, *The Rise and Fall of the White Republic: Class Politics* (London: Verso, 1990); David Roediger, *The Wages of Whiteness: Race and the Making of the American Working Class* (London: Verso, 1991); Vron Ware, *Beyond the Pale: White Women, Racism and History* (London: Verso, 1992); Noel Ignatiev, *How the Irish Became White* (New York: Routledge, 1996); George Lipsitz, *The Possessive Investment in Whiteness: How White People Profit from Identity Politics* (Philadelphia: Temple University Press, 1998).

11 Lipsitz, *The Possessive Investment in Whiteness*, p. 1.

12 See Howard Winant, "Behind Blue Eyes: Whiteness and Contemporary U.S. Racial Politics," *New Left Review*, no. 225 (September–October 1997): 74–75. For an additional intervention, see Robyn Wiegman, "Whiteness Studies and the Paradox of Particularity," *Boundary 2* 26, 3 (1999): 120–122.

13 Winant, "Behind Blue Eyes," p. 75.

14 The critical literature on the internal contradictions in the making of the West, including the Enlightenment project, is extensive, but important contributions and interventions include Max Horkheimer and Theodor Adorno, *Dialectic of Enlightenment*, trans. John Cumming (New York: Seabury Press, 1972), and Paul Gilroy, *The Black Atlantic: Modernity and Double Consciousness* (Cambridge, Mass.: Harvard University Press, 1993). On the whitening of classical civilization, see Martin Bernal, *Black Athena: The Afroasiatic Roots of Classical Civilization*, vol. 1: *The Fabrication of Ancient Greece, 1785–1985* (London: Free Association, 1987).

15 On these elisions and absences in the British and American literary imagination, as well as literary criticism, see Edward Said, *Culture and Imperialism* (New York: Knopf, 1993), and Toni Morrison, *Playing in the Dark: Whiteness and the Literary Imagination* (Cambridge, Mass.: Harvard University Press, 1992).

16 Kenneth Clark, *Civilisation: A Personal View* (New York: Harper and Row, 1969), p. xvii.

17 Ibid.

18 Ibid., p. 2.

19 Ibid., p. 160.

20 Ibid., pp. 248–249. For a useful discussion of the black presence in Hogarth's art, see David Dabydeen, *Hogarth's Blacks: Images of Blacks in Eighteenth Century English Art* (Athens: University of Georgia Press, 1987).

21 Clark, *Civilization*, p. 323.

22 See program segment entitled "Heroic Materialism."

23 Clark, *Civilization*, p. 323. On the connection between Africa and violence, see Patrick Brantlinger, "The Genealogy of the Myth of the 'Dark Continent,'" *Critical Inquiry* 12 (Fall 1985): 166–199.

24 To view the painting at the Wilberforce House, go to http://www.hullcc.gov.uk/wilberforce/images/effigy.jpg.

25 Clark, *Civilisation*, p. 309.

26 Ibid., p. 324.

27 Ibid., p. 268.

28 Ibid., p. 347.

29 "TV: A Masterful Series on Rise of Western Man," *New York Times*, September 9, 1970, p. 95.

30 Jack Gould, "What's a 12-Letter Word For 'Extraordinary'?" *New York Times*, October 18, 1970, Section II, p. 21.

31 George Gent, "Kenneth Clark Basks in '*Civilisation's*' Success," *New York Times*, November 17, 1970, p. 90.

32 For a selection of reviews, see Oswell Blakeston, "Sir Kenneth Clark's Civilization" in *Books and Bookmen*, September 1971: v. 16, p. 69; Theodore K. Rabb, "The Scenic Tour," *Commentary*, June 1971: 111–115; Charles Rosen, "TV Guide," *New York Review of Books*, April 7, 1970: 25–28; John Russell, *New York Times Review of Books*, April 26, 1970, pp. 6–7; "Editorial: *Civilization*," *Social Education*, May 1971: 427–428; "More Civilized than Thou," *Studio International*, March 1970: 125–126.

33 At the same time, this initiative reflected an early installment by the Corporation for Public Broadcasting (CPB), a nonprofit independent corporation created by Congress in 1967, to broaden the appeal of public television by expanding the range of programming.

34 As cited in *Minorities and the Media*, p. 5. See also Archer, *Black Images in the American Theater*, and Dates and Barlow, eds., *Split Image*. For a more recent study, see Robert M. Entman and Andrew Rojecki, *The Black Image in the White Mind: Media and Race in America* (Chicago: University of Chicago Press, 2000).

35 NET subsidized the only black national current affairs monthly (and later weekly), *Black Journal*. See Dates, "Public Television," p. 331. On the *Black Journal* as a site for the making of an alternative black cinema, see Tommy Lee Lott, "Documenting Social Issues: *Black Journal*, 1968–1970," in Phyllis R. Klotman and Janet K. Cutler, ed., *Struggles for Representation: African American Documentary Film and Video* (Bloomington: Indiana University Press, 1999), pp. 71–95.

36 Lott, "Documenting Social Issues," p. 24.

37 See Minutes of the Editorial Policy Committee of the Public Broadcasting Laboratory, August 16, 1967, in Av Westin Papers, The PBL Years: Correspondence and Memoranda, Box 6, Folder 16. State Historical Society of Wisconsin.

38 See note 1.

39 On the rightward shift in American politics, see Dan T. Carter, *From George Wallace to Newt Gingrich: Race in the Conservative Counterrevolution, 1963–1994* (Baton Rouge: Louisiana State University Press, 1996).

40 On the Cleveland election, see Kenneth Weinberg, *Black Victory: Carl Stokes and the Winning of Cleveland* (Chicago: Quadrangle Books, 1968), and Carl B. Stokes, *Promises of Power: A Political Autobiography* (New York: Simon and Schuster, 1973).

41 In George Dent, "29 of 119 Stations Drop First TV Laboratory Show," *New York Times*, November 6, 1967, sec. 2, p. 94.

42 See Minutes of the Editorial Policy Board, August 16, 1967, p. 2. The minutes also reported that "all hands agreed this is perhaps the most important subject on the current scene today."

43 Ibid., September 13, 1967, p. 1. The articulateness of the black nationalist on the program challenged the stable caricatures of the movement in network programming. See J. Fred MacDonald, *Blacks and White TV*, pp. 137–144, and Lott, "Documenting Social Issues," p. 74.

44 See Minutes of the Editorial Policy Board, December 6, 1967, p. 1.

45 Ibid., p. 2.

46 Quoted in Dent, "29 of 119 Stations," p. 94.

47 Quoted in Jack Gould, "Georgia U. Will Not Carry TV Lab's First Show," *New York Times*, November 5, 1969, p. 84.

48 Dent, "29 of 119 Stations," p. 94.

49 Jack Gould, "A Noble Experiment: Nowhere to Go but Up," *New York Times*, November 12, 1967, sec. 2, p. 26.

50 Av Westin Papers, The PBL Years, Programming: Program Rundown — Program Nos. 17 and 18 ("National Advisory Commission on Civil Disorders") and 21 ("Poor People's March"), Box 7, Folder 1. State Historical Society of Wisconsin.

51 Ibid.

52 Ibid., Program No. 7, Box 7, Folder 1.

53 Ibid., Program No. 16, Box 7, Folder 1.

54 Ibid., Program No. 21, Box 7, Folder 1.

55 Jack Gould, " 'Forsyte Saga' Will Unfold on Channel 13," *New York Times*, October 4, 1969, p. 70.

56 For network programs, see Tim Brooks and Earl Marsh, eds., *The Complete Directory to Prime Time Network and Cable T.V. Shows, 1946 to the Present*, 6th ed. (New York: Ballantine Books, 1995).

57 Jack Gould, "Galsworthy's Social Trilogy, 'Forsyte Saga,' Here from Britain," *New York Times*, October 6, 1969, p. 94.

58 Quoted in "Notes and Comment: Talk of the Town," *New Yorker*, January 10, 1970, p. 16.

59 The competing commercial programs are found in Hugh Malcolm Beville Jr., *Audience Ratings: Radio, Television and Cable* (Hillsdale, N.J.: Lawrence Erlbaum, 1985).

60 For a list of programs for the first ten years, see Alistair Cooke, *Masterpieces: A Decade of Masterpiece Theatre* (New York: Knopf, 1981).

61 Ibid.

Selected Bibliography

Adas, Michael. "From Settler Colony to Global Hegemon: Integrating the Exceptionalist Narrative of the American Experience into World History." *American Historical Review* 106, 5 (December 2001): 1692–1720.

Ageron, Charles-Robert. *France coloniale ou parti colonial?* Paris: PUF, 1978.

Aguilar-San Juan, Karin, ed., *The State of Asian America*. Boston: South End Press, 1994.

Ahmad, Aijaz. "Jameson's Rhetoric of Otherness and the 'National Allegory.'" *Social Text* 17 (1987): 3–25.

Alexander, M. Jacqui, and Chandra Mohanty, eds. *Feminist Genealogies, Colonial Legacies, Democratic Futures*. New York: Routledge, 1997.

Anderson, Benedict. *Imagined Communities: Reflections on the Origin and Spread of Nationalism*. 2d ed. London: Verso, 1991.

Anderson, David M., and David Killingray, eds. *Policing the Empire: Government, Authority, and Control, 1830–1940*. Manchester: Manchester University Press, 1991.

———. *Policing and Decolonisation: Politics, Nationalism, and the Police, 1917–1965*. Manchester: Manchester University Press, 1992.

Appadurai, Arjun. *Modernity at Large*. Minneapolis: University of Minnesota Press, 1996.

Armitage, David. "Greater Britain: A Useful Category of Historical Analysis?" *American Historical Review*, April 1999: 427–455.

Ashcroft, Bill, Gareth Griffiths, and Helen Tiffin, eds. *The Post-Colonial Studies Reader*. London: Routledge, 1995.

Auerbach, Jeffrey A. *The Great Exhibition of 1851: A Nation on Display*. New Haven, Conn.: Yale University Press, 1999.

Balakrishnan, Gopal, ed. *Mapping the Nation*. London: Verso, 1996.

Balibar, Étienne, and Immanuel Wallerstein. *Race, Nation, and Class: Ambiguous Identities*. London: Verso, 1992.

Ballantyne, Tony. *Orientalism and Race: Aryanism in the British Empire*. London: Palgrave, 2001.

Barkin, J. Samuel. "The Evolution of the Constitution of Sovereignty and the Emergence of Human Rights Norms." *Millennium: Journal of International Studies* 27 (1998): 229–252.

Bartov, Omer. "Defining Enemies, Making Victims: Germans, Jews, and the Holocaust." *American Historical Review* 103 (1998): 771–816.

Basker, James. "The Next Insurrection: Johnson, Race, and Rebellion." In *The Age of Johnson*, vol. 10. New York: AMS Press, 2000, pp. 37–51.

Bayly, C. A. *Empire and Information: Intelligence Gathering and Social Communication in India, 1780–1870*. Cambridge: Cambridge University Press, 1996.

Betts, Raymond. *Assimilation and Association in French Colonial Theory*. New York: Columbia University Press, 1961.

Bhabha, Homi. "Of Mimicry and Man: The Ambivalence of Colonial Discourse." *October* 28 (1984): 125–133.

Bolton, Geoffrey, gen. ed., *The Oxford History of Australia*. 4 vols. Melbourne: Oxford University Press, 1987–1994.

Bonnell, Victoria E., and Lynn Hunt, eds. *Beyond the Cultural Turn*. Berkeley: University of California Press, 1999.

Bonilla-Silva, Eduardo, and Tyrone Forman. "'I Am Not a Racist But . . .': Mapping White College Students' Racial Ideology in the USA." *Discourse and Society* 11, 1 (2000): 50–85.

Brennan, Timothy. "Masterpiece Theater and the Uses of Tradition." *Social Text* 12 (fall 1985): 102–111.

Brewer, Anthony. *Marxist Theories of Imperialism: A Critical Survey*. London: Routledge, 1980.

Briggs, Asa. *A Social History of England*. New York: Viking, 1983.

Brimelow, Peter. *Alien Nation: Common Sense about America's Immigration Disaster*. New York: Random House, 1995.

Bullard, Alice. *Exile to Paradise: Savagery and Civilization in Paris and the South Pacific, 1790–1900*. Stanford, Calif.: Stanford University Press, 2000.

Burton, Antoinette. *At the Heart of the Empire: Indians and the Colonial Encounter in Late-Victorian Britain*. Berkeley: University of California Press, 1998.

———. *Burdens of History: British Feminists, Indian Women, and Imperial Culture, 1865–1915*. Chapel Hill: University of North Carolina Press, 1994.

———. "Tongues Untied: Lord Salisbury's 'Black Man' and the Boundaries of Imperial Democracy." *Comparative Studies in Society and History* 43, 2 (2000): 632–659.

———, ed. *Gender, Sexuality and Colonial Modernities*. London: Routledge, 1999.

Butterfield, Herbert. *The Englishman and His History*. Cambridge: Cambridge University Press, 1944.

Campt, Tina, Pascal Grosse, and Yara-Colette Lemke-Muniz de Faria. "Blacks, Germans, and the Politics of the Imperial Imagination, 1920–60." In *The Imperialist Imagination: German Colonialism and Its Legacy*. Ed. Sara Friedrichsmeyer, Sara Lennox, and Susanne Zantop. Ann Arbor: University of Michigan Press, 1999, pp. 205–232.

Cannadine, David. *Ornamentalism: How the British Saw Their Empire*. New York: Oxford University Press, 2001.

Chakrabarty, Dipesh. *Provincializing Europe: Postcolonial Thought and Historical Difference*. Princeton, N.J.: Princeton University Press, 2000.

Chang, Gordon H. "History and Postmodernism: Thinking Theory in Asian American Studies." *Amerasia Journal* 21, 1 and 2 (1995): 89–94.

Chatterjee, Partha. *The Nation and Its Fragments: Colonial and Postcolonial Histories.* Princeton, N.J.: Princeton University Press, 1993.

Chaturvedi, Vinayak, ed. *Mapping Subaltern Studies and the Postcolonial.* London: Verso, 2000.

Chaudhuri, Nupur, and Margaret Strobel, eds. *Western Women and Imperialism: Complicity and Resistance.* Bloomington: Indiana University Press, 1992.

Clancy-Smith, Julia, and Frances Gouda, eds. *Domesticating the Empire: Race, Gender, and Family Life in French and Dutch Colonialism.* Charlottesville: University Press of Virginia, 1998.

Clark, C. M. H. *A History of Australia.* Vol. 1. Melbourne: Melbourne University Press, 1963.

———. "Rewriting Australian History." In Clark, *Occasional Lectures and Speeches.* Melbourne: Fontana, 1980.

———. *A Short History of Australia.* New York: New American Library, 1963.

Clark, J. C. D. *Samuel Johnson: Literature, Religion and English Cultural Politics from the Restoration to Romanticism.* Cambridge: Cambridge University Press, 1994.

Clark, Kenneth. *Civilisation: A Personal View.* New York: Harper and Row, 1969.

Clarke, Peter. *Hope and Glory: Britain 1900–90.* London: Penguin, 1996. Penguin History of Britain.

Cohen, William B. *The French Encounter with Africans: White Response to Blacks 1530–1880.* Bloomington: Indiana University Press, 1980.

Cohn, Bernard S. *Colonialism and Its Forms of Knowledge: The British in India.* Princeton, N.J.: Princeton University Press, 1996.

Conklin, Alice H. "Boundaries Unbound: Teaching French History as Colonial History and Colonial History as French History." *French Historical Studies* 23, 2 (spring 2000): 215–238.

———. *A Mission to Civilize: The Republican Idea of Empire in France and West Africa, 1895–1930.* Stanford, Calif.: Stanford University Press, 1997.

Coombes, Annie E. *Reinventing Africa: Museums, Material Culture, and Popular Imagination in Late Victorian and Edwardian England.* New Haven, Conn.: Yale University Press, 1994.

Cooper, Frederick, and Ann Laura Stoler, eds. *Tensions of Empire: Colonial Cultures in a Bourgeois World.* Berkeley: University of California Press, 1997.

Coronil, Fernando. "Beyond Occidentalism: Toward Non-Imperial Geohisorical Categeories." *Cultural Anthropology* 11, 1 (1996): 51–87.

Dalmia, Vasudha. *The Nationalization of Hindu Traditions: Bharatendu Harishchandra and Nineteenth-Century Banaras.* Delhi: Oxford University Press, 1997.

Damousi, Joy. *Depraved and Disorderly: Female Convicts, Sexuality and Gender in Colonial Australia.* Melbourne: Cambridge University Press, 1997.

Dangerfield, George. *The Strange Death of Liberal England.* Stanford, Calif.: Stanford University Press, 1997.

Daniels, Kay. *Convict Women*. Sydney: Allen and Unwin, 1998.

Davis, Leith. "Origins of the Specious: James Macpherson's Ossian and the Forging of the British Empire." *The Eighteenth Century* 34, 2 (1993): 132–150.

Davis, Mike. *Late Victorian Holocausts: El Niño Famines and the Making of the Third World*. London: Verso, 2001.

Davison, Graeme, John Hirst, and Stuart Macintyre, eds. *The Oxford Companion to Australian History*. Melbourne: Oxford University Press, 1998.

Debord, Guy. *The Society of the Spectacle*. Trans. Donald Nicholson-Smith. New York: Zone, 1995.

Desmond, Jane C., and Virginia R. Domínguez. "Resituating American Studies in a Critical Internationalism." *American Quarterly* 48 (1996): 475–490.

Dixon, Robert *Writing the Colonial Adventure: Race, Gender and Natin in Anglo-Australian Popular Fiction, 1875–1914*. Cambridge: Cambridge University Press, 1995.

Dobson, Michael. *The Making of a National Poet: Shakespeare, Adaptation, and Authorship, 1660–1769*. Oxford: Clarendon Press, 1992.

Docker, E. G. *Simply Human Beings*. Melbourne: Jacaranda Press, 1964.

Doyle, Laura. "The Racial Sublime." In *Romanticism, Race, and Imperial Culture, 1780–1834*. Ed. Alan Richardson and Sonia Hofkosh. Bloomington: Indiana University Press, 1996, pp. 15–39.

Driver, Felix, and David Gilbert, eds. *Imperial Cities: Landscape, Display and Identity*. Manchester: Manchester University Press, 1999.

Duara, Prasenjit. *Rescuing History from the Nation: Questioning Narratives of Modern China*. Chicago: University of Chicago Press, 1995.

Dube, Saurabh. *Untouchable Pasts: Religion, Identity, and Power among a Central Indian Community, 1780–1950*. Albany: State University of New York Press, 1998.

Dubois, Laurent. *Les Esclaves de la République*. Paris: Calman-Lévy, 1998.

Duffield, Ian. "Dusé Mohammed Ali, Afro-Asian Solidarity and Pan-Africanism in Early Twentieth-Century London," in *Essays on the History of Blacks in Britain: From Roman Times to the Mid-Twentieth Century*. Ed. Jagdish S. Gundara and Ian Duffield. Aldershot: Avebury, 1992, pp. 124–149.

Dussel, Enrique. "Beyond Eurocentrism: The World System and the Limits of Modernity." In *The Cultures of Globalization*. Ed. Frederic Jameson and Masao Miyoshi. Durham, N.C.: Duke University Press, 1998, pp. 3–31.

Dyer, Richard. *White*. London: Routledge, 1997.

Edney, Matthew H. *Mapping an Empire: The Geographical Construction of British India, 1765–1843*. Chicago: University of Chicago Press, 1997.

Eley, Geoff, and Ronal Grigor Suny, eds. *Becoming National: A Reader*. London: Oxford University Press, 1996.

Elliott, John H. *Imperial Spain, 1469–1716*. London: Penguin, 1963.

Ellis, John S. "Reconciling the Celt: British National Identity, Empire, and the 1911 Investiture of the Prince of Wales." *Journal of British Studies* 37, 4 (1998): 391–418.

Entman, Robert M., and Andrew Rojecki. *The Black Image in the White Mind: Media and Race in America*. Chicago: University of Chicago Press, 2000.

Evans, Lloyd. *Australia and the Modern World*. Melbourne: Cheshire, 1957.

Foner, Eric. *The Story of American Freedom*. New York: W. W. Norton, 1998.

Ford Foundation. *Minorities and the Media: A Ford Foundation Report*. New York: 1974.

Fradera, Josep M. *Cultura nacional en una societat dividida*. Barcelona: Curial, 1992.

———. *Filipinas, la colonia más peculiar: La hacienda pública en la definición de la política colonial, 1762–1868*. CSIC, 1999.

———. *Jaume Balmes: Els fonaments racionals d'una política católica*. Barcelona: Eumo Editorial, 1996.

Freedman, Carl. "England as Ideology: From 'Upstairs, Downstairs' to *A Room with a View*." *Cultural Critique*, winter 1990–1991: 79–106.

Fukuyama, Francis. *The End of History and the Last Man*. New York: Free Press, 1992.

Gee, Emma, ed. *Counterpoint: Perspectives on Asian America*. Los Angeles: University of California Press, 1976.

Gellner, Ernst. *Nations and Nationalism*. Ithaca, N.Y.: Cornell University Press, 1983.

Gibson, Charles. *The Aztecs under Spanish Rule*. Stanford, Calif.: Stanford University Press, 1964.

Giddens, Anthony. *The Nation-State and Violence*. Berkeley: University of California Press, 1987.

Gilroy, Paul. *Against Race: Imagining Political Culture beyond the Color Line*. Cambridge, Mass.: Harvard University Press, 2000.

———. *The Black Atlantic: Modernity and Double Consciousness*. Cambridge, Mass.: Harvard University Press, 1993.

———. *"There Ain't No Black in the Union Jack": The Cultural Politics of Race and Nation*. London: Hutchinson, 1987.

Gilroy, Paul, and Hazel Carby. *The Empire Strikes Back: Race and Racism in 70s Britain*. London: Hutchinson, in association with the Centre for Contemporary Cultural Studies, Birmingham: 1982.

Gilroy, Paul, Lawrence Grossberg, and Angela McRobbie, eds. *Without Guarantees: In Honour of Stuart Hall*. London: Verso, 2000.

Goldstein, Jan. "The Future of French History in the United States: Unapocalyptic Thoughts for the New Millennium." *French Historical Studies* 24, 1 (winter 2001): 1–10.

Gouda, Frances. *Dutch Culture Overseas: Colonial Practice in the Netherland Indies, 1900–1942*. Amsterdam: Amsterdam University Press, 1995.

Green, Jeffrey. *Black Edwardians: Black People in Britain, 1901–1914*. London: Frank Cass, 1998.

Gregg, Robert. *Inside Out, Outside In: Essays in Comparative History*. New York: St. Martin's Press, 1999.

Grimshaw, Patricia, Marilyn Lake, Ann McGrath, and Marian Quartly. *Creating a Nation*. Melbourne: McPhee Gribble, 1994.

Grosse, Pascal. *Kolonialismus: Eugenik und bürgerliche Gesellschaft in Deutschland 1850–1918*. Frankfurt: Campus, 2000.

Guerra, Ramiro. *Azúcar y población en las Antillas*. Havana: Cultural, 1935.

Guha, Ranajit, and Gayatri Chakravorty Spivak, eds. *Selected Subaltern Studies*. New York: Oxford University Press, 1988.

Hage, Ghassan. *White Nation*. Pluto Press, 1998.

Hall, Catherine. *Civilising Subjects: Metropole and Colony in the English Historical Imagination, 1830–1867*. London: Polity Press, 2002.

——. "Rethinking Imperial Histories: The Reform Act of 1867." *New Left Review* 208 (1994): 3–29.

Hall, Catherine, Keith McClelland, and Jane Rendall. *Defining the Victorian Nation: Class, Race, Gender and the Reform Act of 1867*. Cambridge: Cambridge University Press, 2000.

Hall, Catherine, ed. *Cultures of Empire: Colonizers in Britain and the Empire in the Nineteenth and Twentieth Centuries: A Reader*. Manchester: Manchester University Press, 2000.

Hancock, W. K. *Australia*. Melbourne: Jacaranda Press, 1961 [1930].

Harasym, Sarah, ed. *The Post-Colonial Critic: Interviews, Strategies, Dialogues*. New York: Routledge, 1990.

Hardt, Michael, and Antonio Negri. *Empire*. Cambridge, Mass.: Harvard University Press, 2000.

Harvie, Christopher, and H. C. G. Matthew. *Nineteenth-Century Britain: A Very Short Introduction*. Oxford: Oxford University Press, 2000.

Hasluck, Paul. *Black Australians: A Survey of Native Policy in Western Australia, 1829–1897*. Melbourne: Melbourne University Press, 1942.

Haywood, Ian. *The Making of History: A Study of the Literary Forgeries of James Macpherson and Thomas Chatterton in Relation to Eighteenth-Century Ideas of History and Fiction*. London: Associated University Presses, 1986.

Healy, Chris, *From the Ruins of Colonialism: History as Social Memory*. Melbourne: Cambridge University Press, 1997.

Held, David, and Anthony McGrew, "The Great Globalization Debate: An Introduction." In *The Global Transformations Reader*. Ed. David Held. Malden, Mass.: Blackwell, 2000.

Heyck, Thomas William. *The Peoples of the British Isles: A New History, from 1870 to the Present*. Belmont, Calif.: Wadsworth, 1992.

Hirst, John. *Convict Society and Its Enemies: A History of Early New South Wales*. Sydney: Allen and Unwin, 1983.

Hitchens, Peter. *The Abolition of Britain: From Winston Churchill to Princess Diana*. San Francisco: Encounter Books, 2000.

Hobsbawm, Eric. *Nations and Nationalism since 1780*. Cambridge: Cambridge University Press, 1990.

Hoganson, Kristin L. *Fighting for American Manhood: How Gender Politics Provoked the*

Spanish-American and Philippine-American Wars. New Haven, Conn.: Yale University Press, 1999.

Hope in My Heart: The May Ayim Story. Dir. Maria Binder. Dist. Third World Newsreel. Germany, 1997.

Hopkins, A. G. "Back to the Future: From National History to Imperial History." *Past and Present* 164 (1999): 198–243.

Howe, Stephen. *Ireland and Empire: Colonial Legacies in Irish History and Culture.* Oxford: Oxford University Press, 2000.

Hudson, Wayne, and Geoffrey Bolton, eds. *Creating Australia: Changing Australian History.* Sydney: Allen and Unwin, 1997.

Hughes, Robert. *The Fatal Shore: A History of Transportation of Convicts to Australia, 1787–1868.* Sydney: Collins Harvill, 1987.

Hulme, Peter. *Remnants of Conquest: The Island Caribs and Their Visitors.* Oxford: Oxford University Press, 2000.

Hyslop, Jonathan. "The Imperial Working Class Makes Itself 'White': White Labourism in Britain, Australia, and South Africa Before the First World War." *Journal of Historical Sociology* 12, 4 (1999): 398–421.

Irving, Katrina. *Immigrant Mothers: Narratives of Race and Maternity, 1890–1920.* Urbana: University of Illinois, 2000.

James, C. L. R. *The Black Jacobins: Toussaint L'Ouverture and the San Domingo Revolution.* New York: Vintage, 1989 [1938].

Jameson, Fredric. "Third-World Literature in the Era of Multinational Capitalism." *Social Text* 15 (1986).

Jeffery, Keith, ed. *"An Irish Empire"? Aspects of Ireland and the British Empire.* Manchester: Manchester University Press, 1996.

Jun, Helen Heran. "Contingent Nationalisms: Renegotiating Borders in Korean and Korean American Women's Oppositional Struggles." *Positions: East Asia Cultures Critique* 5, 2 (fall 1997): 325–356.

Kale, Madhavi. *Fragments of Empire: Capital, Slavery, and Indian Indentured Labor Migration in the British Caribbean.* Philadelphia: University of Pennsylvania Press, 1998.

Kaplan, Amy, and Donald E. Pease, eds. *Cultures of United States Imperialism.* Durham, N.C.: Duke University Press, 1993.

Kendle, John. *Ireland and the Federal Solution: The Debate over the United Kingdom Constitution, 1870–1921.* Montreal: McGill-Queen's University Press, 1989.

——. *The Round Table Movement and Imperial Union.* Toronto: University of Toronto Press, 1975.

Kidd, Colin. *Subverting Scotland's Past: Scottish Whig Historians and the Creation of an Anglo-British Identity, 1689–c. 1830.* Cambridge: Cambridge University Press, 1993.

Klor de Alva, J. Jorge. "The Postcolonization of (Latin) American Experience: A Reconsideration of 'Colonialism,' 'Postcolonialism,' and 'Mestizaje.'" In Prakash, ed., *After Colonialism*, pp. 241–278.

Kosambi, Meera, ed. *Pandita Ramabai, through Her Own Words*. Delhi: Oxford University Press, 2000.

Lahiri, Shompa. *Indians in Britain: Anglo-Indian Encounters, Race and Identity, 1880–1930*. London: Frank Cass, 2000.

Lauren, Paul Gordon. *Power and Prejudice: The Politics and Diplomacy of Racial Discrimination*. 2d ed. Boulder, Colo.: Westview Press, 1996.

Lee, Benjamin. "Critical Internationalism." *Public Culture* 7 (1995): 559–592.

Leong, Russell. "Lived Theory (Notes on the Run)." *Amerasia Journal* 21, 1 and 2 (1995): v–x.

Levine, Lawrence W. *The Opening of the American Mind: Cannons, Cultures, and History*. Boston: Beacon Press, 1996.

Lim, Shirley Geok-lin, and Amy Ling, eds. *Reading the Literatures of Asian America*. Philadelphia: Temple University Press, 1992.

Lim, Shirley Geok-lin, ed al., eds. *Transnational Asia Pacific: Gender, Culture, and the Public Sphere*. Urbana: University of Illinois Press, 1999.

Linebaugh, Peter, and Marcus Rediker. *The Many-Headed Hydra: Sailors, Slaves, Commoners, and the Hidden History of the Revolutionary Atlantic*. Boston: Beacon Press, 2000.

Lipking, Lawrence. "Inventing the Eighteenth Centuries: A Long View." In *The Profession of Eighteenth-Century Literature: Reflections on an Institution*. Ed. Leo Damrosch. Madison: University of Wisconsin Press, 1992, pp. 7–25.

Liu, Lydia, ed. *Tokens of Exchange: The Problem of Translation in Global Circulations*. Durham, N.C.: Duke University Press, 1999.

Locher-Scholten, Elsbeth. *Women and the Colonial State: Essays on Gender and Modernity in the Netherlands Indies, 1900–42*. Amsterdam: Amsterdam University Press, 2000.

Loomba, Ania. *Colonialism/Postcolonialism*. New York: Routledge, 1998.

Lorcin, Patricia. *Imperial Identities: Stereotyping, Prejudice, and Race in Colonial Algeria*. London: I. B. Tauris, 1995.

Lowe, Lisa. "On Contemporary Asian American Projects." *Amerasia Journal* 21, 1 and 2 (1995): 41–54.

Lynch, John. *The Spanish American Revolutions, 1808–1826*. New York: W. W. Norton, 1973.

MacDonald, Terrence J. *The Historic Turn in the Social Sciences*. Ann Arbor: University of Michigan Press, 1996.

Macintyre, Stuart. *A History for a Nation: Ernest Scott and the Making of Australian History*. Carlton: Melbourne University Press, 1994.

——. "The Writing of Australian History." In *Australians: A Guide to Sources*. Ed. D. H. Borchardt. Sydney: Fairfax, Syme, and Weldon, 1987, pp. 1–29;

Mackenthun, Gesa. "Adding Empire to the Study of American Culture." *Journal of American Studies* 30 (1996): 263–269.

MacKenzie, John M. *Propaganda and Empire: The Manipulation of British Public Opinion, 1880–1960*. Manchester: Manchester University Press, 1984.

———, ed. *Imperialism and Popular Culture*. Manchester: Manchester University Press, 1986.

MacPherson, Margaret. *I Heard the Anzacs Singing*. New York: Creative Age Press, 1942.

Marable, Manning. *Race, Reform, Rebellion: The Second Reconstruction in Black America, 1945–1990*. Jackson: University Press of Mississippi, 1991.

Martínez Shaw, Carlos. *Cataluña en la carrera de indias, 1680–1756*. Barcelona: Crítica, 1981.

Mbembe, Achille. *On the Postcolony*. Berkeley: University of California Press, 2001.

McClintock, Anne M., Aamir Mufti, and Ella Shohat, eds. *Dangerous Liaisons: Gender, Nation, and Postcolonial Perspectives*. Minneapolis: University of Minnesota Press, 1997.

McLure, John. *Late Imperial Romance*. London: Verso, 1994.

Mignolo, Walter D. *Local Histories, Global Designs: Coloniality, Subaltern Knowledges and Border Thinking*. Durham, N.C.: Duke University Press, 2000.

Miller, Stuart Creighton. *"Benevolent Assimilation": The American Conquest of the Philippines, 1899–1903*. New Haven, Conn.: Yale University Press, 1982.

Morgan, Edmund S. *American Slavery, American Freedom: The Ordeal of Colonial Virginia*. New York: W. W. Norton, 1975.

Morgan, Kenneth. *Twentieth-Century Britain: A Very Short Introduction*. Oxford: Oxford University Press, 2000.

———, ed. *The Oxford History of Britain*. Oxford and New York: Oxford University Press, 1988.

Morgan, Sally. *My Place*. Fremantle: Fremantle Arts Centre Press, 1988.

Mouralis, Bernard. *République et colonies: Entre histoire et mémoire: La République française et l'Afrique*. Paris: Présence Africaine, 1999.

Nairn, Tom. *After Britain: New Labour and the Return of Scotland*. London: Granta, 1999.

Newman, Louise Michele. *White Women's Rights: The Racial Origins of Feminism in the United States*. New York: Oxford University Press, 1999.

O'Halloran, Clare. "Irish Re-Creation of the Gaelic Past: The Challenge of Macpherson's Ossian." *Past and Present* 124 (1989): 69–95.

Okamura, Jonathan. *Imagining the Filipino American Diaspora: Transnational Relations, Identities, and Communities*. New York: Garland, 1998.

Okihiro, Gary. "African and Asian American Studies: A Comparative Analysis and Commentary." Gail M. Nomura, et. al., *Frontiers of Asian American Studies*. Pullman: Washington State University Press, 1991.

Olds, Kris, et al., eds. *Globalization and the Asia-Pacific: Contested Territories*. New York: Routledge, 1999.

Ollivier, Maurice, ed. *The Colonial and Imperial Conferences from 1887 to 1937*. 3 vols. Ottawa: Edmond Cloutier, 1954.

Omi, Michael, and Howard Winant. *Racial Formation in the United States: From the 1960s to the 1980s*. New York: Routledge, 1986.

Ong, Aihwa. *Flexible Citizenship: The Cultural Logics of Transnationality.* Durham, N.C.: Duke University Press, 1999.

Ong, Paul, Edna Bonacich, and Lucie Cheng, eds., *The New Asian Immigration in Los Angeles and Global Restructuring.* Philadelphia: Temple University Press, 1994.

Ortiz, Fernando. *Los negros esclavos.* Editorial de Ciencias Sociales, 1975.

Oxley, Deborah, *Convict Maids: The Forced Migration of Women to Australia.* Melbourne: Cambridge University Press, 1996.

Parekh Bhiku, et al. *The Future of Multi-Ethnic Britain: Report of the Commission on the Future of Multi-Ethnic Britain.* London: Profile Books, 2000.

Patey, Douglas Lane. "Ancients and Moderns." In *The Cambridge History of Literary Criticism,* vol. 4: *The Eighteenth Century.* Ed. H. B. Nisbet and Claude Rawson. Cambridge: Cambridge University Press, 1997, pp. 32–71.

Pearce, Lynne, and Jackie Stacey, eds. *Romance Revisited.* New York: New York University Press, 1995.

Peers, Douglas M. "Is Humpty Dumpty Back Together Again?: The Revival of Imperial History and the *Oxford History of the British Empire,*" *Journal of World History* 13, no. 2 (2002): pp. 451–467.

Phillips, Mike and Trevor. *Windrush: The Irresistible Rise of Multi-Racial Britain.* London: HarperCollins, 1998.

Pike, Douglas. *Australia: The Quiet Continent.* London: Cambridge University Press, 1962.

Pines, Jim, ed. *Black and White in Colour: Black People in British Television since 1936.* London: BFI Publications, 1992.

Pownall, Eve. *Mary of Maranoa: Tales of Australian Pioneer Women.* Sydney: F. H. Johnston, 1959.

Prakash, Gyan, ed. *After Colonialism: Imperial Histories and Postcolonial Displacements.* Princeton, N.J.: Princeton University Press, 1995.

Readings, Bill. *The University in Ruins.* Cambridge, Mass.: Harvard University Press, 1996.

Revel, Jacques and Lynn Hunt, eds. *Histories: French Constructions of the Past.* New York: New Press, 1995.

Rich, Paul B. *Race and Empire in British Politics.* 2d ed. Cambridge: Cambridge University Press, 1990.

Robinson, Portia. *The Women of Botany Bay: A Reinterpretation of the Role of Women in the Origins of Australian Society.* Ringwood: Penguin, 1988.

Rodgers, Daniel T. *Atlantic Crossings: Social Politics in a Progressive Age.* Cambridge, Mass.: Harvard University Press, 1998.

Roediger, David. *The Wages of Whiteness: Race and the Making of the American Working Class.* London: Verso, 1991.

Rosenberg, Emily S. *Spreading the American Dream: American Economic and Cultural Expansion, 1890–1945.* New York: Hill and Wang, 1982.

Rothschild, Emma. "Globalization and the Return to History." *Foreign Policy* 115 (summer 1999): 106–116.

Rüger, Adolf. "Imperialismus, Sozialreformismus und antikoloniale demokratische Alternative: Zielvorstellungen von Afrikanern in Deutschland im Jahre 1919." *Zeitschrift für Geschichtswissenschaft* 23 (1975): 1293–1308.

Said, Edward. *Culture and Imperialism*. New York: Knopf, 1993.

———. *Orientalism*. New York: Vintage, 1978.

San Buenaventura, Steffi. "The Master and the Federation: A Filipino-American Social Movement in California and Hawaii." *Social Process in Hawaii* 33 (1991): 169–193.

Schmidt-Lauber, Brigitta. *Die abhängigen Herren: Deutsche Identität in Namibia*. Hamburg: Lit, 1993.

Schneer, Jonathan. *London 1900: The Imperial Metropolis*. New Haven, Conn.: Yale University Press, 1999.

Scott, David. *Refashioning Futures: Criticism after Postcoloniality*. Princeton, N.J.: Princeton University Press, 1999.

Semmel, Bernard. *Imperialism and Social Reform: English Social-Imperialist Thought, 1895–1914*. Garden City, N.Y.: Anchor, 1968.

Shah, A. B., ed. *The Letters and Correspondence of Pandita Ramabai*. Bombay: Maharashtra State Board of Literature and Culture, 1977.

Sharpe, Jenny. *Allegories of Empire: The Figure of Woman in the Colonial Text*. Minneapolis: University of Minnesota Press, 1993.

———. "Postcolonial Studies in the House of U.S. Multiculturalism." In *A Companion to Postcolonial Studies*. Ed. Henry Schwartz and Sangeeta Ray. London: Blackwell, 2000.

Shaw, A. G. L. *Convicts and the Colonies: A Study of Penal Transportation from Great Britain and Ireland to Australia and Other Parts of the British Empire*. London: Faber, 1966.

Singh, Amritjit, and Peter Schmidt. "Introduction." In *Postcolonial Theory of the United States: Race, Ethnicity, and Literature*. Jackson: University of Mississippi Press, 2000.

Sinha, Mrinalini. *Colonial Masculinity: The "Manly Englishman" and the "Effeminate Bengali" in the Late Nineteenth Century*. Manchester: Manchester University Press, 1995.

Skaria, Ajay. *Hybrid Histories: Forests, Frontiers and Wildness in Western India*. Delhi: Oxford University Press, 1999.

Sked, Alan, and Chris Cook. *Postwar Britain: A Political History, 1945–1992*. 4th ed. London: Penguin, 1993.

Smith, Anna Marie. *New Right Discourse on Race and Sexuality: Britain, 1968–1990*. Cambridge: Cambridge University Press, 1994.

Smith, David A., Dorothy J. Solinger, and Steven C. Topik, eds. *States and Sovereignty in the Global Economy*. London: Routledge, 1999.

Spivak, Gayatri Chakravorty. *Outside in the Teaching Machine*. New York: Routledge, 1993.

Stein, Stanley J., and Barbara H. Stein. *Silver, Trade, and War: Spain and America in the Making of Early Modern Europe*. Baltimore: Johns Hopkins University Press, 2000.

Stoler, Ann Laura. *Race and the Education of Desire: Foucault's History of Sexuality and the Colonial Order of Things*. Durham, N.C.: Duke University Press, 1995.

Stratton, Jon, and Ien Ang, "On the Impossibility of a Global Cultural Studies: "'British' Cultural Studies in an 'International' Frame." In *Stuart Hall: Critical Dialogues in Cultural Studies*. Ed. David Morley and Kuan-Hsing Chen. London: Routledge, 1996, pp. 361–391.

Summers, Anne. *Damned Whores and God's Police: The Colonisation of Women in Australia*. Ringwood: Penguin, 1975.

Tachiki, Amy, et al., eds. *Roots: An Asian American Reader*. Los Angeles: University of California Press, 1971.

Taylor, A. J. P. *English History, 1914–45*. Oxford: Oxford University Press, 1985.

Thiong'o, Ngũgĩ wa. *Homecoming: Essays on African and Caribbean Literature, Culture and Politics*. New York: Lawrence Hill, 1972.

Thompson, Andrew S. *Imperial Britain: The Empire in British Politics, c. 1880–1932*. London: Longman, 2000.

———. "The Language of Imperialism and the Meanings of Empire: Imperial Discourse in British Politics, 1895–1914," *Journal of British Studies* 36, 2 (1997): 147–177.

Thompson, Edward P. *The Poverty of Theory and Other Essays*. New York: Monthly Review Press, 1978.

Thompson, Elizabeth. *Colonial Citizens: Republican Rights, Paternal Privilege, and Gender in French Syria and Lebanon*. New York: Columbia University Press, 2000.

Tinker, Hugh. *Separate and Unequal: India and Indians in the British Commonwealth, 1920–1950*. Vancouver: University of British Columbia Press, 1976.

Trouillot, Michel-Rolph. *Silencing the Past: Power and the Production of History*. Boston: Beacon Press, 1995.

Tyrrell, Ian R. "American Exceptionalism in an Age of International History." *American Historical Review* 96 (1991): 1031–1072.

van der Veer, Peter. *Imperial Encounters: Religion and Modernity in India and Britain*. Princeton, N.J.: Princeton University Press, 2001.

Vilar, Pierre. *La Catalogne dans l'Espagne moderne: Recherches sur les fondements économiques des structures nationales*. 3 vols. SEVPEN Paris: 1962.

Wallerstein, Immanuel. "Fernand Braudel, Historian, 'homme de la conjoncture.'" In Immanuel Wallerstein, *Unthinking Social Science: The Limits of Nineteenth-Century Paradigms*. Cambridge: Polity Press, 1991.

Ward, Russel. *Australia*. Sydney: Horwitz, 1965.

Webb, R. K. *Modern England: From the Eighteenth Century to the Present*, 2d ed. New York: Harper and Row, 1980.

White, Nicholas J. *Decolonisation: The British Experience since 1945*. London: Longman, 1999.

Wilder, Gary. "Practicing Citizenship in Imperial Paris." In *Civil Society and the Political Imagination in Africa: Critical Perspectives*. Ed. John L. and Jean Comaroff. Chicago: University of Chicago Press, 1999.

Williams, Eric. *Capitalism and Slavery*. University of North Carolina Press, 1994.

Williams, Patrick, and Laura Chrisman, eds. *Colonial Discourse and Postcolonial Theory.* New York: Columbia University Press, 1994.

Wolf, Eric. *Europe and the People without History.* Berkeley: University of California Press, 1982.

Wong, Sau-ling. "Denationalization Reconsidered: Asian American Cultural Criticism at a Theoretical Crossroads." *Amerasia Journal* 21, 1 and 2 (1995): 1–28.

Zachernuk, Philip S. *Colonial Subjects: An African Intelligentsia and Atlantic Ideas.* Charlottesville: University Press of Virginia, 2000.

Zantop, Susanne. *Colonial Fantasies: Conquest, Family, and Nation in Precolonial Germany, 1770–1870.* Durham, N.C.: Duke University Press, 1997.

Žižek, Slavoj. *Tarrying with the Negative: Kant, Hegel and the Critique of Ideology.* Durham, N.C.: Duke University Press, 1993.

About the Contributors

TONY BALLANTYNE (Ph.D., Cambridge) taught at the National University of Ireland, Galway and the University of Illinois, Urbana-Champaign, before assuming his current position as Lecturer in South Asian and World History at the University of Otago. He is the author of *Orientalism and Race: Aryanism in the British Empire* (2002) and editor of a special issue of the *Journal of Colonialism and Colonial History* entitled *From Orientalism to Ornamentalism: Empire and Difference in History.* He is currently working on a book exploring the relationship between colonialism and diaspora in the making of modern Sikhism.

ANTOINETTE BURTON is Professor of History at the University of Illinois, Urbana-Champaign, where she is also affiliated with the Women's Studies Program and the Unit for Criticism. She is the author of *Burdens of History* (1994), *At the Heart of the Empire* (1998), and *Dwelling in the Archive: Women Writing House, Home and History in Late-Colonial India* (2003). She is working on a book about empire and Victorian political culture.

ANN CURTHOYS is Manning Clark Professor of History at the Australian National University. She has published widely on aspects of Australian history, including Indigenous history; racial thought and race relations; women's history; and television and journalism. She has also written about historical writing, feminist theory, and national identity. Most recently she is the author of *Freedom Ride: An Australian Journey* (2002). Her current projects include a study of the historical experts and the Australian Federal Court and a book manuscript jointly with John Docker to be entitled "Is History Fiction?"

AUGUSTO ESPIRITU is Assistant Professor of History and Asian American Studies at the University of Illinois, Urbana-Champaign. In 2001–2002 he was a postdoctoral fellow at the University of California, Berkeley. His work in progress is entitled "The Dilemmas of Expatriation: Identity, Power, and Performance in Filipino-American Intellectual Life."

KAREN FANG is Assistant Professor of Film and Literature in the Department of English at the University of Houston. Her teaching and research interests include Asian cinema, nineteenth-century British literature, and imperial and postcolonial culture. Her essay in this volume is part of her ongoing work on the culture of surveillance in contemporary Hong Kong.

IAN CHRISTOPHER FLETCHER teaches history at Georgia State University in Atlanta. He is a co-editor of *Women's Suffrage in the British Empire: Citizenship, Nation, and Race* (2000) and a member of the *Radical History Review* editorial collective.

JOSEP M. FRADERA is Professor of History at the Universitat Pompeu Fabra, Barcelona. He has written extensively on eighteenth- and nineteenth-century Spanish, Caribbean, and Philippine colonial history, as well as nineteenth-century Spanish political and intellectual history, including topics such as nationalism and cultural responses to the liberal revolution. He is currently working on a study of Spain's transition from the early modern empire to the colonial regime of the nineteenth century.

ROBERT GREGG is Associate Professor of History at Richard Stockton College of New Jersey. He is the author of *Sparks from the Anvil of Oppression: Philadelphia's African Methodists and Southern Migrants, 1890–1940* (1993) and *Inside Out, Outside In: Essays in Comparative History* (1999). He is also a co-editor of *The Encyclopedia of Contemporary American Culture* (2001).

TERRI A. HASSELER is an Associate Professor of English and Humanities at Bryant College, Smithfield, Rhode Island. She also coordinates the Women's Studies minor. She has published on Western women in India, on postcolonial Indian writers, and on multiculturalism and composition. She is the vice president of the Northeast Victorian Studies Association and cofounder of the United States Association for Commonwealth Literature and Language Studies.

CLEMENT HAWES is Associate Professor of English at Pennsylvania State University, where he teaches eighteenth-century literature. He is currently at work on two related projects: a monograph entitled "Cannibalizing History: Metalepsis and the British Eighteenth Century" and the British New Riverside edition of *Gulliver's Travels and Other Writings* (forthcoming 2003).

DOUGLAS M. HAYNES is Associate Professor of History at the University of California, Irvine, where he also serves on the steering committee of the Program in African American Studies. His research interests are transatlantic in scope, ranging from the cultural politics of Britishness to the metanarratives of ebola disease in the U.S. mass media to the central place of Victorian imperialism in the making of British medicine and science. His current book project explores the place of Commonwealth doctors of color in the British National Health Service from 1947 to 1978.

KRISTIN HOGANSON is Assistant Professor of History at the University of Illinois, Urbana-Champaign. She is the author of *Fighting for American Manhood: How Gender Politics Provoked the Spanish-American and Philippine-American Wars*. Her current research focuses on international components of U.S. domesticity—including household consumption, cookery, and the fictive travel movement—from roughly 1865 to 1920.

PAULA M. KREBS chairs the English Department at Wheaton College, Norton, Massachusetts. She is the author of *Gender, Race, and the Writing of Empire: Public Discourse and the Boer War* (1999).

LARA KRIEGEL is Assistant Professor of History at Florida International University. She has held postdoctoral fellowships at Brown University's Pembroke Center for Teaching and Research on Women and at the Huntington Library. Her research addresses industry, spectacle, empire, and the marketplace in mid-nineteenth-century Britain.

RADHIKA VIYAS MONGIA is Assistant Professor of Women's Studies at the University of California, Santa Cruz. She is currently working on a monograph, "Genealogies of Globalization: Migration, Colonialism, and the State," which examines Indian migration from 1834 to 1917 in order to chart a history of how colonialism shaped the emergence and consolidation of state control over international migration.

SUSAN D. PENNYBACKER is Associate Professor of History at Trinity College in Hartford, Connecticut, where she has taught since 1983. She is the author of *A Vision for London, 1889–1914* (1995) and is completing *From Scottsboro to Munich: Racial Politics in Britain in the 1930s* (forthcoming). She is the co-author, with James A. Miller and Eve Rosenhaft, of "Mother Ada Wright and the International Campaign to 'Free the Scottsboro Boys,' 1931–4" (*American Historical Review*, April 2001).

JOHN PLOTZ is Assistant Professor of English at Brandeis University and author of *The Crowd: British Literature and Public Politics* (2000). His current project, "Portable Properties: Objects, Persons and Culture on the Move in Victorian Greater Britain," examines object narratives, diamond-centered fiction, and imperially inflected debates about regionalism and provincialism.

CHRISTOPHER SCHMIDT-NOWARA is Assistant Professor of History at Fordham University, Lincoln Center. He is the author of *Empire and Antislavery: Spain, Cuba, and Puerto Rico, 1833–1874* (1999). He is editing, with John Nieto-Phillips, a collection of essays entitled "Interpreting Spanish Colonialism."

HEATHER STREETS is Assistant Professor of History at the Washington State University. She received her PH.D. from Duke University in 1998. She is currently revising a book manuscript entitled "Born Warriors: Martial Races and Masculinity in British Imperial Culture, 1857–1914."

HSU-MING TEO is a postdoctoral research fellow at Macquarie University, Sydney. She completed a PH.D. on British women travelers, 1890–1939, and is currently editing a volume on "Cultural History in Australia" and finishing a book on colonialism, race, and the romance novel. In 1999 she won the Australian Vogel Literary Award for her first novel, *Love and Vertigo*.

STUART WARD teaches history at the University of Southern Denmark, specializing in empire and postcolonialism. His current research interest is the demise of the idea of "Greater Britain" in the twentieth century and the impact of this process on the cohesiveness of the U.K. state. His most recent publications include *Australia and the British Embrace: The Demise of the Imperial Ideal* (2001), as well as an edited collection, *British Culture and the End of Empire* (2001).

LORA WILDENTHAL is Associate Professor of History at Texas A&M University. She is the author of *German Women for Empire, 1884–1945* (2001), a study of race, gender, sexuality, and the German colonial empire. She is currently researching the history of human rights activism in West Germany, 1949–1989.

GARY WILDER is Assistant Professor of History at Pomona College. His book, *The French Imperial Nation-State: Negritude, Colonial Humanism, and Interwar Political Rationality,* is forthcoming from the University of Chicago Press. His current research is on mercenaries, African decolonization, and neoliberalism.

Index

Hybridity, 48
Hygiene, 62

Iberian imperialisms, 165
Illustrated Exhibitor, 232, 236
Illustrated London News, 235, 237
Immigration, 27, 33, 36, 167
Imperial history, 5, 46, 52; new imperial
history, 14, 60; new Imperial Studies,
4, 6
Imperial social formation, 4, 50, 112
Imperial turn: definition of, 2, 57, 59, 68,
217, 218, 219, 227, 246, 261
Indenture, 197, 198
India, 10–11, 32, 114; and emigration,
196–211. *See also* South Asia
Indian Emigration Act (1883), 198–211
Indian National Congress, 200
Indigenous citizenship, 77
Indigenous cultures, 47
Indigenous history, 79
Indigenous peoples, 76, 84
Indonesia, 33, 104
Industrialization, 181
Ireland, 11, 31, 114, 225, 237, 238, 251;
Northern Ireland, 33, 111, 303
Irish nationalism, 246, 252, 253; Celtic im-
perialism, 253; and whiteness, 253–254
Irschick, Eugene, 106
Izard, Miquel, 158

James, C. L. R., 180, 309
Jameson, Fredric, 309, 320
Japan, 202, 255–256; Japanese invasion of
Hong Kong, 302
Jebb, Richard, 45, 46
Jefferson, Thomas, 329
Jewett, Sarah Orne, 317
Job market, 90–100
Johnson, Samuel, 218–228
Jones, Sir William, 115
Joshi, Priya, 93, 94, 95, 96
Journal of American History, 170

Kaiserreich, the, 144
Kale, Madhavi, 240
Kater, Captain Henry, 114
Kaviraj, Sudipta, 111
Kerner Commission, 334
King, Martin Luther, Jr., 333
Kipling, Rudyard, 62, 311, 312, 313
Knight, Joseph, 223
Knoblauch, Edward, 260
Knowledge, colonial forms of, 102–103,
105, 202. *See also* Archives
Komagata Maru, 207, 208
Korea, 187
Korean Americans, 187
Korean Central Intelligence Agency, 189
Kureishi, Hanif, 28

Labor: and the Great Exhibition, 233–
242
Labor history, 80
Lalita, K., 108
Lamming, George, 308–320; *Castle of My
Skin*, 310–311; *Natives of My Person*,
318–319
Landes, David, 51, 52
La Pietra Report, 171–183
Latin America, 159, 161, 165
Laurier, Wilfred, 200, 203, 207, 210
Lawrence, D. H., 71, 74
Lawrence, Stephen, 34
League of Nations, 148, 150
Lebanon, 130
Lee, Wen Ho, 187
Lemann, Nicholas, 39
Leong, Russell, 188
Levi, Primo, 40
Linebaugh, Peter, 179
Linguistic turn, the, 9, 102
Liu, Lydia, 309
Liverpool, 29, 34
Lobo, Father Jerome, 223
London Metropolitan Police Act, 294
Loomba, Ania, 94, 95, 96

Louis, William Roger, 46
Lüders, Else, 149–150
Lynch, John, 161

MacDonald, Terence J., 16
MacKenzie, John M., 49, 110, 112
Macpherson, James, 224–225, 226
MacPherson, Margaret, 71
Maier, Charles, 133
Major, John, 7, 35
Malay peninsula, 115
Malcolme, David, 224
Malouf, David, 314
Mamdani, Mahmood, 135
Mani, Lata, 107–108
Maosim, 304, 305
Marsden, William, 115
Marshall, P. J., 4, 49
Marshall Thesis, the, 4
Marwick, Arthur, 34
Marx, Karl, 231
Marxism, 127, 128; Marxist history, 133–
    134
Masterpiece Theater, 327, 330; program-
    ming, 336–337
Matthew, H. C. G., 37
Mayhew, Henry, 82
Mbembe, Achille, 10
McClintock, Anne, 4
McGrath, Ann, 80
Medicine, 62–64
Meek, Russ, 332, 334
Metals (precious), 163
Migration, 86, 196–211. *See also* Immi-
    gration; Passport, history of
Military-fiscal state, 110
Millennium Dome, 35
Mills and Boon, 280, 282, 283, 286
Milner, Alfred, 45, 246, 247–249, 251,
    256
Moby-Dick, 319
Modern Language Association, 90–100
Modern Review, The, 249

Mohanty, Chandra, 92
Molony, John, 78
Monarchy, 46, 165
Morant Bay, 67
Morgan, Kenneth, 27, 28, 29, 30, 33, 34,
    35, 37
Mughal authority, 110
Multiculturalism, 14, 28, 36, 37, 96–97

Naipaul, V. S., 314, 315, 316
Namibia, 152
Nandi, Ashis, 103
Nation: as fantasy, 6; as investigative mo-
    dality, 8; national histories, 16, 70–86;
    as organizing force in history-writing,
    44–54
National Advisory Committee on Civil
    Disorders, 331, 333
National culture, 111
National Educational Television, 326,
    330, 334
National Health Service, 27
Nationalities and Subject Races Con-
    ference, 256
National Urban League, 332, 334
Native Americans, 287, 288
Nazi racial state, 144
Nazism, 144, 148, 150
New Zealand, 46, 70, 71, 76, 79, 251–
    252, 282
North America, 29
Nostalgia, 5
Nottingham, 33
Notting Hill, 9, 33, 34; and Carnival, 34,
    36

O'Connor, Charles, 225
Omatsu, Glen, 186
Ondaatje, Michael, 28
One Nation Party, 79
Ong, Aihwa, 187
Opium Wars, 238
Ordnance Survey, the, 114, 115

Library of Congress Cataloging-in-Publication Data

After the imperial turn : thinking with and through the nation / edited by
Antoinette Burton.

p. cm.

Includes bibliographical references and index.

ISBN 0-8223-3106-3 (cloth : alk. paper)

ISBN 0-8223-3142-X (pbk. : alk. paper)

1. Postcolonialism.   2. State, The.   3. Imperialism.   4. Internationalism.
I. Burton, Antoinette M.

JV51.A34 2003

325'.3 — dc21   2002151599

*   *   *

Tony Ballantyne's essay, "Rereading the Archive and Opening up the Nation-
State: Colonial Knowledge in South Asia (and Beyond)," has been adapted with
permission from "Archive, Discipline, State: Power and Knowledge in South
Asian Historiography," *New Zealand Journal of Asian Studies* 3, 1 (June 2001).

Radhika Viyas Mongia's "Race, Nationality, Mobility: A History of the
Passport," first appeared in *Public Culture* 11, 3 (fall 1999) and is reprinted with
permission from Duke University Press.

A longer version of Christopher Schmidt-Nowara's essay, "After 'Spain':
A Dialogue with Josep M. Fradera on Spanish Colonial Historiography," appeared
in *Bulletin of the Society for Spanish and Portuguese Historical Studies* 25 (winter–
spring 2001), pp. 2–14, and is reprinted here with permission.

Lora Wildenthal's essay, "Notes on a History of 'Imperial Turns' in Modern
Germany," has been adapted with permission from her essay in *European Studies
Journal* 16 (1999), special issue: *German Colonialism: Another* Sonderweg?